The Spectrum of Ritual

A Biogenetic Structural Analysis

The Spectrum of Ritual
A Biogenetic Structural Analysis

By
Eugene G. d'Aquili
Charles D. Laughlin, Jr.
John McManus

With Tom Burns, Barbara Lex,
G. Ronald Murphy, S.J., and W. John Smith

Columbia University Press/New York/1979

Library of Congress Cataloging in Publication Data

D'Aquili, Eugene G   1940–
  The spectrum of ritual.

  Bibliography: p.
  Includes index.
  1. Rites and ceremonies.   2. Neuropsychology.
3. Neurophysiology.   4. Structural anthropology.
I. Laughlin, Charles D., 1938–   joint author.
II. McManus, John, 1942–   joint author.   III. Title.
[DNLM: 1. Behavior.   2. Neurophysiology.   3. Psycho-
physiology. WL102.3 D212s]
GN473.D36   612'.8   78-19015
ISBN 0-231-04514-X

Columbia University Press
New York   Guildford Surrey

Contents

Contents

Preface

On New Year's Day 1974 most of the authors of this volume met in the library of the department of anatomy of the University of Pennsylvania to discuss the reactions to *Biogenetic Structuralism,* which had become available in November 1973 (Columbia University Press). Although it was too early for that volume to be reviewed, a number of scholars from several disciplines had read the manuscript and had already given us considerable feedback. It is interesting that the response was considerably polarized, being either extremely positive or extremely negative. Furthermore, the polarization did not fall out according to the specific disciplines involved. In other words physical anthropologists, cultural anthropologists, cognitive psychologists, and neurophysiologists were all equally divided about the merits of *Biogenetic Structuralism.* Obviously the work answered a need that was perceived by many scholars and touched a raw nerve for a number of others.

Although almost everyone in the last ten years has paid lip service to a multidisciplinary approach to the behavioral and social sciences, it has been our experience that few scholars actually mean what they say. The others become extremely upset with what they consider tampering with the methodological purity of their individual disciplines and consequently become incensed that anyone would dare to choose data from their disciplines that might be in any way controversial to erect a theoretical interdisciplinary superstructure for the behavioral and social sciences. The furor over E. O. Wilson's *Sociobiology* is fairly analogous to the reception that *Biogenetic Structuralism* received. I am sure it was no accident that *The New York Review of Books* chose to review *Biogenetic Structuralism* with Wilson's *Sociobiology,* an association we found flattering at the time. However, the compliment was counteracted by our being forced to share with Wilson the opprobrium heaped upon us both by disciplinary purists and by those who see any attempt to introduce biology into the social and behavioral sciences as some sort of neofascist plot.

In any case, on that New Year's Day, 1974, the authors of this volume considered an issue on which both our supporters and our critics seemed to agree, namely, that *Biogenetic Structuralism* did not present a sufficiently clear exposition of our methodology in analyzing any given social phenomenon. In other words many of our friends thought that *Biogenetic Structuralism,* while strong in its theoretical foundation derived from the empirical data of several disciplines, was weak in presenting its methodology in terms of practical application. We therefore decided that a second book had to be written that would address itself specifically to this issue. The methodology had to be formally presented, and a practical application of the methodology demonstrated. We decided that the "universal" human cultural institution to which we would apply the methodology of biogenetic structuralism would be ritual behavior. We could just as well have chosen kinship structure, political organization, and so forth, but all of the authors seemed to have an interest in human ceremonial ritual, and we voted to devote our energies to an analysis of that topic.

At that New Year's Day meeting we outlined the book in general, and in subsequent meetings we outlined each chapter. Even though there are seven authors (three major authors and four minor authors) the book was designed from the beginning to represent a unified whole, with a definite continuity of subject matter and theme from beginning to end. We definitely wished to avoid a "reader" with some sort of *post hoc* unity imposed by editors. To some extent at least almost every author contributed to almost every chapter in the book. The three major authors certainly went through every chapter very carefully and consulted with the minor authors, as well as with each other, about both the subject matter and the style of each chapter. In spite of the book's being outlined from beginning to end before anything was written, we all decided that the authors of any given chapter should append to that chapter. Although this may give the book the appearance of an anthology, we emphasize again that the entire work was planned and executed as a unity.

Preface

The first and last chapters of this book extend the theory and present the formal methodology of biogenetic structuralism in general. Chapters 2 through 10 deal exclusively with the practical application of the methodology in the analysis of ritual behavior. Consequently it seems that two kinds of readers will probably be drawn to this book: those interested in biogenetic structuralism as an approach in the behavioral and social sciences or as a movement in the philosophy of science and those specifically interested in ritual behavior. In the latter case we feel we have presented the most nearly comprehensive analysis of human ceremonial ritual published to date. Whether our readers are interested in the more theoretical or applied aspects of this sequel to *Biogenetic Structuralism*, we hope that we have at least communicated in this book the essential nature of our multidisciplinary approach to behavioral and social science.

Eugene G. d'Aquili
University of Pennsylvania
March 1978

════Acknowledgments════

The authors wish to acknowledge the valuable assistance, either direct or indirect, which the following individuals rendered in the preparation of this volume: Dr. Jerome H. Barkow, Professor Ivan A. Brady, Dr. Rodney Byrne, Dr. David K. Caldwell, Ms. Mary Lou d'Aquili, Professor Ward Goodenough, Dr. Bobbi Hall, Dr. Robert Harding, Professor Solomon Katz, Ms. Patricia Kolarik, Dr. Harold Levine, Dr. Allan Mann, Professor Emil Menzel, Mr. John D. Moore, Mr. Terry Morse, Dr. Robert Rubinstein, Professor Donald Stone Sade, Professor Anthony F. C. Wallace. Their help and support was indispensable in producing *The Spectrum of Ritual*.

Most especially the authors wish to thank Ms. Mary-Curtis Briggs for her invaluable assistance in editing the manuscript. It is in large part due to her that the jargon of many disciplines has been translated into comprehensible English. She has rendered a great service both to authors and readers.

The Spectrum of Ritual
A Biogenetic Structural Analysis

One

Introduction

Charles D. Laughlin, Jr.,
John McManus, and
Eugene G. d'Aquili

The actions the human animal performs may appear to be capable of almost infinite variety, but they are more properly regarded as variations on a set of action "themes." These are probably little more in number than the repertoire of fixed action patterns of the nonhuman species.

Eliot Chapple, *Culture and Biological Man*

The spectrum of ritual, like the chromatic spectrum, comes in a vast array of forms and colors. Ritual is never random behavior but is highly organized, encompassing myriad discrete and symbolic elements intertwined in a complex behavioral matrix. Like the spectrum, ritual is structured by a set of organizational principles that are only partially, if ever, comprehended by participants and includes both observed and unobserved elements. Furthermore, there are certain preconditions for ritual, just as there are conditions prerequisite to the appearance of the spectrum.

As scientists we are interested in discovering the principles underlying human ritual, just as scientists three centuries or so ago were interested in discovering the source of the rainbow. Before the age of Newton people were certainly familiar with the chromatic spectrum (see Genesis IX: 12–17). They could marvel at the romantic delicacy of the rainbow after a summer shower. They could prize the brilliance of cut crystal and diamond. They could

1

seek the elusive beauty of a refracted beam of light in water. Yet only when Newton applied the new science of optics to the study of light—placing prisms between light source and blank wall—did we come to understand more nearly fully the principles uniting the chromatic spectrum and ordinary white light.

Just as the spectrum puzzled pre-Newtonian physicists, the phenomenon of human ritual puzzles modern behavioral scientists. Ritual, found in a dazzling variety of forms and practiced in one form or another by all societies, appears to us elusive, complex, and problematic, while at the same time reflecting the very essence of humanity. In this work we not only develop the spectral qualities of ritual behavior but also supply the reader with both unifying theory and empirical "prism," without either of which the problem of human ritual cannot be solved.

Note from the beginning that our primary concern here is with ritual. But, in addition, we are offering a set of theoretical constructs, concepts, and methods far transcending ritual. We are, in fact, offering a particular approach to the complex nature of the phenomenon of man while centering our attention on ritual, for to examine human ritual is to examine man in all his hues: his thought, language, society, physiology, individual and social development, and evolution. We advocate the empirical application of a global theory that has been elaborated in a previous book, *Biogenetic Structuralism.* In the following chapters we apply the theory of biogenetic structuralism to an explanation of human ritual. The theory places certain strict methodological requirements on us. For one thing it demands that we explore the evolutionary progression of man's capacity for ritual.

It also compels us to look at ritual behavior as found in other species and to investigate the biopsychological functions of ritual relative to cognitive and neurophysiological processes. The theory of biogenetic structuralism leads us to consider ritual as practiced by man and his society with constant attention to the biological and evolutionary considerations that have gone before.

Our task in this chapter is to prepare the reader for total participation in the rest of the book. We do this by supplying the reader with the theory and methodology indispensable to the more substantive studies of the spectrum of ritual discussed in subsequent chapters. Thus we give a brief outline of biogenetic structural theory, prefaced and encompassed by a discussion of the structuralist movement in general. With the basic tenets of the theory defined, we construct a more detailed body of conceptual and methodological material relevant to the specific understanding of ritual behavior. Finally we define the phenomenon of ritual in new terms necessitated by and in keeping with the theoretical and methodological approach being taken. Thus, with the shades drawn, the pinpoint light source obtained, and the prisms polished and in their respective places, we are then ready for a detailed and sustained examination of the spectrum of ritual.

Structuralism

Among the many issues that may distinguish one structuralist approach from another are (1) the precise locus of structure (epiphenomenal, cultural, neurophysiological, cognitive, etc.), (2) the methodology requisite to the discovery and exploration of structure, and (3) the various roles of language, perception, and cognition in generating, facilitating, or maintaining structure. A number of these issues are discussed from our own perspective.

Broadly speaking, we may delimit two strains of structuralism in social theory today: *semiotic* and *evolutionary* structuralism. Semiotic structuralism is essentially synchronic in its approach to systems, nonbiological in its empirical and theoretical grounding, and neo-Platonic in its conception of structure. Semiotic structuralism is best exemplified in the work of Claude Levi-Strauss, his followers and some of his antecedents (see Mauss, 1925; Levi-Strauss, 1966, 1969, 1973; Maranda, 1972; Needham, 1973; Rossi, 1974), as well as in the work of other scholars (see Foucault, 1970; Leach, 1961, 1965, 1967, Murphy, 1971; de Saussure, 1916; Robey, 1973; Burnham, 1973).

Evolutionary structuralism, on the other hand, may be characterized as diachronic in its approach to systems, biological in its grounding, and neurophysiological or cognitive in attributing the ontological locus of structure. Examples of contemporary works that might be considered in this second category are those of Piaget (1970a, 1970b, 1971); Teilhard de Chardin (1959); Chapple and Coon (1942); Chapple (1970); Count (1969, 1973, 1974); Pribram (1971); Lenneberg (1967); Jung (1956); Whitehead (1960, 1964); Werner (1948, 1957); Harvey, Hunt, and Schroder (1961); Schroder, Driver, and Streufert (1967); Kohlberg (1969); Witkin et al. (1962); Garner (1962, 1974); Wallace (1970); Whitaker (1971); Holloway (1974); and Laughlin and d'Aquili (1974a). The essential tenets comprising evolutionary structuralism are not, however, recent. They are also to be found underlying much of the work of such earlier scholars as Tyler (1881), Hertz (1909), and Bergson (1911).

One may reasonably ask what set of criteria determines the grouping of such disparate scholars under the rubric of "structuralism." We understand all of these thinkers to hold a fundamental proposition in common, namely, that the explanation of social and psychological phenomena must be in terms of ontologically real, knowable, but rarely observable structures that are (1) systemic in their organization and function, (2) universal in their application, and (3) usually imperceptible to actors (Laughlin and d'Aquili, 1974a; chapter 1; see also Piaget, 1971; Lane, 1970:11ff). In other words, structuralism conceives of phenomena at the level of observables or "surface structure" (i.e., behavior, institution, role, expression) as being manifestations of "deep structures," that is, structures that are barely, if ever, observable and that operate unconsciously to transform patterns at the surface. Patterns at the surface may thus be viewed as content mediated by underlying structure, the arrangement of these surface patterns being termed *transforms* or *transformations*.

Theory of Biogenetic Structuralism

Biogenetic structuralism is an amalgamation of evolutionary, biological, neurophysiological, and structuralist theories.

Within the evolutionary structuralist frame of reference we

may explain more clearly what factors distinguish biogenetic structuralism from other, perhaps complementary, approaches. The easiest way to begin this task is to present two syllogisms combined in an enthymeme, but one that nonetheless reflects the essence of our theory.

    1. All behavior is the manifestation of brain function.
    2. Brain function is the activity of brain structure.
    3. All brain structure develops to some degree under the governance of the genetic code.

All behavior is, therefore, to some degree under the governance of the genetic code.

From the standpoint of biogenetic structuralism the crucial epistemological problem faced by the social and behavioral sciences is how to ascertain empirically the interactions over time among the genetic, environmental, and developmental components that result ultimately in the behavioral set under consideration.

The theory of biogenetic structuralism holds that human behavior, along with the behavior of at least all higher vertebrates, is a function of the interaction between the organism's central nervous system and the organism's environment. We may here productively draw upon Kurt Lewin's (1935, 1936) classic formula:

$$B = f(P, E)$$

where behavior may be conceived as the function (f) of the interaction through time between the organism (P) and its environment (E). We may substitute the organism's central nervous system (N) for P, deriving the modified formula:

$$B = f(N, E)$$

and thus schematize the principal elements involved in most, if not all, of the behavior of interest to anthropology and other behavioral sciences. We return to the Lewinian formula later in this chapter. At this point we note that we use the term *equilibration* to describe the interaction between N and E (after Waddington, 1957; see also Piaget, 1971, 1977). We prefer the term *equilibra-*

tion, rather than the more common term *equilibrium,* for two reasons. First, equilibration involves an active modification of sensory data on the part of the organism, rather than a passive encoding of the figurative aspects of reality. In addition, equilibration involves action, active and sustained compensation on the part of the organism in response to environmental perturbations. Equilibration is thus a process, as opposed to equilibrium, which is a state of balance.[1]

Because it requires recourse to equilibration between the organism and the organism's environment, biogenetic structuralism disallows any arbitrary constraints upon empirical epistemology (Rubinstein and Laughlin, 1977). In particular, we would reject both the antireductionist thesis that sociological (psychological) facts require sociological (psychological) explanations (Durkheim, 1938), and its antithesis, which requires science to reduce to "ultimate constituents," a position associated with the *logical atomism* of Bertrand Russell (1956) and the early Wittgenstein (1961; see also Laughlin and Brady, 1978, chapter 1). The former constraint is based on a naive view of the nature of systems: that "the whole is more than the sum of its parts." The latter position is based on the equally naive view that a sufficiently diligent inquiry will discover the concrete elements on which higher levels of system are formed.

There can be no better response to the quest for ultimate constituents than Whitehead's (1960) philosophy of organism. If the universe is constructed of organismic processes in an infinite concatenation of systems within systems, then the search for a level of ultimate constituents, or "basic units," is not only futile, it is quite impossible. As to the "sociological fallacy," we would respond, in agreement with Buckley (1967), Blalock (1969), and in disagreement with Sutherland (1973), that to comprehend a system one must "reduce," to some extent at least, the parts and relations between the parts comprising the whole. As Robert Hinde has said:

The material with which we start is usually at the behavioral level. If the prediction of behavior, given the antecedent conditions, was the sole aim, there might be no need to reduce to a physiological level: reference to un-

1. For a more detailed discussion of the use of this term, see also Piaget, 1971:25ff.

derlying mechanisms could be unnecessary. But even if the complete prediction of behavior were possible, we should still have advanced only one stage towards its full understanding: a further stage would be reached if the regularities in behavior could be understood in terms of the physiological organization they reflect. Thus hypotheses must be judged not only at the behavioral level, but also in terms of their compatability with lower ones (and higher ones?) (Hinde, 1970:7).

To the degree that the scientist has (1) modeled the constituent subsystems and relations between subsystems comprising the whole, and (2) the relations between those subsystems functioning in concert and the environment, he has modeled the whole. To put this more positively, any explanation of behavior (B) must take into account any and all levels of systemic organization that are efficiently present (are "statistically relevant," in Salmon's 1971 sense) in the interaction between B and the environment or E. Thus, by paraphrasing Lewin's formula, we may schematize the interaction as:

$$B = f\left[[P = f(x,y)],\ E\right]$$

where not only the organism (P) is active in the account, but also its efficient subsystems, which, along with their interactions, comprise the organism $[P = f(x,y)]$. Of course, elements x and y may be further broken down into subsystem elements in an infinite regress. But their regress need not worry us, for, as Whitehead (1960) taught us, the model is sufficient if it contains all and only those levels of systemic organization required to account for the phenomena in our universe of discourse. An added advantage of this view, as we shall see in later chapters, is that it avoids the unnecessary and fallacious conception of social groups as organisms (Cohen, 1971), a mistake repeated time and again in anthropological theory (e.g., Radcliffe-Brown, 1940; White, 1959; Service, 1971). Depending on the phenomenon of concern, our models and research may encompass several or all of the levels of systemic organization relevant to man-science generally—the levels of genetics, physiology and neurophysiology, cognition (as well as perception and affect), personality and individual action, institutions, society, and ecology.

Returning for a moment to our initial syllogism, we spoke of all behaviors being predisposed by the genes. Biogenetic structuralism would hold that there is probably no human behavior that is totally genetically determined *or* totally acquired—that *all* behavior is mediated by neural structures that themselves develop by equilibration of the phenotype with its environment. This means that neural structures are inevitably and simultaneously both genetically predisposed and flexible in adaptation to the environment. With reference to anthropology all human behavior that we customarily call "learned" or "cultural" actually consists of a variety of behaviors mediated by structures that are universal to all men. Unlike the Levi-Straussian "structures," the structural models to which we refer are not epiphenomena but rather are composed of a finite number of neural connections within the central nervous system (CNS) (Laughlin and d'Aquili, 1974a; Hebb, 1949; Cunningham, 1972; Rakic, 1976). These sets of neural connections provide fields of action potentials[2] when the model is activated (Eccles, 1973; Caianiello, 1968)—fields that may have component subfields over a large expanse of cortical and subcortical tissue (Laughlin and d'Aquili, 1974a; Pribram, 1971).

The human neocortex is presumably the most flexible and plastic to be found in the animal kingdom. Yet we would contend that under no circumstance is a neural model totally plastic—that, in fact, in ontogeny there are inevitably (1) an initial, genetically determined precursor to every model and (2) a set of constraints inherent in the initial formulation of the model that ultimately affect the nature and complexity of the adult model. We have termed the initial, genetically endowed formulation of a neural model *neurognosis* (see Laughlin and d'Aquili, 1974a, chapter 5; Laughlin and McManus, 1975 n.d.). This term refers both to the structure and the function of genetically determined neural models. Since the function of a large proportion of neural models is to filter, input, and evaluate information pertaining to the environment and to direct appropriate motor responses to the environment, the notion of neurognosis is intended to denote the neural processes of sensory

2. The term *action potential* refers to the all-or-none propagation of an electrochemical discharge down the full course of the axon of a neuron. The action potential is one means a neuron has of communicating information to other neurons in a network.

input, information storage, retrieval, evaluation, and the assignment of appropriate affect and action relative to stimulus—taken
together, these comprise what we will call cognition, the prime
adaptive function of the brain.

The operation of neurognosis in its purest form (that is, without significant acquired complexity) may best be seen in the
neural models underlying "fixed action patterns" (Eibl-Eibesfeldt,
1970; chapter 3; Hinde, 1970).[3] Such patterns underlie egg rolling
by graylag geese (Lorenz and Tinbergen, 1938) and nest building
by rats (Eibl-Eibesfeldt, 1970:27). With the exception of the infant
sucking and grasping reflexes, most human neurognostic models
remain generally open to modification through interaction with the
environment, although there do appear to be periods (called "critical" or "sensitive" periods by some) of optimal plasticity of particular models or classes of models in the ontogeny of the human
brain. We have described the mechanism of neural model reformulation elsewhere (Laughlin and d'Aquili, 1974a:84ff).

The constraints and predispositions imposed upon cognition
and behavior are quite apparent in a number of universal brain
functions in man and other species. Of the many we might choose
to examine,[4] we shall briefly introduce the following, all of which
will be central to our discussion of ritual later in this chapter: cognitive imperative, cognized versus operational environment, conceptualization and symbolization, and cultural elaboration.

Cognitive Imperative

Many of the culturological concepts commonly used in the social
sciences and philosophy are anthropocentrisms. Concepts such

---

3. The probability is that there exist *no* pure, unmodified neurognostic models in the adult
organism.

4. Among the many human cognitive phenomena that are heavily neurognostically structured are the process of empirical inquiry, ambivalence in sexual identity, maintenance of
the boundaries of conceptual systems, resistance to change of conceptual models with age,
the modeling of recursive events as cycles, the optimization of adaptive intelligence, and
various forms of psychopathology, including phobia, schizophrenia, and depression (also attendant syndromes including anomie, suicide, alcoholism, and "voodoo death"). (See
Laughlin and d'Aquili, 1974a; Laughlin and Brady, 1978; d'Aquili and Laughlin, 1975;
Rubinstein et al., n.d.)

as "thought," "reason," "rationality," and "conceptualization" are often used in such a fashion that they may apply *in principle* only to the actions and neural processes of *Homo sapiens*. The fact is, however, that all of these terms refer to behavioral or subjectively reportable equivalents of neural processes—processes that are neurognostically structured and that are the results of untold millennia of evolution. Knowledge of brain functions via introspection is inevitably biased in favor of those features of which we are aware. Yet it is clear that much neural processing of information—collection, evaluation, association, and storage of information—occurs outside the bounds of normal awareness. Awareness itself is, in all probability, an adaptive function of neurophysiological processing that is poorly equipped for exploring itself but is quite remarkable when exploring aspects of the environment most critical to survival. These facts are particularly evidenced by the set of neural constraints we may term the *cognitive imperative* (d'Aquili, 1972; Laughlin and d'Aquili, 1974a:114ff). This concept refers to the drive in man, other mammals, and birds to order their world by differentiation of adaptively significant sensory elements and events, and to the unification of these elements into a systemic, cognitive whole.

There are a number of hallmarks of the cognitive imperative. Frustration of the imperative due to unyielding environmental novelty may lead to anxiety and eventual system breakdown. The brain of higher organisms tends to strive for a balance between novelty and redundancy in the environment (Berlyne, 1960; Suedfeld, 1964). Too much novelty or complexity is met by attempts to classify it into simpler categories, to reduce it to meaningful bits of information. Too little novelty, on the other hand, leads to boredom, restlessness, and attempts to seek or create greater uncertainty or complexity (Berlyne, 1960; Fiske and Maddi, 1961; Pribram, 1971). When an organism perceives itself to be understimulated or overstimulated, it acts to redress the imbalance. To the extent that redress is seen as feasible, the organism experiences motivation; to the extent that correction is seen as not feasible, the organism experiences feelings of helplessness. What counts is the status of environmental stimulation in relation to the ability of the cognitive and behavioral apparatus to act effectively on the environmental stimulation (Pribram, 1971; see chapter 6 for further discussion).

The unfailing attempt by *Homo sapiens* to identify a novel stimulus is a process that occasionally leads to bizarre results (see Wallace, 1957; also chapter 9). Affect always occurs in the context of the activity of the cognitive imperative. The definition and experience of affective arousal is contingent upon what is occurring in the cognitive processes at the time and consequently influences the behavior addressed to adaptive response (Schacter and Singer, 1962; Beck, 1967; Schacter, 1971; Rosenberg, 1960; Valenstein, 1973; Mahl in Pribram, 1971; Barr, 1971; Berlyne, 1960; Zimbardo, 1969; Lazarus, 1966, 1974).

A particularly useful aspect of the cognitive imperative that we must understand is that the discrimination and differentiation of environmental events occur both spatially and temporally. The cognitive imperative requires the ordering of spatial elements into systematic, recognizable entities and relations between entities. It further requires the ordering of durational processes into causal sequences. The latter function of the cognitive imperative is the most difficult to understand, and yet it presents features of profound importance to the comprehension of anthropological phenomena.

We have already mentioned the dysphoria that often follows on the heels of frustrated gnostic functions. Likewise anxiety is the result of frustration of the imperative to "explain" by imposition of "cause" the occurrence of some set of significant events (earthquake, tornado, etc.). Insofar as the relevant sequence of precursor events is available to perception in the environment, causal relations are readily modeled from available information. The apparent capacity of man to model relations in space and time with ever-increasing extension beyond those relations immediately available to its perception comprises the very essence of his evolutionary course for at least the last 5 million years (see Teilhard de Chardin, 1959; also the discussion of the "cognitive extension of prehension" in Laughlin and d'Aquili, 1974a:90ff). One result of this increased cognitive capacity over lower animals is that man is able to model extension and space where no environmentally created spatial boundaries and temporal termini are empirically given. Under such circumstances the human conceptual system creates subjectively and relatively meaningful boundaries (such as nation, seas, primary kin and ethnic groups) and "first causes" or initial termini (like creator gods, origin myths replete with first heroes, arbitrary times of birth) and imposes these upon the conception of the environment.

The cognitive imperative operating in the causal mode on uncertain stimuli usually results in a corpus of "theoretical entities" that are responsible for the occurrence of significant events. Thus, in all societies there may be found various "spirits," "powers," "gods," as well as "black holes," "viruses," "photons," and "libidos," that operate to "cause" events or to inhibit them, depending on the situation. The locus of uncertainty is not always in the present or past but may also involve the future ramifications of known or suspected events. The human brain strives to remove as much uncertainty as possible. The degree to which certainty is created depends on a number of factors, including the emotional import and the survival value adherent to the situation. At any rate we find various forms of predictive and retrodictive divination to be a virtual human universal (Fortes in Huxley, 1966). The results of this operation of the cognitive imperative are seen in our own society in the upsurge of interest in the occult arts (i.e., Satanism, spiritualism, astrology) in the face of greater and greater social and psychological insecurity (see Ornstein, 1976). All of these operations upon environmental stimuli, as well as the assignment of appropriate affect and behavior in relation to the stimuli, make up the cognized environment of the organism.

Cognized Environment
The cognitive imperative is the assimilating operator whose function is to bring novel environmental stimuli into ordered concert with other events and entities modeled in the organism's *cognized environment* (E_c).[5] The distinction between the organism's cog-

5. In a Piagetian sense, the cognized environment may be viewed as comprising two elements: (1) its level of structural organization and (2) its content or surface transformations of the structural organization.

nized environment and the *operational environment* (E_o) of the organism is critical if we are to understand fully both the limitations and the adaptive success of the brain as the organ of behavior. We are using the terminology of Rappaport in this distinction between the two kinds of environment.

The operational model of the environment is that which the anthropologist constructs through observation and measurement of empirical entities, events, and material relationships. He takes this model to represent, for analytical purposes, the physical world of the group he is studying. . . . The cognized model is the model of the environment conceived by the people who act in it. The two models are overlapping, but not identical. While many components of the physical world will be represented in both, the operational model is likely to include material elements, such as disease germs and nitrogen-fixing bacteria, that affect the actors but of which they are not aware. Conversely, the cognized model may include elements that cannot be shown by empirical means to exist, such as spirits and other supernatural beings (Rappaport, 1967:237–238).

Generalizing from Rappaport's excellent discussion of this critical distinction, we would define the cognized environment of any higher organism as the totality of neural models of space and time, while the operational environment would be that part of space and time that affects the organism's survival in one way or another. Here a number of comments are necessary for a complete understanding of the meaning and scope of this distinction.

1. There is always an adaptively significant overlap between the E_c and E_o of the organism. As a result, regular fluctuations in the operational environment are usually modeled in the organism's E_c (see Laughlin and Brady, 1978, for a discussion of "diaphasis").

2. The E_c is generally simpler than the E_o. That is, if the E_o is defined as all the elements and forces operating to produce phenomena affecting the individual, then his cognition of these factors tends to be less complex and inclusive. Of course, a simple physical process may become cognized in an elaborate, cosmological fashion that may appear more complex than reality itself. The E_c as defined by Rappaport is, however, contingent upon the knowledge and capacities of the observer. In principle, these do not exceed that of the observed. In practice, the model of the E_c is simple in relation to reality.

3. The E_c of any organism operates as a system (Laughlin and d'Aquili, 1974a; Harvey et al., 1961; Piaget, 1971; Powers, 1973; see chapter 6). Thus the organism functions neurophysiologically and cognitively to maintain the integrity of the E_c, or subsystemic portion thereof, by a variety of strategies, including distortion of information for assimilation into this environment (Turiel, 1966; Wallace, 1957); rejection of the information (Wallace, 1957; Hastorf and Cantril, 1956; Festinger et al., 1956); and holding the information within perceptual structure for a period of time without assimilation of that information into the E_c. The reader is reminded that a very large literature exists in social psychology on the issue of "cognitive consistency" (see Festinger, 1957, 1964; Abelson et al., 1968; Feldman, 1966; Heider, 1958; Brehm and Cohen, 1962; see also Rubinstein et al., n.d.; and chapters 6, 7, and 9).

4. The E_c of the organism may contain elements and relations not present in the E_o—indeed, these may have little or no representation in the E_o whatsoever. This is most certainly the case with *Homo sapiens* everywhere. The extent to which this is true for the E_c among other species is not known. It seems that chimpanzees may have a rudimentary capacity for developing nonoperational elements in their E_cs under laboratory conditions (Gardner and Gardner, 1969; Premack, 1971; Menzel, 1971, 1973).

5. The E_c of any higher vertebrate is the result of a complex of ontogenetic development. This aspect of neurophysiological and cognitive functioning is covered in some detail in chapters 6 and 7.

6. An inescapable conclusion reached from these considerations is that the Lewinian formula:

$$B = f(P,E)$$

may also be reformulated as:

$$B = f\left\{P, [E_c = f(P, E_o)]\right\}$$

where the behavior of the organism (B) is a function of the interaction between the organism (P) as a biological entity and its (E_c), which is, in turn, the function of previous interactions between the organism and its (E_o). Again, we direct the reader to chapters 6 and 7 for a more detailed elaboration of this point.

Introduction

Cognition, Conceptualization, and Symbolization

As we use the term here, *cognition* refers to the process by which an entity, event, or relationship perceived by an organism in its E_o becomes assimilated into and organized by the organism's E_c. An observer may or may not be aware that an event has been cognized by an organism or group of organisms when a correlative affect and behavioral response are elicited from the organism in response to the presence of that event or object in its sensory field. Events and entities exist in the E_o of the organism that remain uncognized or that because of their complexity or extension are uncognizable given the conceptual capacity of the organism (see chapter 6). This is as true for *H. sapiens* as it is for other species.

With *H. sapiens,* and perhaps with other species as well, there is, in addition to cognition, the capacity of *conceptualization*. This process is defined here as a neurophysiologically based, evolutionary refinement upon cognition that facilitates the modeling of an event or process in the E_o by: (1) unifying sensory material cross-modally[6]; (2) circumventing the necessary use of the limbic system[7] for immediate sensory associations; and (3) thereby facilitating the potential assignment of symbolic or expressive function to concepts. This process is clearly present in the human species. The extent to which conceptualization characterizes the spontaneous conceptual capacities of other vertebrates (i.e., primates, elephants, and dolphins) is controversial. The only other species that has demonstrated this capacity under laboratory conditions is the chimpanzee (see Fleming, 1974; Gardner and Gardner, 1972; A. Premack, 1974; D. Premack, 1971; Premack and Premack, 1972; Laughlin and d'Aquili, 1974a; chapter 3).

6. "Cross-modal transfer" refers to the neurophysiological capacity for direct exchange of sensory information between the cortical areas mediating particular sensory modalities (i.e., visual, somatosensory, auditory senses) without the limbic system's being involved as a mediator (see also Laughlin and d'Aquili, 1974a:53).

7. The limbic system consists of a number of neural structures at the core of the brain (mentioned later in this chapter) that are known to be intimately associated with the expression of emotion, particularly with the experience of pleasure, pain, and anger. The limbic system covers roughly 34, 27, 28, 23, 24, and adjacent structures on the Brodmann map of the brain (see Lamendella, 1977).

The hallmark of the capacity for conceptualization is action on the part of the organism derived from a cognized model *that is to some extent abstracted from the reality it represents.* This is an important consideration in relation to the evolution of neural functions and thus requires some elaboration here.

1. Lower vertebrates (as well as the rest of the animal kingdom) typically develop E_cs that are to a large extent stimulus bound; that is, the entities and relations cognized depend on the repetitive recurrence of the corresponding entities and relations in the E_o. Furthermore, in such animals the cognized entities and relations tend not to produce behavior *in the absence* of the corresponding entities and relations and relations in the perceptual field.

2. Higher vertebrates capable of conceptualization are able, to some degree, to construct a set of entities and relations within their E_c representing *in toto* a set of diverse episodes in the E_o. As suggested in chapter 3, chimpanzees in the wild may be capable of constructing a total cognized community from the social episodes they experience through time. A chimpanzee may thus conceptualize and operate from the conception of a total social structure, even though the cognized "group" may rarely, if ever, come together physically.

3. The distinction between cognition and conceptualization drawn here is really a more simplified way of presenting the notion of the "cognitive extension of prehension" discussed in an earlier work (see Laughlin and d'Aquili, 1974a, chapter 4), where it was argued that the modeling function of the proto-hominid brain gradually evolved to the point where it was capable of constructing relations in space and time more complex, distant, or inclusive than those present in immediate sensory experience. This process of evolutionary development had the most profound effects on the course of hominid adaptation.

4. Another important point is that the capacity to conceptualize is a necessary, although never a sufficient, condition for the ability to *symbolize* (in the sense discussed in Laughlin, McManus and Stephens, 1978). Man, along with other species, is capable of conceptualizing an event without the concept of that event's involving an expressive component. The equation of concept with expressive symbol has led theorists to a number of

anthropocentric conclusions relative to: (1) language and intelligence, (2) the capacity of speechless species to conceptualize, (3) the proportional ranking of species in the phylogenetic scale, and (4) the relationship between brain size and conceptual capacity. We would argue that the ease with which man (and possibly some of the Cetacea) is able to symbolically communicate conceptual material has required substantial selection over a long period of evolutionary time. The selection in all probability was in favor of the advantage organisms might gain by being able to conceptualize material from the E_o vicariously via communication from conspecifics who had themselves experienced the material directly (Laughlin and d'Aquili, 1974a). It seems probable to us that there exists a number of animal species capable of conceptualizing the E_o without the ability also to communicate that material to conspecifics. At any rate the question of conceptual and linguistic competence among Cetacea remains extremely controversial (Cf. Caldwell and Caldwell, 1972; Lilly, 1961, 1967; Droscher, 1965; Bateson, 1972; Fichtelius and Sjolander, 1972; Krone, 1972).

An important point is that the joint capacities of man to conceptualize and symbolize facilitate conceptual elaboration of both the individual's E_c and his E_o (the latter through active, intentional, and unintentional reconstruction of the E_o) and place a special burden on behavioral scientists attempting to unearth the patterns of adaptation characteristic of the species (see Ardener, 1977; Laughlin, 1977).

Cultural Elaboration

The reader will remember that behavior is in direct response, not to the E_o of the organism, but rather to the E_c, and insofar as the E_c is partially isomorphic[8] with the E_o, the behavior of the organism

---

8. By the term *isomorphic* we refer to a special relationship between two structures T and T'. We may say that T is isomorphic with T' if (1) cardinality is the same for both T and T' and (2) there exists a one-to-one correspondence of relations. Another way to say this is that T is isomorphic with T' if T may be mapped onto T':

$$R_T = T'.$$

We may speak of structure T as being *partially* isomorphic with T' if[f] (1) TCT' and (2) every function in T' is a restriction of a function in T' to T. Another way to say this is that T is partially isomorphic with T' if T may be mapped *into* T':

remains adaptive. It will also be remembered that man's capacity to model entities and relations in space and time has vastly increased over the past several hundred millennia—to the point where he is able to cognize such entities and relations in the absence of any immediately corroborative evidence of their existence in the E_o. Furthermore, man may conceptualize entities and relations and ascribe to them symbolic attributes and thus make them concrete elements within his E_c. The effect of this proliferation of cognized elements has been what we term *cultural elaboration*. We refer here to all the material and nonmaterial elements of surface structure (e.g., behavior, institution, role, expression) that are organized, manipulated, transformed, used and manifested by deep structure. We refer, in other words, to the cultural contents or phenomena that have become, among other things, impedimenta in the search for the underlying deep structure or basic principles of human cognition and social action (Laughlin and Brady, 1978, ch. 1). Too close attention to cultural elaboration leads to a "notes and queries" or "oddities and quiddities" approach to human behavior that is detrimental to the development of a coherent science of man. Isolation of cultural elaboration as the principal subject matter of anthropology has (1) led to theories emphasizing the differences among men, rather than their commonalities; (2) led to a "recreation of the old gap between man and other primates which, it was thought, the adoption of an evolutionary frame of reference would serve to bridge" (Hallowell, 1960:319); (3) elevated the concept of "culture" to the status of an epiphenomenon; and (4) perpetuated the false dichotomy between "nature" and "nurture."

Nevertheless the study of cultural elaboration is not unimportant. Quite the contrary, from a properly phylogenetic and ecological point of view, the analysis of surface content (the product of

---

$$R_T \epsilon T'.$$

With respect to the relationship between the cognized environment (E_c) of an organism and that organism's operational environment (E_o), we may speak of E_c as being *adaptively* isomorphic with E_o under these conditions: (1) N represents the total set of neural models within the brain of the organism, (2) $E_c = N$ $E_o \neq \emptyset$, (3) E_c is partially isomorphic with E_o and (4) $E_c \supset E_o$ is a sufficient condition for the biological survival of the organism.

cultural elaboration) becomes critical to an understanding of human adaptation.[9] For it is often the cultural elaboration that determines the behavioral interface between the individual or group and the E_o. An important point here is that much of the cultural elaboration of a human society's E_c has little or no relevance to the adaptation of the population ("adaptation" being used here in its strict biological sense). In other words, once an optimal adaptation is reached by a society, additional cognized elements may be assimilated into the E_c as long as these elements do not jeopardize the adaptation of the population. Much, if not most, of the cultural elaboration in human society would seem to have little relevance to the optimal effectiveness of population adaptation. A biogenetic structural approach to cultural elaboration of a society's E_c provides a theoretical basis for evaluating the phylogenetic and ecological importance of such phenomena.

Methodology of Biogenetic Structuralism

Although the theory of biogenetic structuralism has been elaborated in great detail in other works, the fundamental methodology logically entailed by the theory has been touched on only casually. It is therefore necessary to set out more explicitly the methodological tenets of the approach to make the organization of this and related works explicable. Roughly speaking, biogenetic structuralism invokes two general and complementary research strategies in its study of human social phenomena (see also Wilson, 1975):

1. Neuroanthropology: the study of the relationship between the brain and sociocultural behavior.
2. Comparative ethology: the study of behavior in a pan-specific and biological context.

The exact nature of the studies that emerge from these two perspectives depends on, among other factors, the time frame

9. For a more detailed examination of the relationship between the surface content (culture) and adaptive infrastructure in human populations, see Laughlin and Brady, 1978.

being encompassed by the phenomena of concern. We may discriminate three principal time frames that have thus far concerned biogenetic structural analyses—time relative to phylogenesis, or evolutionary time; time relative to individual ontogenesis; and time relative to population adaptation. When we place the two approaches (neuroanthropology and ethology) within this temporal context, the variety of concerns may be summarized as in Figure 1.1.

Figure 1.1. The Chief Orientations of Biogenetic Structuralism.

	Neuroanthropology	Ethology
Phylogenetic	Neuroevolution Neurogenetics Comparative neurophysiology	Evolutionary precursors of behavior patterns (anlagen or longitudinal homologies)
Ontogenetic	Developmental neurophysiology	Comparative ontogenesis and socialization
Adaptive	Information processing Conceptual systems Neurology and neuro- pathology	Comparative study of social organization in relation to ecological variance. Cycles in adaptation of particular populations ("biogram") Comparative systems of communication

It is apparent that Figure 1.1 presents the elements of a single perspective or "metadiscipline," although the elements of the perspective have been labeled here according to more orthodox disciplines and subdisciplines. For instance, insofar as the brain is the organ of behavior, and "behavior" is a label for a major function of brain, the distinction between neuroanthropology and human ethology is largely spurious. What all of these approaches are in fact doing is looking at the origin and structure of neural functions under a variety of temporal and contextual circumstances. We have called this analytic process a *biogenetic structural analysis,* an approach that is logically entailed by biogenetic structural theory and that provides us with our much-needed analytical tool.

Introduction

We now present, in outline, the central steps in an ideally complete analysis, a process exemplified and amplified by the analysis of human ritual in subsequent chapters.

1. *Isolation of the phenomenon* (*A*) *to be analyzed.* The selection of a focus for analysis may be based on a variety of considerations: phenomenon *A* is a classic problem in the anthropological literature, *A* is of special interest to the analyst, *A* appears intuitively to be a human universal, and so forth. This step should include an intense but informal evaluation of the phenomenon for its appropriateness to biogenetic structural analysis. This means a quick runthrough of the following substeps before committing *A* for complete analysis.

a. *Operational definition of A.* Phenomenon *A* must be defined operationally so that empirical inclusion of all members (manifestations) of *A* is, in principle, possible, and empirical exclusion of all nonmembers of *A* is equally possible. Any member of set *A* may be an entity or a relation among entities.

Because phenomenon *A* is in all likelihood defined initially in relation to the species *Homo sapiens,* it is critical to a biogenetic structural analysis that *A* not be defined anthropomorphically. That is, the definition of *A* must exclude any entity or relation among entities whose inclusion would render an analysis impossible *in principle* among species other than *H. sapiens.* To give a rather obvious, though cogent, example, it would constitute an anthropomorphism to include the use of material weapons as a necessary condition in the operationalization of the concept of warfare. Such an inclusion would mean that it would be impossible, in principle, to examine the phenomenon of warfare among species that do not fashion and use tools.

b. *Establishment of the universality of A.* The central question here is whether phenomenon *A* is a genuine human universal. This is not as easy to ascertain as was once thought. We are now aware of the phenomenon of *latent processes* (Count, 1973; Sade, n.d.; Piaget, 1970, 1971; Seligman and Hager, 1972; Laughlin and d'Aquili, 1974a). Latent processes may be defined for our purposes as universal neural structures that are not universally manifested in behavior, owing to the absence of an appropriate releaser in the environment operating as a necessary (and perhaps, as in the case of fixed action patterns, also a sufficient) condition for the behavior. Latent processes may be instructively conceived in terms of the Lewinian formula $B = f (P,E)$. Behavior here is the manifestation of latent process. Because behavior is contingent upon the interaction between the organism (P) and the environment (E), three conditions may obtain when the behavior indicating the presence of latent process is in fact absent: (i) the hypothesized latent process does not exist; (ii) it exists within the organism, but that organism is in an environment that does not elicit the latent process; or (iii) the latent process is rudimentarily present but remains developmentally incomplete owing to the lack of ontogenetic encounter with appropriate environmental conditions.

In light of latent processes the often-imposed requirement of behavioral universality for establishing A as a human universal is no longer tenable. The universality of A may be ascertained through a variety of means, including: (i) directly measuring neurognosis through neurophysiological techniques, (ii) experimentally eliciting A in populations in which the underlying neurognosis has remained latent, (iii) ascertaining that A occurs independently of historical and geographical variables (see Driver, 1966), and (iv) ascertaining a strong correlation between A and some set of ecological or social variables, the latter being independent of geographical and historical contingencies.

c. Establishment of the operational environment of A. To discover the biological functions of phenomenon A, it is first necessary to model the (E_o) within whose context A functions. The analyst must distinguish the operational components of the E_o for all populations within his sample manifesting A.[10] It is precisely at this point that evolutionary ecology may make a valuable contribution, including, as that discipline does, a concern for ecosystems and the like.

d. Establishment of the neurognostic bases of A. Ideally, the analyst ascertains, as far as possible, the set of all subsystems operating in concert within the human nervous system (NS) to mediate A. Thus, making sure that no components of

10. Here E_o is, of course, another subset of U. Therefore, the operational components may be entities or relations among entities. They may also be first-, or even second-, order subsets of entities and relations among entities within E_o.

the *NS* are in E_o, and no components of E_o are in the *NS*, we may now further define phenomenon *A* as a set of finite, numbered functions in the interaction between the *NS* and its E_o.

The essence of this step in a biogenetic structural analysis is to determine the exact range and limits of the functions in the interaction between *NS* and E_o.

e.) *Establishment of the ecological relations of A.* If we define the function *f* as any operation of a component of *A* upon the E_o and define the function *g* as any operation of a component of the E_o upon a component or set of components of the *NS*, then we may define the *ecology* (*a*) of *A* by the equation

$$f + g = a$$

at time *t*.

In reality the functions *f* and *g* are enormously complex, and the ecology of *A* normally comprises multiple channels of negative and positive feedback (see Milsum, 1968; Blalock, 1969). Precision in the logic of analysis must be stressed at this point to avoid the pitfalls of orthodox "functional" analysis of the sort that has too often obfuscated anthropological explanation (see Hemple, 1959; Jarvie, 1965). It would be well to state again that a "function" of *A* and a "cause" of *A* are two different things; by *function,* in an ecological sense, we specifically mean the relation just described.

Obviously, then, one may completely model the functional and even the entire ecological relations between *A* and E_o without ever once addressing the question of the cause or causes of *A*. To attribute "cause" to a function is to commit a *post hoc* fallacy—quite a common failing in the anthropological literature.

After the ecological relations of *A* are established, the analysis may proceed in one or more of the following three ways. We list them here in perhaps the most operationally expeditious order.

2. *Comparative neurophysiology of A.* We have already defined *A* as a set of functions of *NS* to E_o in man. The task, at this point, is the explication of the neurognostic structures (neural models) underlying *A* in other species. A fundamental question is whether the neural structure underlying *A* in another species is *homologous* or *analogous*. The neural structure me-

diating A in species S is homologous to that mediating A in man if the component subsystems of S's NS are partially isomorphic with those of man (see footnote 8 for a more precise definition of partial isomorphism).

On the other hand, the neural structure mediating A in species S is analogous to that mediating A in man if and only if there is *no* partial isomorphism between relevant neural components. While analogical relations are of interest to biogenetic structuralists, and to evolutionary biologists in general, we are particularly concerned with establishing homological relations because of their importance in reconstructing the probable precursory structures (or *anlagen,* to use Count's term) of A, as well as the evolutionarily significant events that resulted in differentiation of variants of A. It is theoretically possible to determine a higher order set that contains all the homologous features of the neural structures mediating A among the various species of the animal kingdom. In practice, of course, it is exceedingly difficult, and at times impossible, to make such an ideal reconstruction. The reconstruction should be sufficiently complete, however, to allow an intelligent estimate of the necessary and sufficient conditions for the emergence of the neural model particular to man.

3. *Comparative ontogenesis of A*. A precise and comparative accounting for the process of ontogenesis of A is minimally required by biogenetic structural theory, as well as by Count's (1973) theory of the biogram and by Piaget's (1971) theory of adaptive intelligence. A complete analysis of the ontogenesis of A entails at least three substeps: (i) First it is necessary to discover whether the manifestation of A among adult human beings requires a developmental process. The alternative is, of course, that A is a "fixed action pattern" present from birth or emerging fairly full formed during some sensitive period in development (see footnote 3). (ii) If A proves to require a developmental process for completion of the adult form (the usual case in higher vertebrates), the set of necessary and sufficient conditions for differential and optimal development of A must be ascertained. (iii) From a comparative ethological perspective, enough species manifesting A (mediated by their homologous NSs) need to be observed to discover whether common conditions are required for optimal development of A in all species.

4. *Unified model and explanation of A.* The final step is the unification of information derived from these procedures into a coherent explanation of the occurrence of phenomenon *A* in man. Ideally, the explanation should account for the neurophysiological processes mediating *A*, as well as for the development of neural systems during ontogenesis and phylogenesis. The explanation should also include the environmental variables that account for the presence or absence (or latency) of *A* across species, as well as for the ecological relations accounting for variance within species. Finally, the explanation should ideally be capable of predicting (or retrodicting) the occurrence of *A* with a probability greater than that of competing explanations (Salmon, 1971; Rubinstein and Laughlin, n.d.). In practice the present explanation may be given credence if its predictive power is roughly equivalent to that of competing explanations, while its qualities of completeness, field of coverage, stimulus to comprehension, and understanding and heuristic power surpass those of competing models. For reasons stated elsewhere (Laughlin and d'Aquili, 1974a:144ff), we would urge the analyst toward maximal empirical grounding of his explanation through concentration on increasing the predictive power of his model.

A Biogenetic Structural Theory of Ritual: An Overview

It is not, of course, the intent of this work to critique or denigrate competing analyses of human ritual. It is also not in keeping with the strategy of analysis advocated here to describe the vast ethnographic literature pertaining to ceremonial ritual across the globe.[11] Rather, our purpose is to offer an extended example of a biogenetic structural analysis of a classic problem in anthropology through the application of a methodology logically entailed by that theory. As to the precise problem selected, we might have chosen one of many appropriate topics: descent, language, social power, reciprocity, the family, magic, and so forth. All of the fore-

---

11. For more nearly complete summaries of anthropological treatments of human ceremonial ritual, see Shaughnessy (1973), Wallace (1966), Lessa and Vogt (1972), Goode (1951), and Middleton (1967).

going topics are, we feel, equally amenable to biogenetic structural explanation, and all will likely be given such treatment in the future.[12] We have, however, chosen to render full treatment to the phenomenon of human ritual behavior, with particular emphasis on ceremonial ritual, for a number of theoretical and practical reasons. (1) The principal authors have all been concerned with ritual in relation to the study of religion. (2) The phenomenon is, in keeping with the already stated methodology, generally recognized as a human social universal. (3) The problem of the *causes,* as opposed to the *functions,* of ritual, is a classic one in anthropology, and one, in our opinion, that has yet to be satisfactorily solved. (4) Ritual presents an inevitable behavioral component, a component that may be examined in other species. (5) Ritual and ritualization present problems that are treated differently by anthropology and ethology, and their disparate treatments can be amalgamated to the benefit of both disciplines. (6) In the presence of a vast literature on human ritual, no importance limitations will be placed upon us by a paucity of data.

Sources of Obscurity in the Definition of Ritual

The history of anthropological treatment of ceremonial ritual is quite confusing, for a number of reasons, not the least of which is that few theorists have ever attempted to place ceremonial ritual in phylogenetic and evolutionary perspective (exceptions being Wallace, 1966, and Chapple, 1970). Few, indeed, have ever attempted to ascertain the physiological, especially the neurophysiological, concomitants of ritual. To make matters worse (at least from our perspective), the study of ritual has almost inevitably been linked to the study of religion and the social functions of religion manifested in ethnographic accounts of the world's cultures. Thus, one ordinarily finds the analysis of ceremonial ritual inextricably embedded in accounts of myth, social transition, law, proscriptions and prescriptions, feasting, sacrifice and the like— all of which are part of the stock-in-trade of the practicing ethno-

12. A partial analysis of this sort is presented in Laughlin and Brady (1978) relative to the responses of adaptive infrastructures of human society to fluctuations in the operational environment and basic resource availability.

logist. A result of this orientation is that ritual is defined in such a way that it is undeniably unique to man. Lessa and Vogt (1972:323ff), while avoiding an inclusive-exclusive definition of ritual, emphasize that ritual is a human process involving speech and that "most writers would agree that ritual . . . shows continuities with ceremony and everyday etiquette and for some purposes, it may be useful to call all these kinds of behavior ritual." Obviously, if ritual is inextricably linked to speech, and man is the only creature manifesting speech, then it is fruitless to look beyond human populations for evidence of ritual behavior. Yet the entire thrust of this volume is to deny the ever-present tendency toward anthropomorphism in the "science of man" and to bring to bear an alternative account of the development of man through a close analysis of one of the homologous attributes man shares with other vertebrates.

Although some theorists have begun to view ritual behavior as a kind of communication (Goffman, 1967, 1971; Fischer in Shaughnessy, 1973), we believe it is fair to say that most anthropological writers either explicitly or implicitly deny a panspecies application of the concept of ritual. Leach, in contributing to a conference on ritualization (Huxley, 1966:403), stated, "The ethologists are consistent with one another; Professor Hinde's definition will serve for all: 'ritualization refers to the evolutionary changes which the signal movements of lower vertebrates have undergone in adaptation to their function in communication.' *Such a definition has no relevance for the work of social anthropologists.* Unfortunately, although ritual is a concept which is very prominent in anthropological discourse, there is no consensus as to its precise meaning" (emphasis ours; see also Turner in Huxley, 1966, for a similar stance). As we have explained, the biogenetic structuralist rejects any definition of ritual, or of any other behavioral phenomenon, that renders the concept incapable, *in principle,* of application and test among other species. Anthropomorphic operationalization is the bane of behavioral science, posing as it does a major barrier to an evolutionary account of *Homo sapiens.* Our present problem, then, is to define ritual so that its application to behavioral patterns of other organisms is conceptually and logically possible. Only then will we be able, in subsequent chapters, to trace the precursors (*anlagen*) or evolutionary origins of human ritual and also demonstrate common biological and neurobiological functions of ritual behavior in the societies of man and other organisms.

Ritual in the Context of Social Coordination

Selection in favor of a social adaptation among many organisms is evidenced throughout the animal kingdom. The many and varied advantages of sociality have been enumerated by a number of contemporary theorists, including Wynne-Edwards (1962), Cohen (1971), Allee (1951), and Etkin (1964). Many of these advantages are behavioral and require the coordination of individual action into corporate action to reap an effect, for example, "mobbing" of predators, hunting in concert, maintenance of territory, concerted migration within the group range. The central problem for any species whose primary adaptive techniques depend largely on collective, rather than individual, action, is to develop and maintain social coherence and coordination over time.[13] Social coordination must at all times (or, in the case of socially diaphasic organisms, during particular seasons) be sufficient to facilitate corporate action, often rapidly (in response to imminent environmental press) and efficiently (with a minimum of energy outlay in stimulating coordinated action). Social coordination depends on a finite set of communicatory mechanisms by whose implementation the group, or an adaptively significant portion thereof, may be united in common action.

The mechanisms by which various social organisms maintain the cybernetic flow of information requisite to social coordination and action are many and varied, though they tend to be finite in number for any given species (Marler, 1965; Smith, 1969; and

---

13. The point is made later in the book that the concept of coordination may also be used to characterize the functional arrangement of subsystems *within* the individual organism and that the nature of these coordinations may be discovered through structural analysis. Common principles hold at all levels of organic system organization (see Chapter 6 for further discussion of this issue).

chapter 2). Social action may be triggered very simply by a single alarm call, for example, the baboon two-phase bark (Hall and DeVore, 1965), or by the release of chemical signals (phero-mones) as among insects (Wilson, 1971) and primates (Marler, 1965; Smith 1969; Michael et al., 1971, 1972). Rapid social coor-dination may be elicited through such signals, although most coordination, we suspect, depends on release of fixed action pat-terns.

These examples of social communication are taken from the organizationally simple end of what might be termed the con-tinuum of social communication. Communication mechanisms from the simpler end of this continuum have had the most cover-age in the ethological literature for two reasons: (1) they no doubt predominate in the communicative repertoire of most social ani-mals, especially those at the lower end of the phylogenetic scale, and (ii) they are methodologically easier to describe and analyze in the field. The latter reason has generated a systematic bias in our reconstruction and understanding of animal communication (see also Kummer, 1967). W. John Smith, in his summary of the range of animal communication in chapter 2, demonstrates that communication mechanisms may, in fact, be graded in complex-ity of requisite social interaction and cybernetic flow, depending on: the demographic, the situational, and the physiological vari-ables involved. Smith shows that *formalized behavior*—that is, traditionally or biogenetically derived behavior "specialized to be informative"—may actually range in complexity from single dis-plays by single individuals to intricate systems of behavioral units by a number of individuals.

We are now prepared to define *ritual behavior* as a subset of formalized behavior that involves two or more individuals in active and reciprocal communication and that (1) is structured; (2) is ste-reotyped and repetitive in occurrence over time; and (3) results in greater coordination of conspecifics toward some social action, purpose, or goal (see Chapple and Coon, 1942:398ff.). Criterion three refers to the primary biological function of ritual behavior, which is to facilitate, through the cybernetic flow of information, the synchronization of individual action into corporate action—action directed toward some environmental challenge that may not be met successfully through individual action.[14]

Concerted social action among vertebrates requires coordination at two levels of organization: (1) coordination of subsystems within each participating organism, which may be termed *intraorganismic* coordination, and (2) coordination of the participating individuals into collective and cohesive action, which may be called *interorganismic* coordination. For an individual organism to respond adaptively requires the integration of the sensory-neuroendocrine-motor subsystems of the organism's nervous system. Adequate response further requires the appropriate balance between sympathetic and parasympathetic systems governing levels of arousal (see Schneirla, 1965; Fox, 1974; Lex in chapter 4).

The individual components needed for intraorganismic coordination are known to be neural subsystems of dispersed but particular neural areas. The perceptual and conceptual structures are associated with what are often termed the "higher cortical functions" involving the cerebral cortex. In man, the "seat" of motivation and affect is associated with the limbic system, a diverse structure including the limbic lobe (the subcallosal, cingulate, and parahippocampal gyri of the "old" cortex), as well as the hippocampus proper and the dentate gyrus and subcortical structures such as the amygdaloid body, septal nuclei, hypothalamus, epithalamus, anterior thalamic nuclei, and portions of the basal ganglia (Truex and Carpenter, 1969:538; Nauta and Karten, 1970; Lamendella, 1977). The sympathetic and parasympathetic functions of the reticular formation would appear to be mediated by the limbic lobe through its numerous connections with the hypothalamus. Motor activity is mediated by structures located in the neocortex and in the cerebellum. Intraorganismic coordination requires an intricate integration of these various functions and

---

14. After Etkin (1964:4), we may make the distinction between *aggregated* action, in which groups coalesce temporarily in response to environmental press, and *social* action, in which groups remain together as a response to social attraction. Much of what we say in this volume refers to social groups and social action.

thus mediates sensory input and action. The organism must perceive the relevant stimulus via an orientation response (*OR*) to the stimulus. Information pertaining to the stimulus must reach the perceptual structures that hold the information in short-term memory while a search is made for the correct indentification of the stimulus (i.e., the mechanism of the cognitive imperative). Once an identification of the stimulus is made, the object or event must be evaluated for its relevance to past experience, and then appropriate affect, state of arousal, and, finally, motor response (if required) are elicited.

Failure to act in response to an environmental stimulus may occur at any point in the system. The stimulus may be subthreshold in intensity for sense receptors, or the organism may be sufficiently habituated to the stimulus that the stimulus does not elicit an *OR*. On the other hand, the *OR* may occur but the stimulus be discounted as significant upon initial identification, or the stimulus may be evaluated and found to be associated with null response in past experience.

Interorganismic coordination within a social group requires a type of intraorganismic coordination that we term *synchronization* (see also Chapple, 1970). In order for synchronization of individual sensory-neuroendocrine-motor subsystems to occur, the behavior of significant group members must be communicative in a causal sense—that is, the behavior of one's conspecifics influences one's own internal coordination and resultant behavior. Chance simultaneity of action on the part of a number of conspecifics toward the same environmental stimulus is not due to synchronization. There must exist some minimal channel of information flow that facilitates the coordination of action. The communicative process may be as simple as an alarm call among baboons, who, upon hearing the call from one of their members, may bound as a group into the trees. The call is transmitted simultaneously to all group members within hailing distance and group response is nearly instantaneous. There may, of course, be redundant reinforcement in repetition of the alarm call by other animals. The point is that quite simple communicative interaction is required for concerted action on the part of the group. This is a

simple, direct, unambiguous and efficient response to a stimulus
(let us say a predator) in which rapid and well-coordinated action
is necessary for group survival.

The problem of interorganismic coordination is often not as
simple as depicted in this example. Indeed the communication
required to obtain and regulate social coordination may require
considerably more complex communication. And such is the nature of ritual. *Ritual behavior, as communication eliciting interorganismic coordination, requires a minimal degree of in-
tercalation of the behavior of each participating actor as
information into the intraorganismic coordinations within other
participating actors.* To put this in common ethological parlance,
ritual requires a minimal degree of social facilitation. The role of
each animal in the ritual behavior may or may not be the same.
However, the simplest form of ritual being assumed (in which
every participant's part is in concert with all other participants),
ritual behavior as a paradigm of communication may be schematized as in Figure 1.2, where S represents some environmental
stimulus, and X, the initial perceiver of S. Here we see that the interactions necessary to initiate and maintain coordinated action
have become much more complex.

We have thus far simplified the discussion for the sake of

Figure 1.2

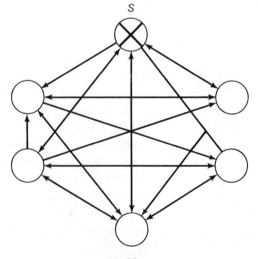

ease in communication with our readers. In reality, S may represent a conceived stimulus, that is, a part of the organism's E_c while not a part of its E_o. Furthermore, S may not be a single entity or event but may be as diffuse as the need to set a direction for group movement (see chapter 3). It may also be quite difficult, if not impossible, to determine the exact nature of S in the field situation. An example that readily comes to mind is the mysterious "star formation" among sperm whales. "The sperm whales gather nose to nose in a large 'star' and wave their flukes. We can speculate as to whether this is some form of communication or protective behavior, but because of our lack of information, the explanation will have to rest there for the moment" (Fichtelius and Sjolander, 1972:138).

We may say then that the primary biological function of ritual behavior is cybernetic: ritual operates to facilitate both intraorganismic and interorganismic coordination. Such coordination is necessary to form coherent, corporate responses, with common motive and drive, for the completion of some effect or task that could not be completed by conspecifics acting alone. Ritual is one mechanism for eliciting what Wilson (1971:297) has termed "group effect." Alarm calls, specific pheromone releasers, formalized displays do not in themselves constitute facilitators of group effects. Ritual interaction does, for it requires time for culmination and propagation of corporate effect.

Ritual behavior operates to coordinate the integrated neuromotor functions of participants. The integration of individual neuromotor systems may be largely genetically determined and present at birth or may emerge or be constructed during some later sensitive period in the ontogenensis of the organism. The behavior pattern resulting from such a closely "prewired" integration has been called by many ethologists a "fixed action pattern" (see Eibl-Eibesfeldt, 1970:15; Hinde, 1970; see also chapter 2). Concomitantly, one of the simplest forms of ritual occurs as a releaser and social modulator of individual fixed action patterns. Such is likely to be the case with concerted intergroup aggression among rhesus monkeys, where the aggressive display used by individual monkeys emerges early in life and requires few, if any, acquired components, but its modulation in the "in line formation" requires more complex cybernetic control (see chapter 3). In such cases it is not the individual component of the ritual that requires a complex ontogenesis for full integration at the adult stage, but rather the mechanism for social modulation of individual responses into a corporate response.

As an example of synchronization of fixed action patterns, let us consider for a moment the reproductive behavior of heterosexual, social organisms. Reproduction in these organisms always consists of at least two phases, the communication phase and the copulatory phase. In higher organisms, such as dolphins and man, there are often three phases, the communicatory, precopulatory (foreplay), and copulatory phases. The communicatory phase functions to inhibit the release of aggression and stimulate the release of copulatory response. In other words, through communication, both animals are brought to the point where direct precopulatory contact and copulation may occur with a minimum of "misunderstanding" of intent and undue agonistic behavior. The range of communications that may be used during the communication phase is vast, including elaborate formalized displays, pheromone release, vocalizations and song, and so forth. In some species the communication may be more complex and interactive—may be, in other words, ritual behavior. The ritual interaction between dolphins before actual copulation may last as long as thirty minutes and offers a remarkable example of the type of synchronization to which we refer:

A male will start paying attention to a particular female by posturing in front of her. Twisting his powerful body into an S-shape, head up, flukes down, he will glide gracefully and slowly under the female until he is directly beneath her tail. His beak is tantalizingly close but not touching her sexual organs at this point. The female responds to these obviously suggestive overtones by patting her amorous swain's head with her flukes. This receptive motion is quite unique, more like the fluttering of a fan than swimming. It also signals that the first stage of courting is drawing to a close (Krone, 1972:100).

The period of foreplay involving direct physical contact and reciprocal manipulation is elaborate, including much ritual interaction before actual copulation. The whole episode culminates in complete synchronization of affect and action, the dolphins using neural structures between which the connections are largely genetically predisposed.

In complex forms of ritual behavior (including sexual interaction in higher vertebrate species) the appropriate integration at the organismic level, as well as the synchronization of interorganismic motivation and action, requires a complex development in ontogenesis. It is precisely here that we may observe a complex feedback interaction between ritual and intraorganismic coordination. That is, the integration of neuromotor functions in the developing individual may pass through a series of developmental stages before reaching the configuration characteristic of an adult. The transformation from one developmental level to another may, in fact, be facilitated by ritual. And the ritual in its turn requires successful developmental transformation for its future propagation (see chapter 6).

A fundamental problem for a society is to maintain through time the potential for group or corporate action. This is no easy matter, as Count (1973), among others, has made clear. Social cohesion in action requires continuous close coordination of roles and classes of roles. Yet the members of society change throughout their lives; the aggregation of group members changes through attrition, birth, and death. For phylogenetically simple social animals (e.g., insects), the continuous coherence is minimally assured genetically. Higher order social organisms (e.g., Cetacea, canids, and primates), on the other hand, are faced with the problem Count (1973) has termed "reverberation," the developmental transformation of status and role differential in social dyads (e.g., parent-offspring). Where effective participation in ritual as an adult requires the acquired entrainment of sensory-neuroendocrine-motor subsystems in ontogenetic development, and where such entrainment must undergo periodic transformations in solution of the problem of reverberation, then *we would expect ritual behavior to have a secondary but crucial biological function: as a mechanism for entraining and transforming the structure of neuromotor subsystems in the developing organism.* Ritual, in other words, becomes a mechanism for *socialization.*

The intimate involvement of ritual in socialization in *H. sapiens* and other higher organisms is dealt with in greater detail in later chapters (chapters 4, 6, and 7). Suffice it to say here that in the higher organisms—organisms that require experiential input from their E_o during ontogeny for the construction of an E_c—ritual is both critically dependent on socialization and intimately involved in the facilitation and structuring of socialization. The problem of maintaining social cohesion and coordination in action arises anew with each generation. The process of socializing the young into adaptive roles in ritual is an alternation between active and passive involvement. The young animal perceives innumerable occurrences of repetitive ritual during which he learns to integrate (1) the stimulus S with the resultant ritual response, (2) the precise sequencing of behaviors comprising the ritual, (3) the affective states linked to those behaviors, (4) the significant perceptual events emphasized through the orientations of ritual participants, and (5) the events and results occurring subsequent to the ritual. Whether this process for the young is inculcated passively or actively depends on whether the young are allowed to participate in the ritual or must stand by as observers. Yet, even if the young are excluded from active participation in adult ritual but are allowed to perceive it, they may enact the ritual, or crucial aspects of it, during peer play and thus further integrate the neural associations on which adequate functioning of adult ritual depends.

The Spectrum of Ritual

Human ceremonial ritual is not a simple institution unique to man but rather a nexus of variables shared by other species. All component variables have evolutionary precursors (or *anlagen*) dating far back in hominid phylogenesis and beyond. Specifically, we would suggest that ceremonial rituals (ceremonies, rites) are strips of often complex ritual behavior that (1) are included in the collective E_c of a society, (2) are conceptualized by members of the society, (3) become a locus of symbolization for members of the society, and (4) may have effects on the E_o, some of which are modeled within the E_c, and some of which are not. The evolutionary development of human ritual has been a function of the evolution of the neurophysiological bases of conceptual structure and communication (Laughlin and d'Aquili, 1974a). One may trace the evolutionary progression of ritual behavior from the emergence of formalization through the coordination of formalized communicative behavior and sequences of ritual behavior to the conceptualization of such sequences and the assignment of symbols to them by man. Very specifically, we would hypothesize that evolutionary development of conceptual complexity (the result of enhanced "corticalization" of the brain) provides a necessary, but not sufficient, condition for the development of complexity in communication. Communication itself is a function of conceptual capacity and a number of other environmental, biogenetic, and social factors too extensive to discuss here. Ritual behavior per se is characteristic of vertebrates, and more specifically mammals and birds, these being the two taxa that have developed the most complex conceptual facilities known. Let us now look briefly at the evolutionary processes that have thus far culminated in the capacity of human ceremonial ritual.

Formalization

The process of formalization is discussed in detail in chapter 2. Suffice it to say here that it is the evolutionarily fundamental process in the development of more complex forms of communication in animals. Formalized displays are a major component of vertebrate communication, and the rudiments of formalization remain in a number of nonverbal displays in man such as tongue showing (Smith, et al., n.d.), as well as a number of other facial gestures (Darwin, 1872; Andrew, 1963, 1965; Van Hooff, 1972), emotional expressions (Eibl-Eibesfeldt, 1972), and general body gestures, posture, and distancing (see Birdwhistell, 1970; Hall, 1966). Most formalized displays remain cognized, but beyond awareness, in human communication and interaction.

Ritual Behavior

More than any other scholar, Erving Goffman (1959, 1967, 1971) has made us aware of the prevalent role of ritual behavior in asserting and maintaining a person's public role (or "face"). Human beings are both persons and actors in a social system, and to perform one's role in society successfully, one must be equipped to participate in appropriate ritual. The ritual aspects of role behavior may or may not be components in the person's E_c—certainly many rituals remain outside the cognized world of the actor, as does the process by means of which these rituals are acquired during ontogenesis. As a matter of fact one may become aware of the rituals only when they are in some sense violated.

Many categories of information may be transmitted through social ritual by what Goffman (1967:77ff) calls *demeanor:* "that element of the individual's ceremonial behavior typically conveyed through deportment, dress, and bearing, which serves to express to those in his immediate presence that he is a person of certain desirable or undesirable qualities." In addition we may rapidly ascertain a person's social status, profession, education, nationality and location of birth, and a number of other attributes merely by observing that person closely during the initial greeting ritual.

A major variable determining whether a ritual becomes a component in the E_c of a person or society is whether or not the ritual becomes integral in defining a difference or set of differences between groups or classes within a group. A set of ritual behaviors may become cognized as "our" or "their" custom. For example, we may cognize the ritual inherent in meal "courses" when we become aware that the French customarily eat their salad after, rather than before, their entree.

Conceptualized Ritual

Human ritual behavior becomes conceptualized—becomes, in other words, a ceremony, a ritual, or a rite—when that complex of behaviors is conceptually delimited and differentiated from contiguous behavior (Chapple, 1970). Ritual thus conceptually isolated is usually modified so as to exaggerate the differentiation-modifications often taking the form of cultural elaborations on the basic behavioral pattern (see Wallace, 1966:162 in relation to this for revitalization ritual). In keeping with the process of antithesis of formalized displays first described by Darwin (1872), the elements of conceptualized ritual may be severely contrasted, forming antinomies (see chapter 5). With respect to communicative and formalized behavior such antinomies underscore the message inherent in the behavior and reduce confusion in the display or ritual (Sade, 1973).[15] The cultural elaboration of conceptualized ritual may become extremely complex, resulting in much of the exotic material and behavioral culture that has for so long been dear to the ethnographer's heart. Such elaborations have quite often drawn the eyes of the anthropologist away from the structural and panspecific, homologous features of ritual behavior. Semiotic structuralists like Levi-Strauss (1966) have gone far in explaining the manipulation of many of these surface, symbolic elements in ritual. Yet here is an excellent example of the differences of approach between semiotic and evolutionary structuralism. Unlike the semiotic structuralist, we are less interested in the structures mediating discrete surface symbology than in discovering the evolutionary precursors and neurognostic features of ritual behavior itself.

Conceptualized ritual is, by definition, a part of the E_c. And man is capable of generating a considerable disparity between his E_c and his E_o. Indeed he is capable of modeling entities and relations that do not belong to the E_o. A major result of this capability is that, unlike ritual behavior in other animals (as far as we know), ritual behavior in man may be directed to effects, goals, and tasks having little or no biologically adaptive value to the population. We would, however, urge caution here; it must never be assumed that, because the *cognized* purpose of a ritual would seem to have no biologically adaptive importance to the population, the ritual behavior per se has no adaptive significance. The critical importance of this understanding has been brought home to us in the excellent work of Rappaport (1968) in showing that Tsembaga ritual functions biologically to regulate relations occurring outside the cognized model of ritual held by the Tsembaga themselves.

There is one further issue that needs to be introduced, although it, too, is addressed in a later chapter (see chapter 5): the

15. For a discussion of the neurognostic substrate for antinomous thinking, see Laughlin and d'Aquili, 1974a.

relationship between ceremonial ritual and myth. We must remind the reader again of the distinction between the E_c and E_o. In constructing an E_c, man is confronted by phenomenal effects in the E_o, whose phenomenal causes are too complex or spatio-temporally removed for him to model from inductive extrapolation alone. He is required by the cognitive imperative to deduce the entities and relations that might account for the effects he has experienced. The annual inundation of prime agricultural land by the Nile River was for ancient Egyptians a significant and cognized event. Yet as far as we know, Egyptians were unaware of the precise causes of the annual flood on which their economic well-being so greatly depended. Instead they deduced one or another religious "cause" for the event—causes requiring critical ritual attention on the part of cult priests (see Gardiner, 1961). We call the range of disparity between man's ability to experience effects and his inability to isolate causes ("prehend"; see Laughlin and d'Aquili, 1974a; chapter 4) the *zone of uncertainty* in the E_c.[16] Conceptual models constructed in man's brain to account for relations in the zone of uncertainty are precisely the realm of "religion." Because this is the realm of greatest uncertainty, it is precisely the locus of models and actions of "ultimate concern" (Tillich, 1963) to a society. The expression of these conceptual models through the medium of language is termed *myth,* and ritual behaviors conceptualized in relation to models within the zone of uncertainty are "religious" ceremonies. Thus we may see that: (1) There is an almost inevitable association between myth and ceremonial ritual in religious expression and action and (2) there may be complex ceremonial rituals having little or no religious consequence at all (e.g., a formal ball, a football game, a school graduation ceremony). Traditional classes of ceremonial ritual such as "rites of passage" (Van Gennep, 1960) or "rites of intensification" (Chapple and Coon, 1942) may or may not exhibit religious components.

What we emphasize is that ritual, inclusive of ceremonial ritual, is an evolutionary, ancient channel of communication that

16. We are especially grateful to Ivan Brady for this notion. See also Laughlin and Brady (1978).

Introduction

operates by virtue of a number of homologous biological functions (i.e., synchronization, integration, tuning, etc.) in man and other vertebrates. It is the conceptual matrix in which a particular ritual is embedded, rather than the biogenetic structure of the ritual itself, that determines whether the ritual is religious or secular.

Conclusion

We have accomplished a number of things in this introductory chapter. First, we have placed the theory of biogenetic structuralism within a general historical frame called evolutionary structuralism and have contrasted that approach with more orthodox structuralist theory. Second, we have sketched the fundamental tenets of biogenetic structuralism as we presently understand them. Third, by logical extension of the theory, an appropriate biogenetic structural methodology has been presented—one that, although admittedly ideal in scope, is sufficiently grounded in the needs of the science of man to act as an overall guide to basic research and interpretation. Quite obviously there are questions—even classic ones in all the behavioral and social sciences—that for one reason or another may resist a full biogenetic structural analysis. Nonetheless, we cannot know this to be the case until we attempt such analyses.

Fourth, we have presented an outline of a biogenetic structural theory of human ritual behavior that we feel succeeds in accounting for (1) the full range of ritual behavior in man, (2) the universality of ritual behavior among human societies, (3) certain universal functions of ritual behavior among human societies, (4) several important links between the individual neurophysiological and cognitive systems and ritual behavior at the social level, (5) the systemic principles underlying ritual behavior in man and other creatures, (6) the evolutionary origins and widespread occurrence of ritual behavior in man and other creatures, and (7) the relationship between ontogenesis in the individual and the social interaction involved in ritual behavior. In short, we feel that we have constructed an explanatory model of human ritual, one that

41

not only is amenable to empirical testing in the field but that also facilitates—even requires—the rational linkage of data and theoretical materials heretofore segregated in disparate disciplines. And yet, the work presented in this and subsequent chapters is much farther ranging than a mere account of human ritual. Within individual substantive chapters the authors have touched on many aspects of the lives of other animal species. Implicit in a biogenetic structural explanation of ritual are similar accounts of such issues as the evolutionary origins of language, the nature of mythology, the universal attributes of political organization, the logical and empirical relations obtaining between the economy and complexity of social interaction—indeed, our model implies a similar model of human society as a whole.

The following substantive chapters have been explicitly designed to explore, explain, and elaborate the more important aspects of ritual behavior among animal societies, with a principal orientation toward understanding the origin and functioning of ritual in human society. The chapters have been arranged progressively beginning with a general discussion of the animal kingdom and ending with an analysis of a single human ceremonial ritual, the Roman Mass. In chapter 2 W. John Smith discusses the general field of the ethology of communication. He provides us with many of the fundamental concepts and relationships used in subsequent chapters. He also places ritual behavior within the context of communication between organic systems. The biological and ethological perspective becomes somewhat more focused in chapter 3, in which Charles Laughlin and John McManus demonstrate the operation of ritual among higher mammals (principally primates). Included in their treatment is an account of the evolutionary progression in the nature and complexity of ritual up the hominoid and hominid phylogenetic scale. They conclude their chapter by presenting some scientifically grounded speculations pertaining to ritual among the australopithecines.

Emphasis on human ritual begins in chapter 4, in which Barbara Lex discusses autonomic system functioning during ritual trance. Her explication of the process of "tuning" becomes pivotal in the accounts offered in later chapters of social interaction and individual ontogenesis in relation to ritual behavior. Then, in chapter 5, Eugene d'Aquili and Charles Laughlin discuss some evolutionary and neuropsychological concomitants of ritual and myth.

Providing this treatise with a crucial developmental perspective, in chapters 6 and 7 John McManus presents a theoretical framework for considering the relationship between individual ontogenesis and the universal attributes of ritual. He explicitly relates the theory of biogenetic structuralism to Jean Piaget's *genetic epistemology* and the *conceptual systems theory* group. These chapters also provide concepts and relations necessary for a more thorough understanding of the discussions of several social functions of ritual found in the subsequent three chapters. In chapter 8, Tom Burns and Charles Laughlin develop a theoretical framework within which ritual, particularly ceremonial ritual, may be seen as a universal and important social power resource. Laughlin and d'Aquili then turn in chapter 9 to an analysis of the role of ritual in societies under ecological stress. Finally, Ron Murphy, himself a Jesuit priest, applies biogenetic structural analysis in chapter 10 to the structure and functions of the Roman Mass.

The extent to which we have been able to match our explanation of human ritual behavior with the format of an ideal biogenetic structural analysis presented in this chapter is evaluated in the book's concluding chapter (chapter 11). A number of other issues are also explored in the final chapter, including the necessity for further field research, the implications of biogenetic structuralism for the training of scholars, and some speculations about the future of the science of man.

The Problem of Epistemological Esthetics

Before proceeding to this analysis of the spectrum of ritual, we must append a few words about the appropriateness of an interdisciplinary enterprise such as this book. Before going to press, the manuscript was read and critically evaluated by a number of respected experts in the fields of neurobiology, ethology, psychology, and anthropology. To our astonishment it was greeted either by enthusiasm or by condemnation. This polarity was exhibited by experts in each of the fields mentioned, and the emotional overlay in most cases was surprising at both poles. As best the authors can determine, the emotional quality of the reactions stems from a priori judgments arising from what might be called, for want of a better term, epistemological esthetics. Put simply, some scholars wish to know almost everything about an extremely circumscribed area with 95 percent-plus certainty, while others (including many neurobiologists) are more than happy to approach the current confusion in the behavioral and social sciences with a unifying theory having somewhat less certainty but capable of generating testable hypotheses. In other words we are apparently dealing with a matter of scientific taste. Although it is fashionable these days to praise "interdisciplinary efforts" in theory, very few scholars actually attempt them, so that *practical* prejudice on the part of some scientists need not ordinarily surface. This work attempts to unify the results of solid, respected research in a number of traditional disciplines into a coherent interdisciplinary whole. In building the bridges between the disciplines, however, there was bound to be a certain amount of speculation, although every effort was made to keep such speculation to a minimum.

References

Abelson, R. et al. 1968. *Theories of Cognitive Consistency*. Chicago: Rand McNally.

Allee, W. C. 1951. *Cooperation Among Animals*. New York: Henry Schuman.

Andrew, R. T. 1963. "Evolution of Facial Expression." *Science* 142(3595):1034–1041.

—— 1965. "The Origins of Facial Expressions." *Scientific American* 213(4):88.

d'Aquili, E. G. 1972. *The Biopsychological Determinants of Culture*. Reading, Pa.: Addison-Wesley.

d'Aquili, E. G. and C. D. Laughlin. 1975. "The Biopsychological Determinants of Religious Ritual." *Zygon* 10(1).

Ardener, E. 1977 "Some Outstanding Problems in the Analysis of Events." Paper presented at the *Fundamentals of Symbolism* conference, Burg Warterstein, Austria.

Barr, H. L. 1971. *LSD: Personality and Experience*. New York: Wiley.

Bateson, G. 1972. "Problems in Cetacea and Other Mammalian Communication," in *Steps to an Ecology of Mind* (G. Bateson). New York: Ballantine Books.

Introduction

Beck, A. 1967. *Depression*. New York: Hoeber.

Berlyne, D. 1960. *Conflict, Arousal, and Curiosity*. New York: McGraw-Hill.

Birdwhistell, R. L. 1970. *Kinesics and Context*. Philadelphia: University of Pennsylvania Press.

Blalock, H. M. 1969. *Theory Construction*. Englewood Cliffs, N.J.: Prentice-Hall.

Brehm, J. and A. R. Cohen. 1962. *Explorations in Cognitive Dissonance*. New York: Wiley.

Buckley, W. 1967. *Sociology and Modern Systems Theory*. Englewood Cliffs, N.J.: Prentice-Hall.

Burnham, J. 1973. *The Structure of Art*. New York: George Braziller.

Caianiello, E. R. 1968. *Neural Networks*. New York: Springer-Verlag.

Caldwell, D. K. and M. C. Caldwell. 1972. *The World of the Bottlenosed Dolphin*. New York: J. B. Lippincott.

Chapple, E. D. 1970. *Culture and Biological Man*. New York: Holt, Rinehart, and Winston.

Chapple, E. D. and C. S. Coon. 1942. *Principles of Anthropology*. New York: Henry Holt.

Cohen, J. E. 1971. *Casual Groups of Monkeys and Men*. Cambridge, Mass.: Harvard University Press.

Count, E. W. 1969. "Animal Communication in Man—Science: An Essay in Perspective," in *Approaches to Animal Communication* (T. A. Sebeols and A. Ramsay, eds.). The Hague: Mouton.

—— 1973. *Being and Becoming Human*. New York: Van Nostrand Reinhold.

—— 1974. "Homination: Organism and Process." *Bevolkerungsbiologie*. Stuttgart: Gustav Fischer Verlag.

Cunningham, M. 1972. *Intelligence: Its Organization and Development*. New York: Academic Press.

Darwin, C. 1872. *The Expression of the Emotions in Man and Animals* (1965 ed.). Chicago: University of Chicago Press.

Driver, H. E. 1966. "Geographic-Historical vs. Psycho-Emotional Explanation." *Current Anthropology*, 7(1).

Droscher, V. B. 1965. *The Mysterious Senses of Animals*. New York: Dulton.

Durkheim, E. 1938. *The Rules of Sociological Method* (1966 ed.). New York: Free Press.

Eccles, J. C. 1973. *The Understanding of the Brain*. New York: McGraw-Hill.

Eibl-Eibesfeldt, I. 1970. *Ethology*. New York: Holt, Rinehart, and Winston.

—— 1972. "Similarities and Differences Between Cultures in Expressive Movements," in *Non-Verbal Communication* (R. A. Hinde, ed.). Cambridge, England: Cambridge University Press.

Etkin, W. 1964. *Social Behavior and Organization Among Vertebrates*. Chicago: University of Chicago Press.

Feldman, S. 1966. *Cognitive Consistency*. New York: Academic Press.

Festinger, L. 1957. *A Theory of Cognitive Dissonance*. Stanford: Stanford University Press.

—— 1964. *Conflict, Decision, and Dissonance*. Stanford: Stanford University Press.

Festinger, L., H. Ricker, and S. Schacter. 1956. *When Prophecy Fails*. New York: Harper and Row.

Fichtelius, K. E. and S. Sjolander. 1972. *Smarter Than Man? Intelligence in Whales, Dolphins, and Man*. New York: Random House.

Fiske, D. and S. Maddi. 1961. *Functions of Varied Experience*. Homewood, Illinois: Dorsey Press.

45

Fleming, J. D. 1974. "Field Report: The State of the Apes." *Psychology Today* 7(8):31ff.

Foucault, M. 1970. *The Order of Things*. New York: Random House.

Fox, M. W. 1974. *Concepts in Ethology: Animal and Human Behavior*. Minneapolis: University of Minnesota Press.

Gardner, R. A. and B. T. Gardner. 1972. "Teaching to a Chimpanzee." *Science* 165:664–672.

Garner, W. R. 1962. *Uncertainty and Structure as Psychological Concepts*. New York: Wiley.

—— 1974. *The Processing of Information and Structure*. New York: Lawrence Erlbaum Associates.

Goffman, E. 1959. *The Presentation of Self in Everyday Life*. Garden City, N.Y.: Doubleday.

—— 1967. *Interaction Ritual*. Garden City, N.Y.: Doubleday.

—— 1971. *Relations in Public*. New York: Harper and Row.

Goode, W. J. 1951. *Religion Among the Primitives*. New York: Free Press.

Hall, E. T. 1966. *The Hidden Dimension*. New York: Doubleday.

Hall, K. R. L. and I. DeVore, 1965. "Baboon Social Behavior," in *Primate Behavior* (I. DeVore, ed.). New York: Holt, Rinehart, and Winston.

Hallowell, A. I. 1960. "Self, Society, and Culture in Phylogenetic Perspective," in *Evolution After Darwin* (S. Tax, ed.), vol. 11. Chicago: University of Chicago Press.

Harvey, O. J., D. E. Hunt, and H. M. Schroder. 1961. *Conceptual Systems and Personality Organization*. New York: Wiley.

Hastorf, S. and E. Cantril. 1956. "They Saw a Game: A Case Study," *Journal of Abnormal and Social Psychology* 49:129–134.

Hebb, D. O. 1949. *The Organization of Behavior*. New York: Wiley.

Heider, F. 1958. *The Psychology of Interpersonal Relations*. New York: Wiley.

Hemple, C. G. 1959. "The Logic of Functional Analysis," in *Symposium of Sociological Theory* (Llewellyn Gross, ed.). New York: Row Peterson.

Hertz, R. 1909. *Death and the Right Hand* (1960 ed.). Aberdeen, Scotland: Cohen and West.

Hinde, R. A. 1970. *Animal Behavior* (2nd ed.). New York: McGraw-Hill.

Holloway, R. L. 1974. "The Casts of Fossil Hominid Brains," *Scientific American* 231(1):106ff.

Huxley, Sir J. 1966. Symposium "A Discussion on Ritualization of Behavior in Animals and Man," *Philosophical Transactions of the Royal Society of London* Series B, 251:247–526.

Jarvie, I. C. 1965. "Limits to Functionalism and Alternatives to It in Anthropology," in *Functionalism in the Social Sciences* (D. Martindale, ed.). Philadelphia: American Academy of Social and Political Science.

Jung, C. G. 1956. *Symbols of Transformation*. Vol. 5 of *Collected Works*. London: Routledge and Kegan Paul.

Kohlberg, L. 1969. "Stage and Sequence: The Cognitive Developmental Approach to Socialization," in *Handbook of Socialization Theory and Research* (D. Goslin, ed.). Chicago: Rand McNally.

Krone, C. 1972. *The World of the Dolphin*. New York: Belmont/Tower Books.

Kummer, H. 1967. "Tripartite Relations in Hamadryas Baboons," in *Social Communication Among Primates* (S. A. Altmann, ed.). Chicago: University of Chicago Press.

Lamendella, J. T. 1977. "The Limbic System in Human Communication," in *Studies in Neurolinguistics,* vol. 3 (H. and H. Whitaker, eds.). New York: Academic Press.

Lane, M. 1970. *Introduction to Structuralism.* New York: Basic Books.

Laughlin, C. D. 1974. "Myth, Language, and the Brain: The Evolutionary Importance of Vicarious Experience." Mimeo.

—— 1977. "Symbolism and Canalization: Reflections on Ardener's P Structures." Paper presented at the Colloque France-Canada III conference, Quebec.

Laughlin, C. D. and E. G. d'Aquili. 1974. *Biogenetic Structuralism.* New York: Columbia University Press.

Laughlin, C. D. and I. A. Brady. 1978. *Extinction and Survival in Human Populations.* New York: Columbia University Press.

Laughlin, C. D. and J. McManus. 1975. "The Nature of Neurognosis." Paper presented to the American Anthropological Association Meetings, San Francisco.

Laughlin, C. D., and J. McManus, and C. Stephens. 1977. "The Evolution of Brain and Symbol." Presented at the *Fundamentals of Symbolism* conference, Burg Wartenstein, Austria.

Lazarus, R. S. 1966. *Psychological Stress and the Coping Process.* New York: McGraw-Hill.

—— 1974. "Cognitive and Coping Process in Emotion," in *Cognitive Views of Human Motivation.* (B. Weiner, ed.). New York: Academic Press.

Leach, E. R. 1961. *Rethinking Anthropology.* London: Athlene Press.

—— 1965. *Political Systems on Highland Burma.* Boston: Beacon Press.

—— 1967. "The Structural Study of Myth and Totemism," A. S. A. Monograph 5. London: Tavistock.

Lenneberg, E. H. 1967. *Biological Foundations of Language.* New York: Wiley.

Lessa, W. A. and E. Z. Vogt. 1972. *Reader in Comparative Religion.* New York: Harper and Row.

Levi-Strauss, C. 1966. *The Savage Mind.* Chicago: University of Chicago Press.

—— 1969. *The Raw and the Cooked.* New York: Harper and Row.

—— 1973. *From Honey to Ashes.* New York: Harper and Row.

Lewin, K. 1935. *A Dynamic Theory of Personality.* New York: McGraw-Hill.

—— 1936. *Principles of Typological Psychology.* New York: McGraw-Hill.

Lilly, J. C. 1961. *Man and Dolphin.* New York: Doubleday.

——1967. *The Mind of the Dolphin.* New York: Doubleday.

Lorenz, K. and N. Tinbergen. 1938. *Taxis und Instinkthandlung in der Eirollbewegung der Graugans. Z. Tierpsychol.* 2:1–29.

Maranda, P. 1972. *Mythology.* Baltimore: Penguin Books.

Marler, P. 1965. "Communication in Monkeys and Apes," in *Primate Behavior* (I. DeVore, ed.). New York: Holt, Rinehart, and Winston.

Mauss, M. 1925. *The Gift* (1967 English ed.). New York: Norton.

Menzel, E. W. 1971. "Communication About the Environment in a Group of Young Chimpanzees," *Folia Primatologica* 15:220–232.

—— 1973. "Precultural Primate Behavior," *Symposia of the Fourth International Congress of Primatology,* vol. 1. Basel: S. Karger.

Michael, R. P., E. B. Keverne, and R. W. Bonsall. 1971. "Pheromones: Isolation of Male Sex Attractants from a Female Primate," *Science* 172:964–966.

Michael, R. P., O. Zumpe, E. B. Keverne, and R. W. Bonsall. 1972. "Neuroendocrine Factors in the Control of Primates' Behavior," *Recent Progress in Hormone Research* 28:665–706.

Middleton, J. 1967. *Gods and Rituals*. Garden City, N.Y.: Natural History Press.

Milsum, J. H. 1968. *Positive Feedback*. Oxford: Pergamon Press.

Murphy, R. F. 1971. *The Dialectics of Social Life*. New York: Basic Books.

Nauta, W. J. H. and H. J. Karten. 1970. "A General Profile of General Vertebrate Brain, with Sidelights on the Ancestry of Cerebral Cortex," in *The Neurosciences: Second Study Program* (F. O. Schmitt, ed.). New York: Rockefeller University Press.

Needham, R. 1973. *Right and Left*. Chicago: University of Chicago Press.

Ornstein, R. E. 1976. "The Container Versus the Contents." *Psychology Today*, pp. 36–43.

Piaget, J. 1970. *Structuralism*. New York: Harper and Row.

—— 1970b. *Genetic Epistemology*. New York: Columbia University Press.

—— 1971. *Biology and Knowledge*. Chicago: University of Chicago Press.

—— 1974. *Understanding Causality*. New York: Norton.

—— 1977. *The Development of Thought: Equilibration of Cognitive Structures*. New York: Viking Press.

Powers, W. T. 1973. *Behavior: Control of Perception*. Chicago: Aldine.

Premack, A. 1974. *Chimps Who Read*. New York: Harper and Row.

Premack, D. 1971. "Language in Chimpanzee?" *Science* 172:808–822.

Premack, A. and D. Premack. 1972. "Teaching Language to an Ape." *Scientific American* 227(4).

Pribram, K. H. 1971. *Language of the Brain*. Englewood Cliffs, Prentice-Hall.

Radcliffe-Brown, A. R. 1940. "On Social Structure." *Journal of the Royal Anthropological Institute* 70.

Rakic, P. 1976. *Local Circuit Neurons*. Cambridge: MIT Press.

Rappaport, R. A. 1968. *Pigs for the Ancestors*. New Haven: Yale University Press.

Robey, D. 1973. *Structuralism: An Introduction*. London: Oxford University Press.

Rosenberg, M. 1960. "An Analysis of Affective-Cognitive Consistency," in *Attitude Organization and Change* (M. Rosenberg et al., eds.). New Haven: Yale University Press.

Rossi, I. 1974. *The Unconscious in Culture*. New York: Dulton.

Rubinstein, R. A. and C. D. Laughlin. 1974. "Bridging Levels of Systemic Organization," *Current Anthropology* 15:459–481.

Rubinstein, R. A. and C. D. Laughlin, n.d. "Rethinking Anthropological Explanation."

Rubinstein, R. A., C. D. Laughlin, and J. McManus, n.d. "One Relation of Kuhn's Paradigmatic Science to Cognitive Psychological Theory."

Russell, B. 1956. "The Philosophy of Logical Atomism," in *Logic and Knowledge* (R. C. Marsh, ed.). New York: Macmillan.

Sade, D. S. 1973. "An Ethogram for Rhesus Monkeys. I. Antithetical Contrasts in Posture and Movement," *American Journal of Physical Anthropology* 38(2):537–542.

—— n.d. "Latent Processes and the Biological Bases of Social Organization." Mimeo.

Salmon, W. 1971. *Statistical Explanation and Statistical Relevance*. Pittsburgh: The University of Pittsburgh Press.

deSaussure, F. 1916. *Course in General Linguistics* (1966 English edition). New York: McGraw-Hill.

Schacter, S. 1971. *Emotion, Obesity, and Crime*. New York: Academic Press.

Schacter, S. and T. E. Singer. 1962. "Cognitive, Social and Physiological Determinants of Emotional States," *Psychological Review* 69:379–397.

Schneirla, T. C. 1965. "Aspects of Stimulation and Organization," in *Approach/Withdraw Processes Underlying Vertebrate Behavioral Development*, in *Advances in the Study of*

Animal Behavior (D. S. Lehrman, R. A. Hinde, E. Shaw, eds.). New York: Academic Press.

Schroder, H. M., M. Driver, and S. Streufert. 1967. *Human Information Processing*. New York: Holt, Rinehart, and Winston.

Seligman, M. and J. Hager. 1972. *Biological Boundaries of Learning*. New York: Appleton-Century-Crofts.

Service, E. R. 1971. *Cultural Evolutionism*. New York: Holt, Rinehart, and Winston.

Shaughnessy, J. D. 1973. *The Roots of Ritual*. Grand Rapids, Mich.: William Eirdmans.

Smith, W. J. 1969. "Messages of Vertebrate Communication," *Science* 165:145–150.

Smith, W. J. et al. n.d. "Tongue Showing: A Facial Display of Humans and Other Primate Species." Mimeo.

Sperber, D. 1975. *Rethinking Symbolism*. Cambridge: Cambridge University Press.

Suedfeld, P. 1964. "Conceptual Structure and Subjective Stress in Sensory Deprivation," *Perceptual and Motor Skills* 19:896–898.

Sutherland, J. W. 1973. *A General Systems Philosophy for the Social and Behavioral Sciences*. New York: George Braziller.

Teilhard de Chardin, P. 1959. *The Phenomenon of Man*. New York: Harper and Row.

Tillich, P. 1963. *Systematic Theology*. Chicago: University of Chicago Press.

Truex, R. C. and M. B. Carpenter. 1969. *Human Neuroanatomy* (6th ed.) Baltimore: Williams and Wilkins.

Turiel, E. 1966. "An Experimental Test of the Sequentiality of Developmental Stages in the Child's Moral Judgements," *Journal of Personality and Social Psychology* 3(6):611–618.

Tyler, E. B. 1881. *Anthropology* (abridged ed.). Ann Arbor: The University of Michigan Press.

Valenstein, E. 1973. *Brain Control*. New York: Wiley.

Van Gennep, A. 1960. *The Rites of Passage*. Chicago: University of Chicago Press.

Van Hooff, J. A. R. A. M. 1972. "A Comparative Approach to the Phylogeny of Laughter and Smiling," in *Non-verbal Communication* (R. A. Hinde, ed.). Cambridge: Cambridge University Press.

Waddington, C. H. 1957. *The Strategy of the Genes*. London: Allen and Urwin.

Wallace, A. F. C. 1957. "Mazeway Disintegration: The Individual's Perception of Socio-Cultural Disorganization," in *Human Adaptation to Disaster* (N. J. Demerath and A. F. C. Wallace, eds.). *Human Organization* Special Issue 16(2):23–27.

—— 1966. *Religion: An Anthropological View*. New York: Random House.

—— 1970. *Culture and Personality*. 2nd ed. New York: Random House.

Werner, H. 1948. *Comparative Psychology of Mental Development*. New York: International Universities Press.

—— 1957. "Concept of Development from a Comparative and Organismic Point of View," in *Concept of Development* (D. Harris, ed.). Minneapolis: University of Minnesota Press.

Whitaker, H. A. 1971. *On the Representation of Language in the Human Brain*. Edmonton, Canada: C.I.L.L.

White, L. A. 1959. *The Evolution of Culture*. New York: McGraw-Hill.

Whitehead, A. N. 1960. *Process and Reality*. New York: Macmillan.

—— 1964. *The Concept of Nature*. Cambridge, England: Cambridge University Press.

Wilson, E. O. 1971. *The Insect Societies*. Cambridge, Mass.: Harvard University Press.

—— 1975. *Sociobiology: The New Synthesis*. Cambridge, Mass.: Harvard University Press.

Witkin, H. A. et al. 1962. *Psychological Differentiation*. New York: Wiley.

Wittgenstein, L. 1961. *Tractalus Logico-Philosophicus*. New York: Humanities Press.

Wynne-Edwards, V. C. 1962. *Animal Dispersion in Relation to Social Behavior*. New York: Hafner.

Zimbardo, P. G. 1969. *Cognitive Control of Motivation*. Glenview, Ill.: Scott Foresman.

Two

Ritual and the Ethology of Communicating

W. John Smith

Let us now consider man in the free spirit of natural history, as though we were zoologists from another planet completing a catalogue of social species on Earth. In this macroscopic view, the humanities and social sciences shrink to specialized branches of biology; history, biography, and fiction are the research protocols of human ethology; and anthropology and sociology together constitute the sociobiology of a single primate species.

Edward O. Wilson, *Sociobiology*

Whatever else the term may mean, *ritual* connotes for both biologists and anthropologists behavior that is formally organized into repeatable patterns. Perhaps the fundamental and pervasive function of these patterns is to facilitate orderly interactions between individuals, between an individual and his notion of a deity, or between an individual and himself across a span of time. Ritual behavior facilitates interactions because it makes available information about the nature of events, and about the participants in them, that each participating individual must have to interact without generating chaos.

It is in the recognition of this fundamental characteristic of ritual—that it provides individuals with some predictive grasp of

I am indebted to Thomas A. Sebeok and the Wenner-Gren Foundation for introducing me to anthropological concepts of ritual, and to Erving Goffman, Joel Sherzer, Adam Kendon, and Charles Laughlin for guidance as I learned about these concepts and about the field of human nonverbal communication. Funding during the period in which this chapter was written was provided by National Science Foundation grant GB 36772.

their circumstances and thus enables them to make choices about their subsequent behavior—that theories from biology and anthropology are beginning to converge. Both disciplines have long been interested in some of the behavior of interacting individuals, even though both have been oddly unconcerned until recently with the processes by which interaction is controlled. The acts that have received attention have been striking ones—stereotyped and often elaborate. They have been traditionally interpreted in terms of origins, effects, and the motives of their users. However, the fact that they are tools of communication and can be studied to help us understand the general characteristics of that process has not been a dominant theme in research. Perhaps, if this orientation had emerged earlier, biology and anthropology would have recognized their common interests more clearly and would have differed less in their conceptual approaches to ritual.

Formalized Behavior

Communication, in a very broad sense, involves any sharing of information. When individuals interact, there are many potential sources for this information. For instance, information is inherent in all the features of an interaction's setting; its place in time and space, and its immediate physical, ecological, and social environment. The very appearance of the participants in an interaction is informative: their sizes, sexes, and apparent ages. Every aspect of their behavior can be informative, from their individual maintenance acts such as foraging or resting, to their orientations, approaches, pauses, and withdrawals.

The pertinence of each of these potential sources differs enormously in the development of different interactions. However, some of the participants' behavior, including some aspects of the acts just mentioned, is especially likely to be pertinent. There is, in addition, a class of acts that has been specialized for the function of making potentially useful information available. These special acts can be extremely important in determining the course of an interaction, largely because without them some of the information that is most significant in guiding each individual's behavior remains essentially private, inaccessible to the other participants. This information has to do with the individual's physiological state, store of knowledge, and genetic predispositions. The task of behavior that is specialized for signaling is to give some public indication of the private information that is directly affecting an actor's selection of behavior.

What anthropologists call "ritual" belongs to this special class of behavior. Further, biologists, and in particular ethologists, speak of behavior belonging to this class as having been "ritualized." Unfortunately, anthropologists differ over what phenomena to include in their concept of ritual, while ethologists (although they have borrowed an anthropological term) use it to specify an evolutionary process that accounts for only a part of the sources of human rituals.

Although anthropologists are not agreed on the operational limits of the concept of ritual, there is an orthodox convention, which is well represented by Turner's definition of ritual as "prescribed formal behavior for occasions not given over to technological routine, having references to beliefs in mystical beings or powers" (1967:19). In this view, rituals are complex, usually prolonged performances by groups concerned with such major human events as puberty, marriage, or death, or with major environmental events such as the changes of seasons, planting, or harvesting. More closely related to biological concerns, however, is the broader view held by social scientists such as Goffman, who views ritual as embracing formal behavior in both ceremonial situations and in the ordinary social intercourse of daily life. Goffman finds "interpersonal ritual" in the exchange of glances in a minimal greeting (1963), in the handholding of a boy and girl (1971), and, in fact, in all interaction.

All anthropological concepts of ritual recognize one characteristic that is not part of related biological concepts. This is the notion that rituals necessarily make reference to supernatural causes. Even Goffman (1971) contends that interpersonal rituals attest to the "sacredness" of certain individuals. Perhaps this assumption arose because the rituals traditionally studied by anthropologists were collective occasions whose central function was to affirm the position of the participants and other elements of social structure on a cosmic compass. Furthermore, even our lesser, interpersonal rituals are not formed by rational action. In acting them out we do not move step by step in logical and analytic response to the apparent needs of each situation, but rather, we adhere to formats we did not plan. Because the formats work—that is, produce expected results—we may use them habitually in an effectively "superstitious" way, usually without examining them. However, although the idea that ritual is nonrational behavior has significant psychological implications, this need not be a central issue in considering ritual behavior as a tool of communication. The nonrational nature of ritual is more a matter to be considered along with motives and the internal mechanisms governing an individual's use of ritual, rather than as a mechanism governing the course of interactions.

Much more important in examining communication is that ritual provides its participants with specialized frameworks for interaction: frameworks of expectancy (Douglas, 1966) within which these participants can reliably anticipate certain kinds of behavioral order and thus respond appropriately to the situation. Both Turner and Goffman agree that the usefulness of jointly performed rituals is in helping their participants to remain within the bounds of familiar relationships and activities. Rituals provide information about the part each participant accepts and will adhere to in an interaction (i.e., his temporary "social persona"; see Goodenough, 1965).

Ethologists recognize behavior comparable to human ritual, but by their term *ritualization* they refer to an evolutionary process—that process by which behavior specialized to be informative becomes differentiated from behavior that is informative only incidentally to its other functions (Tinbergen, 1952; Blest, 1961). Although the ethologists have found that features of some of this specialized behavior are learned, the process they describe is basically that of natural selection guiding genetic evolution (see, e.g., Hinde and Tinbergen, 1958; Huxley, 1966; Lorenz, 1966).

The types of biological ritualization that have been studied most are signal acts performed by individuals and known as "displays." It has also been recognized that some kinds of interactions appear to have rather stereotyped forms, and ethologists have sometimes termed these "ceremonies" or even "rituals." Neither of the latter terms seems to have been widely sanctioned with a specific definition, however, and both are sometimes used so loosely that they overlap with the term *display* (see Huxley, 1966).

Biologists have studied relatively little signaling behavior that is peculiar to small populations of individuals or that is dependent for most of its specialized form on nongenetic evolutionary processes relying on learning to transmit their results. On the other hand, the form of ritual behavior studied by anthropologists, particularly that studied in the orthodox tradition, is largely a product of nongenetic factors. Some of its components, and the tendency for it to be used in certain situations (e.g., greetings, courtship), may derive from roots laid in our species' genetic evolution, but the forms of specific rituals differ greatly from group to group and are clearly traditional. This leads to the unfortunate result that, if ethologists remain strictly faithful to the way they have used the term *ritualization,* they would have to admit that it is not the process by which most such human rituals evolve.

This problem in terminology is minor and should not conceal the basic fact that behavior specialized to be informative has evolved in man and other animals both by processes of genetic evolution (the biologists' "ritualization") and by processes of tradition (which we might call "conventionalization"). Because the products of both processes have the same general function, suppose we embrace both with one term: *formalization.* Formal behavior is specialized to make information available, whether it functions primarily as a mnemonic device used by an individual to remind himself of a complex procedure at some later time, or whether it operates in more obviously social circumstances.

Terminology aside, this class of formalized behavior is obviously heterogeneous in that it comprises more than one kind of behavioral unit. At one extreme the units are single or compound acts performed by single individuals. At the other they are cooperative performances by two or more individuals. Ethology has stressed the first with its concept of display behavior,[1] and anthropology the second with its concept of ritual. Nonetheless, the different kinds of units are all behavioral tools of communicating, and the whole range must be studied if we are to understand how interactions are managed. The next two sections of this chapter are devoted to, first, display behavior, and second, the cooperative activities that can be termed "formalized interactions." The final section considers ritual in an evolutionary perspective.

Displays

The behavioral unit central to most ethological research on communicating has been the display. The concept was used by Darwin (1872), and consistent use of the term goes back at least to Huxley (1914), although displays were not defined until Moynihan (1956, 1960) described them as acts specially adapted "in physical form or frequency to subserve social signal functions." As traditionally recognized, not only do displays have the formal stability needed by the basic units of any system of communication, but also most of their characteristics tend to be stable from generation to generation and to be set by genetic inheritance. Yet some of their features, such as dialectal differences among the vocal displays of different populations or idiolectal differences in the styles of individuals, can be stabilized by tradition and other

1. This refers primarily to vertebrate ethology and the ethological study of the "nonsocial" invertebrates. Social invertebrates such as ants, termites, and honeybees have highly integrated colonies within which a phenomenon known as "mass communication" (Wilson, 1971) occurs. In mass communication (not to be confused with human "mass media communication," which it resembles only in part), information that a single individual could not provide to another individual is made available by groups of communicators. For example, when a foraging fire ant finds a source of food, it lays a chemical ("pheromonal") trail from the food back to its nest. The number of ants needed to harvest the food source cannot be known from this trail alone, but if the source is large, other ants that follow the trail will also deposit pheromone upon it as they return to the nest with their part of the harvest. As the trail accumulates more pheromone, it becomes more attractive to yet other foragers. Saturation is reached when the number of foragers harvesting from the source makes access to it difficult—additional workers will turn back without reaching the food, and they will not lay trails. The concentration of pheromone in the trail is thus matched to the size of the food source, making it the joint communicative product of a group of individuals.

nongenetic mechanisms. Thus the concept is open to include cultural products.

Displays, in as many sensory modalities as are usefully available, are part of the behavioral property of virtually all animals. Most people are familiar with representative samples: the singing of birds or caterwauling of cats; the arched, tail-raised, fur-on-end stance of a Hallowe'en cat or the flattened ears of the dog that stalks it; the dog's urinating on special sites during its daily rounds of its neighborhood. And we know many human examples, from laughing and crying, or smiling and frowning, to the tactile display of gently patting a child or a friend on the back.

Ethology, having originated in evolutionary biology, has been much concerned with ritualization—the genetic evolution of displays. Ethologists have found that ritualization appears to act by altering precursor acts in response to social, ecological, and physical selection pressures.

Display acts, like any products of evolution, do not arise *de novo*. Ethologists have been able to discern a variety of potential precursor behaviors that can provide the sources of at least visible displays. One important class has been called "intention movements," that is, incompletely performed patterns of initiating locomotion, turning, striking, or other acts. For instance, careful observation shows that a bird bends its legs, lowers its chest, and draws its head back toward its shoulders before springing into flight (Daanje, 1950). These movements signal preparation for flying, even though a bird may make them when still undecided about whether or not to fly. Because they are informative and readily seen, such actions are appropriate precursors for evolutionary modifications that enhance their capacity to give information about the acts the animal may soon perform. Acts need not, however, be incomplete to provide good precursors for displays. For instance, apparently protective movements such as lowering the eyebrows above the eyes in attacking (Andrew, 1963) may have been sources of facial displays, and autonomic responses such as those that reduce heat accumulation, for example, vasodilation (in blushing) and erecting bodily hair or feathers, also seem to have been modified for communication in many species (Morris,

1956a). Other acts are completed but redirected from their usual objectives (Moynihan, 1955), for example, striking one's cupped palm with one's fist when threatening—much as a bull tule elk threatens another bull by attacking a nearby bush with his antlers (McCullough, 1969). Yet other acts occur reliably in situations in which they appear to be irrelevant; for example, an individual may groom his hair by running his fingers through it when he is "nervous" and indecisive, and a drake may make jabbing movements of preening at colorful feathers in his wing as he courts a duck. Actions in this last category have been called "displacement activities" (see Tinbergen, 1952) and are a "mixed bag" over which there has been considerable controversy (see Hinde, 1970).[2]

Although not fully understood, these several classes of activities appear to provide most of the evolutionary sources for visible displays, and the sources for tactile displays would seem to be at least as evident. Sources for vocal displays or for displaying by releasing chemicals (pheromones) are more conjectural but are also, in principle, detectable acts that initially correlate with directly functional behavior patterns in a way that renders them usefully informative.

The effect of evolution on the precursors of displays, that is, the effect of ritualization and of the broader formalization process, is to enable acts to be more effective in making information available to recipient individuals (see Smith, n.d.). Of several ways in which this is achieved the most striking is usually the development of novel characteristics of form, the display movements be-

---

2. It is not clear, for instance, that many acts thought to be "displacement" are actually irrelevant. The judgment of relevance is made by an ethologist, who may fail to realize that an animal can be behaving more appropriately by turning to an activity of secondary importance in an event than (when blocked by circumstances from its more obvious responses) by doing nothing at all. Further, the judgment is normally made with respect to an act that is assumed to be only the precursor of some display. The postulated act may well be irrelevant in the circumstances but wrongly postulated—and other possible precursors of the display may be acts that are relevant (see Bastock, Morris, and Moynihan, 1953). On the whole, many of the displays for which irrelevant acts have been postulated as evolutionary precursors have probably been derived either from acts of secondary importance that were likely to occur in close temporal conjunction with social encounters (e.g., grooming movements, see Moynihan, 1955) or from acts that appear irrelevant because, in being redirected and exaggerated, they have become difficult for an ethological observer to recognize.

coming more exaggerated than their precursors and perhaps either elaborated or simplified—changes that make them more conspicuous and hence more likely to attract attention. All vocalizations, for instance, are novel and exaggerated modifications of the sounds of breathing; many postural displays and exaggerated movements are likewise novel alterations of their precursors' forms. Exaggeration is not inevitable, however. Other displays or components of displays differ from their precursors only in being used more often than is necessary to achieve just the original direct functions of the acts. For instance, black-tailed deer have a rub-urinating display in which the act of urinating is repeated much more often (and in briefer bouts) than is required just to void urine and is done in a novel posture that gets the urine on the hind legs (Muller-Schwarze, 1971), where it presumably evaporates from the fur as a pheromonal signal. Nestling birds hold their mouths open as if to admit food when no food is being offered and thus signal their readiness to ingest. Yet other displays, such as the hand and body movements that accompany human speech, become specialized through their correlation with changes in the patterns of other activities, and others (commonly involving the deposition of pheromones in urine or feces) become restricted to use only when the communicator is in specific locations where they can serve as marking functions.

The evolutionary differentiation of display behavior is constrained and directed in various ways. To begin with, of course, the physical characteristics of the communicating animal determine the limits within which it can perform and receive signals. Its habitat provides other limitations—for example, a communicator may be obscured by foliage; blanketed by noise from wind, waves, or other individuals; or concealed from the kinds of predators that the environment harbors. Various pressures hone the distinctiveness of each display; it must be recognizably different from other displays in the species' repertoire, from the displays of other species that live in the same immediate region, and often also in some ways from the displays of other conspecific individuals (to the extent that interactions are based on the mutual recognition of individuals and dependent on displays for this information). Different sorts of social organization affect the characteristics of displays; for instance, in species in which individuals are continuously and closely together, displays are often more variable in form and more likely to intergrade than they are in species in which individuals have much less intimate and frequent access to each other.

Ethologists have not restricted their interest in display behavior to its evolutionary origins. They recognize it as just one member of a broader class initially called *fixed action patterns*. These patterns are relatively stereotyped units, each of which appears to comprise a set of muscular contractions that have a fixed relationship to one another. The set can be foreshortened or reoriented, but its components cannot be rearranged. Behavior classified as fixed action patterns has included hunting procedures, antipredator defenses, nest-building acts, egg-retrieval sequences, and even the stereotyped movements idiosyncratically developed by individuals. Displays have been among the most conspicuous and strange-looking acts so classified. The fixed-action-pattern concept set a major perspective for ethological research, although it has proved to be a mixed blessing.[3]

That behavior should evolve in such chunks as fixed action patterns has always puzzled ethologists and led them to pay a great deal of attention to these units. As a result, they have obtained detailed descriptions of both displays and the conditions that elicit them: external stimuli and internal motivation states. There developed, unfortunately, a preoccupation with the most salient simuli and with a very limited set of motivational causes. This led, on the one hand, to underestimating the importance to animals of relationships among external stimuli, and on the other to attempts to explain the "causation" of most displays in terms of aggression, fear, and sex. As hypothetical causal mechanisms, each of these three is complex, and together they comprise only a fraction of whatever motivational processes do underlie display behavior. In recognition of the difficulties inherent in using pri-

---

3. Hinde (1970:chapter 3) has reviewed the concept in detail and has explained its uses and the difficulties encountered in work with the effects of peripheral stimuli on the course of sequences of muscular contractions that are often labeled as fixed action patterns.

marily behavioral clues as indices of unknown internal states, Hinde (1955, 1956, 1970) proposed that we avoid oversimplified explanatory hypotheses. He suggested that we use instead descriptive intervening variables, which he called "tendencies." Tendencies imply that there are internal mechanisms that control behavior but do not specify their properties. One of the advantages of this descriptive device is that it permits the recognition of diverse states not adequately represented by the traditional trio of motivations (i.e., aggression, fear, and sex). The focus remains, however, on the internal mechanisms controlling individual behavior, and not on the mechanisms controlling the orderliness of interactions (see Smith, ms.).

The traditional ethological interest in the motivational states of individuals who display is only indirectly relevant to the study of communication. It is more relevant and more appropriate to ask of behavioral studies what kinds of information displays make available to those individuals who may interact with the communicator and, further, how that information contributes to the mechanisms used in managing the processes of interacting.

The kinds of information made available by displays comprise, first, messages about the communicator's behavior—the behavioral selections in which it is engaged or the options it may choose, the relative probabilities of these choices, and some indication of how it will perform them. Second, there are messages about some nonbehavioral attributes of the communicator—its identity and sometimes its location.

The behavioral messages encoded in the displays of many vertebrate species appear to belong to a rather limited message set that the species hold in common (see Chart 2.1). Some behavioral selection messages can be translated readily into standard motivational categories—the messages of attack and escape, for example. Others cannot. Examples of the latter include the messages predicting behavior that falls within such broad categories as locomotion or interaction.

All behavioral selection messages, but most especially the broadly predictive ones, are meaningless to a recipient except as evaluated in terms of additional information. This information is

Chart 2:1. Messages that are Widely Encoded in the Displays of Diverse Species of Vertebrate Animals

I. BEHAVIORAL MESSAGES

    A. Behavioral Selection Messages

locomotion: walking, running, flying, swimming, and so forth, with no specification of particular functional classes such as running to escape or to join.

general set: unspecified kinds of activities that always or usually are alternatives physically incompatible with other behavioral selections encoded by a display. (For example, a prairie dog does a jump-yip display when the probability that it will flee or continue to flee becomes less than the probability that it will do something like resting, foraging, or grooming that is incompatible with escape behavior—but which selection it will make within this "general set" is not specified by the display.)

attack: attempting to inflict injury.

escape: attempting to withdraw or avoid. (Often encoded in the same displays that encode some probability of attacking and some probability of continuing to vacillate—see below.)

copulation: attempting to inseminate, be inseminated, or to carry out the functionally equivalent act of fertilization characteristic of each species.

indecisive: vacillating or hesitating between other selections. (This message is very commonly encoded, since most displays correlate with the probability that the communicator will select between at least two incompatible options and will behave "indecisively" while choosing.)

interaction: attempting to interact or to avoid interaction of any of several kinds that may include attack, copulation, association, and other possibilities. (This message does not specify which kind of interaction is relevant in any particular event. It is encoded, for instance, by the "songs" of many birds, used by males ready to challenge or fight with intruders, or court, associate with, or copulate with females.)

association: remaining in the company of another individual.

remaining with site: restricting movements to a particular neighborhood. (Also encoded by many bird songs, sung only by males remaining within their territories.)

seeking: attempting to gain the opportunity to perform some other selection such as interaction or escape.

receptive: prepared to accept some other selection such as copulation or caregiving. (The latter may not itself be a widespread behavioral selection message.)

attentive: paying attention to a stimulus; monitoring. (For example, a prairie dog will "bark" for as long as it continues to watch some source of disturbance and while attentive remains ready to flee or otherwise avoid interacting.)

B. Behavioral Supplemental Messages
probability: the likelihood that a given behavioral selection will be made.
intensity: the forcefulness, rapidity, and so forth, with which a given selection will be performed. (Not a unitary message category: this will require subdivision when more research has been done.)
relative stability: a measure of the expected persistence of a given selection. (Such information is encoded, for instance, by the duration and regularity of intervals between a prairie dog's barks.)
direction: the direction a given behavioral selection will take (e.g., toward or away from some other individual).

II. NONBEHAVIORAL MESSAGES

A. Identifying Messages
population classes: species, subspecific populations, individual.
physiological classes: maturity, breeding state, sex.
bonding classes: pairs, families, troops.

B. Location Message
A single category of information that enables the sources of a display to be pinpointed.

A behavioral selection message is information that indicates what kinds of activities, from the whole behavioral repertoire available to it, a displaying animal is making or possibly about to make. A behavioral supplemental message provides additional information about that selection: how likely it is to be performed, the direction it may take, and so on. Nonbehavioral messages specify who the communicator is (to varying degrees of explicitness) and, in the case of at least most vocal displays, where the communicator is.

The chart is based on Smith (1969) and on a detailed revision (n.d.).

available from sources that are contextual to the use of any particular display, and these contextual sources are usually abundant. They include other displays and nonformalized activities of the communicator, the site and circumstances in which an event occurs, and even the history that a recipient brings with it to that event. In other words, although displays are important sources of information about a communicator's behavior, responses to displays have to be context dependent.

The evolution of messages only broadly predictive of a communicator's behavior, and even the fact that such messages are few and may be largely shared among very diverse species, is likely due to the quite small display repertoires that seem characteristic of all species (Smith, 1969). By traditional criteria there are usually not more than about forty displays per species (Moynihan, 1970). Furthermore, these displays are divided into several sets suited to different sensory modalities—sets that overlap each other in the information they make available. Whatever the reasons for their limited display vocabularies, species are faced with an evolutionary choice between providing either information that is precise or information that can be used in many different circumstances but that must therefore depend on those circumstances to provide sufficient additional information to make the message useful. To some extent species have chosen both routes. Where fully appropriate and immediate responses are necessary, narrowly specific information may be supplied by a display. For instance, when a communicator has sighted a predator, it can signal that there is a high probability that it is escaping; in response, recipients of the signal will flee or freeze. But in more common, less menacing circumstances, the diplays that are used sacrifice precision and provide primarily broadly predictive information.

Although only the most preliminary attempts have yet been made to catalogue human displays, it is already clear that we use displays extensively even when also using our special communicative tool, speech. In fact, in normal circumstances, speech leans considerably on display behavior to provide crucial sources of contextual information (see, e.g., Kendon, 1967; Birdwhistell, 1970), and some of our human displays appear to be specialized to accompany speech. Whether these comprise an "extra" allotment of displays is not yet known, although there is as yet no reason to think that the size of our display repertoire greatly exceeds that of other primates (Smith, ms.). The displays accompanying speech may provide information not found in the displays of other species, but many of our other displays likely share the set of messages that is widespread among nonhuman species. Only a single human display has as yet, however, been subject to a thorough message analysis, showing the tongue (Smith, Chase, and Lieblich, 1974). Tongue showing is done in quite diverse circumstances and encodes the messages of interaction (with a depressed probability, i.e., interaction or some aspect of it is likely to be shunned) and the general set of incompatible alternatives (see Table 2.1). A fuller picture of the display repertoire of our species can be expected to emerge in the next few years, for there is a great deal of current research on what is often called human "nonverbal behavior" (see Hinde, 1972; and an annotated collection by Weitz, 1974).

The display concept is important in studying the formalized behavior of human beings, just as it is for other species. Yet displays are not the only formalized behavioral units of importance in communicating, and the traditional display concept is now in need of revision.[4] Some of its problems are of tangential interest to us here. Displays can be difficult to recognize when they are only slightly or partly formalized, or when their form varies and, at one extreme, they intergrade freely with each other. A matter closer to this book's concern with ritual is the existence of compound formal units in which displays are used simultaneously or in orderly sequences. But it is of even more interest that formalization extends beyond displays and their compounds to behavior patterns that cannot be performed by single individuals alone. Just as it takes "two to tango," it takes two (or more) to greet and to perform various other little ceremonies that have been called "rituals" by both ethologists and some anthropologists. Formalization provides the framework and patterns for these cooperative interactions, giving their participants preestablished parts to play.

Formalized Interactions

When individuals cooperate to manage interactions in accordance with preestablished, formal procedures, each steps into a part or role and accepts the rules that accompany it. The behavior of the participants is not rigidly fixed, at least not in most vertebrate animals, but is directed into repeatable patterns of acts that serve the requirements of that particular kind of interaction. As each participant plays its part it affects the ways others play

---

4. A detailed discussion of the inadequacies of the traditional display concept, along with an expanded definition of ''display'' behavior, is presented by Smith (ms.). This work can also be consulted for numerous examples of displays and for a more detailed examination of most of the ethological concepts dealt with in this chapter.

theirs, and each individual may be required to make specific kinds of accommodation to the others in support of the progress of their interaction. The key feature of a formalized interaction that is apparent to an observer is thus the *recurrence of a pattern* in the cooperative behavior of two or more participants, a pattern with regular, classifiable moves and responses that are characteristic of the parts being played, even though the details differ from event to event.

The formal characteristics are often most readily seen in the mutual overtures that are necessary when individuals are establishing, reaffirming, or testing their relationships. Each individual is then especially uncertain about the other, prepared to respond to its attack or to flee, and trying to maneuver it into more specific responses. Among the kinds of interactions in which these conditions prevail is what ethologists have traditionally called "courtship," a term they do not restrict to pair-bonding activities. Because the signaling patterns used in courting must unambiguously identify the participants, they are often among the most conspicuous and bizarre of a species' displays.

Formalized courtship interactions can be found in many species of insects, in which their main function is, not to control attack and escape, but simply to synchronize the responses of the two sexes. The sequences of moves and responses of a male and a female may fall into patterned chains, as in the courting sequence of a butterfly called the silverwashed fritillary (reviewed by Bastock, 1967). A male finds and then circles closely around a flying female; next they perform a spectacular joint flight in which the male repeatedly glides below and then darts up in front of her while she adheres to a very straight flight path. Then the female alights, the male joins her, and they both posture and exchange special scents. The whole sequence has seven male acts plus appropriate female responses but may begin without the aerial steps if a male finds an already receptive female.

Interactional sequences are usually less fixed in the courting of vertebrate animals, but they remain orderly and largely predictable even while permitting considerable adjustment to the circumstances of each occasion. Especially detailed cases have been described for some fish (e.g., the nine-spined stickleback, see Morris, 1956b) and birds (e.g., African weaver birds, see Crook, 1963). Steps in the sequences may be repeated or interpolated by an individual out of the "usual" or idealized order but are never very far from the responses that most frequently correlate with them. In other species there may be little appearance of fixed order, although the component actions are remarkably stereotyped and complicated; the courtship sequences of ducks are familiar examples. Yet even here, where sequencing is extremely variable, the synchrony among males in the performance of some of their displays is extraordinarily precise (Weidmann and Darley, 1971). Other, asynchronously used displays cue the start of synchronous performance and indicate to us some of the rules that govern these interactions.

In many kinds of birds the formalized interactions used in establishing pair bonds are retained and used in greetings after mates have been temporarily apart. They are also used for reassuring and appeasing functions when one or both mates has been upset. For example, the male may dispute with a territorial intruder and then turn aggressively on his mate, or the female may drive the male away from the immediate vicinity of her nest. In general, the longer two mates have been paired, the more easily they adjust to difficult circumstances with little or no use of formalized interactions. Nonetheless, it is often fairly easy to cause a pair to bring these performances back into use by a simple experiment. If, for instance, a stuffed owl is placed in the vicinity of the nest of an eastern king bird, the male attacks it and then turns on his mate as she joins him. She forestalls his attack by using a wing-fluttering display and a vocalization to which he replies in kind (Smith, 1966).

Among the most elaborate greeting performances of birds yet known are those Tinbergen and his students have described for gulls (summarized by Tinbergen, 1959; and Moynihan, 1962). The male may begin a greeting interaction by effectively challenging his mate with a display called the long call. They then align in parallel with each other and use another vocalization called the mew call. Remaining in parallel they both proceed through a variable succession of progressively less "agonistic" (i.e., less involved with attack and escape) postural displays, terminating the interaction with mutual head flagging, in which they stiffly turn their heads away from each other. Although the exact sequence of displays is subject to omissions and some changes in order, the participants largely adhere to a cooperative rule, each performing the same display as its mate does.

The orientations assumed by greeting kingbirds or gulls are quite limited, usually parallel or carefully oblique. Such orientations can be maintained only by mutual cooperation and are part of the formal structure of greeting and appeasing interactions. They are more elaborate in geese, whole families of which may maneuver into oblique orientations to each other and to their gander when he is returning from a squabble with another gander and is engaging them in a so-called triumph ceremony (see Fischer, 1965). In these family performances the postural displays differ from those used by the ganders in threatening each other only in the mutual orientations of the participants.

While greetings are formal interactions that enable their participants to interact more freely, some formal interactions reaffirm relationships of individuals whose cooperation is limited to placing reasonable bounds on their competitive encounters. Two territorial birds, for instance, may engage each other in a "countersinging duel" from opposite sides of the boundary between their territories. The dominant male black-tailed prairie dogs of neighboring coterie groups may challenge at their border, facing each other and chattering their teeth, or each in turn presenting anal glands for the other to sniff (King, 1955; Smith et al., 1973). Neighboring male wildebeest have a much more complicated "challenge ritual" (Estes, 1969) with about thirty possible component steps that can vary considerably in their sequence and require an average of six or seven minutes a day to complete. It begins with one male's entering his neighbor's territory and proceeds through various mutual orientations varying from a reverse parallel standing or circling to kneeling with horns confronted.

Courting, greeting, and challenging patterns are elaborate in many species of vertebrate animals, and human beings would seem to be no exception. In a very thorough study of naturally occurring human greetings at parties and in a few other kinds of social occasions recorded on cinefilm in the northeastern United States, Kendon and Ferber (1973) demonstrated many minutely detailed patterns of mutual organization, timing, and sequencing. They found, for instance, that when two greeting individuals are initially some distance apart, there are typically two successive exchanges of "salutation displays."

The first or "distance salutation" is exchanged shortly after each individual perceives the other. One displays, commonly performing a head toss and perhaps also a wave and some suitable vocalization. The head toss is actually a compound of such display units as raising the eyebrows and smiling, and it appears from preliminary observations by Eibl-Eibesfeldt (1968) to be used by diverse ethnic groups around the world in one form of greeting at a distance. Having performed distance salutations, the individuals may either not interact further or may approach each other. While approaching, they shift their gazes, scanning here and there, and a quick but distinct aversion of the gaze is common just before they begin the "close salutation." This part of the sequence is very likely to incorporate smiling and vocalizing. Each participant assumes one of a small number of distinctive head postures, and they halt face to face, usually within about two meters of each other. They then do something from a large range of highly formalized acts such as handshaking, embracing, and exchanging remarks in a fashion that simulates a verbal exchange of information. Although often perfunctory, this preliminary exchange can be prolonged and can incorporate true speech exchanges, but it is at least initially part of the greeting performance. Even if conversation then continues, the greeting itself is formally closed by the participants' moving apart and adopting a changed orientation to each other. That is, greeting is formally terminated before further interaction is developed. Formal terminations seem to be common in human interactions and much less so in the behavior of other species.

That greeting interactions appear to have a formal structure does not imply that they are inflexible. Indeed, even within the limited ethnic and situational sample that Kendon and Ferber obtained, greetings were very variable within the limits of this outline. Differences in the degree of familiarity between participants, in their status, in familial or other relationships, their sex, the kind of social occasion, time elapsed since last meeting, and other variables all had effects.

Goffman has proposed a concept that subsumes the formal structure of greetings within a much more broadly defined interactional unit, the "interchange" (1967, 1971). An interchange is a basic unit of everyday ritual, a pattern of two or more moves by two or more participants: for example, "excuse me"—"certainly" (1967:20). In that interchanges are formal structures that guide behavior in specific kinds of cooperative interactions, the concept is effectively identical with that of "formalized interactions."

Almost every kind of interaction among human adults is opened and closed by interchanges (Goffman, 1971). An encounter begins with a "supportive interchange" in which one individual indicates readiness to be involved with another, and the second indicates receipt of the signal(s) and acceptance of the implied relationship with the first person. A class of comparable importance, because it helps participants to accommodate to one another, is that of "remedial interchanges." These restore order to encounters after infractions of social rights and obligations and involve mutually performed patterns of challenging the misconduct (a step that may be omitted) and a correcting response, followed by acceptance and then sometimes expressions of gratitude for the acceptance. Supportive and remedial interchanges are so pervasive that Goffman contends that one or the other of them comprises almost all brief human encounters. They also provide the procedures for initiating and closing more extended encounters, becoming "ritual brackets" that mark transitions first to the state of increased access of individuals to one another, and later to the state of diminished access (Goffman, 1971:79). And they function in many additional ways. At various junctures in an interaction the supportive can provide reassurance of diverse sorts, and the remedial can even close an encounter by letting an individual apologize, as it were, for reducing the other person's access to him. The many forms of both supportive and remedial interchanges are specific to different kinds of interactional needs, and all are as highly conventionalized and automatically used as are the displays that provide some of their component acts.

One very abundantly used kind of human interaction that is bounded by supportive or remedial interchanges and controlled in its unfolding by successive ritual interchanges of various sorts is not found in the behavior of other species—the conversation. Conversing depends on cooperation—on the participants' sharing a "working consensus" (Goffman, 1959), on the conversation's topic, on who will guide it at any time, on the acceptable level of emotionality, and various other features. Each participant has to accommodate to the other's style, and they must jointly establish what Argyle and Kendon (1967) termed the "standing features" or orientations, distances apart, and postures that both facilitate interacting and indicate the agreement by each individual to continue. The extent to which such standing features are formalized remains largely untested in natural circumstances, but there are many formalized "dynamic features" that determine the flow of conversational interactions. These include utterances, movements, and patterns of looking that indicate the direction and shifts of the attention of each participant, the control of turn taking as speaker and listener, and the participants' continuing adherence to their working agreement for managing the interaction (Argyle and Kendon, 1967).

Conversations are extraordinarily intricate interactions, replete with gestures, postural changes, nonverbal utterances, and speech and often proceeding and shifting phases very rapidly. Observations made in real time cannot begin to cope with the many interrelated patterns of activities that occur, and analysis of samples recorded on film is extremely time consuming. A particularly detailed analysis, based on frame-by-frame study of film, was done by Kendon on the start of a conversation involving six participants (1973). Five were seated, awaiting the other's arrival to chair an informal discussion. He came, sat down, made a few remarks, and then looked at each participant in turn. Each gave him a brief nod of the head. He then lowered his head (thus averting his gaze while he formulated what he was about to say) and leaned forward. From this position he reached for a cup on a table. As he touched it, but before he picked it up, he rotated his head toward one participant and, looking directly at her, asked a question. At precisely the moment he began to turn his head, she began to turn to look at him—that is, they began simultaneously to form an axis of interaction, as if she had known in advance that he would next address her. Kendon checked back on the film and found that she had slightly raised her eyebrows, then lowered her head and looked away from him as he had looked at her while scanning the whole group. As he had leaned toward his cup, she had again averted her head but had also tilted it forward as he began to reach. She was by then sharing his rhythm of movement. This indicated her attentiveness and increased the likelihood that he would address her—which he did when they were directly facing one another. In this and other work Kendon (1970) has found that moving into synchrony with another person is a common move that communicates readiness to interact and does so without risking the commitment entailed in a verbal request.

The axis of interaction between members of a conversing dyad is established and maintained through joint orientation and repeated visual scanning, with brief meetings of their gazes. The posture adopted by the axial listener is often similar to ("congruent" with, see Scheflen, 1964) the speaker's. At appropriate points in the flow of his speech such a listener will nod, change facial expression, and make other movements that appear to be formalized signals of continued attention. Such movements may lead to "interactional synchrony," in which the positions held by the two participants are shifted simultaneously, the listener mirroring the speaker's postural changes (Condon and Ogston, 1967). The two individuals apportion roles when necessary by "turn-taking signals" (Duncan, 1972). For instance, the speaker can signal readiness to yield by drawling as he speaks a terminal clause, decreasing the loudness of his words, relaxing a hand he has held in a fixed position, or uttering a formalized verbalization such as "or something," or "you know"; alternatively, he can attempt temporarily to keep his listener from taking a speaking turn by continuously gesticulating. Such signaling behavior comprises displays or essentially display-like formalizations that make each participant's behavior more predictable within the framework of the interactional formalization of conversing.

Ritual: An Evolutionary Perspective

In nonhuman animals, displays, their compounds, and formalized interactions are the whole set of formal behavioral tools available for social communication. Man has, of course, the additional tool of language, which enormously extends his capacities for sharing information. Yet the evolution of linguistic behavior began in a primate that already had displays and formalized patterns of interacting, and these were not discarded. Far from it. The displays must have determined, in part, the directions language evolution would take, and they functioned in various contextual relationships with it—as they still do. They also continue to function independently of speech in many circumstances. Many of their old messages and functions remain. We can greet, court, and challenge, for instance, entirely with glances, eyebrow raisings, blushes, fist wavings, growls, and other displays, if we remain within the established frameworks of such interactions. Even when we add words, they are often in stereotyped units divorced from literal meanings. "How are you" is not a question about health or even a question; it is a salutation we can replace with "Hi" if the participants' relationship permits. This is to say, not that speech does not greatly enrich the interactions people can have, but that the procedures of interacting are still organized to a significant extent on what came before and that the procedures still employ the old behavioral tools. These tools are displays, the formalized units of behavior by which an individual can share information about himself, and formalized interactions, the cooperative units within which groups of two or more participants can coordinate their behavior to yield coherent, serviceable encounters.

That the ethological concept of "formalized interactions" and the anthropological concept of "interchange" appear to represent fully comparable phenomena has already been noted. This implies that what Goffman and others see as everyday human ritual is a class of behavior rooted in biological evolution. Further, the grander rituals with which anthropologists have more often been concerned may be primarily traditional, highly conventionalized elaborations of this class, fitted to culturally and structurally defined requirements. Such rituals resemble the formalized interactions of nonhuman species in very fundamental ways. Each, for instance, has a nonrational structure that engages its participants in cooperative acts. Each ritual conveys to its participants and other recipients a consistent assortment of information and is used in a variety of circumstances just as one nonhuman formalized interaction may be used in, say, courting, greeting, and appeasing. This renders a recipient's use of a ritual's information in any event very dependent on other information from contextual sources (Turner, 1967).

In addition, the "ritual acts" contributed by participants in human rituals are communicative analogues of displays; in everyday rituals many of them are displays. Ritual acts are only one member of the class that Turner (1966; 1967:19) refers to as "symbols." Other symbols are the formal physical accoutrements of rituals: objects, scents, sites, and the like. These also have antecedents in the communication of nonhuman animals (Smith, ms.), but to simplify the issue they are ignored in this chapter; their incorporation would not affect its basic arguments. Each ritual symbol has its consistent information content and functions differently when used in different contexts (Turner, 1966; 1967; Leach, 1966). For example, any ritual dealing with spirits appears to be made up of ritual acts, each of which is a highly stereotyped set of gestures that serves a "meaningful unit" and can be variously combined with other such units in different rituals (Sapir, 1970). The units of Sapir's spirit-directed rituals are also comparable to displays in that the use of each correlates, not with external entities such as the kinds of spirits being sought, but with the communicator's behavior in dealing with the spirit—for example, by making a sacrifice, taking medicine, or washing.

Finally, for any one human population there are limited numbers of symbols and of rituals. Leach argues that this is because all the knowledge of nonliterate peoples must be incorporated in the stories and rituals familiar to the living generation, and these must be few enough to be learned and remembered (1966). This numerical limitation forces ritual symbols to become specialized for use in many different circumstances, generating as many of what Leach calls "alternative meanings" as the sources of information contextual to them vary. The effect on the kinds of information encoded is the same as the effect of the small display repertoire available to each species on the kinds of messages its displays can provide (Smith, 1969).

In summary, it appears that the ritual acts (and other symbols), everyday interpersonal rituals, and rituals of religious and major occasions that human beings perform have their ultimate sources in the displays (and comparable nonbehavioral specializations) and the formalized interactions characteristic of nonhuman animals. Such displays are products of biological evolution, which creates genetic predispositions to behave in specialized ways, ways that in some species can be considerably elaborated by learned traditions. That this continuity between human beings and other species in the behavior with which they communicate has been less than obvious is due in part to a divergence between biology and anthropology in the kinds of behavior they have usually studied. Ethology is a branch of evolutionary biology, and ethologists have been centrally concerned with the genetic theory of evolution. Thus they have considered the adaptive values of behavior to individuals (since natural selection works on individual phenotypes) and have tended to pay relatively little attention to behavioral units that cannot be performed in their entirety by single individuals. Nonetheless, even the basic individual behavioral unit, the display, is adaptive only if it elicits an appropriate response; it evolves in intraspecific repertoires only in conjunction with the evolution of response behavior. Cooperative acts have, however, been, on the whole, much nearer to the focus of anthropologists as they studied the structure and workings of societies and the combined contributions of individuals to unit structures of a higher order. Once it is realized that evolutionary specializations for communicating have produced both units that individuals perform and units that groups perform (on the basis of individual contributions, still readily subject to natural selection), then the relationships between the ethological concept of display and the anthropological concept of ritual are more easily seen.

This proposal that human ritual is not a fundamentally new class of communicative behavior peculiar to our species does not imply that it has no human peculiarities (see Huxley, 1966). The enormous cultural elaboration of our rituals correlates with their extension into peculiarly human enterprises such as worship and government. Human beings have reflected upon rituals, their causes, and their uses and have modified them to adjust their functioning. It would be fallacious to assume that human rituals are nothing more than elaborate versions of nonhuman ones, simply because a common origin is claimed. Human social behavior, managed with the highly specialized tool of language, is much more intricate than that of any other species. From studying biological origins and from comparing diverse species, we can gain insights into the properties of such classes of behavior as displays and formalized interactions. But to discover what human beings can do with such classes and how human activities are constrained by them, we must study human behavior.

References

Andrew, R. T. 1963. "Evolution of Facial Expressions." *Science* 142:1034–1041.

Argyle, M. and A. Kendon. 1967. "The Experimental Analysis of Social Performance," in *Advances in Experimental Social Psychology*, 3:55–98. (L. Berkowitz, ed.). New York: Academic Press.

Bastock, M. 1967. *Courtship: An Ethological Study*. Chicago: Aldine Press.

Bastock, M., D. Morris, and M. Moynihan. 1953. "Some Comments on Conflict and Thwarting in Animals." *Behavior* 6:66–84.

Birdwhistell, R. 1970. *Kinesics and Context*. Philadelphia: University of Pennsylvania Press.

Blest, A. D. 1961. "The Concept of Ritualization," in *Current Problems in Animal Behavior* (W. H. Thorpe and O. L. Zangwill, eds.). Cambridge, England: Cambridge University Press.

Condon, W. S. and W. D. Ogston. 1967. "A Segmentation of Behavior." *Journal of Psychiatric Research* 5:221–235.

Crook, J. H. 1963. "Comparative Studies on the Reproductive Behavior of Two Closely Related Weaver Bird Species (*Ploceus cucullatus* and *Ploceus nigerrimus*) and Their Races." *Behavior* 21:177–232.

Daanje, A. 1950. "On the Locomotory Movements in Birds and the Intention Movements Derived from Them." *Behavior* 3:49–98.

Darwin, C. 1872. *The Expression of the Emotions in Man and Animals.* London: Appleton.

Douglas, M. 1963. *Purity and Danger: An Analysis of Concepts of Pollution and Taboo.* London: Routledge and Kegan Paul.

Duncan, S., Jr. 1972. "Some Signals and Rules for Taking Turns in Conversations." *Journal of Personality and Social Psychology* 23:283–292.

Eibl-Eibesfeldt, I. 1968. "Zur Ethologie Menschlichen Grussverhalten I. Beobachtungen an Balinesen, Papuas und Samoanern nebst Vergleichenden Bemerkungen." *Zeits. Tierpsychol.* 25:727–744.

Estes, R. D. 1969. "Territorial Behavior of the Wildebeest (*Connochaetes taurinus,* Burchell, 1823) *Zeits. Tierpsychol.* 26:284–370.

Fischer, H. 1965. "Das Triumphgeschrei der Graugans (*Anser anser*). *Zeits. Tierpsychol.* 22:247–304.

Goffman, E. 1959. *Presentation of Self in Everyday Life.* New York: Doubleday.

—— 1963. *Behavior in Public Places.* New York: Free Press.

—— 1967. *Interaction Ritual.* Garden City, N.Y.: Anchor Books.

—— 1971. *Relations in Public.* New York: Basic Books.

Goodenough, W. H. 1965. "Rethinking 'Status' and 'Role' toward a General Model of the Cultural Organization of Social Relationships." Association of Social Anthropologists, Monograph 1, The Relevance of Models for Social Anthropology, 1–24.

Hinde, R. A. 1955. "A Comparative Study of the Courtship of Certain Finches (*Fringillidae*)." *Ibis* 97:706–745.

—— 1956. "A Comparative Study of the Courtship of Certain Finches (*Fringillidae*)." *Ibis* 98:1–23.

—— 1970. *Animal Behavior. A Synthesis of Ethology and Comparative Psychology.* 2d ed. New York: McGraw-Hill.

—— 1972. *Non-Verbal Communication.* Cambridge, England: Cambridge University Press.

Hinde, R. A. and N. Tinbergen. 1958. "The Comparative Study of Species-Specific Behavior," in *Behavior and Evolution* (A. Roe and G. G. Simpson, eds.). New Haven: Yale University Press.

Huxley, J. 1914. "The Courtship Habits of the Great Crested Grebe (*Podiceps cristatus*); with an Addition to the Theory of Sexual Selection." *Proceedings of the Zoological Society* 35.

—— 1966. "A Discussion on Ritualization of Behavior in Animals and Man." Introduction, in *Philosophical Trans. Royal Society* B (25) 251:249–271.

Kendon, A. 1967. "Some Functions of Gaze-Direction in Social Interaction." *Acta Psychologica* 26:22–63.

—— 1970. "Movement Coordination in Social Interaction: Some Examples Described." *Acta Psychologica* 32:100–125.

—— 1973. "The Role of Visible Behavior in the Organization of Face-to-Face Interaction," in *Movement and Communication in Man and Chimpanzee* (M. von Cranach and I. Vine, eds.). New York: Academic Press.

Kendon, A. and A. Ferber. 1973. "A Description of Some Human Greetings," in *Comparative Ecology and Behavior of Primates* (R. P. Michael and J. H. Crook, eds.). New York: Academic Press.

King, J. A. 1955. "Social Behavior, Social Organization, and Population Dynamics in a Black-Tailed Prairie Dog Town in the Black Hills of South Dakota." *South Dakota University Mich. Contr. Lab. Vert. Biol.* 67:1–123.

Leach, E. R. 1966. "Evolution of Ritualization in the Biological and Cultural Spheres." *Philosophical Transcriptions of the Royal Society* B 251:403–408.

Lorenz, K. 1966. "Evolution of Ritualization in the Biological and Cultural Spheres." *Philosophical Transcriptions of the Royal Society* B 251:273–284.

McCullough, D. R. 1969. "The Tule Elk: Its History, Behavior, and Ecology." *University of California Publ. Zool.* 88:1–191.

Morris, D. 1956a. "The Feather Postures of Birds, and the Problem of the Origin of Social Signals." *Behavior* 9:75–113.

—— 1956b. "The Function and Causation of Courtship Ceremonies," in *L'instinct dans le Comportement des Animaux et de l'homme* (M. Autori, ed.). Paris: Masson.

Moynihan, M. 1955. "Remarks on the Original Sources of Display." *Auk* 72:240–246.

—— 1956. "Notes on the Behavior of Some North American Gulls, I. Aerial Hostile Behavior." *Behavior* 10:126–178.

—— 1960. "Some Adaptations Which Help to Promote Gregariousness." *Proceedings of the 12th International Ornithological Congress* (Helsinki, 1958):523–541.

—— 1962. "Hostile and Sexual Behavior Patterns of South American and Pacific Laridae." *Behavior* Supplement VIII:1–365.

—— 1970. "The Control, Suppression, Decay, Disappearance and Replacement of Displays." *Journal of Theoretical Biology* 29:85–112.

Muller-Schwarze, D. 1971. "Pheromones in Black-Tailed Deer (*Odocoileus hemionus columbianus*)." *Animal Behavior* 19:141–152.

Sapir, J. D. 1970. "*Kujaama*: Symbolic Separation Among the Diola-Fogny." *American Anthropologist* 72:1330–1348.

Scheflen, A. E. 1964. "The Significance of Posture in Communication Systems." *Psychiatry* 27:316–331.

Smith, W. John. 1966. "Communication and Relationships in the Genus *Tyrannus*." *Nuttall Ornithological Club Publication* 6:1–250. Cambridge, Mass.

—— 1969. "Messages of Vertebrate Communication." *Science* 165:145–150.

—— n.d. "The Behavior of Communicating: An Ethological Approach."

Smith, W. John, J. Chase, and A. K. Lieblick. 1974. "Tongue Showing: A Facial Display of Humans and Other Primate Species." Mimeo.

Smith, W. John, S. L. Smith, E. C. Oppenheimer, J. G. deVilla, and F. A. Ulmer. 1973. "Behavior of a Captive Population of Black-Tailed Prairie Dogs: Annual Cycle of Social Behavior." *Behavior* 46:189–220.

Tinbergen, N. 1952. " 'Derived' Activities: Their Causation, Biological Significance, Origin and Emancipation During Evolution." *Quarterly Biological Review* 27:1–32.

—— 1959. "Comparative Studies of the Behavior of Gulls (*Laridae*): A Progress Report." *Behavior* 15:1–70.

Turner, V. W. 1966. "The Syntax of Symbolism in an African Religion." *Philosophical Transcriptions of the Royal Society* B 251:295–304.

—— 1967. *The Forest of Symbols*. Ithaca, N.Y.: Cornell University Press.

Weidmann, U. and J. Darley. 1971. "The Role of the Female in the Social Display of Mallards." *Animal Behavior* 19:287–298.

Weitz, S. 1974. *Nonverbal Communication*. New York: Oxford University Press.

Wilson, E. O. 1971. *The Insect Societies*. Cambridge, Mass.: Harvard University Press.

—— 1975. *Sociobiology*. Cambridge: The Belknap Press of Harvard University Press.

Three

Mammalian Ritual

Charles D. Laughlin, Jr.
and John McManus

> As a reaction against the assertions of marvels made by
> inspired *dilettanti*, there has arisen among animal psycholo-
> gists a distinct negativist tendency, according to which it is
> considered particularly exact to establish *non*-performance,
> *non*-human behavior, mechanically-limited actions, and stu-
> pidity to animals. Is not too much honour paid to the errors
> we are combating by this negative attitude? Let us not, in
> avoiding *one* error, be led to the opposite extreme.
>
> Wolfgang Köhler, *The Mentality of Apes*

A major goal of this book is to trace the *anlagen* of human ritual in
phylogenesis. W. John Smith, in defining ritual behavior (chapter
2) as the most complex form of communication to be found among
animals, established the capacity for ritual coordination as integral to the vertebrate biogram (see Count, 1973). We note that ritual is manifested in its more elaborate forms among social birds
and mammals and that it is always communication that may func-

The authors express their heartfelt appreciation for the hours of pleasant and informative discussion they had with the following persons on Cayo Santiago: Janet C.
Dunaif, Kathy Cushing, Jay Ross Kaplan, Douglas Leigh Rhodes, Richard G. Raw-
lins, Carol Berman, Saroj Datta, and Diana Sade. Profound thanks are offered to
Professor Donald Stone Sade, Scientist in Charge of the Cayo Santiago rhesus
monkey colony, for his kind permission to visit his research facilities and for his
unselfish aid in completing this project. We also thank Dr. Bobbi Hall and Terry
Morse for many useful ideas. None of these people should be held accountable for
the ideas and interpretations contained herein.

tion either in preparation for social action or as social action. In the present chapter we examine the range of ritual behavior among the higher mammals with the view to making grounded speculations about the possible nature of australopithecine ritual as the link between ritual behavior among lower animals and more advanced hominid ritual.

Before launching ourselves into the vast and fascinating range of mammalian ritual, let us briefly recall the Lewinian formula: $B = f(P,E)$. At the group level, P may be conceived as including the complexity and arrangement of roles, the permutations of roles, the level of cooperation within the group, and the range of differential access to basic resources.[1] In turn, E is determined by the number of basic resources available to the organism in any particular environmental niche, the number of alternative niches available to the organism within its range, the number and nature of predators and competitors operating in that range, and the change of all of these through time (see Schaffer in Schaffer, 1971). It is quite critical, then, to ascertain, not only the constraints and alternatives inherent to the organism, but also the environment that provides the context for action.

We would claim that the maximal complexity encompassed by P in the Lewinian formula becomes progressively greater with each step in the phylogenetic scale. This progressive emergence of complexity is reflected in the organization of the cognized environment (E_c) and results in more complexity and variety in social structure and more complexity and variation in modes of communication (flexibility in communicative displays and lessening of the constraints imposed by "typical intensity").[2] Increased complexity of the E_c may even be sufficient to increase the range of

1. The concept of "basic resources" may be defined as those raw materials present in the environment that are exploited through the prevailing level of information and technology in a given society and on which survival of a viable reproductive population depends (see Laughlin and Brady, 1978; also chapter 9).

2. The term *typical intensity* (see Morris, 1957) refers to the stereotyped force with which a display is delivered by the signaling animal. "Whereas the motivational factors which underlie the signal movements presumably fluctuate continuously, the signal movements themselves have more limited variability: this stereotype presumably aids recognition" (Hinde in Huxley, 1966:286).

the operational environment (E_o) and thus increase the number and types of environmental forces operating in the ecosystem of the organism. This latter development can have at least three consequences: (1) It may result in widening the appropriate environmental niche of the organism. (2) It may effect actual change in the E_o. (3) It may effect a convergence between E_c and E_o through a more accurate reading of the E_o.

The Range of Ritual Behavior

There seems to be no a priori reason for ascribing to nonhuman primates the capacity for more complex ritual behavior than that of other taxa. Indeed, there would appear to be a number of nonprimate mammals with social and communication systems matching, and even surpassing, that of most nonhuman primates. As evidence becomes available pertaining to social organization among the Cetacea, Canidae, and felines, it becomes increasingly clear that the capacity for complex communication has had a parallel development in a number of taxa and that selection has favored the operation of this capacity according to similar principles—principles retained and elaborated from those already present and operating adaptively in the generalized vertebrate biogram.

As we have made clear, we support the thesis that society is an adaptive strategy—a strategy that facilitates, through various channels of communication, adaptation through corporate action. The central concept we shall use in explaining the mechanisms that make society an adaptive strategy will be that of *coordination* (chapter 1).

The increase in reliance on social action as an adaptive strategy in mammals is related to an increased range of intragroup personality differentiation, including wider differentiation in temperament (Fox, 1974), greater role differentiation, a longer period of time for development of adult patterns in ontogeny, and more variation in autonomic system tuning (see chapter 4). All of this provides, within any taxonomic classification, an optimal range of social responses to varying environments and thus an optimal range of complexity in communication. Thus, we would expect to find ritual behavior predominating as a mechanism for coordination among those species most reliant on social action as an adaptive strategy. Conversely, we would expect to find ritual behavior *less* predominant or nonexistent among species relying least on the social order.

The chasm that has existed between the anthropological and ethological treatments of ritual is fortunately now being bridged. Those working on problems of social coordination among higher vertebrates are beginning to recognize that a mere enumeration of the formalized displays of a species may often not account for all the complex social actions encountered in the wild. Crook (1970), for example, has vehemently opposed the imposition of simplistic unidimensional theories of social coordination in ethological studies and has shown that we require a much more complex picture of a number of variables to predict such things as role differentiation, coordination of group movement, and the like (Menzel, 1968; Gartlan, 1968; Kummer, 1968; and Donald Stone Sade and Richard Rawlings, personal communication, have made similar statements). Furthermore, a number of researchers have become aware that ethology has perpetuated a systematic bias in the data by concentrating on the simpler elements of communication, notably formalized displays and vocalizations (see Crook, 1970; Carpenter, 1964; Mason, 1964; Menzel, 1973a, 1974; Kummer, 1971b, and Altmann, 1967).

Complementing this shift in emphasis, scholars have begun to look at various forms of nonverbal communication in man and animals and to trace such things as facial displays and other formalized components of human communication to their origins in the vertebrate biogram (see various articles in Hinde, 1972; Smith et al., 1973; Andrew, 1965). We would predict that when the chasm is completely bridged, the picture will reflect a continuum of complexity in communicative capacity, correlated closely with the evolutionary development of neural and social complexity— the latter developments facilitating increase in flexibility of social form in relation to ecological variation and change (Crook, 1970; Fox, 1975b; Denham, 1971).

Ritual behavior, then, being one of the more complex mechanisms for social coordination, is more easily observed in the communicative behavior of higher mammals—mammals such as the canids, felines, and higher primates.

Ritual and Social Coordination Among the Canidae

Probably no taxon provides so clear a range of complexity in patterns of social organization, adaptation, and communication as does *Canidae*. As Fox (1971, 1974, 1975a) has shown, canid capacity for social organization and coordination ranges on a continuum from species characterized as solitary, except during mating and parental seasons (e.g., the red fox), to species exhibiting permanent, demographically stable, and complex social groups (e.g., wolf, Cape hunting dog; Fox, 1975a). When wolf society is compared to that of the red fox, the relative complexity of wolf society may be seen along a number of interesting dimensions: (1) Wolves exhibit greater heterogeneity of temperament, even as cubs, than foxes do (Fox, 1974:33). (2) Wolves exhibit more role differentiation than foxes do. (3) Wolves rely heavily on social cooperation in hunting and pack movement, whereas foxes do not. (4) Wolves show a greater tendency toward intragroup sharing and altruism than foxes do, even to the extent of sharing food with injured adult members of the group (Fox, 1974:40). (5) Wolves exhibit much less "typical intensity" in their formalized displays than foxes do (Fox, 1975a:436). (6) Wolves show the entire range of complexity in social organization and action, whereas foxes do not. (7) Wolves consistently show play behavior into adulthood; foxes do not. Taken together, these distinctions describe the wolf pattern of social relations as more adaptively flexible than that of the fox, allowing the wolf a much greater range of predation strategies and patterns of resource distribution. This increased flexibility requires, however, the potential for greater complexity in communication. This is already evidenced for the wolf in the "more subtle intensity gradation" of his displays and in the flexibility with which such displays may be elaborated into more complex arrays (Fox, 1975a:436). It is not surprising, then, that evidence for ritual communication occurs primarily among wolves and less among foxes and other less social canids.

84

A number of rituals among wolf packs appear to be enactments of the ideal social order. In one ritual (Schenkel, 1947; Fox, 1971), the leader of the pack "will seize some food item or an interesting object such as a bone or a piece of caribou skin and parade with it before the entire pack; then he will approach the pack, drop the object, and leave it. The entire pack briefly investigates the 'gift' and then ignores it" (Fox, 1974:39).

Another such ritual is frequently exhibited when wolves greet the pack leader. "Typically, wolves wake up, stretch, greet each other, and focus much attention on the leader, licking his face, nibbling and jawing his muzzle, wagging their tails, and whining. The leader might in turn growl and seize various individuals around the muzzle or pin them to the ground and hold them there for a few seconds" (Fox, 1974:38).

The social-adaptive functions of collective singing among wolves and other social canids are less certain than those of the rituals already described. Nonetheless, collective singing shows all the hallmarks of ritual behavior: "the dawn and dusk choruses of coyotes and jackals, and the choirs of wolves. In coyotes, it is often a family that engages in choral singing, and in both coyote and wolf, is accompanied by much reciprocal greeting, face-licking, and muzzle-biting. . . . It often occurs, for example, prior to the assembly going off to hunt" (Fox, 1975a:439–440).

Another example of social ritual is the common prehunt interaction among wolves described by Murie (1944) as a "ceremonial" involving a good deal of tail wagging and occasionally ending in a group howl. According to Estes and Goddard (1967) a similar ritual occurs among African wild dogs. Mech (1970, and Fox, 1975a) has interpreted these rituals as a mechanism for motivating the pack leaders for a hunt. The exact nature of the complex communications requisite for coordination during the actual hunt by wolves is not clearly understood. Descriptions in the literature are, however, illustrative:

Haber has found clear evidence of hunting strategy; one or more wolves will drive Dall sheep down a hillside to others waiting lower down in ambush. Alternatively one may act as a distracting decoy, presenting itself conspicuously to a moose or caribou and even howling, while other members of the pack creep up behind the unsuspecting prey. He also saw a hunting party approach a moose *and then on some cue,* all but the leader lay down and waited while the leader got round behind the prey; then the others drove the prey towards the leader, *again on some undetectable cue.* Wolves also cooperate when attacking mother and calf, making simultaneous and timed attacks to separate calf from mother (Fox, 1971:139; emphasis ours).

It is crucial to our understanding of the full range of communication that certain information be obtained on the nature of communication in highly concerted, complex social coordination. Our hypothesis would be that much of the coordination alluded to in the passage just quoted depends on ritual behavior. And it seems quite certain, as well, that such ritual communication requires a complex development in ontogenesis. "In young wolves playing together, there are clear patterns of ambush, stalking, cutting off and otherwise anticipating the movements of one peer that is being chased by the others. Dominance roles are often reversed during play (in play chasing and play fighting) so that a dominant individual may assume a submissive role and allow a subordinate to chase and roll it over" (Fox, 1971:140).

Ritual and Social Coordination Among Felines

An analogous, although less well-documented, gradient in social behavior exists among the cats, with leopards at the solitary pole and lions at the social pole (Schaller, 1972:356). With respect to lions, "group existence is a form of life insurance. Sick or crippled lions, unable to kill for themselves, can subsist for months by joining others on their kills. Cubs whose mothers fail to produce enough milk can supplement their diet by suckling on other lactating females, and in the event of a lioness's death, her cubs remain with the pride" (Schaller, 1972:358). Many of the same adaptive advantages that characterize the wolf pack also characterize the lion pride: more efficient use of resources, more effective protection from predation and competition, a greater range of alternative hunting strategies, greater role differentiation, and division of labor.

Lions have a large repertoire of communicative displays and vocalizations (Schaller, 1972:83ff). Evidence of ritual interactions is, however, partial at best, possibly owing to the difficulties of observation and description. Clearly, pride members form a close-knit corporate unit, relying heavily upon corporate action for adaptation. A number of interactions characterize the social order among lions. As with Canidae and primates, aggression is highly stylized and, in the case of lions, infrequent. More typical is peaceful "social licking." Most licking and rubbing among lions is between adult female and young (Schaller, 1972:89).

Concerted social action is most evident during group hunts. There seems to be some disagreement about the complexity of coordination exhibited by lions when they hunt in a body (Cf. Schaller, 1972; Stevenson-Hamilton, 1954; Roosevelt and Heller, 1922). There is little doubt, however, that group coordination is at times required in the hunt. A typical pattern of approach to potential prey is for a number of lions to fan out into as wide a "front" as possible and to approach the prey simultaneously and thus create the highest probability of at least one lion bringing the prey to ground (Schaller, 1972). Communication in such hunting strategies seems to be based on visual information—individuals at times are obviously keeping track of the pursuit by watching their huntmates' progress. If lions do, in fact, use more complex hunting strategies than the group stalk (a distinct possibility in our estimation), such as game drives and encirclement, the means of communication used to coordinate such social action remains a mystery. Our knowledge of social coordination in play is little better. As with other higher vertebrate species, lion adults (principally females) play, as well as the young animals do. Play would at least seem to offer development of social facilitation, if not ritual enactment of group hunting coordination. Play (discussed by McManus, chapter 6) would seem to be essential for social coordination. Species not exhibiting play among conspecifics when they are young tend not to be organizationally complex. Data also exist indicating that animals socialize with others with whom they have had early interactions. Fox (1974) cites studies with beagles and with rhesus monkeys that demonstrate that under three rearing conditions—rearing by human beings, by conspecifics, or under mixed conditions—animals spontaneously group themselves with conspecifics reared under conditions similar to their own.

Ritual Among Nonhuman Primates

It is most germane to the course of this book to lay the foundations of ritual behavior at the level of the primate biogram (see also Wallace, 1966). Through study of homologous features of primate ritual behavior among a variety of species, we may arrive at the precursors that must have been characteristic of the protohominoid and protohominid capacity for ritual (see Tinbergen, 1962; Wickler, 1972).[3]

Optimal cognitive functioning, constrained by the genetically predisposed structure of the brain, inevitably constrains the optimal capacity for communicative complexity in any species or individual (see also Kummer in Altman, 1967; Schaffer in Schaffer, 1971). For a variety of neurophysiological reasons discussed elsewhere (Laughlin and d'Aquili, 1974), we consider the optimal cognitive capacity of the anthropoid apes (especially the chimpanzee) to be markedly superior to that of the *Cercopithecidae*. We thus would expect the complexity of communicative capacity among chimpanzees to be greater than among monkeys. We have found this to be the case in comparing what data exist relative to ritual in these two taxa. Again, of course, we have been hampered by the inherent bias of ethologists toward the description of communicative fixed action patterns to the exclusion of more complex

3. We have already established that the complexity of ritual, when it is in fact manifested by a species or local variant, is a function of the complexity of the social organization, this being in turn a function of a number of variables, including species-specific genetic endowment, ecological flexibility, and level of cognitive and conceptual functioning (see Kummer, Vogel, Durham, Nagel articles in Kummer, 1971b; Gartland in Menzel, 1973a; Fox, 1974; Kummer 1971b; Bernstein in Schrier and Stollnitz, 1971). The latter variable itself is in turn a function of interaction between the organism's genetic endowment and its environment (Harlow et al. in Jarrard, 1971; Harvey, Hunt, and Schroder, 1961; Menzel, 1968; Menzel et al., 1970; McManus, chapter 6; Piaget, 1971; also a significant literature exists concerning the effects of early environmental restriction on both human beings and animals. Some of these studies are discussed in Fox, 1974, and Seligman, 1975).

forms of communication. The results are, however, at the very least, suggestive of the evolutionary trends we are espousing. We turn first, therefore, to a description of ritual communication among the *Cercopithecidae,* and secondly to that among chimpanzees. Finally, we make some speculations about ritual behavior among the australopithecines, on the basis of what we know about the biology of their brains and their level of social adaptation.

Ritual Behavior Among Monkeys
Social action in a primate society requires constant coordination. Among the species for which there are sufficient data, social organization may differ widely from group to group in relation to ecology, demography, and other variables (see Denham, 1971; Miyadi, 1967; Kummer, 1971b; Itani and Suzuki, 1967; Bernstein in Schrier and Stollnitz, 1971). The maintenance of primate society depends, as Kummer (in Eisenberg and Dillon, 1971:222) has so nicely put it, on maintaining a balance between social attraction and aggressive repulsion among group members. Such a balance among all members of a group requires both a cognized model of the social order within each member and channels of communication sufficiently complex to reinforce that cognized model and readjust it in relation to change.

Aggression Ritual. The role of ritualized aggression is well known in relation to territorial defense and the maintenance of optimal demographic-geographic balance (see Eibl-Eibesfeldt, 1970:314ff). The problem of aggression among conspecifics becomes exacerbated when conspecifics form groups and begin to exploit the environment by social strategies. In this regard, dominance ranking, found in a majority of primate societies, may be conceived as one of a set of alternative patterns for the imposition of *cognized space* between group members. A change in the demographic-geographical relations involving a primate group furthermore necessitates either a positive or a negative shift in the intensity and incidence of ritual aggression.

We would suggest that intragroup aggression ritual operates to enact the cognized social order of the group. We would also suggest that in all likelihood the incidence of aggression ritual as reinforcement of the cognized social order is necessary for the optimal operation of long-term memory capacity of the particular species in functional relation to the complexity of the social order and environment of change operating on the particular group. All things being equal, we would expect less frequent and intense intragroup aggression ritual among chimpanzees than among macaque monkeys—this being a function of differential temporal lobe development between the species. A number of authorities have noted the remarkable *infrequency* of aggressive interactions among a variety of primate species in the wild, and the all but inevitable "ritualized" form that aggression takes when it in fact occurs (see Leskes and Acheson in Kummer, 1971a; Etkin, 1964:19; Southwick, 1967:182; Waterhouse and Waterhouse, 1973; Hall, 1962; Gartlan, 1968). Indeed, some writers have even suggested that a major function of ritual aggression is the reduction of actual damage to "combatants" (see Huxley, Crane, and Eibl-Eibesfeldt in Huxley, 1966). Huxley (1966) has gone so far as to term bouts of ritual aggression "tournaments."

At a deeper structural level, ritual aggression would seem to provide a sufficient channel of communication for maintenance of differences in temperament—crucial biopsychological differences that likely underlie social role differentiation in society (Fox, 1974). Individual central nervous system (CNS) components may be integrated and reintegrated ("tuned," see next chapter) in relation, not only to environmental vicissitudes, but also to other conspecifics in the group. We would maintain that a major function of ritual aggression in all highly social vertebrates is precisely the synchronization of CNS functions (including tuning of autonomic and neuroendocrine components, particularly the plasma testosterone level; see Rose et al., 1972) necessary for endurance of cognized social order and effective social action. Heart rate and other biological processes, for example, correlate significantly with dominance ranking in some species, and predictions of future rank may be made from vital signs during infancy (Fox, 1974:36ff). Although genetically based, this relationship may be behaviorally altered. Candland et al. (1970) have found that, when a high-ranking monkey is taken from one group and placed in a group where it is low-ranking, its basal heart rate drops. Similar data are cited in Pribram (1971). There may be limits to the flexibility of CNS reintegration in all individuals so that potentially high-ranking animals (particularly males) may have to leave or be driven from the group to existence on the periphery or as solitary animals.

The synchronization of temperament in a social group entails establishing and maintaining distancing through balance of affect. Activation of positive affect decreases distancing among conspecifics, while activation of negative affect increases distancing. These systems may create spacing in the geographical sense, as with territorial animals that seem to become more ferocious and defensive toward the center of their territories (Count, 1973). The systems may also create distancing in the cognized social environment of the individual members of the group—indeed, with Sade (1974), we would consider the two structures of distancing to be transformations of the same structure.

With the corticalization apparent in the hominoids, and especially in the hominids, the differentiation of affect becomes greater and thus facilitates a more subtle array of affect among (say) chimpanzees than among macaques, and among hominids than among chimpanzees.

Affect occurs only in a cognitive context, and the degree to which it is differentiated depends on the sophistication of the cognitive system (Gellhorn and Loofburrow, 1963; also see a number of studies cited in Beck, 1967; Lazarus, 1974; McManus, chapter 6; and Pribram, 1971). Thus affect itself, linked with cognition, may facilitate a greater range of temperament and a more complex set of social alignments, the higher the organism is on the phylogenetic scale, just as temperamental variation seems to influence cognitive capacity and affective range.

Society is precisely a set of roles, usually ranked in one way or another. Yet there is constant change within the social group through birth, development, attrition, and death—change resulting in social reverberation. The dynamics of social adaptation require some set of mechanisms by means of which the individual member may assume a change in role or status with a minimum of bloodshed—mechanisms that, to use Levi-Strauss's metaphor, allow for the cooking of the individual in the social stew. In rhesus monkeys "males who remain with their natal group are inhibited from mating with their mothers by the reverberance of the role of infant in their adult relationships with their mothers. The role of infant is cognitively incompatible with the role of mate when the same female is the object. The mother's superior dominance is a key part of the relationship, for if the son can successfully challenge his mother's dominance, the inhibition is broken and he will mate with her" (Sade, 1968:36). Another example of this is in the rank reversal of female rhesus siblings (Sade, 1969). In Group *F* of the Cayo Santiago colony, females tend to rise in rank above their older female siblings by the end of their fifth year. In other words each young female monkey ends up ranking just below her mother and just above her older sisters. This movement in ranking is accompanied by an increase in the incidence of aggression between siblings. Thus aggressive interactions, most of which are formalized as aggression ritual, may operate to coordinate the crucial neural subsystems in such a way as to maintain the social fabric. Variation in temperament corresponds to variation in role at the social level, and the concept of reverberation should be functionally applicable at the biological level as well.

Ritual aggression is particularly evident in intergroup encounters in some species of monkeys, as well as in social action directed against predators. Aggression ritual may then take the form of "mobbing" or "line formation" behavior. The latter has been described by Hausfater for Cayo Santiago rhesus monkeys as follows:

Violent intergoup squabbles involved virtually all of the members of group F and were marked by sustained fighting in "line formation." . . . In line formation 2-20 . . . animals faced off with individuals of an opposing group and reciprocally lunged, batted, and growled across the boundary so formed, though with a minimum of actual physical contact. Additional . . . animals stood grunting . . . behind the line of more active participants and rushed forward to lunge at the opponents, then quickly returned to the rear. Participants in the line were most often adult female and 2- to 5-year old males, while older males tended to pace back and forth behind the line (1972:82–83).

The present authors can verify this description from personal observations of Cayo Santiago monkeys. Each animal participating in the line formation alternates between making threatening gestures at the opposite "camp" and turning his head to watch what his fellow group members are doing. Much of the communication necessary for coordination of the line formation seemed to us to be visual, although auditory information would increase in importance in heavy bush.

The line formation is one of a variety of aggression rituals that might be cited as examples of ritual response to other groups of conspecifics in the environment. Furthermore, this formation would seem to be at least minimally homologous to much ritual "warfare" among human populations (see Matthiessen, 1962; Rappaport, 1968, for descriptions of ritual aggression among human groups in the New Guinea highlands). All such social action among primates requires enlistment of participants through allelomimetic arousal. Although the fundamental affect and motor patterns of aggression may be present in primates as fixed action patterns, the intraorganismic and interorganismic coordination of these into social aggression ritual requires a developmental process to mature. This issue is discussed in more detail later here and in a subsequent chapter (see chapter 7).

Allogrooming as Ritual. Whereas various biological and quasibiological functions have been attributed to intensive social grooming among primate species, most theories ignore the effects of grooming on the organism's nervous system (NS).[4] Evidence exists that grooming behavior among primates and other species operates as an arousal mechanism for parasympathetic activity (see Schneirla, 1965; Fox, 1974; see also chapter 4). As ritual, grooming may operate in two ways. First, it may decrease the social distance between conspecifics, in both the participants'

---

4. The connection between allogrooming and autonomic functioning has also been noted by van Lawick-Goodall (1968; 71ff) and Fox (1974:62ff).

E_o and E_c. Second, it may inhibit arousal of sympathetic activity potentially leading to aggressive confrontation.

Evidence for the first function is plentiful for virtually all primate species, particularly baboons and macaques, among whom allogrooming is all but incessant. Especially notable are bouts of allogrooming as ritual "markers" punctuating the initiation of approach under a variety of circumstances, for example, initiation of contact between animals of different rank, of play sequences, and of copulatory sequences (discussions of allogrooming among various primate and other species may be found in van Lawick-Goodall, 1968; Fox, 1974; Schaller, 1972; Hall and DeVore, 1965; Sade, 1965, 1972; and Crook in Eisenberg and Dillon, 1971).

The present authors observed intermittent allogrooming among members of rhesus kin groups at rest on Cayo Santiago, especially during the hot part of the day. This often took the form of mutual grooming among a number of animals.

The evidence in the literature for the second function—that of allogrooming an individual in anticipation of an aggressive outburst—is less available. Yet the data are exceedingly suggestive, for they derive from other nonprimate social vertebrates as well (see Fox, 1974). Donald Stone Sade (1965:8) has noted the use of allogrooming among rhesus monkeys to anticipate and alleviate potential aggression within the troop. Van Lawick-Goodall (1968:283) has noted the same use of allogrooming ritual among chimpanzees.

Ritual allogrooming may thus be seen as a complex of behaviors that may include other communicative components such as submissive-aggressive gestures and visual cuing. A primary biological function of such behavior is to reestablish parasympathetic tuning in counteraction against potential or overt aggression and to reduce social distancing between participants in the ritual exchange (see chapter 7 for discussion of allogrooming in a broader, adaptive context).

Ritual Behavior and Social Decisions. The communication needed for cohesive group movement is often highly complex and poorly understood by researchers (Donald Stone Sade and Richard Rawlings, personal communication; Kummer, 1968; Menzel,

1971, 1973a). Yet it is precisely here, in the realm of coordinated social action, that we would expect ritual behavior to flourish. Probably the best work done on this subject among Old World monkeys is that of Kummer (1968; in Altmann, 1967; in Eisenberg and Dillon, 1971). Specifically, Kummer (in Altmann, 1967) has examined more complex types of interaction within Hamadryas baboon troops, complex interactions of the kind he terms "tripartite relations." Such a relation "is composed of sequences in which three individuals simultaneously interact in three essentially different roles and each of them aims its behavior at both of its partners" (Kummer in Altmann, 1967:64). An excellent example of ritual behavior among Hamadryas baboons is found in Kummer's description of so-called *I-D* interaction, often used in setting direction of movement:

Common travel by several one-male units is coordinated by the unit leaders. In this situation it becomes apparent that two adult males of different age often have an especially close relationship and lead their units together. The development of such *two-male teams* can be reconstructed from the observable stages. In the fully developed team, the younger leader initiates movements in a certain direction by walking ahead (I-role). The older male, who usually brings up the rear of the two units, accepts or rejects the indicated direction by following or by remaining seated (D-role). The leaders "notify" each other by a set of presentation gestures when they change their relative locations (1968:149–150).

In actual operation over a period of time, the *I-D* interaction is quite complex and exemplifies again the main attributes of ritual behavior, combining formalized gestures and other, non-formalized components such as the movement of female members of the units into a repetitive, stylized, and communicative set of interactions. The reader is directed to Kummer's description of *I-D* ritual in operation for an excellent example of the necessity of *context* in relation to patterns of communication, a point stressed by many students of natural communication systems (see Count in Sebeok and Ramsay, 1969:76; Jolly, 1966:131).

Kummer has also recognized the efficacy of particular patterns of communication at different levels of demographic organization within the troop. The larger the group concerned, and the more complex the role structure, the more complex the system of communication used in intragroup coordination. Determining the direction of Hamadryas troop movement during decamping at the sleeping rock is a case in point. Direction of movement must be determined for as many as 500 or 750 animals (Kummer, 1968:21). The direction may be set in one of two ways (Kummer, 1968:138ff): (1) singly, by the definitive action of one old male (who "will stand up in the center of the troop and instead of advancing just a few meters as usual, he moves with a peculiar rapid swinging-gait towards the troop's periphery. . . . His neighbors respond immediately with contact grunts and accompany him in rapidly increasing numbers. Many of the males at the fronts are seen looking at him. Within a few seconds the entire troop will move out in the indicated direction whereby the starter never arrives at the lead" [Kummer, 1968:139]); (2) jointly, by the formation and reformation of "pseudopods" composed of male leaders and their units. These pseudopods form on the periphery of the troop and indicate a particular direction. If the pseudopod continues to draw males and their units from the core of the troop, the direction of travel is determined by that pseudopod. Other pseudopods may form, however, indicating other directions.

Frequently . . . a pseudopod will become stationary and no longer gets reinforcements from the rear. In the meantime another pseudopod may arise, independently of the first, in another direction. Often, the first pseudopod will withdraw while the second is being formed; the males at the back of the initial pseudopod going back first, followed by those at the front. A troop will form two, rarely three, such pseudopods which independently of each other advance and withdraw until the center flows into one of them, thus provoking the actual departure in this direction.

As we shall see again when we discuss chimpanzee ritual behavior, the coordination by social animals of movement in space is a source of potentially useful information on ritual as communication.

Ritual and Play. For vertebrates, society is a major adaptive strategy whose sine qua non is flexibility of organization in relation to environmental variation. This means that a range of coordinations may be expected in the repertoire of a social species, and this includes variation in the elements, arrangement of elements, and context of ritual communication. The role of ontogeny in facilitating adaptive flexibility among the highly social vertebrates becomes pivotal in "social learning." Ethologists have recognized this fact in emphasizing that true play occurs only among some social birds and mammals (Eibl-Eibesfeldt, 1970:240; Hinde, 1970; Loizos in Jewell and Loizos, 1966; Menzel et al., 1970; Etkin in Etkin, 1964). Of particular note is that play carries over into adulthood only among the more phylogenetically advanced social mammals; for example, wolves (Fox, 1971, 1973), lions (Schaller, 1972; Schenkel in Jewell and Loizos, 1966), dolphins (Lilly, 1967; Krone, 1972; Caldwell and Caldwell, 1972) and chimpanzees (van Lawick-Goodall, 1968:247; also see Huxley, 1966).

We emphasize the necessity of play interaction in the refinement of certain types of ritual behavior observed among primates and other species. Whereas the rough motor patterns utilized in individual behavior may be present from birth, or soon after, the coordination of these patterns into effective ritual behavior requires development in a social context (Menzel, 1968). Furthermore, the more complex the pattern of synchronized adult action in a species, the more complex we would expect social play to be (Thorpe in Huxley, 1966). Indeed, we do find social play to be notably more complex among wolves, chimpanzees, and dolphins than in the rest of the animal kingdom, except human beings. And yet play in even the most complex social species amounts to repetition of very stereotyped patterns of behavior (Thorpe in Huxley, 1966).

Of particular note is the importance of social play in shaping and refining aggression ritual in the development of young animals. In most species the action patterns associated with individual aggression appear to be "wired-in" at or soon after birth. Yet it is quite apparent from field and experimental research that these patterns of aggression must be refined before they become consonant with social action (Eibl-Eibesfeldt, 1970:243). Experimental evidence on social deprivation of infant monkeys is enlightening here (see Hinde in Schrier and Stollnitz, 1971, for an excellent review). A young animal deprived of peer interaction for a significant period of development and then returned to the peer group is inevitably hyperaggressive and less sharing and affectionate in relation to others in his peer group (Harlow and Harlow, 1969). In field research Kummer has made it quite clear that the essential elements of adult social behavior among Hamadryas baboons are developed during ontogeny (Kummer in Altmann, 1967; Kummer, 1968). This includes the structuring of aggressive interaction. Hamadryas one-year-old play groups, for example, coalesce near a subadult male who does not take part in play but who does place strict constraints on the extremes of play, especially aggression. If aggressive interaction gets out of hand and one participant runs screaming into the subadult's arms, he threatens the aggressor. Young baboons learn through such involvement both the bounds of appropriate aggression and the value of conspecific support in aggressive engagements (Kummer in Altmann, 1967:64). The latter coordination is necessary for the kind of complex aggression ritual we described in the "line formation" earlier. Rhesus monkey play is characterized by an alternation between periods of relatively peaceful individual exploration of the environment and explosive bouts of peer interaction often marked by allelomimetic ("social facilitory") affect (Sade, personal communication; personal observation by the authors). It seems highly likely to us that the involved coordination of action and enlistment of support characteristic of the in-line formation requires this kind of alternation in ontogeny (see alternation section of chapter 6).

Chimpanzee Ritual

It was once believed, on the basis of preliminary studies, that the chimpanzee exhibited a quite simple social organization. Chimpanzee aggregations of varying size were seen as highly unstable and were termed "temporary associations" by one fieldworker (van Lawick-Goodall, 1968:211). Such groupings in loose association were assumed to typify the species as a whole (see van La-wick-Goodall, 1968; Reynolds and Reynolds, 1965). However, as a result of research by Japanese scholars (Itani and Suzuki, 1967; Sugiyama, 1972:156), as well as more intensive work on the part of van Lawick-Goodall and her associates in the Gombe reserve (van Lawick-Goodall, 1971; and in Menzel, 1973a; Teleki, 1973a), a more complex picture of chimpanzee social organization has begun to emerge. If we may be allowed to extrapolate from partial data, chimpanzee social organization appears to be character-ized by the following attributes: (1) The proximal group structure (group of conspecifics in close physical proximity to each other) is highly flexible and probably varies in relation to ecological vari-ables. (2) Relations between individual animals appear to have multivariable determination. (3) The cognized group (termed "community" by van Lawick-Goodall in Schaffer, 1971) is rarely coterminous with the proximal group, especially in a forest envi-ronment. (4) The cognized group is retained in long-term memory independent of geographical proximity.

Because the work by the Japanese is thus far tentative, and because most work on communication in the wild has centered on formalized displays and vocalizations, our knowledge of chimpan-zee ritual behavior is as yet rudimentary. What we do know from field research and experimentation, however, is more than suggestive. For one thing it is quite clear that social action on the part of the chimpanzee proximal group (perhaps even portions of the cognized community; see footnote in Teleki, 1973a:85) is de-pendent on very complex and informative communication (see Menzel, 1971, 1973b, 1974; also article in Menzel, 1973a). Men-zel, in a series of ingenious experiments with a group of young chimpanzees dwelling in a one-acre compound, has discovered that one chimpanzee can communicate a number of pieces of in-formation that he alone knows to the rest of the group and thus in-fluence their behavior. One chimpanzee might, for example, be carried around the field and shown a number of caches of food and concealed novel objects. While the chimpanzee is being shown these locations, others in the group are locked in a retain-ing cage. The chimpanzee, once it has been shown the various interesting locations, is put back in the cage with his fellows, and then the whole group is released into the compound. The chimpanzee that has seen the hidden items (up to 18 locations: see Menzel, 1973b) is invariably able to "lead" the rest of the group to those locations in such a way that it is obvious he has communicated the (1) presence or absence of an object, (2) direction of the object, (3) number of objects, (4) class of object (e.g., food or interesting object, threatening or safe object), (5) relative quantity of food in each location, (6) distance to object, and (7) type of food (Menzel in Menzel, 1973a). Much of this communication occurs through nuances of social action, rather than through vocalization or display. Any pattern of repetitive and communicative (formalized, in Smith's terms) social action that occurs within a group of chimpanzees, with or without display components, would form a ritual. As we shall see, there is some evidence that this process has occurred, at least minimally, in the wild.

Of considerable importance are the results of a number of research projects that have successfully taught chimpanzees to communicate with human researchers, some using *American Sign Language* (Gardner and Gardner, 1969, 1971, 1975; Fouts, 1973; Miles, 1975; Petitto and Terrace, 1975), symbolic objects (Premack, 1971a, also in Jarrard, 1971; Premack and Premack, 1972), and computerized symbols (see Yerkes project in Fleming, 1974; Rumbaugh and von Glasersfeld, 1973a, b). One significant result of all the chimpanzee language research projects has been evidence that the chimpanzee is capable of conceptualization, at least under optimal experimental conditions (neurophysiological evidence for chimpanzee conceptualization is discussed in Laughlin and d'Aquili, 1974). We suspect that chimpanzees are quite capable of spontaneous conceptualization in the wild, probably at a level equivalent to preoperations in the Piagetian scheme, although the evidence in favor of such an assertion is quite scanty. The major evidence for spontaneous conceptualization rests partially on Menzel's experiments cited earlier and partially on the unfolding picture of chimpanzee social organization described earlier. Chimpanzees in the Gombe rarely assemble in groups larger than ten (van Lawick-Goodall, 1968:211), and yet each animal in the Gombe reserve knows its status in relation to every other animal upon meeting (van Lawick-Goodall, 1971)—this with a minimum of overt or ritual aggression. It is not too farfetched to suppose (partly on the basis of the language research) that all adult animals are capable of conceptualizing a "community" or cognized social structure comprising all animals in the reserve (and perhaps beyond), although there may never have been a time when all members of that community were joined in a proximal social group (see also Köhler, 1927:276).

In light of these issues, it is not surprising to find some evidence of quite complex ritual behavior among chimpanzees in the wild. Furthermore, these issues raise the interesting question of whether chimpanzees are capable, not only of cognized ritual, but also of conceptualized ritual. If, indeed, chimpanzees carry out conceptualized ritual, then we would have to accept immediately the fact that chimpanzees perform ceremonies, whether or not they are capable of elaborating those ceremonies with other symbolic material. In this regard Leach and Turner (in Huxley, 1966) have perpetuated the all too common error of equating symbolic expression with conceptualization (see Laughlin, McManus and Stephens, 1977).

The classic example of chimpanzee ritual, incorporating many of the elements we have now come to look for in ritual across many species (e.g., allelomimetic arousal, alternating sympathetic-parasympathetic tuning, fixed action elements, synchronized and repetitive action, and role differentiation), is that described by van Lawick-Goodall under the label of "rain dance":

At about noon the first heavy drops of rain began to fall. The chimpanzees climbed out of the tree and one after the other plodded up the steep grassy slope toward the open ridge at the top. There were seven adult males in the group, including Goliath and David Graybeard, several females, and a few youngsters. As they reached the ridge the chimpanzees paused. At that moment the storm broke. The rain was torrential, and the sudden clap of thunder, right overhead, made me jump. As if this were a signal, one of the big males stood upright and as he swayed and swaggered rhythmically from foot to foot, I could just hear the rising crescendo of his pant-hoots above the beating of the rain. Then he charged

101

off, flat-out down the slope toward the trees he had just left. He ran some thirty yards, and then swinging round the trunk of a small tree to break his headlong rush, leaped into the low branches and sat motionless.

Almost at once, two other males charged after him. One broke off a low branch from a tree as he ran and brandished it in the air before hurling it ahead of him. The other, as he reached the end of his run, stood upright and rhythmically swayed the branches of a tree back and forth before seizing a huge branch and dragging it farther down the slope. A fourth male, as he too charged, leaped into a tree and, almost without breaking his speed, tore off a large branch, leaped with it to the ground, and continued down the slope. As the last two males called and charged down, so the one who had started the whole performance climbed from his tree and began plodding up the slope again. The others, who had also climbed into trees near the bottom of the slope, followed suit. When they reached the ridge, they started charging down all over again, one after the other, with equal vigor.

The females and youngsters had climbed into trees near the top of the rise as soon as the displays had begun, and there they remained watching throughout the whole performance. As the males charged down and plodded back up, so the rain fell harder, jagged forks or brilliant flares of lightning lit the leaden sky, and the crashing of the thunder seemed to shake the very mountains.

My enthusiasm was not merely scientific as I watched, enthralled, from my grandstand seat on the opposite side of the narrow ravine, sheltered under a plastic sheet. In fact it was raining and blowing far too hard for me to get at my notebook or use my binoculars. I could only watch, and marvel at the magnificence of those splendid creatures. With a display of strength and vigor such as this, primitive man himself might have challenged the elements.

Twenty minutes from the start of the performance, the last of the males plodded back up the slope for the last time. The females and youngsters climbed down from their trees and the whole group moved over the crest of the ridge. One male paused, and with his hand on a tree trunk, looked back—the actor taking his final curtain. Then he too vanished over the ridge (1971:52–54).

Although this complex "rain dance" was observed by van Lawick-Goodall only three times in ten years (1971:54), a number of its elements have been discovered by Wolfgang Köhler in a group of captive chimpanzees—patterns of behavior that Köhler was tempted to call the "primitive stages of dancing":

One lovely fresh morning Tschego and Grande were playing together on a box. Presently Grande rose upright, and with bristling hair (a sign of sympathetic activity), in her characteristic, pompous, and would-be-terrible manner, began to stamp first one foot and then the other, till the box shook. Meanwhile, Tschego slipped from the box, rose upright, and slowly revolved round her own axis in front of Grande, springing clumsily and heavily—but springing—from one foot to the other. They appeared to incite each other to these strange antics and to be in the best of tempers. I have frequent notes of such behavior. Any game of two together was apt to turn into this "spinning-top" play, which appeared to express a climax of friendly and amicable *joie de vivre*. The resemblance to a human dance became truly striking when the rotations were rapid, or when Tschego, for instance, stretched her arms out horizontally as she spun round. . . . The whole *group* of chimpanzees sometimes combined in more elaborate *motion-patterns*. For instance, two would wrestle and tumble about playing near some post; soon their movements would become more regular and tend to describe a circle round the post as a center. One after another, the rest of the group approach, join the two, and finally they march in an orderly fashion and in single file round and round the post. The character of their movement changes; they no longer walk, they trot, and as a rule with special emphasis on one foot, while the other steps lightly; thus a rough approximate rhythm develops, and they tend to "keep time" with one another. They wag their heads in time to the steps of their "dance" and appear full of eager enjoyment of their primitive game (1927:314–315).

It seems clear that the coordinated social action characteristic of the "rain dance" ritual would require the kind of bouts of allelomimetic arousal in play described by Köhler. What is not so clear is the function of the "rain dance" ritual; that is, to what end, if any, is it directed? How does the ritual "fit in" with the rest of their cognized environment? Any answer to this question must at best be speculation, and yet it would seem critical here to make what sense we can of the data at hand. An additional source of data will be useful in this pursuit, namely, the excellent descriptions offered by Kortlandt (1962, 1965, 1966, 1967, 1973) of wild chimpanzee response to potential predators. In a set of remarkable experiments using an electrically animated stuffed leopard, Kortlandt (1965; Kortlandt and Kooij, 1963) observed the typical response of chimpanzee groups to the sudden appearance of their dangerous enemy. Briefly, members of a chimpanzee band "mob" the enemy, forming a semicircular "line formation." In formation, or by synchronized individual charges, the animals stamp the ground, scream in unison, and brandish (or throw) uprooted trees, broken branches, and other "clubs" at the leopard. Whether or not they are effective in wielding a club depends, according to Kortlandt, on whether the group dwells on the savanna or in the forest, the savanna dwellers being notably better clubfighters than their forest-dwelling cousins. Nissen (1931) reported something like a "war dance" directed against his native helpers, and Kortlandt (1973) saw the same sort of outburst as "predator control" among large groups of chimpanzees, often performed before retiring to sleep at dusk.

All of these bits and pieces, when collated, provide a tentative basis for a hypothesis about the nature of van Lawick-Goodall's "rain dance." We suggest that within the repertoire of ritual behaviors of many (if not all) wild chimpanzee communities is one that might be termed the *danger ritual*. The full performance of this ritual among adult members of a chimpanzee society depends on the development of allelomimetic coordination in ontogenesis and combines a number of more common motor patterns such as tree shaking, pant hooting, bipedal running, and other aggressive displays. The ritual may occur in any situation conceived by chimpanzees as potentially dangerous to themselves. The set of stimuli that will elicit spontaneous ocurrence of the danger ritual includes such things as recognized and dangerous predators, thunderstorms, and strange and frightening apparitions. The total membership of the set of dangerous stimuli is not known and should be researched further. We would predict that what each stimulus holds in common with all other stimuli is that it is modeled in the chimpanzee cognized environment as dangerously problematic, unknown, or unpredictable. The set may include stimuli as vague as the perception that dusk is a probable condition for a leopard attack. The really intriguing question is *whether the danger ritual, originally effective against predation, has been generalized to phenomena that represent, for chimpanzees, a zone of uncertainty,* that is, phenomena, like thunder and lightning, that are cognized, but whose causes are not comprehended.

A similar phenomenon occurs among Cayo Santiago rhesus monkeys at the appearance of low-flying planes. The strange noise evokes display activity consisting of vigorous branch shaking and ritualized displays appropriate to aggressive encounters. This appears to be an intense, general response to stimuli of unknown origin and is not as rigidly performed as pure aggressive displays. One hypothesis about chimpanzee responses to such stimuli is that display elements are reorganized and formalized out of elements that are themelves ritualizations in the narrow sense and that such formalization has characteristics specific to unfamiliar situations. We would expect to find, then, some difference between formalized response to danger that is identifiable (i.e., predators) and to danger that is novel or ambiguous. As with rhesus monkeys these uncertainty responses may show a lesser degree of genetic predisposition and therefore more variability or individual idiosyncracy. The concomitant question, as raised earlier in this discussion, is whether the danger ritual is also conceptually distinct for chimpanzees—whether they are capable of conceptualizing their responses to such stimuli in varying situations as the same, rationally appropriate set of behaviors.

The latter question arises anew when one considers the means of distributing meat among members of a group of chimpanzees after a successful kill (see Teleki, 1973a, b). During the "consuming period" a great deal of social interaction and exchange occurs—much more than would be necessary if the sole purpose was the consumption of meat. Meat exchange would seem to be a ritual of the sort termed an "intensification ritual" by Chapple and Coon (1942), in which ideal social cooperation and dependence are acted out. The *exchange ritual* usually involves four to fifteen individuals, the mean average being eight per occurrence (Teleki, 1973a:138), and may take from 1.5 to 9.0 hours (mean around 3.5) to complete (Teleki, 1973a:137). Activity during exchange centers on one or more animals that have been able to obtain a major portion of the kill during the first few minutes of the capture. "When chimpanzees are sharing meat, their behavior is generally relaxed and uncompetitive. The pieces of the prey animal are consumed in a leisurely fashion and are evidently relished" (Teleki, 1973b:41). The distribution of meat is quite orderly, involving an entire complex of communications:

A variety of vocal and gestural signals occurs in connection with the sharing of a carcass. The sounds, gestures, and facial expressions seen during this stage are not specific to predation, though some may appear more frequently in this than in any other behavioral context. Request signals, for example, occur very frequently during distribution: 395 begging interactions, containing three to four times as many discrete signals, were observed in the 43 hours of meat consumption during 1968–69 (Teleki, 1973a:146).

Of the 395 requests for meat observed during that period, 114 (29 percent) were successful (1973b:41). Of the 616 attempts by one animal to get meat from another by all means (including meat requests), 335 (54 percent) were successful (1973a:147). That is, sufficient transfer of meat occurs to make it worthwhile for an animal to persist in his attempt to get some. Indeed, most animals in the Gombe community participated in the exchange ritual during the year of explicit observations reported by Teleki (1973a:138). Note also that all of this exchange occurs in the strict absence of aggression between the meat requestor and meat controller—even when the requestor is of much higher rank than the controller (Teleki, 1973a:156). Menzel (1974) mentions that, if one animal takes an object away from another, all the chimpanzees in the group become upset and scream at the "thief."

Chimpanzee exchange ritual would seem to fulfill many of the same functions as many human exchange rituals (see Suttles, 1960, and Piddocke, 1968, on the *potlatch* among Northwest Coast Indian groups), that is, the reinforcement of the structure of cooperation, coordination, and exchange and the redistribution of scarce resources on bases other than who happens to be strongest. In other words, combined with other types of social communication, the exchange ritual would reinforce the cognized community through motor action and perceptual information. The ritual may have this effect with or without actual conceptualization of the ritual. Yet a number of features of the exchange ritual would point to the possibility that chimpanzees conceptualize the sequence as distinct from other types of interaction: (1) the rigid exclusive of aggression as a means of obtaining meat, even during the initial splitting of the carcass (compare this with the frequent aggressive encounters over meat among lions; Schaller, 1972); (2) the remarkable length of time it takes for the group to consume even the smallest kill; (3) the strict adherence to role during the exchange; (4) the inordinate amount of social communication occurring during the exchange period—far more than is necessary for consumption of the meat; (5) the fact that sooner or later every animal in the community participates in the consumption of meat; and (6) the fact that very often it is *after* chimpanzees have eaten their fill that they participate in predation and exchange. All of these factors seem to indicate to us that chimpanzees recognize the entire period of predation—capture, carcass division and meat exchange—as conceptually distinct from other forms of interaction. To what degree the exchange ritual is also a source of symbolization still remains unknown. It is not entirely unreasonable to hypothesize that the meat itself (with the exception of brain tissue; see Teleki, 1973a:142) takes on the conceptual status of symbol for chimpanzee participants.

Australopithecine Ritual

A very pertinent question at this juncture would be what the nature and importance of ritual behavior were among the earliest homminids. Obviously we are incapable of reconstructing australopithecine social behavior from any observational evidence, and anything less would be indecisive. Yet we do have indirect evidence both from comparative ethology and from comparative neurophysiology, and being somewhat habituated to the effects of controversy, we would like to speculate a bit about the capabilities of *Australopithecus* in this regard.

The neurophysiological processes underlying biological intelligence are in themselves a root issue (see Piercy, 1964; Holloway, 1970; Passingham, 1973; van Valen, 1975), and there is little space here in which to discuss the question. Some aspects of the issue are discussed in chapter 5 and have been discussed in Laughlin and d'Aquili (1974) in relation to speech and "culture" among the australopithecines. Suffice it to say here that we agree with Holloway (1970) that, although frontal lobe development has reached hominid proportions in the chimpanzee, the functioning of the frontal lobes among the hominids would be more complex owing to reorganization necessitated by differentially greater development in other components of the hominid brain. We would explicitly call the reader's attention to the differentially greater development of the parieto-occipital area (termed the "inferior parietal lobule" by Geschwind, 1965) among the hominids, and in particular in *Australopithecus* over and above the chimpanzee brain (LeGros Clark, 1963, 1964). Now, the parieto-occipital area (on the dominant side in human beings) is recognized as a primary mediator of cross-modal transfer of information, conceptualization, and logicomathematical relations among concepts (Goldstein and Gelb, 1924; Weigl, 1927; Conrad, 1932; Zucker, 1934). Semmes et al. (1955) reported multimodal spatial disorientation in many patients after sustaining lesions in either or both parietal lobes and thus implicated bilateral parietal functioning in biological intelligence. Relative decrease in the proportion of primary association cortex and increase in the proportion of association cortex in *Australopithecus* is evidenced by the location of the lunate sulcus (see LeGros Clark, 1947; Holloway, 1972).

It has been argued elsewhere that the development of a fully functioning inferior parietal lobule must have been a necessary condition for the development of speech (Laughlin and d'Aquili, 1974). However, because speech requires the development of other neural elements, parieto-occipital development was not a sufficient condition for speech. There are insufficient data from australopithecine endocasts to determine the extent of development of some of these other elements. It is distinctly possible that *Australopithecus* communicated by speech. On the other hand, Gordon Hewes (1973) has offered an alternative hypothesis: that *Australopithecus* and subsequent hominids specialized in a gestural system of communication that became quite complex and refined—much as the *American Sign Language* has become refined—and that it has superseded by speech only in the Upper Paleolithic among advanced *H. sapiens.* Although we find some problems with this thesis, we believe that it is not disconsonant with our own position. And, as a matter of fact, if *Australopithecus* did take this route to a systematic expressive system through gestures, we would reason that that development could have occurred much earlier in the neural development of the organism than if the movement had been directly to speech.

Perhaps more to the point, we believe that the evidence outlined here indicates a high probability that *Australopithecus* was biologically *capable* of complex, conceptualized, and probably even symbolized ritual behavior. We emphasize "capability" because we are speaking here of potentiation, not behavioral inevitability. The evidence from comparative ethology, especially the growing corpus of data on variation of social forms within primate species, indicates that a characteristic feature of primate society is flexibility in relation to environment. Thus, to speak of *Australopithecus* or any other stage in hominid evolution as being characterized by a single type of socioeconomic structure (e.g., "big game hunter"; see articles in Lee and DeVore, 1968) is antithetical to our view of the course of evolution commonly exemplified by higher vertebrates. Rather, we would hold, with Teleki (1973a), that australopithecine socioeconomic structure reflected, if anything, *more* flexibility in form than present-day chimpanzee society does. It is therefore necessary that we speak of optimal capacity of the australopithecines relative to ritual behavior, for it is quite possible that many australopithecine societies under certain environmental conditions did not manifest this capacity to the optimum. Yet it seems equally certain that *some* australopithecine societies expressed maximal complexity in their ritual—especially if the development of ritual was conjoined, as Hewes would have us believe, with the development of a gestural system.

Assuming our reconstruction is near the mark, what might we posit as the characteristics of optimally developed australopithecine ritual? The answer is fivefold:

1. As has been reasoned elsewhere (Laughlin and d'Aquili, 1974), owing to enhanced "corticalization," *Australopithecus* had reached the point where he could model a world of entities and relations beyond the boundaries of immediate perception. This means that he likely conceived of a number of problems in causality and spatial relations whose solutions were not present in his world of perception. Thus, *Australopithecus* had a zone of uncertainty extending well beyond the capability of a chimpanzee but certainly not as extensive as that of subsequent hominid species. Ritual—certainly conceptualized ritual, and perhaps symbolized ritual as well—would have been directed in response to problems predominant in their zone of uncertainty. Although very speculative, it is not inappropriate to consider that *Australopithecus* might have directed conceptualized ritual at such problems as the vicissitudes of basic resource availability, the death of fellow group members, the curing of disease, the distribution of meat and other scarce resources, and the maintenance of relations between groups.

2. The emotionality or affect incorporated in australopithecine ritual would have been somewhat more differentiated than that of the chimpanzee but much less differentiated than that of *H. sapiens*. This is due again to evolutionary developments occurring in the australopithecine brain. With enhanced cerebralization in the hominid line the neural structures underlying conceptual systems ("higher cortical functions") developed as a whole with positive allometry in relation to the neural structures (the structures of the limbic system) mediating affect. It is the neocortex that both interprets states internal to the organism and is responsible for the assignment of affect to environmental stimuli (see Gellhorn and Loofbourrow, 1963:40; MacLean, 1958; Count in Sebeok and Ramsey, 1969). With a more complexly arranged neocortex *Australopithecus* must have had a more complex repertoire of affect—hence the affective content of his ritual would have been more complex than, say, that of the chimpanzee.

3. It is likely that ritual would have been maximally relied on in maintenance of australopithecine cognized communities in environments conducive to such organization. It is not beyond the realm of probability that ceremonial gatherings occurred from time to time, perhaps ostensibly to distribute some scarce

resource or in response to some repetitive environmental event. It is possible that populations dwelt in an environment necessitating seasonal fission-fusion and that the occasions of bifurcation and reunification were marked by ritual reenactment of the ideal social order.

4. It is furthermore likely that at least some australopithecine societies used ceremonial ritual to solve the problem of reverberation in role and status recurring in the ontogenesis of group members. How these "rites of passage" might have been structured is anyone's guess. Judged by the prevalence of "puberty rites" among human groups, such rites could have been a major source of ritual transformation for australopithecines as well.

5. Finally, it seems likely that, all else being equal, aggression ritual both within and between groups was more infrequent for the australopithecines than for chimpanzees. This suggestion is based on the assumption that greater long-term memory ("time-binding") capacity facilitated by further development of the temporal lobes evident in australopithecine endocasts would necessitate less frequent reinforcement of the cognized social order.

Conclusion

The material in this chapter has been highly selective, both in terms of the range of animal species discussed and in terms of the orientation toward the evidence. A number of other animal species might have been chosen, such as elephants (see Douglas-Hamiltons, 1975) or members of Cetacea, but the requirements of space and the paucity of relevant data have limited our coverage. The orientation has been in the direction of explaining the complex relationships between ritual behavior and intraorganismic or interorganismic coordination, and also the evolution of these relationships over the course of hominoid evolution. The chapters that follow focus their attentions on *Homo sapiens,* with only tangential reference to the data on other species. Yet they all presuppose the relationship between *H. sapiens* and his phylogenetically simpler forebears and cousins.

References

Altmann, S. A. (ed.) 1967. *Social Communication Among Primates*. Chicago: University of Chicago Press.

Andrew, R. T. 1965. "The Origins of Facial Expressions." *Scientific American* 213(4):88.

Beck, A. 1967. *Depression: Causes and Treatment*. Philadelphia: University of Pennsylvania Press.

Caldwell, D. K. and M. C. Caldwell. 1972. *The World of the Bottlenosed Dolphin*. Philadelphia: J. B. Lippincott.

Candland, D. et al. 1970. "Squirrel Monkey Heart Rate During Formation of Status Orders." *Journal of Comparative and Physiological Psychology* 70:417–23.

Carpenter, C. R. 1964. *Naturalistic Behavior of Nonhuman Primates*. University Park, Pa.: Pennsylvania State University Press.

Chapple, E. D. and C. S. Coon. 1942. *Principles of Anthropology*. New York: Henry Holt.

Conrad, K. 1932. "Versuch einer psychologischen Analyse des Pareitalsyndromes." *Monatsschrift für Psychiatrie und Neurologie* 84.

Count, E. W. 1973. *Being and Becoming Human*. New York: Van Nostrand Reinhold.

Crook, J. H. 1970. "The Socioecology of Primates," in *Social Behavior in Birds and Mammals* (J. H. Crook, ed.). New York: Academic Press.

Denham, W. W. 1971. "Energy Relations and Some Basic Properties of Primate Social Organization." *American Anthropologist* 73(1):77–95.

Douglas-Hamilton, I. and O. Douglas-Hamilton. 1975. *Among the Elephants*. New York: The Viking Press.

Eibl-Eibesfeldt, I. 1970. *Ethology: The Biology of Behavior*. New York: Holt, Rinehart, and Winston.

Eisenberg, J. F. and W. S. Dillon. 1971. *Man and Beast: Comparative Social Behavior*. Washington, D.C.: Smithsonian University Press.

Estes, R. D. and J. Goodard. 1967. "Prey Selection and Hunting Behavior of the African Wild Dog." *Journal of Wildlife Management* 31:52–70.

Etkin, W. 1964. *Social Behavior and Organization Among Vertebrates*. Chicago: University of Chicago Press.

Fleming, J. D. 1974. "Field Report: The State of the Apes," *Psychology Today* 7(8):31ff.

Fouts, R. 1973. "Acquisition and Testing of Gestural Signs in Four Young Chimpanzees." *Science* 180:978–980.

Fox, M. W. 1971. *Behavior of Wolves, Dogs, and Related Canids*. New York: Harper and Row.

—— 1973. Social Dynamics of Three Captive Wolf Packs. *Behavior* 47:240–301.

—— 1974. *Concepts in Ethology: Animal and Human Behavior*. Minneapolis: University of Minnesota Press.

—— 1975a. "Evolution of Social Behavior in Canids," in *The Wild Canids* (M. W. Fox, ed.). New York: Van Nostrand Reinhold.

—— 1975b. *The Wild Canids*. New York: Van Nostrand Reinhold.

Gardner, B. T. and R. A. Gardner, 1971. "Two Way Communication with an Infant Chimpanzee," in *Behavior of Non-Human Primates* (A. Schrier and G. Stollnitz, eds.). New York: Academic Press.

Gardner, R. A. and B. T. Gardner. 1969. "Teaching Sign Language to a Chimpanzee," *Science* 165:664–672.

——— 1975. "Early Signs of Language in Child and Chimpanzee," *Science* 187:752–53.

Gartlan, J. S. 1968. "Structure and Function in Primate Society." *Folia Primatologica* 8:89–120.

Gellhorn, E. and G. N. Loofbourrow. 1963. *Emotions and Emotional Disorders: A Neuro-physiological Study*. New York: Harper and Row.

Geschwind, N. 1965. "Disconnection Syndromes in Animals and Man." *Brain* 88:237–294, 585–644.

Goldstein, K. and A. Gelb. 1924. "Uber Farbennamenammesie." *Psychologische Forschung* 6.

Hall, K. R. L. 1962. "The Sexual, Agonistic and Derived Social Behavior of the Wild Chacma Baboon, *Papio ursinus*." *Proceedings of the Zoological Society of London* 139:283–327.

Hall, K. and I. DeVore. 1965. "Baboon Social Behavior," in *Primate Behavior* (I. DeVore, ed.). New York: Holt, Rinehart, and Winston.

Harlow, H. F. and M. K. Harlow. 1969. "Effects of Various Mother-Infant Relationships on Rhesus Monkey Behaviors," in *Determinants of Infant Behavior* (B. M. Foss, ed.). Vol. 4. London: Methuen.

Harvey, O. J., D. Hunt, and S. Schroder. 1961. *Conceptual Systems and Personality Organization*. New York: Wiley.

Hausfater, G. 1972. "Intergroup Behavior of Free-Ranging Rhesus Monkeys (*Macacas mulatta*)." *Folia Primatologica* 18:78–107.

Hewes, G. W. 1973. "Primate Communication and the Gestural Origin of Language." *Current Anthropology* 14(1–2):5–24.

Hinde, R. A. 1970. *Animal Behavior*. 2d ed. New York: McGraw-Hill.

——— 1972. *Non-Verbal Communication*. Cambridge, England: Cambridge University Press.

Holloway, R. L. 1970. "Neural Parameters, Hunting and the Evolution of the Human Brain," in *The Primate Brain* (C. R. Noback and W. Montagna, eds.). New York: Appleton-Century-Crofts.

——— 1972. "Australopithecine Endocasts, Brain Evolution in the Hominoidea, and a Model of Hominid Evolution," in *The Functional and Evolutionary Biology of Primates* (R. Tuttle, ed.). Chicago: Aldine.

Huxley, Sir J. 1966. *A Discussion on Ritualizations of Behavior in Animals and Man*. (*Philosophical Transactions of the Royal Society of London*, Series B). 251:247–524.

Itani, J. and Suzuki, A. 1967. "The Social Unit of Chimpanzees." *Primates* 8:355–381.

Jarrard, L. E. 1971. *Cognitive Processes of Nonhuman Primates*. New York: Academic Press.

Jewell, P. A. and C. Loizos. 1966. *Play, Exploration and Territory in Mammals*. (*Symposia of the Zoological Society of London* 18). London: Academic Press.

Jolly, A. 1966. *Lemur Behavior*. Chicago: University of Chicago Press.

Köhler, W. 1927. *The Mentality of Apes*. 2d ed. London: Routledge and Kegan Paul.

Kortlandt, A. 1962. "Chimpanzees in the Wild." *Scientific American* 206(5):128–138.

——— 1965. "How Do Chimpanzees Use Weapons When Fighting Leopards?" *Yearbook of the American Philosophical Society*, pp. 327–332.

——— 1966. "On Tool-use Among Primates." *Current Anthropology* 7:215–216.

——— 1967. "Experimentation with Chimpanzees in the Wild," in *Progress in Primatology* (D. Starck, R. Schneider, H. J. Kohn, eds.). Stuttgart: Gustav Fischer.

——— 1973. "Comment on Article by G. W. Hewes." *Current Anthropology* 14 (1–2):13–14.

Kortlandt, A. and M. Kooij. 1963. "Protohominid Behavior in Primates," in *Symposia of the Zoological Society of London*, 10:61–88.

Krone, C. 1972. *The World of the Dolphin*. New York: Belmont/Tower Books.

Kummer, H. 1968. *Social Organization of Hamadryas Baboons* Basel: S. Karger.

—— 1971a. *Behavior*. (*Proceedings of the Third International Congress of Primatology*, vol. 3). Basel: S. Karger.

—— 1971b. *Primate Societies*. Chicago: Aldine-Atherton.

Laughlin, C. D. and E. G. d'Aquili. 1974. *Biogenetic Structuralism*. New York: Columbia University Press.

Laughlin, C. D., and I. Brady, 1978. *Extinction and Survial in Human Populations*. New York: Columbia University Press.

Laughlin, C. D., J. McManus, and C. Stephens. 1977. "The Evolution of Brain and Symbol." Paper presented at the Fundamentals of Symbolism Conference, Burg Wartemsteom. Austria.

Lee, R. B. and I. DeVore. 1968. *Man the Hunter*. Chicago: Aldine.

LeGros Clark, W. E. 1947. "Observations on the Anatomy of the Fossil Australopithecinae." *Journal of Anatomy* 81:300.

——1963. *The Antecedents of Man*. New York: Harper and Row.

——1964. *The Fossil Evidence for Human Evolution*. Chicago: University of Chicago Press.

Lilly, J. C. 1967. *The Mind of the Dolphin*. New York: Avon Books.

MacLean, P. D. 1958. "Contrasting Functions of Limbic and Neocortical Systems of the Brain and Their Relevance to Psychophysiological Aspects of Medicine." *American Journal of Medicine* 25:611–626.

Mason, W. A. 1964. "Primate Sociability and Social Organization," in *Advances in Experimental Psychology*, Vol. 1 (L. Berkowitz, ed.). New York: Academic Press.

Matthiessen, P. 1962. *Under the Mountain Wall*. New York: Ballantine.

Mech, L. D. 1970. *The Wolf: The Ecology and Behavior of an Endangered Speices*. Garden City: Doubleday.

Menzel, E. W. 1968. "Primate Naturalistic Research and Problems of Early Experience." *Developmental Psychobiology* 1 (3):175–184.

——1971. "Communication About the Environment in a Group of Young Chimpanzees." *Folia Primatologica* 15:220–232.

——1973a. *Precultural Primate Behavior*. (*Symposia of the Fourth International Congress of Primatology*, vol. 1), Basel: S. Karger.

——1973b. "Chimpanzee Spatial Memory Organization." *Science* 182:943–945.

——1974. "Communication and Aggression in a Group of Young Chimpanzees," in *Communication and Affect: Communication of Aggression* (T. Alloway, L. Kranes, P. Pliner, eds.). Plenum Press.

Menzel, E. W., R. K. Davenport, and C. M. Rogers. 1970. "The Development of Tool-Using in Wild-Born and Restriction-Reared Chimpanzees." *Folia Primatologica* 12:273–283.

Miles, L. 1975. "Sign Language and Natural Gesture Combinations in Chimpanzee Communications: A Preliminary Report," paper presented before the annual meeting of the Northeastern Anthropological Association. Potsdam, New York.

Miyadi, D. 1967. "Differences in Social Behavior Among Japanese Macaque Troops," in *Progress in Primatology* (D. Sturck, R. Schneider, H. J. Kuhn, eds.). Stuttgart: Gustav Fischer.

114

Morris, D. 1957. " 'Typical Intensity' and Its Relation to the Problem of Ritualization."
Behavior 11:1–13.

Murie, A. 1944. *The Wolves of Mount McKinley*. National Parks Fauna Series 5, Washington, D. C.

Nissen, H. W. 1931. "A Field Study of the Chimpanzee." *Compartive Pscyhology Monographs* 8(1).

Passingham, R. E. 1973. "Anatomical Differences Between the Neocortex of Man and Other Primates." *Brain, Behavior, and Evolution* 7:337–359.

Petitto, L. and H. Terrace. 1975. "Reception and Production of American Sign Language by an Infant Chimpanzee," paper presented before the annual meeting of the Northeastern Anthropological Association. Potsdam, New York.

Piaget, J. 1971. *Biology and Knowledge*. Chicago: University of Chicago Press.

Piaget, J. and B. Inhelder. 1969. *The Pscyhology of the Child*. New York: Basic Books.

Piddocke, S. 1968. "The Potlatch System of the Southern Kwakiut: A New Perspective," in *Economic Anthropology* (E. E. LeClair and H. K. Schneider, eds.). New York: Holt, Rinehart, and Winston.

Piercy, M. 1964. "The Effects of Cerebral Lesions on Intellectual Function: A Review of Current Research Trends." *British Journal of Psychiatry* 110:310–352.

Premack, D. 1971a. "Language in Chimpanzee?" *Science* 172:808–822.

—— 1971b. "On the Assessment of Language Competence in Chimpanzees," in *Cognitive Processes in Non-Human Primates* (A. Schrier and F. Stollnitz, eds.). New York: Academic Press.

Premack, A. J. and D. Premack. 1972. "Teaching Language to an Ape." *Scientific American* 227 (4).

Pribram, K. H. 1971. *Language of the Brain*. Englewood Cliffs, N.J.: Prentice-Hall.

Rappaport, R. A. 1968. *Pigs for the Ancestors*. New Haven, Conn.: Yale University Press.

Reynolds, V. and F. Reynolds. 1965. "Chimpanzees of the Budongo Forest," in *Primate Behavior* (I. DeVore, ed.). New York: Holt, Rinehart, and Winston.

Roosevelt, T. and E. Heller. 1922. *Life Histories of African Game Animals*, Vol. 1. London: John Murray.

Rose, R. M., T. P. Gordon, and I. S. Bernstein, 1972. "Plasma Testosterone Levels in the Male Rhesus: "Influences of Sexual and Social Stimuli." *Science* 178:643–645.

Rumbaugh, D. and E. von Glasersfeld. 1973a. "Reading and Sentence Completion by a Chimpanzee." *Science* 182:731–733.

—— 1973b. "Computer Controlled Language Training System for Investigating Language Skills of Young Apes." *Behavioral Research Methods and Instruments* 5(5):385–392.

Sade, D. S. 1965. "Some Aspects of Parent-Offspring and Sibling Relations in a Group of Rhesus Monkeys with a Discussion of Grooming." *American Journal of Physical Anthropology* 23 (1):1–17.

—— 1968. "Inhibition of Son-Mother Mating Among Free-Ranging Rhesus Monkeys." *Science and Psychoanalysis* 12:18–38.

—— 1969. "An Algorithm for Dominance Relations Among Rhesus Monkeys: Rules for Adult Females and Sisters." Paper presented at the American Association of Physical Anthropologists meetings. Mexico City.

—— 1972. "Sociometrics of *Macaca mulatta* I, Linkages and Cliques in Grooming Matrices." *Folia Primatologica* 18:196–223.

—— 1974. "The Vertebrate Ego." Paper presented at the American Anthropological Association meetings. Mexico City.

115

Schaffer, H. R. 1971. *The Origins of Human Social Relations*. New York: Academic Press.

Schaller, G. B. 1972. *The Serengeti Lion*. Chicago: University of Chicago Press.

Schenkel, R. 1947. "Ausdrucks-studien an Wolfen." *Behavior* 1:81–129.

Schneirla, T. C. 1965. "Aspects of Stimulation and Organization in Approach/Withdrawal Processes Underlying Vertebrate Behavior Development," in *Advances in the Study of Animal Behavior* (D. S. Lehrman, R. A. Hinde, E. Shaw, eds.). New York: Academic Press.

Schrier, A. M. and F. Stollnitz. 1971. *Behavior of Non-Human Primates*. New York: Academic Press.

Sebeok, T. A. and A. Ramsay. 1969. *Approaches to Animal Communication*. The Hague: Mouton.

Seligman, M. 1975. *Helplessness*. San Francisco: W. H. Freeman.

Semmes, J. et al. 1955. "Spatial Orientation in Man After Cerebral Injury. I. Analysis by Locus of Lesion." *Journal of Psychology* 39:227–244.

Smith, W. J., J. Chase, A. K. Lieblich. 1973. "Tongue Showing: A Facial Display of Humans and Other Primate Species" Mimeo.

Southwick, C. H. 1967. "An Experimental Study of Intragroup Agonistic Behavior in Rhesus Monkeys (*Macaca mulatta*)." *Behavior* 28:182–209.

Stevenson-Hamilton, J. 1954. *Wild Life in South Africa*. London: Cassell.

Sugiyama, Y. 1972. "Social Characteristics and Socialization of Wild Chimpanzees," in *Primate Socialization* (F. E. Poirier, ed.). New York: Random House.

Suttles, W. 1960. "Azzinal Ties, Subsistence, and Prestige Among the Coast Salish." *American Anthropologist* 62:296–305.

Teleki, G. 1973a. *The Predatory Behavior of Wild Chimpanzees*. Lewisburg, Pa.: Bucknell University Press.

——1973b. "The Omnivorous Chimpanzee." *Scientific American* 228:33–42.

Tinbergen, N. 1962. "The Evolution of Animal Communication—A Critical Examination of Methods." *Symposia of the Zoological Society of London* 8:1–6.

van Lawick-Goodall, J. 1968. "The Behavior of Free-Living Chimpanzees in the Gombe Stream Reserve." *Animal Behavior Monographs* 1(3):161–311.

——1971. *In the Shadow of Man*. Boston: Houghton Mifflin.

van Valen, L. 1975. "Brain Size and Intelligence in Man." *American Journal of Physical Anthropology* 40:417–424.

Waterhouse, M. J. and H. B. Waterhouse. 1973. "Primate Ethology and Human Social Behavior," in *Comparative Ecology and Behavior of Primate* (R. Michael and J. Crook, eds.). London: Academic Press.

Weigl, E. 1927. "Zur Psychologie der sogenannten Abstraktionsprocesse," *Zeitschrift für Psychologie* 103.

Wickler, W. 1972. *The Sexual Code*. Garden City, N.Y.: Doubleday.

Zucker, K. 1934. "An Analysis of Disturbed Function in Aphasia." *Brain* 57.

Four

The Neurobiology of Ritual Trance

Barbara W. Lex

It is a fundamental premise . . . that all functions of the body, mental and emotional as well as the more obvious "physical" functions, depend on alterations in the patterns of materials of which the body is built. Protoplasm, cells, tissues, organs and organisms represent patterns of materials which at other times, in other arrangements, are different things, both animate and inanimate. Mental and emotional phenomena are inconceivable in the absence of a neural substrate, and function without an alteration of substrate pattern is incomprehensible.

Ernst Gellhorn and G. N. Loofbourrow,
Emotions and Emotional Disorders

For many years ethnographers have returned from the field with intriguing reports of unusual behavior by participants in rituals. These reports, although far from agreement in their labeling, interpretation, or rigor of observation, point to the impact of patterned, repetitive acts on the human nervous system. The purpose of this chapter is to bring neurobiological data to bear on the observed phenomena, which I collectively term *ritual trance*. It is my

This is a revised version of an article, "Physiological Aspects of Ritual Trance," which appears in the *Journal of Altered States of Consciousness 2* (2), 1975. The author gratefully acknowledges receipt of a Western Michigan University Faculty Research Fellowship that permitted investigation of psychophysiological research at the Langley Porter Neuropsychiatric Institute in 1973. Eliot D. Chapple, William F. Kiely, and Charles H. Long have provided useful comments and suggestions on the earlier version of this chapter, but, of course, the author assumes the final responsibility for the contents herein.

aim to demonstrate that ritual trance, known by many names and manifested in numerous forms, arises from manipulation of universal neurophysiological structures of the human body, lies within the potential behavior of all normal human beings, and functions as a homeostatic mechanism for both individuals and groups.

Ritual trance may constitute a hitherto neglected cultural universal. Using Murdock's Ethnographic Atlas (1967), Bourguignon identifies institutionalized forms of "dissociation" in 437 societies, 89 percent of the 488 societies for which adequate ethnographic data are available (1972:418). On the basis of this evidence, one of Bourguignon's students, Goodman, asserts that "we are dealing with a capacity common to all men" (1972:70). Near-universality of these experiences suggests a human biological substrate or propensity (see chapter 1); this interpretation is confirmed by observable changes in motor behavior, speech patterns, and response to external stimuli in trance states reported both by laymen and by scientifically trained observers.

Previously, approaches termed "physiological and psychological" (Firth, 1969:x), "neurophysiological and biocybernetic" (Bourguignon, 1973:6), and "biopsychological" (Shack, 1972:xi) have been applied to the study of ritual trance, with varying degrees of insight, thoroughness, and success. Generally speaking, anthropologists have not equipped themselves to understand and apply perspectives from the biological and psychological sciences to ethnographic observations; the subjects of inquiry, theories, and methods of these disciplines do not readily coincide with traditional anthropological interests in culture or social structure. Instead, anthropologists usually elect either to confine their disquisitions of trance phenomena to social or cultural matters or to rely uncritically on the few findings of other scientists that directly treat ritual trance, incorporating these narrowly focused, and often ethnocentric, interpretations into their analyses.

One notable exception is recent work on ceremonial possession by Walker (1972), including chapters on pertinent research in neurophysiology and hypnosis. However, the bulk of Walker's emphasis is on experiments that demonstrate effects of repetitive stimuli on the brain. Although brain structures undeniably play an important role in response to stimuli, other components of the nervous system are involved in acts that facilitate trance. For example, emetics stimulate the vagus nerve of the parasympathetic nervous system by inducing vomiting, and, as will be demonstrated later, the parasympathetic nervous system mediates responses in the viscera and in the striated muscles, as well as in the brain.[1]

The nervous system operates as a unit, encompassing all levels from the myotatic reflex (tonic contraction of the muscles in response to a stretching force) to higher cortical functions (for example, reason and foresight). Thus, to exclude from discussions of central nervous system (CNS) excitation either the parasympathetic or sympathetic nervous systems, both of which are subsystems of the autonomic nervous system (ANS), not only is arbitrary but also belies the integration of the nervous system necessary for maintenance of homeostasis. In brief, investigation of ritual trance cannot be restricted to brain behavior, because the organs of the body are homeostatically interconnected by the nervous system.

Particularly fertile for neurophysiological analysis of ritual trance and the effects of cultural practices that facilitate trance states is the concept of CNS tuning advanced by Gellhorn and his colleagues, as well as recent investigations of specialization in the two cerebral hemispheres conducted by several researchers in the neurosciences; these findings complement the results of several decades of anthropological research on the effects of interaction on human biological rhythms performed by Chapple. But a thorough outline of the physiological bases of human behavior, including ritual trance, would be exceedingly complex. Although specialists may fault this necessarily oversimplified account, data presented herein identify pertinent structures and provide explanations that both increase our current understanding of these phenomena and indicate domains requiring further investigation.

---

1. Those who wish to accord primacy to cortical activity of the brain need only to contemplate the effects of seasickness on both thought and motor behavior to see their arguments topple.

Ritual

Chapple speaks of rituals as fixed, precisely performed emotional-interaction forms (1970:292–295). From this perspective ritual behavior (by definition) consists of a sequence of repetitive acts. Although not all rituals evoke states of trance, rhythmic stimuli and fixed interaction tend to produce these states. As will be demonstrated, such factors entrain[2] biological rhythms, synchronizing these to respond to environmental exigencies. By eliminating, correcting, or avoiding dysphasias, entrainment enhances survival opportunities in all species (Chapple, 1970:29).

According to Chapple (1970), dysfunctional, disparate emotional states among members of a group—what he terms "emotional asynchronies"—cause disequilibria. Ordinary events, as well as life crises, disrupt usual, basal patterns, evoking dysphasic emotional responses. Repetitive, evocative sequences of behavior in the separation, transition, and reincorporation phases of rites of passage and rites of intensification establish similar emotional states in participants, restoring individual and group equilibria (Chapple and Coon, 1942; Chapple, 1970).

Moreover, from the perspective of communications theory (Leach, 1966; Birdwhistell, 1970), multifarious stimulations provide redundant messages and thereby reduce ambiguity. Exposure to manifold, intense, repetitive, emotion-evoking stimuli ensures uniformity of behavior in ritual participants. Further, attainment of ritual trance is both an inward and outward manifestation of desired emotional states. If emotional synchrony is the goal of actions in rituals, then exhibition of behaviors attainable only when one is experiencing the appropriate inner state overtly attests to the existence of such a state. Deeds, rather than words, which may constitute falsehoods as well as truth,[3] demonstrate the

2. Entrainment refers to the process by which biological rhythms are synchronized by environmental stimuli. Chapple (1970:27) notes that three major synchronizers of circadian rhythms are light, temperature, and interaction. This presents an example of intraorganismic coordination discussed in chapter 1.

3. However, in rituals certain utterances are simultaneously also actions. To illustrate, in the Iroquois Thanksgiving address, linguists identify performative segments, distin-

authenticity and magnitude of one's faith, control of supernatural forces, or contact with spirit worlds. Extraordinary behaviors, such as "speaking in tongues" (glossolalia), handling fire, behaving like a supernatural entity, or exhibiting unusual feats of endurance, so radically depart from and contrast to mundane experiences that they are ordinarily deemed sacred. In the absence of exact configurations of neural excitation—that is, degree of intensity of stimulation in specific loci, including autonomic and motor responses—these states are difficult to simulate.[4]

A broad variety of methods have been used to facilitate ritual trance. Lewis provides an overview:

As is well known, trance states can be readily induced in most normal people by a wide range of stimuli, applied either separately or in combination. Time-honoured techniques include the use of alcoholic spirits, hypnotic suggestion, rapid overbreathing, the inhalation of smoke vapours, music and dancing, and the ingestion of such drugs as mescaline or lysergic acid and other psychotropic alkaloids. Even without these aids, much of the same effect can be produced, although usually in the nature of things more slowly, by such self-inflicted privations as fasting and ascetic contemplation (e.g., "transcendental meditation"). The inspirational effect of sensory deprivation, implied in the stereotyped mystical flight into the wilderness, has also been well-documented in recent laboratory experiments (1971:39).

Similar examples are provided by Wallace (1966), and all of these cultural practices suggest directions for productive neurobiological investigation. Goodman terms such techniques "driving behaviors," after the repetitive photic stimulations employed in electroencephalography to assess ictal (seizure) propensities in the rhythms of the cerebral cortex (1972:74). However, the list pro-

---

guished—semantically and morphologically as well as syntactically—by a shift in tense, wherein "words are transformed into actions." Typically, these Iroquoian performatives refer to the emotional states of thankfulness and gratitude (Foster, 1974).

4. However, through simulation one may accomplish the same end by cultivating the capacities of the human body and thus facilitate learning by imitation of the appropriate behavioral configurations. Kildahl (1972), for example, describes the efforts of "guides" who assist people "seeking the Holy Spirit" to achieve glossolalia by manipulating their bodies and repeating strings of syllables.

vided by Lewis obviously includes procedures that additionally excite other structures of the body. Systematic examination of driving behaviors categorized according to the structures they affect not only clarifies the role of these techniques in facilitating ritual trance but also demonstrates the extent to which knowledge of physiological function is applied by primitive people.

Repetitive Stimuli and Brain Function

Several anthropologists have noted the significance of repetitive stimuli in ritual contexts. Needham asks "Why is noise that is produced by striking or shaking so widely used in order to communicate with the other world?" (1967:606) and notes that rhythmic sounds are identified with the transition phase of rites of passage (1967:613). Chapple sees musical rhythms as synchronizers entraining free-running body rhythms, commenting:

Voodoo drums, the regular and driving rhythms of revivalistic ceremonies, the incessant beat of jazz or its teenage variants in rock and roll, must synchronize the rhythms of muscular activity centered in the brain and nervous system.

Combined with the dance or with other rhythmic forms of synchronized mass movement—stamping the feet or clapping the hands over and over again—the sound and action of responding as the tempo speeds up clearly ''possess'' and control the participant. The external rhythm becomes the synchronizer to set the internal clocks of these fast rhythms (1970:38).

In their explanations Sturtevant (1968), Walker (1972), and Goodman (1972) report the laboratory investigations of Neher (1961; 1962) into the effects of repetitive photic and auditory stimuli on the electrocortical rhythms of the human brain.

In the research laboratory and as a medical diagnostic procedure electroencephalograph recordings from the scalps of individuals exposed to an intense flashing light approximating the frequency of the alpha, or resting, scanning brain rhythm (usually around ten cycles per second)[5] show increased wave amplitude. Light is a primary synchronizer of biological rhythms in all species (Luce, 1971:121; Chapple, 1970:27). Entrainment of brain rhythms via a rhythmic photic stimulus is quickly established and spreads throughout the brain, so that changes in the frequency at which the light is flashed alter the frequency of the brain waves (Neher, 1962:153).

In seizure-prone individuals photic stimulation evokes the characteristic spike waves presaging an epileptic episode, but even normal persons experience unusual sensations, strong emotions, pseudoperceptions, or myoclonic jerks. Auditory stimulation emanating from drums, producing innumerable frequencies and harmonics, elicits similar results, including temporal distortion (Neher, 1961; 1962). Comparable findings are reported by Walter and Walter (1949).

Drumming rhythms vary sufficiently in a given performance to evoke a response in most hearers so that individual differences in basal rhythms are potentially accommodated (Neher, 1962). In rituals, contrary to Neher's assessment, dancing may produce visual flicker effects due to shifts in ocular focus and the movement of dancers between an individual and a light source. Photic, and auditory, stimuli can spontaneously elicit seizures in susceptible individuals (Gastaut et al., 1949), so that the intense rhythmic photic and auditory stimulations generated by dancing to particular musical tempos and instruments appear to be sufficient synchronizers to effect entrainment of brain rhythms. Moreover, sustained motion also stimulates proprioceptors of the body and can result

5. A great deal of mystique surrounds the alpha rhythm, but no special states of consciousness can be directly attributed to alpha production per se; rather, this brain wave frequency is usually associated with muscular relaxation, absence of visual scanning, or lack of ocular focus (Mulholland, 1972). (Furthermore, the localized specialization of brain structures engaged in processing specific types of information requires extreme precision in electroencephalographic recording—including exclusion of extraneous signals—and stipulation of the exact locus of particular wave frequencies is necessary for any significant interpretation of output.) In fact, rather than eliciting an exalted state of human consciousness, the alpha frequency not only is found in other mammals but also prosaically identifies cessation or "diminution of information processing activity in a given area of the brain" (Ornstein, 1972:199).

in dizziness with accompanying disturbances in vestibulary centers in the ear and baroreceptors in the carotid sinuses, both of which maintain equilibrium or balance; muscle tension or relaxation additionally affects emotional states (Gellhorn, 1967; 1968a; 1969). Further, as Neher observes (1962:156), in rituals not only does rhythmic stimulation often occur simultaneously in several sensory modes, but also adjunctive aids—such as fasting, breathing vapors, or hyperventilation—contribute to alterations in the biochemical environment of the body. All of these physiological manipulations, complexly combined in the context of a ritual, effectually generate stimulus bombardment of the human nervous system.

As Lewis observed, absence or blocking of stimuli, as in sensory deprivation or some meditation techniques, also perturbs the equilibrium of ordinary life situations (see also Naranjo and Ornstein, 1971). There seems to be a range of sensory stimulation, subject to cultural variation and individual differences, with upper and lower thresholds beyond which excitation in neural structures is altered and behavior of an organism is directly modified. In certain types of ritual trance, transcendental meditation, for example, a number of impinging stimuli are reduced or held constant. Ornstein (1972) asserts that the many forms of ritual trance, including meditation, as well as hyperkinetic behaviors, share characteristic evocation and predominance of the special capacities of the right cerebral hemisphere.

Recently, systematic inquiries into the capacities and functions of the cerebral hemispheres have expanded previous contributions made by Neher to the study of brain responses in ritual trance. In the last several years a number of specialists in the neurosciences, directing their attention to the neurobiologic foundations of human consciousness, have discovered a new domain for investigation in the right cerebral hemisphere, previously thought to be unspecialized and subordinate to the "dominant" left (in most right-handed and in the majority of left-handed individuals) hemisphere (Sperry, 1969; Bogen, 1969a, b, c; 1972; Galin and Ornstein, 1972; Morgan et al., 1971; Dimond, 1972; Gazzaniga, 1972; Levy, 1972; Kimura, 1973; Tunnell, 1973;

Nebes, 1974; see also Laughlin and d'Aquili, 1974:59ff). Ample evidence, carefully garnered from study of normal individuals, as well as of patients in whom the cerebral hemispheres have been surgically disconnected by transection of the intermediary neural structures (the corpus callosum and anterior commissure), documents the existence of two distinct modes of thought (Ornstein, 1972). Bogen summarizes the impact of these new findings: "Our present recognition is that the hemispheres are not as much 'major' or 'minor' as that they are complementary, and that each hemisphere is capable of thinking on its own, in its own way" (1972:194).

Briefly stated, in most human beings the left cerebral hemisphere functions in the production of speech, as well as in linear, analytic thought, and also assesses the duration of temporal units, processing information sequentially. In contrast, the specializations of the right hemisphere comprise spatial and tonal perception, recognition of patterns—including those constituting emotion and other states in the internal milieu—and holistic, synthetic thought, but linguistic capability is limited and the temporal capacity is believed absent. Specific acts involve complementary shifts between the functions of the two hemispheres (Bogen, 1969a, b; Dimond, 1972; Ornstein, 1972; Kimura, 1973).

In Ornstein's view (1972) the traditional concept of human consciousness as wholly rational, logical thought disrupted by interference from "lower" (phylogenetically earlier) structures controlling emotion is supplanted by a perspective in which there is alternation between the modes particular to each cerebral hemisphere; the left hemisphere is the domain of logic, the right hemisphere is that of emotion. Further, Ornstein argues that the exceptional feelings distinctive of ritual trance reside in the special abilities of the right hemisphere.

A shift from the time-binding, verbal, linear mode of thought into a timeless, oceanic gestalt, although it adds greater complexity to an already intricate model of human neurobiology, not only accords with Neher's research on auditory driving but also provides an explanation for subjective reports of temporal distortion and unusual sensations—often inexpressible experiences—presented by persons who have undergone ritual trance. Indeed, Leach notes that in "primitive and less primitive thinking," the concept of time is often rendered as "a repetition of repeated reversal, a sequence of oscillations between polar opposites," with the duration of rituals encompassing one sort of time period, "sacred," and differentiated from that of ordinary, "profane," time (1961:126:127). This interpretation is independently supported by Ornstein (1972), who describes many ritual practices that, in his estimation, evoke and place in preeminence right hemisphere functions and at the same time inhibit or hold constant the capacities of the left hemisphere. For example, in certain meditation techniques reduction of sensory inputs by means of repetition of a *mantram,* a mellifluous sound,[6] has the effect of monopolizing the verbal-logical activities of the left hemisphere, leaving the right hemisphere to function freely.[7] Conversely, response to the rhythms of chanting and singing, dancing, handclapping, and percussion instruments engages right-hemisphere capabilities, concomitantly evoking the "timeless" quality of the attendant experience (Ornstein, 1972).

Studies of hemispheric specialization, particularly investigations of linguistic function, illuminate another aspect of trance behavior. For example, among the characteristics of "altered states of consciousness," Ludwig (1968:77–83) names ineffability and memory disturbances, and Prince (1968:121) subsumes ritual trance phenomena under "psychomotor amnesiac states." Data are lacking that might indicate whether "amnesia" results from total absence of memory or from differences in language capacity between the two cerebral hemispheres. Prince, although he supports his classification system with evidence from electroencephalograph recordings of patients diagnosed as suffering psychomotor epilepsy or hysterical fugue states, as well as of sleepwalking subjects, does not identify recording procedures in the experiments he reports. This ommission is crucial because in

6. Although Ornstein describes *mantra* as meanin*gless,* serious students of Hindu and Buddhist philosophies contend that *mantra* are meanin*gful* in mystical senses (Bharati, 1970:101ff). I am indebted to Oliver B. Lerch, Jr., for this emendation.

7. This process seems analogous to Deikman's (1966) concept of "deautomatization."

some cases, for convenience, only unilateral recordings are taken.

Research on language function in the right hemisphere emphasized recognition or production of written words in literate subjects; these findings may not be comparable to results gained from nonliterate or preliterate subjects. Existing research does, however, suggest that, although not completely deficient in verbal ability, the right hemisphere appears to be better at recognition of nouns and adjectives than of verbs; available evidence is somewhat contradictory, owing to the differing laboratory procedures of the investigators (Nebes, 1974:5). However, if the capacity to conceptualize motion and process is absent in the right hemisphere, then the inabilty to describe trance experiences points to right-hemisphere dominance in such states. In this light, ineffability, as well as the "mystical" content of imageries used to explain trance phenomena, are products of interpretation within the verbal limits of a symbol system. Moreover, if the expressive qualities of art forms derive from right-hemisphere functions—as Ornstein and Bogen suggest—then these symbolic representations may reveal more about trance experiences than any necessarily constrained verbal descriptions.[8]

Other forms of nonverbal expression may be inferred from right cerebral hemisphere capacities and functions. Bogen reports right-hemisphere superiority in kinesthetic perception and the "awareness of human disability" (1969b:142, citing Luria, 1966:90), suggesting that this cerebral hemisphere is important in self-recognition of illness and in general perception of internal body states. Baldwin asserts that the majority of hallucinations (sensory pseudoperceptions) are the result of impaired right-hemisphere function; they occur under the effects of LSD-25, sleep deprivation, nutritional deprivation, metabolic dysfunction, and in body temperatures above 40° C or below 34° C (1970:3–8). Taken together, these conditions involve subcortical, as well as cortical, neural structures. Indeed, Fischer (1972) contends that

8. Ornstein (1972) also argues that interhemispheric communication results in creativity—under certain conditions syntheses that occur in the right hemisphere are sequentially analyzed and verbally expressed by the left. The implications of this idea for specialists in anthropology and in artificial intelligence are discussed by West (1974).

hallucinations are the "language" by which the "mute" right hemisphere communicates ideas.

To extend the commentary, I submit that oceanic feelings, ineffability, or pseudoperceptions emanating from right-hemisphere preeminence, evoked by stimulation of subcortical and cortical centers, may also underlie concepts such as "mana," "faith," "power," and other labels for both personified and impersonal supernatural forces. This hypothesis, that these terms are attempts to verbalize about extraordinary sensations experienced in ritual trance, could be systematically investigated by ethnoscientists. Similarly, glossolalia, often comprising rhythmic patterns of meaningless sounds and stereotyped utterances, also merits examination as a behavior that predominantly emanates from the right cerebral hemisphere;[9] existing laboratory studies, such as Palmer's (1966), are inconclusive because of the small sample size. Empirical investigation should resolve the question of whether glossolalia appears only in trance, as Goodman (1972) contends, or is produced outside trance states, as Samarin (1972) argues.

Ornstein's assertions about the significance of right-hemisphere capabilities in trance phenomena might have been anticipated by a little-noticed result of Neher's experiments. In auditory driving, "a rather surprising finding was predominantly unilateral response in the right hemisphere of three subjects . . . one possible explanation is cerebral dominance (all subjects were right-handed)" (1962:449). Although in their comparison of spatial with verbal performance Galin and Ornstein conclude that the alpha, or resting, frequency preponderates in the hemisphere less involved in a task (1972:200), Morgan et al. (1971) observe that right-hemisphere activity is usually characterized by the alpha frequency and that tasks specific to that hemisphere only proportionately reduce alpha output. Neher's work strongly suggests that

9. Support for this observation is found in the earliest discussions of specializations of the cerebral hemispheres; in 1874 Hughlings Jackson argued that activity in the right cerebral hemisphere is the source of emotive and ''automatic'' speech (Benton, 1972:228). For a comprehensive treatment of the phylogenesis of human speech, see Count (1973); a review of neurophysiological contributions to linguistics is in Dingwall and Whitaker (1974).

one significant effect of auditory driving is enhancement of the alpha rhythm, especially in the right hemisphere, with consequent entrainment of cortical rhythms at that frequency.

However, reports of fairly continuous alpha frequencies in the right hemisphere may reflect culturally determined inhibition; laboratory subjects in these experiments are almost invariably white, male, middle-class college students from a cultural background emphasizing sequential verbal-logical reason rather than holistic synthetic perceptions. Although laboratory investigation has scarcely broached the topic, Ornstein (1972), analyzing ethnographic accounts of ritual trance, suggests that hemisphere alternation may be culturally influenced, and Bogen (1972:50), reporting preliminary findings from tests administered to Hopi Indians and to blacks, considers that "hemisphericity," "a tendency to rely more on one hemisphere than the other," may be culturally determined. This hypothesis cannot be evaluated until persons from a variety of cultural backgrounds are the subjects of research on functional hemisphere alternation, as Bogen (1972:51) freely admits.[10]

Another possible interpretation is that generally in the human species the right hemisphere has characteristics, including electrocortical activity, dramatically different from those of the left hemisphere. In contradiction Kinsbourne (1973) questions the validity of assertions that unusual, exalted, or mystical states of consciousness are the result of (temporary) right-hemisphere dominance, basing his objections on the total absence of such states in the behaviors and subjective reports of patients who have undergone surgical transection of the corpus callosum. However, these criticisms disregard several weighty factors. First, the pa-

10. Certainly, despite numerous cross-cultural studies designed to identify cognitive capacities and processes (for example, see Price-Williams, 1970), the tests, methods, and assumptions of these experiments remain open to question (Cole and Scribner, 1974). The concept of hemisphericity may enable both anthropologists and psychologists to sharpen the focus of their research on cognitive processes and to clarify issues of cognitive capacities. Bogen intimates that hemisphericity may bias the outcome of intelligence tests (1972:51), and the same tendency possibly accounts for assertions that primitive thought qualitatively differs from that of civilized peoples (for example, Levy-Bruhl's concept of "prelogical mentality").

tients are invariably residents of a society unusually distrustful of any state of consciousness that departs from a normative central tendency (see Wallace, 1959). Second, and correlatively, ritual trance experiences, insofar as they are institutionalized, are both explained and supported by intricate shared belief systems (*Ibid.*). Third, although the "split-brain" subjects provide singular opportunities for study of differences in capacity and function between the two cerebral hemispheres, their unique clinical status precludes direct and uniform behavioral comparison with other individuals. Fourth, and finally, overemphasis on the cerebral cortex in discussions of trance states omits from consideration the impact of multifarious stimuli on subcortical centers. If my conclusions are correct, driving behaviors during rituals, with their manifold excitement of numerous neural structures, subcortical as well as cortical, evoke greater accentuation of right-hemisphere activity than usually prevails. However, to examine comprehensively the pertinent neurobiological factors in ritual trance—and to avoid Cartesian notions of mind-body distinctions—the roles of the emotions and body rhythms in these states must also be examined.

Emotions and Biological Rhythms

As I have shown, in rituals the entire body, not merely the brain, receives repetitive stimulation. However, alteration in biological rhythms, or, more properly, entrainment, also occurs through interaction (Chapple, 1970:27). Participants in rituals are additionally exposed to the precisely performed acts of their fellow participants, as well as to the symbolic meaning of these acts. The effects of these interactions and of symbols on the nervous system are examined in the following discussion.

Both symbols and behavior derive from neurophysiological states and are accompanied, if not underlain, by inextricable emotional configurations. For example, Chapple asserts that symbols are "cultural shapings" of "neurophysical events" (1970:60) and that "coincident changes in physiological states on which fixed action patterns are based are to be called 'emotional reactions' " (1970:59; also, see Count, 1973, for a discussion of the neurobiological bases of the symbolic process). Further, he assumes that adaptive behavior is not simply confined to the "overt, observable changes in the skeletal-muscle activity," but, contrary to popular usage, includes "internal biochemical and physiological states" which mediate observable behavior (*Ibid.*). Observations similar to Chapple's are enunciated by Gray (1973), a psychologist employing a general systems approach. To summarize, symbols and behavior both result from excitation in neurophysiological structures and are associated with emotional states. Consequently, while attempts to separate one sector of an integrated neurobiological system, for other than heuristic purposes, are common, they are misleading distortions.

Hence, although the discussion now turns to the ANS, the neural subsystem that largely controls emotions and vegetative functions, we are examining only one part of a complex, interactive whole. Moreover, in spite of the fact that the ANS has been relegated to subsidiary status in conventional assessments of nervous system organization and operation, recent research in the neurosciences has revealed that this system is not completely "automatic" in its functions, that modifications in excitation in the system can be achieved through voluntary efforts—although the exact mechanisms by which these changes are effected are as yet unknown—and that the system plays an integral role in states of ritual trance.

As the major system maintaining homeostasis in the internal milieu, the ANS rapidly responds to changes in stimuli, both intrasomatic and extrasomatic, by appropriate excitations in the sympathetic or parasympathetic (sub)systems. These two neural structures are not independent; rather, with few exceptions organs are reciprocally innervated by both. Although qualitatively different in structure, stimulation of one subsystem dampens or inhibits functioning of the other.

Anatomical and neurochemical differences account for the distinct functions particular to each. Characterized by internal connectedness, the entire sympathetic nervous system (SNS) can be excited by stimulation of only a few nerves. Moreover, intense sympathetic response is synergistic, for neural stimulation in this system in turn triggers the release of adrenal hormones, as well as the neurohumors epinephrine and norepinephrine. Manifesting less internal connectedness, the parasympathetic nervous system, (PNS), releasing acetylcholine and serotonin, reacts *in toto* only in response to relatively simultaneous stimulation of its components (Leukel, 1972). Among other inputs, cold and fear excite the sympathetic system, while sweatbaths, emetics, and purgatives excite the parasympathetic system.

Up to a specific threshold, stimulation of the PNS generally results in more pleasurable states such as sleep, digestion, grooming, and relaxation, although intense stimulation results in discomforts such as frequent urination, fainting, voiding of the bowel, peptic ulcers, and other visceral disorders. Alert wakefulness is largely mediated by the SNS; fear and anger involve greater sympathetic excitation. Cannon, a pioneer of modern neurophysiology, described intense sympathetic response in terms of preparation for emergency situations (1929). In "fight or flight" contexts some arteries relax while others contract, shunting blood from the viscera to the somatic (skeletal) muscles. Blood pressure and heart rate rise, respiration increases, digestive activity ceases, and body cooling is achieved via increased perspiration. In short, the SNS mobilizes an organism by simultaneously arming the muscle structures and halting or reducing activity in organs not immediately necessary for escape or combat.

Continuous mobilization is dysfunctional; therefore parasympathetic compensation or rebound often follows and inhibits sympathetic reactivity, resulting in slowed respiration and heart rate, as well as diversion of blood to the viscera from the striated muscles, enabling restorative rest and renewal of energy—action of significant biological survival value.

A dynamic equilibrium between sympathetic and parasympathetic arousal usually prevails (Pribram, 1967:6); as one subsystem of the ANS is stimulated, excitation in the other, inhibiting, system is concomitantly evoked. Leukel writes: "A balance between SNS and PNS arousal is, therefore, always present, a balance that depends on individual differences in ANS sensivity and on the current stimulus situation" (1972:91). With regard to individual differences, each person has a central tendency, termed "automatic balance," toward oscillation in autonomic function that potentially affects emotional characteristics.

As a result of longitudinal research, Wenger and Callen (1972) have identified five configurations or patterns of functional automatic factors in American subjects. Global application of these findings, based on examination of fourteen neurobiological variables, is only suggestive, for systematic cross-cultural studies are lacking, but the presence of five types of autonomic balance in a heterogeneous population raises questions about the number of patterns that might be found in more homogeneous social groups. The existence of several types of autonomic balance may alone explain the variety of techniques to facilitate trance found among the world's cultures, and individuals with anomalous autonomic balance may also provide an explanation for the failure of some persons to achieve trance states by employing the techniques used in rituals of their society. However, in the absence of definitive cross-cultural research (Kugelmass, 1972), and also because the variables used to discern autonomic balance are at best measures of central tendencies (Wenger and Cullen, 1972:567), at this time the foregoing observations are both speculative and indicative of the need for further investigation of this topic.

Although one might expect that a large repertoire of physiological states is necessary to account for the vast array of emotional nuances that individuals experience—and that artists in all media celebrate—empirical evidence contradicts this notion. Cannon (1929), for example, suggested that only a few basic states underlie the entire range of human experience, and more recently his work has been supported, although refined, by that of Orne and Scheibe (1964), Schacter and Singer (1962), and Johnson (1970). Moreover, autonomic reactions do not appear to be essential to the experience of emotion in adults, for paraplegics who cannot perceive visceral sensations still have emotional feelings (Leukel, 1972:366), and the autonomic effects of neurohumors such as epinephrine do not invariably result in predictable emotional responses unless the individual associates the experience with particular symbolic content (Schacter and Singer, 1962). Discussing the available evidence, Leukel concludes: "Although autonomic reactions seem *unnecessary* to emotional experience and behavior, they *can* initiate both, depending on how the subject interprets them" (1972:366). Cortical and subcortical centers controlling autonomic responses appear to become conditioned to react to emotional stimuli, and once learning has occurred, autonomic fluctuations are no longer essential to emotional experience. This may explain the onset of trance in response to only a single cue, as reported by Goodman (1972:85), as well as the observation that novices seem to be less able to control their behavior than experienced trancers (Lee, 1968:41–42; Walker, 1972:31; Katz, 1973:144–145).

Control of the PNS, which stimulates the pancreas to secrete insulin, originates in the anterior and central hypothalmus, and control of the SNS, which stimulates adrenal hormones, in the posterior and lateral hypothalmus. Internal conditions of brain tissue are affected by edema or dehydration, blood sugar level, and salinity, as well as amount of blood available to brain tissue. Decrease in cortical excitability and control over subcortical centers, which is important to facilitation of ritual trance, can be brought about by various agents—fatigue, insulin shock, hypoglycemia, compensated acidosis, and hypoxia are a few examples (Cohen, 1967)—directly or indirectly via driving behaviors.

Central Nervous System Tuning:
The Function of Ritual

Autonomic or vegetative excitation does not occur independent of other neurobiologic systems. Indeed, among other structures each subsystem of the ANS is integrated with the brain and the skeletal muscles, and generally only under special circumstances (in laboratory experiments or under pathological conditions) are these somatic responses separable from autonomic function (Lacey, 1967). Moreover, stimulation of any segment of the nervous system evokes a response in the total, integrated system (Lacey and Lacey, 1970:205). With the model provided by Hess (1925), which emphasizes the interconnectedness and inseparability of these structures, it is appropriate to speak of autonomic-somatic integration in the ergotropic and trophotropic systems. The names of these two systems reflect the oscillating needs of an organism, inexorably shifting from energy-expending behavior to energy-conserving behavior.

Ergotropic response consists of augmented sympathetic discharges, increased muscle tonus, and excitation in the cerebral cortex manifested as "desynchronized" resting rhythms; the *trophotropic* pattern includes heightened parasympathetic discharges, relaxed skeletal muscles, and synchronized cortical rhythms (Gellhorn and Kiely, 1972). Kiely (1974:2) points to an interconnected "tripartite hub"—the limbic system, hypothalmus, and reticular formation of the paleocortex are its members—as comprising the mechanism that integrates purposive, foresighted behavior in man by mediating subcortical responses in the ergotropic and trophotropic systems. In his review of neurophysiological mechanisms, Kiely presents a table summarizing the effects of stimulation in each system; a modified version is provided in Table 4.1.

Fundamental to human perception is the ergotropic orienting reflex or "what-is-it?" response, which, as Sokolov (1963) indicates, involves complex body reaction, including muscular movements (turning toward the stimulus and focusing the eyes), autonomic changes (heart rate, circulation pattern, pupillary dilation), and shifts in cortical activity (from resting rhythms to desynchronized differentials in wave frequency and amplitude). Coordination of cultural and idiosyncratic patterns, which identify certain stimuli as appropriate for attention and others as superfluous, ensures that only a small proportion of the "deluge of raw information" from external and internal environments reaches the threshold of response, attesting to the brain's effectiveness as a filter of input (Smith, 1972:335). Habituation, attenuation of the orienting reflex that results when stimuli cease to be novel, is a product of trophotropic reactivity (Gellhorn and Kiely, 1972:401).

Table 4.1* Some Effects of Stimulation of the Ergotropic and Trophotropic Systems

Stimulation of the Ergotropic System	Stimulation of the Trophotropic System
Autonomic Effects	
Augmented Sympathetic Discharges	Augmented Parasympathetic Discharges
Increased heart rate, blood pressure, sweat secretion; pupillary dilation; inhibition of G.I. motor and secretory function	Reduction in heart rate, blood pressure, sweat secretion; pupillary constriction; increased G.I. motor and secretory functions
Somatic Effects	
Desynchrony of EEG, increased skeletal muscle tone, increased secretion of catabolic hormones: epinephrine, norepinephrine, cortisol, thyroxine, growth hormone, ADH, aldosterone	Synchrony of EEG, loss of skeletal muscle tone, blocking of shivering response, increased secretion of insulin, estrogens, androgens
Behavioral Effects	
Arousal, heightened activity, and emotional responsiveness	Inactivity, drowsiness, and sleep

* After Kiely (1974).

Hence, a shifting ergotropic-trophotropic equilibrium characterizes processing of intrasomatic and extrasomatic stimuli. Furthermore, although ergotropic excitation lowers thresholds of perception if, for example, pain or loud, fast music is sustained, trophotropic rebound results (Oswald, 1959); the seeming paradox can be attributed to tuning and reversal in the CNS.

A consideration of tuning and reversal phenomena is vital to comprehension of the nature and subsequent effects of ritual trance. According to Gellhorn and his colleagues most life situations, whether novel or habitual, have their effects on the internal milieu and contribute to a condition termed *tuning* (Gellhorn and Loofbourrow, 1963; Gellhorn, 1968b; 1969; Gellhorn and Kiely, 1973) "which refers . . . to the sensitization or facilitation of particular centers" (Gellhorn and Loofbourrow, 1963:91). Tuning may be accomplished by direct stimulation of either the sympathetic or parasympathetic system, use of drugs that activate or block one or the other system, or mental activity. Driving behaviors employed to facilitate ritual trance are actually elaborate methods of tuning the CNS.

Three stages of tuning are recognized (Gellhorn, 1970; Gellhorn and Kiely, 1973). In the first stage, response in one system increases while at the same time reactivity in the other system decreases. Augmented reactivity of the sensitized system continues; in the second stage of tuning, reached after stimuli exceed a threshold, not only is inhibition of the nonsensitized system complete, but also stimuli that usually elicit a response in the nonsensitized system instead evoke a response in the sensitized system. Behaviors resulting from this second stage of tuning are termed *reversal phenomena*. If stimulation continues, increased sensitization in this second stage can lead to a third, wherein reciprocal relationships fail and simultaneous discharges result (Gellhorn, 1970; Gellhorn and Kiely, 1973). The third stage of mixed discharges prevails as a product of chronic or intense excitation, as in prolonged or excessive stress (see chapters 5 and 9), and as characteristic of normal physiological states such as orgasm (Beltrami, 1973) and rapid eye movement (REM), or paradoxical, sleep; learned behaviors, including Zen and Yogic meditation and ecstasy states (Gellhorn and Kiely, 1972); and pathological states such as experimental and clinical neuroses, psychosomatic disorders, and psychoses (Gellhorn and Kiely, 1972).

These states are similar because of the shared occurrence of mixed discharges, although the source and degree of excitement in particular centers vary from one state to another, as do individuals' resultant symbolic interpretations. Superficial resemblances have engendered much confused but needless debate about correspondences between trance and sleep, trance and sexual activity, and trance and various pathological conditions (Beltrami, 1973). If each of these states is studied from a neurobiological perspective, as Walker (1972) urges in the case of trance, then the confusion can be resolved. It is, however, presently impossible to count the states of consciousness potentially available in human neurophysiology. For heuristic purposes Bourguignon's (1973) differentiation of "trance" from "possession trance" and Goodman's (1972) polar types, "hypoarousal and hyperarousal," constitute gross trial approximations and are misleading because in the former case the categories are based on cultural distinctions (that is, content, rather than structure) and in the latter are derived solely from observations of motor behavior. A synthesis combining Fischer's (1972) iconic model and Gaarder's (1971a, b) multivariate homeostatic control system would yield a more nearly comprehensive and realistic representation of the complex dynamics involved in human consciousness.

To date no laboratory research has specifically examined ritual trance requiring movement, such as dancing, although strategies for dealing with the problem have been proposed (Prince, 1968). Hence, evidence that ritual trance involves shifts in hemisphere dominance and trophotropic-ergotropic balance is extrapolated from neurobiological analyses of Yogic and Zen meditation and ecstasy, rather than from direct inquiry. Ornstein (1972) subsumes Zen and Yogic practices, as well as ritual trance including more active motor behavior, under a general rubric called "esoteric traditions," but in his view excitation of the right cerebral hemisphere is the fundamental basis for all of these behaviors. However, in the analysis of Gellhorn and Kiely (1972:403), who have devoted extensive research to the effects of tuning on the nervous system in both lower animals and man, meditation constitutes a shift in balance in the direction of trophotropic dominance with some degree of ergotropic excitation,[11] combining relaxation of the skeletal muscles with cortical alertness, while in ecstasy both relaxation and mental activity are further heightened. In these states learning has occurred in the nervous system (*Ibid.*).

Certain types of mixed discharges are therapeutic. Few neuroscientists would dispute the necessity of REM sleep for continued health, and Gellhorn and Kiely (1972) join Wallace and Benson (1971) in encouraging meditation practices as valuable in release from stressors. With regard to ritual trance, among anthropologists Walker (1972) most patently eschews notions of pathology and, instead, details the integrative and salutary benefits of ceremonial possession.

---

11. Wallace and Benson (1971:131) view transcendental meditation as the hypometabolic antithesis of the "defense-alarm reaction" ("fight or flight response"); in sum, in their analysis this process is wholly trophotropic.

Keeping in mind that trophotropic response refers to anabolic processes,[12] techniques to facilitate ritual trance generally employ trophotropic tuning, directly or indirectly via rebound to provide means to allay stress and to restore homeostatic functioning adaptively. Stiff, jerky limb and trunk movements (pseudocerebrate rigidity) and facial contortions, as well as twitches, all involve increased muscle tonus and are aspects of ergotropic activation, which, if intensified or sustained, can result in trophotropic rebound. Among other consequences, trophotropic tuning produces increased sensitivity to hyperventilation (Gellhorn and Loofbourrow, 1963:332), and hence chanting and singing augment trophotropic responses in this regard, in addition to providing repetitive proprioceptive and exteroceptive stimulation. Trophotropic tuning also reduces sensitivity to pain, which explains the ability of individuals to withstand adjudicative "autonomic ordeals" such as those described by Roberts (1967:170),[13] with response probably altered in the hypothalamus (Gellhorn and Loofbourrow, 1963:291).

Reversal phenomena appear to account for the seemingly paradoxical responses to temperature extremes reported by observers of certain ritual trances. For example, cold may be experienced as warmth and heat experienced as cold (Jesuit Relations, 17:175–79; 21:153). Reversal phenomena may also underlie "rites of reversal" analyzed by Gluckman (1965) and Norbeck (1967), among others. Taken together, prosaic behaviors and rites of reversal seem to demarcate the extreme boundaries of oscillations in temporal, social, and biological rhythms in human experience.[14]

12. An anabolic process is one of constructive metabolism, as opposed to catabolic, or destructive, metabolism.

13. According to Roberts, "autonomic ordeals" are those instances "in which the judgment of success or failure, guilt or innocence, is dependent upon involuntary physiological responses such as scalding or blistering of the person or persons tested in the course of 'trials' or 'decision-making processes.' " Among these responses he includes "bleeding, burning, scalding, vomiting, floating . . ." (1967:170).

14. Leach (1961) discusses several ways in which rites of reversal exhibit temporal and social oscillations.

Ritualized reversals, on close scrutiny, often do not seem to be true opposition (nor, for that matter, do binarily opposed categories; see Laughlin and d'Aquili, 1974:105; also chapter 5). Besides innate biological limits' prohibiting exact inversions, the periods of license in which reversals occur are more correctly described as temporal intervals during which certain unusual acts are permitted and encouraged, rather than as explicit, consistent transpositions of biocultural behaviors. Moreover, it seems likely that emotions evoked by these exceptional and ordinarily forbidden behaviors resemble exhilaration accompanying risk taking and thus entail mixed trophotropic-ergotropic discharges. Reversals can be viewed as experienced behavior patterns that wrench individuals or groups away from prior neurobiologic, as well as social, equilibria, instituting qualitatively different patterns in their stead.

Alert attention to detail is required for perfect execution of rituals, and thus performance engenders a certain degree of ergotropic activation. In addition, attention to detail in contexts requiring behavior explicitly contrary to routine patterns, whether in opposition to ordinary actions or to behaviors essential in other types of ritual, further heightens awareness by interrupting the trophotropic responses that prevail in habitual acts. For the novice, such external and internal stimulations are necessary for experiencing requisite emotions and manifesting socially approved behaviors appropriate to a specific ritual; for experienced participants, who have internalized the essential configurations of behavior, evoked responses may appear less significant but are, nevertheless, indispensable for establishing the proper setting for the ritual.

Turner's (1969) concept of *communitas* hints at a perception of shared emotional states among persons having presently or historically, individually or collectively, experienced equivalent conditions by common response mediated through human neurobiological structures. Ambivalence, created by oscillation between opposing emotional states, characterizes these "liminal" states wherein *communitas* prevails. Moreover, whether in the transitional phase of rites or in institutionalized deviant social roles, the liminal individual is simultaneously a part of and not a part of the ongoing social order; in like fashion alternation of categories of time, sacred and profane, constitutes the temporal pattern of a particular culture—neither category of time is less important or "real," for one cannot exist without contraposition of the other. Implicit in liminality is a recognition of contrast between part-whole (or figure-ground) perception of individual and collective experiences. This schizoid state is the condition of man, for acknowledgment that both alternatives exist is necessary so that individuals or groups may deliberately shift from one mode to the other; people return to the mundane world from the sacred and journey from their ordinary plane of existence to mystical realms.

Embedded in rites of passage (and rites of intensification) is the deliberate goal of change in neurophysiological functioning. In Chapple's words: "It seems quite evident, but little studied, that the rites have evolved, in part at least, as structured means through which equilibrium, in all its complex emotional-interactional patterns, is reestablished. In so doing, they discharge the emotional tensions which the sympathetic nervous system has built up" (1970:317). Gellhorn's discussion of the neurobiological processes operant in abreaction provides the insight that ritual trance is a form of catharsis. Apart from these rites, mixed neural discharges, but in different loci, appear to underlie psychosomatic disorders, including folk illnesses. Examples of this are magical fright as described by Gillin (1948), and the therapies employed by native curers and psychotherapists alike. This interpretation is in no sense contradictory; both disorder and treatment are symbolic expressions of the properties and relationships of human anatomical structures. Furthermore, neurobiological analyses of therapeutic techniques illuminate the disorders that are treated, as well as the dynamics of ritual trance.

Abreaction is probably the best known of the therapeutic procedures that manipulate neurobiological structures. The mechanism is described as "a process of reviving the memory of a repressed unpleasant experience and expressing in speech and actions the emotions related to it, thereby relieving the personality of its influence" (Gellhorn and Loofbourrow, 1963:297). The techniques for this therapy were developed to alleviate effects of battle fatigue or emotional shock; barbiturate or nitrous oxide is administered to patients who are then encouraged to relive a traumatic event under conditions of altered cortical functioning. Gellhorn's interpretation suggests that intense emotional excitement followed by exhaustion are at work in this form of therapy (*Ibid.*) Sargant (1957) compares the resultant condition to Pavlov's concept of "transmarginal inhibition," whereby prior conditioned reflexes are lost or reversed. In abreaction, patients frequently exhibit alternate laughing and crying, indicating autonomic fluctuations; these behaviors are sometimes also observed in trance or meditation. Of greatest import, however, is Gellhorn's contention that during abreaction oscillations in ergotropic-trophotropic functioning often lead to a "new setting of the level of autonomic balance," a hysteretic change described as "relatively long-lasting" (Gellhorn and Loofbourrow, 1963:297). In other words, abreaction helps the individual to reexperience, under controlled conditions, intense emotional responses to stress-provoking stimuli, permitting discharge of affect with accompanying physiological readjustments. The heightened tensions excite the ergotropic system to the extent that trophotropic rebound results, establishing a new configuration of internal functioning (Gellhorn and Kiely, 1973:256). Sargant (1957, 1974), although focusing on the impact of abreaction on excitation of the cerebral cortex, contends that faith healing and mystical experiences are products of physiological processes that occur when there is a neural "spillover" of impulses; in his view religious conversion and ritual trance are clearly forms of abreaction, although employed in sacred contexts.

Employing similar neurophysiological principles, implosion therapy, by bombarding the patient with sustained fear-evoking stimuli, initially elicits strong ergotropic excitation, and, ultimately, the emotional "flooding" so exhausts the person that trophotropic rebound occurs (Gellhorn and Loofbourrow, 1963:225). However, the closest secular analogue to ritual can be found in group-interaction therapies. For these techniques Gellhorn and Kiely note the efficacy of "systematically practicing and modifying expressive movements such as posture, gesture, speech, and singing" in altering disturbed behavior patterns, citing the work of Born (1953).

In group-interaction therapies feedback from proprioceptors, as in singing and dancing, seems to evoke new patterns of affective response in the hypothalamus, limbic system, and neocortex (Gellhorn and Kiely, 1973:257). Instead of employing

anxiety-provoking stimuli, action therapies avoid primary emphasis on perceptual, cognitive, and affective experience and address themselves to overt, objectively observable behavioral changes. They assume that changes in thinking and feeling may best be effected by modifying the way one acts, rather than the reverse. The physiological experiments demonstrating the effect of proprioceptive impulses on hypothalamic activity and upon the T-E balance support this interpretation (1973:256).

This form of therapy provides important clues for an assessment of the neurophysiological changes that occur in ritual trance.

In rituals, symbolic content, although certainly present, is highly standardized, designed to evoke similar emotional responses in all participants. More importantly, for individual or group variations in interpretations of symbols appear inevitable (Chapple, 1970:314–317), behavior is also fixed. To excite the appropriate neurophysiological centers—and thus rest trophotropic-ergotropic balance—the performance or a ritual requires strict adherence to patterned posture, gesture, speech, and (perhaps) singing modes that are traditionally sanctioned rather than innovative.

The absence of extreme stress, characteristic of both abreaction and implosion therapies, also points to the similarity of rituals to group-interaction therapies. Although attention to performance increases awareness of interactive cues (Chapple, 1970:317), strong anxiety could produce mixed neural discharges in inappropriate centers, resulting in dysphasia. The disruptive power of anxiety also explains the reluctance to change rituals and the general conservative tendency of primitive society, with its strong emphasis on ritual drama, [features detailed by Diamond (1974:137–138; 150–159)] for individualistic alterations in ritual would be likely to lead to greater stress—and under acute stress organisms are less able to learn and to adapt with new behaviors.

Moreover, the very term *life crisis* conjures a picture of a threatened, ergotropically tuned individual or group in need of nurturance, and nurturant behavior elicits trophotropic response. To establish equilibria, standardized mobilization of all or significant numbers of persons must take place. As Chapple observes:

In rites of passage, and, in a less obvious and dramatic sense, in rites of intensification, performance of the rites, in almost every society, is obligatory. Not only must everyone be present, but one is required to carry out the interaction forms . . . whatever their idiosyncratic tendencies, the participants must carry out the interaction forms even if, as often has been observed, they have to be dragged through the motions by others (1970:317)

If the ritual is conducted correctly, the result is easing of tension or strain (*Ibid.*). Significantly, another relevant aspect of ritual is the shift to the mode of consciousness characteristic of the right cerebral hemisphere, associated, according to Ornstein (1972:178), with perceptions of unity and holism. Hence, individuals, eager or reluctant, are integrated into a group, not only by the sharing of pleasurable emotions through participation in formalized, repetitive, precisely performed interaction forms, but also by a mode of thought that reinforces feelings of solidarity.

Conclusion

The *raison d'être* for rituals is the readjustment of dysphasic biological and social rhythms by manipulation of neurophysiological structures under controlled conditions. Rituals properly executed promote a feeling of well-being and relief, not only because prolonged or intense stresses are alleviated, but also because the driving techniques employed in rituals are designed to sensitize or "tune" the nervous system and thereby lessen inhibition of the right hemisphere and permit temporary right-hemisphere dominance, as well as mixed trophotropic-ergotropic excitation, to achieve synchronization of cortical rhythms in both hemispheres and evoke trophotropic rebound.

Furthermore, it is difficult to separate the impact of repetitive behaviors on the brain from their influence on the rest of the nervous system because the various driving techniques simultaneously excite numerous neural centers. In a given ritual one specific practice alone may be sufficient to establish a state of trance; that several techniques are engaged concomitantly or sequentially indicates redundancy, to guarantee reliability, potentially affecting the entire group of participants. In other words, manifold driving techniques accommodate individual differences in experience and genetic makeup. However, any complete interpretation of ritual trance also recognizes the symbolic qualities of human behavior, since other biologically based activities, such as eating, sleeping, and reproduction, are not confined to mere satisfaction of biological necessities but are also embellished with other behaviors.

Driving practices, whether involving ingestion or exposure to substances that alter the body's biochemical milieu, manipulation of neural reflexes, or symbol systems, function as follows:

1. by either blocking sequential information processing of the left hemisphere via bombardment of repetitive stimuli and thus holding activity in that hemisphere constant or by providing stimuli that the right hemisphere is especially suited to process, or both;

2. by promoting trophotropic dominance, often through direct stimulation of the PNS, or intense activation of the ergotropic system to elicit trophotropic rebound, or both;

3. by lessening motor activity and thus facilitating trophotropic dominance through relaxation of the skeletal muscles or by increasing motor activity, resulting in ergotropic excitation to the extent that trophotropic rebound eventually results.

Various combinations of these procedures characterize ritual trance, but until systematic investigations of autonomic balance are done in geographically distant populations, one can only speculate that the adoption of particular driving techniques is at least partially derived from genetically based autonomic factors.

The impact of different life-styles on unknown configurations of autonomic balance is even more obscured by lack of data and therefore merits extensive cross-disciplinary research.

In summary, although concrete empirical data from neurobiological studies of ritual trance incorporating extensive body motion are unavailable, one can extrapolate from general principles of neurophysiological function and the limited observations of sedentary ritual trance that neuroscientists have reported. Several working hypotheses derive from the foregoing discussion:

1. Each individual has a characteristic trophotropic-ergotropic balance, acquired from genetic inheritance and influenced by experience.

2. Life circumstances, including conflict, disturb this balance, resulting in ergotropic tuning, and in extreme cases, trophotropic rebound or mixed discharges.

3. Dysphasias in trophotropic-ergotropic balance generate maladaptive behavior.

4. Alleviation of dysphasic neurobiologic function is necessary for the conduct of concerted actions and the reduction of conflict within a group.

5. Seeking homeostasis, rituals entrain or synchronize biological rhythms, establishing equilibria.

6. In rituals, as in other forms of therapy, interaction patterns counter dysphasias by the use of tuning.

7. Tuning requires intense or sustained excitation of the ergotropic-trophotropic system, and hence driving techniques augment neurophysiological responses.

8. Driving techniques facilitate right-hemisphere dominance, resulting in gestalt, timeless, nonverbal experiences, differentiated and unique when compared with left-hemisphere functioning or hemisphere alternation.

9. Rebound in the trophotropic-ergotropic system, which results from tuning via driving techniques, shifts balance in the trophotropic-ergotropic system toward life-conserving trophotropic function via exhaustion.

10. Rebound from tuning establishes a new balance; new patterns of right-left hemisphere integration can also result.

This analysis, although admittedly preliminary, points to the need for further research, on the part of anthropologists as well as neuroscientists, to refute, support, or revise evidence provided by the author. Although the opinion has often been advanced that ritual trance behaviors are not amenable to holistic study in laboratory contexts, this belief retards thorough, systematic research characteristic of scientific investigation that can eventually illuminate the neurophysiological bases of trance.

References

Beltrami, E. 1973. *Orgasm and Ecstasy: Neurophysiological Differences.* Ms.

Benton, A. L. 1972. "Hemispheric Dominance and Somesthesis," in *Psychopathology: Contributions from the Social, Behavioral, and Biological Sciences* (M. Hammer, K. Salzinger, S. Sutton, eds.). New York: Wiley.

Bharati, A. 1970. *The Tantric Tradition.* New York: Doubleday.

Birdwhistell, R. L. 1970. *Kinesics and Context: Essays on Body Motion Communication.* Philadelphia: University of Pennsylvania Press.

Bogen, J. E. 1969a. "The Other Side of the Brain I: Dysgraphia and D Dyscopia Following Cerebral Commissurotomy." *Bulletin of the Los Angeles Neurological Society* 34:73–105.

—— 1969b. "The Other Side of the Brain II: An Appositional Mind." *Bulletin of the Los Angeles Neurological Society* 34:135–162.

—— 1969c. "The Other Side of the Brain III: The Corpus Callosum and Creativity." *Bulletin of the Los Angeles Neurological Society* 34:191–220.

—— 1972. "The Other Side of the Brain IV: The A/P Ratio." *Bulletin of the Los Angeles Neurological Society* 37:49–61.

Born, H. Z. 1953. "Reversibility of Psychosomatic Processes as a Basis for a Principle of General Therapy." *Arztleche Forschung* 7:25–31.

Bourguignon, E. 1972. "Dreams and Altered States of Consciousness in Anthropological Research," in *Psychological Anthropology* (2nd ed.) (F. K. L. Hsu, ed.). Homewood, Ill.: The Dorsey Press.

—— 1973. "Introduction: A Framework for the Comparative Study of Altered States of Consciousness," in *Religion, Altered States of Consciousness, and Social Change* (E. Bourguignon, ed.). Columbus: Ohio State University Press.

Cannon, W. B. 1929. *Bodily Changes in Pain, Hunger, Fear and Rage: An Account of Researches into the Function of Emotional Excitement.* New York: Appleton-Century.

Chapple, E. D. 1970. *Culture and Biological Man.* New York: Holt, Rinehart and Winston.

Chapple, E. D. and C. S. Coon. 1942. *Principles of Anthropology.* New York: Holt.

Cohen, S. 1967. "Psychotomimetic Agents." *Annual Review of Pharmacology* 7:301–318.

Cole, M. and S. Scribner. 1974. *Culture and Thought: A Psychological Introduction.* New York: Wiley.

Count, E. W. 1973. *Being and Becoming Human: Essays on the Biogram.* New York: Van Nostrand.

Deikman, A. J. 1966. "Deautomatization and the Mystic Experience." *Psychiatry* 29:324–338.

Diamond, S. 1974. *In Search of the Primitive: A Critique of Civilization.* New Brunswick, New Jersey: Transaction Books. Distributed by E. P. Dutton.

Dimond, S. 1972. *The Double Brain.* London: Churchill Livingston.

Dingwall, W. D. and H. A. Whitaker. 1974. "Neurolinguistics." *Annual Review of Anthropology* 3:323–356.

Firth, R. 1969. "Foreword," in *Spirit Mediumship and Society in Africa* (J. Beattie and J. Middleton, eds.). New York: Africana.

Fischer, R. 1972. "Reply from Dr. Fischer." *R. M. Bucke Memorial Society Newsletter-Review* 5:42–45.

Foster, M. K. 1974. "When Words Become Deeds: An Analysis of Three Iroquois Longhouse Speech Events," in *Explorations in the Ethnography of Speaking* (J. Sherzer and R. Bauman, eds.). New York: Cambridge University Press.

Gaarder, K. 1971a. "Control of States of Consciousness I: Attainment through Control of Psychophysiological Variables." *Archives of General Psychiatry* 25.429–435.

—— 1971b. "Control of States of Consciousness II: Attainment through Internal Feedback Augmenting Control of Psychophysiological Variables." *Archives of General Psychiatry* 25:436–441.

Galin, D. and R. Ornstein. 1972. "Lateral Specialization of a Cognitive Mode: An EEG Study." *Psychophysiology* 9:412–418.

Gastaut, H., J. Roger, J. Corriol, and Y. Gastaut. 1949. "Epilepsy Induced by Rhythmic, Intermittent, Auditory Stimulation or Epilepsy 'Psyphogenique.'" *Electroencephalography and Clinical Neurophysiology* 1:121.

Gazzaniga, M. S. 1972. "One Brain—Two Minds?" *American Scientist* 60:311–317.

Gellhorn, E. 1967. *Principles of Autonomic-Somatic Integration: Physiological Basis and Psychological and Clinical Implications.* Minneapolis: University of Minnesota Press.

—— 1968a. "Attempt at a Synthesis: Contribution to a Theory of Emotion," in *Biological Foundations of Emotion: Research and Commentary* (E. Gellhorn, ed.). Glenview, Ill.: Scott, Foresman.

—— 1968b. "Central Nervous System Tuning and Its Implications for Neuropsychiatry." *Journal of Nervous and Mental Diseases* 147:148–162.

—— 1969. "Further Studies on the Physiology and Pathophysiology of the Tuning of the Central Nervous System." *Psychosomatics* 10:94–104.

—— 1970. "The Emotions and the Ergotropic and Trophotropic Systems." *Psychologische Forschung* 34:48–94.

Gellhorn, E. and W. F. Kiely. 1972. "Mystical States of Consciousness: Neurophysiological and Clinical Aspects." *Journal of Nervous and Mental Diseases* 154:399–405.

—— 1973. "Autonomic Nervous System in Psychiatric Disorder," in *Biological Psychiatry* (J. Mendels, ed.). New York: Wiley.

Gellhorn, E. and G. N. Loofbourrow. 1963. *Emotions and Emotional Disorders: A Neurophysiological Study.* New York: Harper and Row.

Gillin, J. 1948. "Magical Fright." *Psychiatry* 11:387–400.

Gluckman, M. 1965. *Politics, Law and Ritual in Tribal Society.* Chicago: Aldine.

Goodman, F. D. 1972. *Speaking in Tongues: A Cross-Cultural Study of Glossolalia.* Chicago: University of Chicago Press.

Gray, W. 1973. "Emotional Cognitive Structures: A General Systems Theory of Personality." *General Systems* 18:167–174.

Hess, W. R. 1925. *On the Relations Between Psychic and Vegetative Functions.* Zurich: Schwabe.

Neurobiology of Ritual Trance

Jesuit Relations, 1896–1901. *The Jesuit Relations and Allied Documents.* 73 vols. (R. G. Thwaites, ed.) Cleveland: Burrows.

Johnson, L. C. 1970. "A Psychophysiology for All States." *Psychophysiology* 6:501–516.

Katz, R. 1973. "Education for Transcendence: Lessons from the !Kung Zhu/Twasi." *Journal of Transpersonal Psychology* 2:136–155.

Kiely, W. F. 1974. *From the Symbolic Stimulus to the Pathophysiological Response.* Ms.

Kildahl, J. P. 1972. *The Psychology of Speaking in Tongues.* New York: Harper and Row.

Kimura, D. 1973. "The Asymmetry of the Human Brain." *Scientific American* 299:70–78.

Kinsbourne, M. 1973. *Hemispheric Collaboration and Competition.* Ms.

Kugelmass, S. 1972. "Psychophysiological Indices in Psychopathological and Crosscultural Research," in *Psychopathology: Contributions from the Social, Behavioral, and Biological Sciences* (M. Hammer, K. Salzinger, and S. Sutton, eds.). New York: Wiley.

Lacey, J. I. 1967. "Somatic Response in Patterning and Stress," in *Psychological Stress: Issues in Research* (M. H. Appley and R. Trumball, eds.). New York: Appleton.

Lacey, J. I. and B. C. Lacey. 1970. "Some Autonomic-Central Nervous System Correlates," in *Physiological Correlates of Emotion* (P. Black, ed.). New York: Academic Press.

Laughlin, C. D., Jr. and E. G. d'Aquili. 1974. *Biogenetic Structuralism.* New York: Columbia University Press.

Leach, E. R. 1961. *Rethinking Anthropology.* London: The Athlone Press.

—— 1966. "Ritualization in Man in Relation to Conceptual and Social Development." *Philosophical Transactions of the Royal Society of London* 251(B):403–408.

Lee, R. B. 1968. "The Sociology of !Kung Bushman Trance Performances," in *Trance and Possession States* (R. Prince, ed.) Montreal: R. M. Bucke Memorial Society.

Leukel, F. 1972. *Introduction to Physiological Psychology.* St. Louis: Mosby.

Levy, J. 1972. "Lateral Specialization of the Human Brain," in *The Biology of Behavior* (J. A. Kiger, ed.). Corvallis: Oregon State University Press.

Lewis, I. M. 1971. *Ecstatic Religion: An Anthropological Study of Spirit Possession and Shamanism.* Middlesex, England: Penguin Books.

Luce, G. G. 1971. *Biological Rhythms in Human and Animal Physiology.* New York: Dover Publications.

Ludwig, A. M. 1968. "Altered States of Consciousness," in *Trance and Possession States* (R. Prince, ed.). Montreal: R. M. Bucke Memorial Society.

Luria, A. R. 1966. *Higher Cortical Functions in Man.* New York: Basic Books.

Morgan, A. H., P. J. McDonald, and H. McDonald. 1971. "Differences in Bilateral Alpha Activity as a Function of Experimental Task." *Neuropsychologia* 9:459–469.

Mulholland, T. B. 1972. "Can You Really Turn On With Alpha?" *R. M. Bucke Memorial Society Newsletter-Review* 5:32–40.

Murdock, G. P. 1967. "Ethnographic Atlas: A Summary." *Ethnology* 6.

Naranjo, C. and R. E. Ornstein. 1971. *On the Psychology of Meditation.* New York: Viking Press.

Nebes, R. D. 1974. "Hemispheric Specialization in Commissurotomized Man." *Psychological Bulletin* 81:1–14.

Needham, R. 1967. "Percussion and Transition." *Man* 2:606–614.

Neher, A. 1961. "Auditory Driving Observed With Scalp Electrodes in Normal Subjects." *Electroencephalography and Clinical Neurophysiology* 13:499–451.

—— 1962. "A Physiological Explanation of Unusual Behavior in Ceremonies Involving Drums." *Human Biology* 34:151–161.

Barbara W. Lex

Norbeck, E. 1967. "African Rituals of Conflict," in *Gods and Rituals: Readings in Religious Beliefs and Practices* (J. Middleton, ed.). New York: Natural History Press.

Orne, M. and K. Scheibe. 1964. "The Contributions of Non-deprivation Factors in the Induction of Sensory Deprivation Effects: The Psychology of the Panic Button." *Journal of Abnormal Social Psychology* 68:3–12.

Ornstein, R. 1972. *The Psychology of Consciousness*. San Francisco: Freeman.

Oswald, I. 1959. "Experimental Studies of Rhythm, Anxiety and Cerebral Vigilance." *Journal of Mental Science* 105:269–294.

Palmer, G. 1966. "Trance and Dissociation: A Cross-Cultural Study in Psychological Physiology." Master's thesis, University of Minnesota.

Pribram, K. H. 1967. "Emotion: Steps Toward a Neuropsychological Theory," in *Neurophysiology and Emotion* (D. C. Glass, ed.). New York: The Rockefeller University Press and Russell Sage Foundation.

Price-Williams, D. R. 1970. *Cross-Cultural Studies*. Baltimore: Penguin.

Prince, R. 1968. "Can the EEG Be Used in the Study of Possession States?" in *Trance and Possession States* (R. Prince, ed.). Montreal: R. M. Bucke Memorial Society.

Roberts, J. M. 1967. "Oaths, Autonomic Ordeals, and Power," in *Cross-Cultural Approaches: Readings in Comparative Research* (C. S. Ford, ed.). New Haven, Conn.: HRAF Press.

Samarin, W. J. 1972. *Tongues of Men and Angels: The Religious Language of Pentacostalism*. New York: Macmillan.

Sargant, W. 1957. *The Battle for the Mind*. New York: Doubleday.

—— 1974. *The Mind Possessed: A Physiology of Possession, Mysticism and Faith Healing*. Philadelphia: Lippincott.

Schacter, S. and J. Singer. 1962. "Cognitive, Social, and Physiological Determinants of Emotional States." *Psychological Review* 69:379–399.

Shack, W. A. 1972. "Preface," in *Ceremonial Spirit Possession in Africa and Afro-America: Forms, Meanings, and Functional Significance for Individuals and Groups* (S. S. Walker). Leiden, Netherlands: Brill.

Smith, C. U. M. 1972. *The Brain: Towards an Understanding*. New York: Capricorn Books.

Sokolov, Y. N. 1963. *Perception and Conditioned Reflex*. New York: Macmillan.

Sperry, R. 1969. "A Modified Concept of Consciousness." *Psychological Review* 76:532–536.

Sturtevant, W. C. 1968. "Categories, Percussion and Physiology." *Man* 3:133–134.

Tunnell, G. G. 1973. *Culture and Biology: Becoming Human*. Minneapolis: Burgess.

Turner, V. W. 1969. *The Ritual Process: Structure and Anti-Structure*. Chicago: Aldine.

Walker, S. S. 1972. *Ceremonial Spirit Possession in Africa and Afro-America: Forms, Meanings, and Functional Significance for Individuals and Social Groups*. Leiden, Netherlands: Brill.

Wallace, A. F. C. 1959. "Cultural Determinants of Response to Hallucinatory Experience." *Archives of General Psychiatry* 1:58–59.

—— 1966. *Religion: An Anthropological View*. New York: Random House.

Wallace, R. K. and H. Benson. 1971. "The Physiology of Meditation," in *Altered States of Awareness: Readings from Scientific American*. San Francisco: Freeman.

Walter, V. J. and W. G. Walter. 1949. "The Central Effects of Rhythmic Sensory Stimulation." *Electroencephalography and Clinical Neurophysiology* 1:57–86.

Wenger, M. A. and T. D. Cullen. 1972. "Studies of Autonomic Balance in Children and Adults," in *Handbook of Psychophysiology* (N. S. Sternbach and R. A. Greenfield, eds.). New York: Holt, Rinehart and Winston.

West, S. A. 1974. *Creativity, Altered States of Awareness, and Artificial Intelligence.* Ms.

Five

The Neurobiology of Myth and Ritual

Eugene G. d'Aquili and
Charles D. Laughlin, Jr.

Thus symbolism, including the symbolic transference by which it is effected, is merely one exemplification of the fact that a unity of experience arises out of the confluence of many components. This unity of experience is complex, so as to be capable of analysis. The components of experience are not a structureless collection indiscriminately brought together. Each component by its very nature stands in a certain potential scheme of relationships to the other components. It is the transformation of this potentiality into real unity which constitutes that actual concrete fact which is an act of experience.

Alfred North Whitehead, *Symbolism*

Introductory Summary

The preceding three chapters have considered in some detail both the origin of human ritual from an evolutionary perspective and the probable neurophysiological mechanisms underlying the affective and trance states associated with ritual. These affective states appear to provide the reinforcing mechanism for maintaining human ritual, especially ceremonial ritual, as a viable cultural institution. In the last chapter Professor Lex alluded in passing to the importance of integrating the functions of the human neocortex into this model and further suggested that some of the recent research in lateralization of brain functioning may provide the necessary clue for such an integration. The focus of this chapter is precisely to integrate the ethological data from chapters 2 and 3, Professor Lex's treatment of autonomic tuning, and our own work relating the evolution of neocortical functioning to the development of cultural institutions.

Simply, we attempt to explain from a neuroevolutionary point of view why human ceremonial ritual is inevitably embedded within a mythic structure. It is indeed a fact that all human ceremonial rituals possess a cognitive rationale related to the generation of the affective or dissociative states described by Professor Lex. In other words we attempt to integrate the material presented thus far with recent research concerning the nature of higher cortical functioning, to present a coherent neurobiological model for human ceremonial ritual, before we move on in subsequent chapters to a consideration of cognitive developmental and social aspects of ritual.

In many ways the most difficult task in doing a biogenetic structural analysis of human ceremonial ritual is to present a neural model for the development of myth in which human ritual is embedded. Yet the biogenetic structural methodology presented in chapter 1 requires that all the major facets of a cultural institution be at least tentatively explained in terms of a neuroanatomical/neurophysiological model if sufficient data can be found to support the construction of such a model. Those who are well versed in the neural sciences may find fault with our choosing one set of data and interpretations rather than another in certain areas that are as yet controversial. The reader who may not be well versed in the neural sciences should be clearly aware that there are a number of such controversial areas in neurobiology. While biology may be a "hard" science compared to the social sciences, the "hardness" is only relative. At any rate, in areas where there is still legitimate controversy, we have chosen the data and interpretations that are most consonant with the evidence from ethology, psychology, and other sciences presented elsewhere in this volume. Methodological purists from within the neural sciences may occasionally find this choice of data objectionable. But the entire thrust of biogenetic structuralism is an interdisciplinary approach to the social sciences, and, as such, an inter-disciplinary methodology (such as that developed in chapter 1) must be followed. What such a methodology lacks in rigor it makes up for in scope, which is precisely the great need in the social sciences today. What follows, therefore, is not presented as scientific dogma, but rather as the most probable neural model, based on valid neurophysiological investigation and consonant with the evidence from other sciences, which can explain the generation of myth and its relationship to human ceremonial ritual.

Up to this point we have been considering those aspects of ceremonial ritual that man appears to have in common with lower animals. It is not sufficient for a biogenetic structural analysis of a human cultural institution merely to consider the evolution of the traits of man's behavior shared with lower animals. It is incumbent upon such an analysis to explain the differences as well. Furthermore those differences should be explained, if possible, in terms of evolution of the central nervous system (CNS), and in terms of the adaptive value that such accretions to the phylogenetically antecedent behavior have for *Homo sapiens* (see chapter 1).

Since this attempt to provide a comprehensive neurobiological model for human ceremonial ritual involves the integration of data from various disciplines, and since the argument providing the basis for this model may appear at times somewhat difficult to follow, it is necessary to summarize some of the material from the preceding three chapters, but with perhaps some shift of emphasis, to provide a smooth exposition.

Let us begin our argument by considering the problem of those aspects of human ritual that man shares with other animals versus those aspects of human ritual, particularly its mythic basis, that appear to be unique to man. We would be the first to agree that cultic ritual as practiced by *Homo sapiens* has many unique characteristics. As we shall see, however, these unique characteristics, although an integral part of ritual as performed by man, can be viewed as being derived from other neurobiological systems that had selective advantages totally separate from those of ritual behavior. These unique elements of human ritual, particularly the myth structure or cognitive matrix in which ritual is embedded, ap-

154

pear to have been, as it were, grafted on the mainstream of the evolution of ritual behavior. While it is dangerous not to perceive the unique aspects of human ritual, particularly as exemplified in ceremonial ritual, it is even more dangerous to ignore those of its aspects that man has in common with other species. Tinbergen (1965) has strongly argued for the importance of homologous features in the study of origins of communicative behavior. To refuse to consider human ritual behavior within an evolutionary perspective is to commit the rankest of anthropocentrisms.

Let us return to a theme touched upon in chapter 2, that is, a consideration of ritual behavior across species, but from a slightly different perspective. A major problem for any organism whose adaptation depends on cooperation with one or more conspecifics is to decrease the distancing between itself and others so that some form of cooperation can be achieved. A number of ethologists such as Lorenz (1966), Tinbergen (1965), and Lehrman (1965) have observed that a certain amount of distance is normally maintained among vertebrates, probably to preserve the integrity of the individual's survival functions. Jay (1965), Chance (1965), and others have noted the importance of "social space" among nonhuman primates. Much has recently been written about personal space in man. There is increasing evidence that most vertebrates under normal conditions maintain a degree of distance or separateness. Most frequently this distancing is spatial, but it may also be relational in terms of hierarchy within a group.

If two or more animals must cooperate in a task, the most basic of which is the copulative function, their usually adaptive distancing becomes maladaptive. Some way must be found to circumvent the problem to permit greater spatial or relational proximity. One way in which proximity is achieved is by the performance of ritual behavior by one or more members of the group. Lorenz (1966), Lehrman (1965), Tinbergen (1965), and others have noted that such ritual courtship behavior prior to coition is common among many species and seems to aid the elimination of the distancing between the two individuals, allowing coition to take place. Ritual behavior before cooperative group action is also extremely common. Lorenz (1966) makes the important point that ritual behavior appears to be the trigger for much of the cooperative behavior within species for which cooperation is essential for survival. More importantly, Lorenz (1966) sees these same functions operative within culturally elaborated religious rituals in man. He notes:

> In cultural ritualization, the two steps of the development leading from communication to the control of aggression and, from this, to the formation of a bond, are strikingly analogous to those that take place in the evolution of instinctive rituals . . . The triple function of suppressing fighting within the group, of holding the group together, and of setting it off, as an independent entity, against other, similar units, is performed by the developed ritual in so strictly analogous a manner as to merit deep consideration (1966:74).

At this point we must reiterate what is meant by ritual behavior. We have defined it as a sequence of behavior that (1) is sequentially structured (patterned) (2) is repetitive and rhythmic (to some degree at least)—that is, it tends to recur in the same or nearly the same form with some regularity; (3) acts to coordinate affective, preceptual (cognitive in man and other higher vertebrates), and motor processes within the CNS of individual participants; and, most particularly, (4) coordinates and synchronizes these processes among the various individual participants. Manley (1960) has considered this coordinating function of ritual among the black-headed gull in some detail. It appears, from the work of Schein and Hale (1965) with the domestic turkey, of Tinbergen (1951) with three-spined sticklebacks and queen butterflies, and of Rosenblatt (1965) with cats, that there is something about the repetitive or rhythmic emanation of signals from a conspecific that generates a high degree of limbic arousal. With respect to this rhythmicity of ritual Lorenz (1966) notes:

> The display of animals during threat and courtship furnishes an abundance of examples, and so does the culturally developed ceremonial of man. The deans of the university walked into the hall with a "measured step"; pitch, rhythm, and loudness of the Catholic priests chanting during mass are all strictly regulated by liturgic prescription. The unambiguity of the communication is also increased by its frequent repetition. Rhyth-

mical repetition of the same movement is so characteristic of very many rituals, both instinctive and cultural, that it is hardly necessary to describe examples (1966:72).

Walter and Walter (1949), and Gellhorn and Kiely (1972; 1973) have shown that such repetitive auditory and visual stimuli can drive cortical rhythms and eventually produce an intensely pleasurable, ineffable experience in man (see also Abraham, 1976). Furthermore, Gellhorn and Kiely (1972; 1973) cite evidence that such repetitive stimuli can bring about simultaneous intense discharges from both the sympathetic and parasympathetic nervous systems in man. Lex has reviewed the evidence for these phenomena in detail in the preceding chapter.

When one considers the evidence taken from the animal literature, together with the limited studies that have been done on man, one can infer that there is something about repetitive rhythmic stimuli that may, under proper conditions, bring about the unusual neural state of simultaneous high discharge of both autonomic subsystems. We would ask the reader to keep in mind the three stages of tuning of the sympathetic-parasympathetic subsystems (Gellhorn, 1967; Gellhorn and Kiely, 1973). In the first state, response in one system increases while, at the same time, reactivity in the other system decreases. If augmented reactivity of the sensitized system continues, the second stage of tuning is reached after stimuli exceed a certain threshold. At this point, not only is inhibition of the nonsensitized system complete, but also stimuli that usually elicit a response in the nonsensitized system evoke instead a response in the sensitized system. These behaviors comprise the "reversal phenomena" that Lex alluded to. If stimulation continues beyond this stage, increased sensitization can lead to a third stage characterized by simultaneous discharges in both systems. Normally, either the sympathetic or the parasympathetic system predominates, and the excitation of one subsystem inhibits the other. In the special case of prolonged rhythmic stimuli one can postulate that the simultaneous strong discharge of both autonomic systems creates a state of stimulation of the median forebrain bundle, generating not only a pleasurable sensation but, under proper conditions, a sense of union or oneness with conspecifics.

The simplest paradigm to explain the situation in man is the feeling of union that occurs during orgasm. During orgasm as during other states we shall consider later, there is intense simultaneous discharge from both of the autonomic subsystems. We are postulating that the various ecstasy states that can be produced in man after exposure to rhythmic auditory, visual, or tactile stimuli produce a feeling of union with other members participating in that ritual. In fact, social unity is a common theme running through the myth associated with most human rituals. Although it is very difficult to extrapolate from a human model to an animal model, it is clear that a homologous affective state is produced by rhythmic repeated ritual behavior in other species. This state may vary in intensity but always has the effect of unifying the social group.

Put simply, there is increasing evidence that rhythmic or repetitive behavior coordinates the limbic discharges (that is, affective states) of a group of conspecifics. It can generate a level of arousal that is both pleasurable and reasonably uniform among the individuals so that necessary group action is facilitated. We must note at this point that we have said nothing about the communicative aspect of this rhythmic signaling as separate from the affective responses. There is a body of evidence that many of these rhythmic stimuli serve as nonaffective communication as well. The position of most ethologists is that rhythmicity evolved in lower animal species is in the service of communication. However, many ethologists maintain that rhythmicity evolved an autonomous effect of its own separate from its signaling function. Thus Lorenz (1966) states:

Both instinctive and cultural rituals [together termed "formalized behavior" by Smith in chapter 2] become independent motivations of behavior by creating new ends or goals towards which the organisms strive for their own sake. It is in their character of independent motivating factors that rituals transcend their original function of communication and become able to perform their equally important secondary tasks of controlling aggression and of forming a bond between certain individuals (1966:72).

It is by no means certain that rhythmicity evolved first in the service of signaling and only secondarily developed its function of affective arousal. One may just as well maintain that the affective arousal is primary and that signaling became grafted onto the already present rhythmicity, using those very patterns of rhythmicity as signals. Whether signaling or affective arousal was first in the evolutionary sequence, however, is relatively unimportant. What is important is that we can distinguish two aspects of ritual behavior, one involving affective arousal as a result of rhythmic stimuli, and the other involving nonaffective communication using patterns of rhythmic stimuli, although both elements in fact seem inextricably woven together.

What we are suggesting in this chapter, on the basis of the behavioral observations of ethologists, is that the rhythmic quality in and of itself produces positive limbic discharges resulting in decreased distancing and increased social cohesion. Even at the level of birds the communication quality of the signaling can be regarded as added to the effect of the rhythmicity on the nervous systems of the animals involved. Certainly in man the communicative quality of many aspects of ritual becomes very important and can enhance, or on occasion suppress, the immediate neural effect of the rhythmic or periodic stimuli. Similarly, in man, the cognitive, as opposed to the simply perceptual aspects of ritual behavior become extremely important. But the basic and relatively simple effect of ritual, that is, limbic coordination among conspecifics, is just as present in human ritual behavior as it is among other animals.

In higher organisms that require experiential input from their social environment for the adaptive potential of ritual behavior to reach fruition, ritual performed by adult members of the group has the secondary effect of socializing the young. A consideration of the adaptive significance of ritual becomes more complicated in this case, for the problem of obtaining social cohesion as an adaptive response arises anew with each generation. The process of socialization requires both passive and active participation by the young. The young may passively perceive innumerable occurrences of a repetitive ritual during which they learn to associate

(1) the set of stimuli requiring or initiating the ritual, (2) the precise sequencing of behavioral events comprising the ritual, (3) affective states linked to the ritual behavior, (4) significant perceptual entities emphasized through the orientation of ritual participants, and (5) corporate group action concurrent with, or subsequent to, the ritual. In higher organisms, and especially among the primates, the young may enact the ritual during peer group play and thus further concretize the neural associations on which adequate functioning of the adult ritual depends.

Thus far, we have presented a partial review and integration of much of the material of the last three chapters. We have presented the final common denominator of ritual behavior based on the exigencies of survival and crossing species lines. Let us now consider the problem of religious ritual in man. To do so we have to leave the theme that we have been considering up to this point to consider the aspects of ritual that appear to be unique to human religious action. We shall, however, return to the common biological theme toward the end of this chaapter.

Human Religious Ritual

The facet of religious ceremonial ritual that appears to be distinctly human is its seemingly inevitable association with myth. That is, religious ritual is always embedded in a cognitive matrix—a web of meaning, in Geertz's (1973) terms—that allows members of the society to interpret the conceptual significance of certain behavior. As numerous structural theorists have pointed out (Levi-Strauss, 1963b; 1964; Maranda, 1973; Maranda and Maranda, 1971), mythic structure presents a problem that requires solution. In this regard it is the function of myth to supply a solution to the problem raised at the conceptual level and the function of concomitant ritual to supply a solution at the level of action. Man, who is at the mercy of certain forces of nature, must elaborate a cognitive structure that provides an explanation of those forces, the reasons why they affect him, and, most importantly, the means by which they may be controlled. An explanation generally takes the form of an elaborate story having the universal characteristics of employing powers, demons, personified forces, gods, or a supreme god as an integral element. The precise form the personalized power may take is limited only by the creative imagination of man. Elsewhere (d'Aquili, 1972; Laughlin and d'Aquili, 1974; see also chapter 1) we have suggested that man has a drive (termed the "cognitive imperative") to organize unexplained external stimuli into some coherent cognitive matrix. This matrix generally takes the form of a myth in nonindustrial societies and a blend of science and myth in western industrial societies.

The solution at the level of action posed by a myth may (and usually does) require the ritual unification of the group, or a priestly representative of the group, with a personified being in such a fashion that the society gains some measure of control over the forces controlled by the being. All of this has been clearly delineated by Levi-Strauss (1963a, b; 1964), among others. Thus, for example, the concepts of a Christ figure or a solar hero represent cognitive solutions to problems posed by the myths within which they are embedded as structural elements. Orthodox structuralists have, however, tended to deemphasize the role of ritual in organism-environment equilibration in favor of a stress on the analysis of the internal dialectics of mythic structure. There is, of course, much evidence supporting the contention that antinomies differentiated by myth are also in part resolved by myth. However, as Levi-Strauss admits:

And since the purpose of the myth is to provide a logical mode capable of overcoming a contradiction (an impossible achievement if, as it happens, the contradiction is real), a theoretically infinite number of states will be generated, each one slightly different from the other. Thus, myth grows spiral-wise until the intellectual impulse which has produced it is exhausted. Its *growth* is a continuous process, whereas its *structure* remains discontinuous (1963a:226).

We can see that, considering the mythic process alone, complete psychological satisfaction of the inherent problem is never forthcoming. The process continues as long as the "intellectual impulse" remains unexhausted. Our contention is that total psychological resolution of the ambiguity contained in myth is never achieved within the confines of the structure of the myth per se, but rather by the articulation of the mythic structure with a mechanism specifically affecting limbic and autonomic functions. In other words the process of resolution requires some mechanism extraneous to the myth but intimately united with mythic expression through action. The mechanism must be capable of facilitating and sustaining a psychologically fulfilling resolution to problematic antinomies, thus providing active reinforcement of the mythic structure itself.

We contend that the only resolutions that are psychologically powerful to both individuals and groups are those that have an aspect of existential reality. We show in this chapter that such a powerfully affective resolution arises primarily from ritual or meditation and rarely, if ever, from a cognitive unification of antinomies alone. The *ultimate* union of opposites that is the aim of all human religious ritual is the union of contingent and vulnerable man with a powerful, possibly omnipotent force. In other words we propose that man and a personified power or powers represent the ultimate poles of much mythic structure and that polarity is the basic problem that myth and ritual must solve. Side by side with this basic antinomy are usually other correlative antinomies that frequently must be resolved according to the specific myth before the basic god/man antinomy can be resolved. Such polar opposites include heaven/hell, sky/earth/good/bad, left/right, strong/weak, as well as an almost endless series of other polarities that recur in human myths.

Since we have stated a hypothesis that bases human religious ritual, in part, at least, on the evolution of the CNS, and since the structure of human religious ritual behavior arises directly out of its mythic structure, we must try to explain how man formulates myth.

The capacity to mythologize involves at least three critical higher cortical functions: conceptualization, abstract causal thinking, and antinomous thinking. First, all myths are couched in terms of named categories of objects that we call concepts or ideas. Second, all myths, like all other rational thoughts, involve causal sequences. Third, myths involve the orientation of the uni-

162

verse into multiple dyads of polar opposites. This latter characteristic is also present in everyday thought but is more markedly obvious in mythic structures. Indeed, it is this quality of human
thought that has entranced psychologists and anthropologists
from Jung to Levi-Strauss to such a degree that other aspects of
myth structuring have often been neglected.

At the risk of appearing overly simplistic, we note that all
three of these higher cortical functions involve, in one way or
another, a specific area of the brain. This area in man is composed of the supramarginal and angular gyri, as well as of certain
adjacent areas. It can best be visualized as the area of overlap
between the somesthetic, visual, and auditory association areas. It
is, so to speak, an association area of association areas. It allows
for direct transfer across sensory modalities without involvement
of the limbic or affective system. It is as if three computer systems,
one for each of the three major sensory modalities mentioned,
were hooked into each other and the information from each became available to all. Such a system allows classes of objects to
be set up that are vastly more inclusive than any classifying system possible within each individual sensory modality.

Ever since Goldstein's work in the 1940s it has been felt that
the brain area we have described was intrinsically involved in
conceptualization. After a period of research neglect, this position
became powerfully supported by the evidence of Geschwind in
his new classic monograph "Disconnection Syndromes in Animals
and Man" (1965). Geschwind refers to this general area of the
brain as the *inferior parietal lobule* (see chapter 1). Soviet researchers refer to roughly the same area as simply the parieto-occipital area, and Luria (1966) notes that it is intimately involved in
the formulation of basic logical grammatical categories. Luria and
others have shown that destruction of parts of this area of the brain
inhibits the use of the comparative degree of adjectives. One object, for example, cannot be set off against another object in comparison. Such statements as "larger than," "smaller than," or "better than" become impossible for patients with lesions in portions
of this area. Furthermore, such patients are not able to name the
opposite of any word presented to them.

Although not conclusive, such evidence indicates that the inferior parietal lobule not only may underlie conceptualization but also may be responsible for man's proclivity for abstract antinomous thinking. Of course, a devastating lesion that destroys most or all of this area not only wipes out antinomous thinking but also drastically interferes with concept formation. The intellectual sequelae of such a lesion are profound. Furthermore, there is increasing evidence that the reciprocal connections between the anterior convexity of the frontal lobe on the dominant side and the inferior parietal lobule are intimately related to abstract causal thinking (Luria, 1966). Indeed Basso, De Renzi, Faglioni, Scotti, and Spinnler (1973) have presented impressive neurophysiological evidence for the existence of cerebral areas critical to the performance of "intelligence tasks." After reviewing the pertinent literature, as well as their findings, they conclude that:

. . . there is one region of the brain, overlapping the language area, which plays a major role in several different intellectual tasks, independent of their specific features. This might mean that several intellectual abilities are focally organized in this area, or more likely, that the area subserves a superordinate ability entering into every intelligent performance and identifiable with the factor designated as "g" by psychologists.

We propose that this area comprises the inferior parietal lobule, the anterior convexity of the frontal lobes, and their reciprocal interconnections. It has long been known that the anterior portions of the frontal lobes, particularly on the dominant side, are involved in ordering not only sequential movement but also perceptual and cognitive elements in both space and time. Lesions of the anterior convexity of the frontal lobe or its connection with the inferior parietal lobule interfere drastically with causal thinking. The implications of the work of W. Grey Walter (1973) on the relationship of the Contingent Negative Variation (CNV) to anticipated causal behavior involving abstract causal sequencing tends to confirm the importance of the frontal lobes to the process of abstract causal thinking. Furthermore, the research of Livanov, Gavrilova, and Aslanov (1973) on correlation of biopotentials of the frontal cortex with mental activity involving causal sequencing further supports the position that the areas of the frontal lobes, particularly the anterior frontal convexity, are intimately related to processing information in terms of what we have called abstract causality. Furthermore, more recent work by Luria (1973) and Pribram (1973) not only adds evidence of the importance of the frontal regions in performing abstract causal operations but also seems to involve them in the modification and maintenance of the cognitive structures that govern the interrelationship of the human organism with its environment.

It is impossible in this presentation to trace the evolution of conceptualization, language, causal thinking, and antinomous thinking. We have done this elsewhere (Laughlin and d'Aquili, 1974). We are aware that such a brief presentation opens one to the charge of being a naive localizer of cerebral functioning. We are also fully aware of the problems of attempting specific and exact localization of higher cortical functions. Nevertheless, it appears to be true that, phylogenetically, with the evolution of the inferior parietal lobule, the anterior convexity of the frontal lobes, and their reciprocal interconnections, man as "culture bearer" began to develop. It is interesting that, ontogenetically, these areas of the brain are the last to myelinate, and their myelination corresponds to the development of Piaget's formal operations and the perfection of linguistic ability. We are not claiming that these areas are the sole explanation for spoken language. Other areas of the brain needed to evolve as well, in order for spoken language to develop. But these areas (anterior convexity of the frontal lobe, the inferior parietal lobule and their interconnections) appear to be involved in the critical elements of mythologizing, that is, conceptualization, abstract causal thinking, and abstract antinomous thinking.

As LeGros Clark (1963) and others have pointed out, the posterior and inferior areas of the parietal lobe are much enlarged in the endocasts of *Australopithecus* over homologous areas of the nonhominid primate brain. This expansion took place at the expense of the occipital cortex, causing the latter to curve medially inward. This area of the australopithecine endocranial casts appears to represent the evolution of what we are calling the inferior parietal lobule in *Homo sapiens.* It is true that this structure is present in rudimentary form in the chimpanzee, and it is undoubtedly this structure that is responsible for the cross-modal transfer underlying the chimpanzee's now proved ability to develop a nonverbal language. With the development of the australopithecine grade, this area of the brain became sufficiently developed to appear grossly on endocranial casts. But the inferior parietal lobule did not reach its modern level of gross morphologic development until the advent of the genus *Homo.* Nevertheless, it is clearly discernible in *Australopithecus.*

This finding, coupled with the fact that the anterior convexity of the frontal lobes had evolved to essentially modern proportions relative to brain/body ratio in *Australopithecus,* makes it reasonable to infer that man's australopithecine ancestor was probably capable of rudimentary spontaneous conceptual thinking and abstract causal thinking, in spite of his relatively small cranial capacity (see chapter 3). Furthermore, if we are to believe Luria's (1966) findings concerning the antinomous function of this area of the brain, *Australopithecus* was probably ordering his world in rudimentary conceptual opposites. Not only are the conceptual-causal faculties essential for mythmaking and attendent ritual behavior, but also, as we have pointed out elsewhere (Laughlin and d'Aquili, 1974), they are the minimal requirements for the development of "culture." In spite of the small brain of *Australopithecus,* one should not be surprised to find primitive stone implements associated with him, since he apparently had the requisite neural organization for abstract problem solving and toolmaking, no matter what the size of his brain.

The question arises whether it is probable that *Australopithecus* developed myth and religious ritual. In theory, at least, the minimal neural requirements were present for these behaviors. It is conceivable that a mythic structure could be developed in terms of abstract symbols rather than verbal language (see chapter 3). We feel, however, that it is unlikely that any elaborated myths developed in the absence of spoken language. We feel that it is improbable that the australopithecines possessed speech, even though they were capable of a certain degree of abstract thought. We base this contention on the findings of the endocranial casts. *Australopithecus* shows minimal development of the inferior frontal convolution, where Broca's area would be located in the genus *Homo,* as well as minimal development of the middle temporal convolution, where Wenicke's area is located in *Homo.* In our view this makes it very improbable that the australopithecines possessed anything like fluent verbal language. Although myth structure and ritual are theoretically not completely dependent on verbal language, language is sufficiently important in the development and elaboration of myths for us to regard it as unlikely that the australopithecines either elaborated myths or practiced elaborate religious ritual.

With the advent of the genus *Homo,* however, the story becomes quite different. *Homo erectus* shows considerable elaboration of the inferior frontal convolution and middle temporal convolutions, as well as further development of the inferior parietal lobule. While we consider it improbable that *Australopithecus* was a complex mythmaker and religious ritual practitioner, we think it probable that *Homo erectus* was both. We do not wish at this time to be drawn into the controversy over the recent Leakey finds from East Rudolf. If, indeed, the East Rudolf skull represents the genus *Homo,* then we simply push the cognitive, mythic, and ritual functions back from about 750,000 years ago to perhaps 2.5 million years ago or more. In any case we doubt that many physical anthropologists would disagree that, even if *Homo* were present on the earth 2 million years ago, he nevertheless had probably evolved from an australopithecine-like creature. The latter australopithecine types and *Homo* probably evolved from a common early australopithecine ancestor. Whenever it occurred, with the advent of the genus *Homo,* we get our first approximation of what we would probably recognize as human intellectual functioning, including both speech and the various abstract thinking faculties discussed previously.

At this point we must return briefly to a topic we mentioned in passing earlier—that is, what we call the "cognitive imperative." The abstract problem solving that the evolution of these neural structures made possible aided man's adaptation to any environment. It permitted him to look for the causes of the phenomena that were occurring around him and to attempt to control them. Such problem-solving ability enhanced human adaptation from the arctic region to the tropical belt. It is not surprising, therefore, that, once these neural systems evolved, they rapidly spread over the globe. In this chapter it is not possible to trace in detail the evolution of each of these neural mechanisms and the probable original selective pressures on them. Suffice it to say that in the aggregate these neural systems represent man's highest and most universal adaptive capability.

Their importance for survival is demonstrated by man's almost instinctive need to organize unknown or unexplained stimuli into some sort of cognitive framework. Work by Adler (1973), Harvey, Hunt, and Schroder (1961), and others, as well as our own work involving people's responses to the Philadelphia earthquake several years ago (accompanied by numerous other studies by cognitive psychologists), all support the hypothesis that man automatically, almost reflexly, confronts an unknown stimulus by the question "What is it?" Affective responses such as fear, happiness, or sadness and motor responses are clearly secondary to the immediate cognitive response (see chapters 1 and 6). This appears to be true whether a person has normal intellectual functioning, is grossly psychotic, or has minimal to moderate brain damage. In all cases the immediate attempt of the human organism in the face of an unknown stimulus is the attempt to organize it within a known framework. It is this universal adaptive drive, related to abstract problem solving, that we have called the cognitive imperative. Such cognitive organization of external stimuli into a linear, causal, verbal mode of consciousness is an effect of the neural mechanisms whose evolution we have just described, all operating primarily within the dominant hemisphere of the brain. It is this linear analytic and verbal form of cognition that precisely constitutes man's most efficient form of adaptation to certain environments.

That there is a drive for organizing data in this distinctively human manner, together with an affective reward, is supported by the experiments of Terziaix and Cecotto (1959; 1960), Rosadini and Rossi (1961), Alema and Rosadini (1964), and Hommes and Panhysen (1971). In summary these workers have demonstrated, among other things, that an intracarotid injection of sodium amytal on the dominant side of the brain, which interferes with the verbal and analytic functions that we have been discussing, and which prevents the organization of percepts into an analytical and verbal mode, results in a dramatic reaction that includes a sense of guilt and unworthiness, worries about the future, and a sense of loss of mastery over the environment. In a word such a chemical inhibition of the functions of the dominant hemisphere (analytic functioning) results in depression. On the other hand, injection of sodium amytal into the carotid artery on the nondominant side, in effect, releases the dominant analytic side from certain inhibiting influences and yields a state of very clear euphoria.

In the face of such evidence it is hard to deny the biological importance of ordering sensory data within an analytic framework. It is not hyperbole to speak of the need for order as a cognitive imperative. The point of all this is that man is driven to understand the world around him. He cannot do otherwise. He has no choice in the matter whatsoever. All the higher cognitive functions that we have described necessarily operate on incoming data—that is, percepts are categorized, organized, and modified into concepts, and concepts and percepts are both organized in causal chains and arranged in terms of antinomies or polar dyads. Strips of reality that can be understood within the bounds of given data are so understood and a model of reality is so constructed. If, however, the data available do not explain any unusual phenomenon, the machinery of the brain is not turned off. It still automatically constructs models of reality out of juxtaposed material drawn from the various sensory memory banks. It is here that Western science differs from myth formation. Ideally, Western science imposes a limitation on the functioning of the gnostic machinery of the brain and thus refuses to include in a model of reality elements that are not derived from observed data or that are not immediately inferable from such data.

At this point we should return to man's ability to think in terms of abstract causality. We have already discussed the relationship of the anterior convexity of the frontal lobe to the inferior parietal lobule in terms of the ability to juxtapose concepts in linear sequences. For convenience we refer to the anterior convexity of the frontal lobe, the inferior parietal lobule, and their reciprocal interconnections as the *causal operator*. The causal operator treats any given strip of reality in the same way that a mathematical operator functions. It organizes that strip of reality into what is subjectively perceived as causal sequences, back to the initial terminus of that strip or forward toward some desired final terminus. In view of the apparently universal human trait, under ordinary circumstances, of positing causes for any given strip of reality, we postulate that, if the initial terminus is not given by sense data, then the causal operator grinds out an initial terminus automatically.

Here again, we may note how Western science may differ from the more usual form of human cognizing. Science ideally refuses to postulate an initial terminus or first cause of any strip of reality unless it is observed or can be immediately inferred from observation. Under more usual conditions the causal operator grinds out the initial terminus or first cause of any strip of reality. This is a mental construct drawn from elements encoded in memory and characterized by the operator's nature itself. That is, the construct causes or in some sense has the power to generate the strip of reality. What we are implying is that gods, powers, spirits, personified forces, or any other causative ingredients are automatically generated by the causal operator. Note that in speaking of Western science *we have not been speaking of Western scientists*. The restrictions imposed on human thought are social and contractual in Western science. However, the brain of the scientist functions no differently from anyone else's brain. Although the scientist may reject the idea of gods, spirits, demons, or any other type of personified power, he nevertheless experiences them in his dreams and fantasy life. Any practicing psychiatrist or clinical psychologist can point to these phenomena in the fantasy life of the most rational man. The causal operator simply operates spontaneously on reality, positing an initial causal terminus when none is given. When the strip of reality to be analyzed is the totality of the universe, then the initial terminus or first cause that is automatically produced by the causal operator is Aristotle's First Mover Unmoved.

If the foregoing analysis is correct, then human beings have no choice but to construct myths to explain their world. The mythic materials may be social, or they may appear individually in dreams, daydreams, or fantasies. Nevertheless, so long as human beings ponder their existence in what often appears to be a capricious universe, then they must construct myths to orient themselves within that universe. This is inherent in the obligatory functioning of the neural structures considered earlier. Since it is highly unlikely that man will ever know the first cause of every strip of reality observed, it is highly probable that man will always create gods, powers, demons, or other entities as first causes to explain what he observes. Indeed, man cannot do otherwise. Myths are structured either socially or individually, according to the analytic and verbal mode of consciousness of the dominant hemisphere. Myths entail the codification of unexplained reality in terms of antinomies and of causal explanatory sequences.

The development of these higher cortical functions may be regarded as a major adaptive advance, insofar as they allow man abstract problem solving, an advantage in virtually any environment. They can, however, also be regarded as a curse. Because man can think abstractly and causally, he can transcend the world of his immediate perceptual field (see the "cognitive extension of prehension" in Laughlin and d'Aquili, 1974). From experience he can postulate probable events under given circumstances. Most of all, these functions make him acutely aware of his own mortality and of the contingency of his existence in an unpredictable world (Becker, 1973). This is the basis of the existential anxiety that all men bear. It is to relieve this "curse of cognition," this existential anxiety, that man first seeks mastery over his environment by attempting to understand it (see "zone of uncertainty" in chapter 1). He organizes reality into a cognitive framework. Often the organization is by means of a myth. But in and of itself, this organization of reality into mythic structures does not give man genuine control over the overwhelming forces of nature that confront him.

Satisfying the cognitive imperative, although necessary, is not sufficient. Since man ultimately attempts mastery of his environment by motor action, he tries to achieve mastery over disease, famine, and death by some form of motor activity as well. It is thus that religious ritual (i.e., mythically based, conceptualized ritual) necessarily arises out of the structuring of a myth. It can be argued that religious ritual is, in practice, no more effective in overcoming the grim forces of man's existential condition than cognitive organization is. To explain the persistence of religious ritual, Skinner and other behaviorists have proposed a model based on irregular scheduling of rewards. For example, if a ritual is performed often enough, a famine may be relieved in the natural course of events and the ritual is given the credit for it. It is certainly known from animal experimentation, as well as from observation of human behavior, that chance rewards may often sustain a behavior that is causally linked to the reward only in the cognized environment (E_c) of the subject. But religious ritual has persistence and intensity that seem to transcend the Skinnerian model. What really appears to maintain the force and persistence of religious ritual is the ineffable experience, the intense positive affect experienced by a participant, associated with the resolution of a crucial antinomy, usually the resolution of the god/man antinomy. How elements that are intrinsically opposite can at the same time be merged, and how this experience is joined with an ineffable affective experience, we now attempt to delineate.

Religious Ritual and Cerebral Assymetry

Over the last eight years or so the work of Sperry et al. (1969), Nebes and Sperry (1971), Gazzaniga (1970), Gazzaniga and Hillyard (1971), Bogen (1969), Levy-Agresti and Sperry (1968), and others has strongly pointed to what appears to be a rather startling situation in neuroanatomy and neurophysiology. Until these workers performed their experiments on split-brain animals and studied split-brain conditions in human beings, it had always been assumed that the higher cortical functions we have been considering, namely, language ability, conceptualization, abstract causal thinking, and certain basic logical processes such as abstract antinomous thinking were pretty much all that was important in terms of higher cortical functioning. It had been known since the middle of the nineteenth century that, for the most part, these functions are lateralized to one hemisphere of the brain called the "dominant" hemisphere.

One can understand the prejudices regarding the prominence of these functions. Since they underlie abstract problem solving, and, to a great extent, most of human "culture," they were considered of paramount importance. The nondominant or "minor" hemisphere was usually ignored and even relegated to the status of a vestigial organ. By severing the connections between the two hemispheres in animals—that is, by severing the corpus callosum, the anterior commissure, and the optic chiasm—these workers were able to demonstrate that both sides of the brain could be taught different tasks and could respond differently to the same stimuli under appropriate conditions. To speak anthropomorphically, it was as if these animals possessed two minds or two spheres of consciousness.

The studies in relation to man were much more dramatic. In studying individuals with the corpus callosum severed to prevent the spread of epilepsy, it soon became clear that such individuals also acted as if they had two minds or spheres of consciousness, each independent of the other. This had not been noted before, because tests of the nondominant or minor hemisphere were usually given in terms of verbal questions requiring verbal answers. Since such verbal ability is almost completely lateralized to the dominant hemisphere, it is impossible to get accurate information concerning the minor or nondominant hemisphere, because both sides of the brain function essentially independently in these patients. By designing tests that did not require verbal responses it became possible to study functions of the minor hemisphere in split-brain patients.

At the risk of oversimplifying the situation it appears that the dominant hemisphere, as has been known for many years, is responsible for analytic, causal, verbal thought, and probably for discrete perception. In other words the neural mechanisms we have been discussing function primarily, although not solely, within the dominant or major cerebral hemisphere. What is new is the discovery that the so-called minor hemisphere has extremely important nonverbal, nonanalytic functions. First of all, it is related to the perception of visual-spatial relationships. Over and above this, there is good evidence that the minor hemisphere perceives the world, not in terms of discrete entities, but in terms of gestalts or nondiscrete holistic perceptions. The perception of wholeness or unity controlled by this hemisphere is extremely important to this discussion. Furthermore, there is evidence that the minor hemisphere may be chiefly responsible for creative or artistic ability.

Levy (personal communication) and Trevarthen (1969) are obtaining evidence that in the normally functioning individual both hemispheres may operate in solving problems via a mechanism of reciprocal inhibition controlled at the brain stem level. Put simply, the world is approached by a rapid functional alternation of each hemisphere. One is, as it were, flashed on, then turned off; the second flashed on, then turned off; the first flashed on, and so forth, in rapid alternation. The rhythm of this process, and the predominance of one side or the other, may account for various cognitive styles, from the extremely analytic and scientific to the extremely artistic and synthetic.

There is some evidence (see chapter 4) that this duality of cerebral functioning may parallel the duality of autonomic functioning we considered in the first part of this chapter. Actually it is conceptually easier to integrate the two modes of consciousness into a more general duality of patterning within the CNS. Professor Lex has done this by using Hess's (1925) model of an energy-expending (or ergotropic) system and an energy-conserving (or trophotropic) system operating in a manner complementary to the human organism (see chapter 4). In this model the ergotropic system consists not only of the sympathetic nervous system, which governs arousal states and fight or flight responses, but also of any energy-expending process within the nervous system. Conversely, the trophotropic system includes not only the parasympathetic nervous system, which governs basic vegetative and homeostatic functions, but also any CNS process that maintains the baseline stability of the organism. Thus the ergotropic/trophotropic model represents an extension to the CNS of the autonomic nervous system's functioning. We are now presenting an extended model according to which the minor or nondominant hemisphere is identified with the trophotropic or baseline energy state system, and the dominant or major hemisphere that governs analytical verbal and causal thinking is identified with the ergotropic or energy-expending system.

Alteration in the tuning of these systems has been offered as an explanation for various altered states of consciousness by varying investigators, including Gellhorn (1967), Gellhorn and Kiely (1972; 1973), and Ornstein (1972; see also chapter 4). These investigators present evidence that, at maximal stimulation of either the trophotropic or ergotropic system, there is, as it were, a spillover into the opposite complementary system. It has been postulated that the rhythmic activity of ritual behavior supersaturates the ergotropic or energy-expending system to the point that the trophotropic system not only is simultaneously excited by a kind of spillover but also on rare occasions may be maximally stimulated, so that, briefly at least, both systems are intensely stimulated. The positive, ineffable affect that this state produces was alluded to in the first part of this chapter.

In man, we propose that, with the simultaneous stimulation of the lower aspects of both systems, their cerebral representations—that is, both hemispheres of the brain—may function simultaneously. This is manifested cognitively with the presentation of polar opposites by the analytic hemisphere (that is, the presentation of a problem to be solved in terms of the myth structure) and the *simultaneous* experience of their union via the excitation or stimulation of the minor hemisphere. This explains the often-reported experience of individuals solving paradoxical problems during certain states of meditation or during states induced by some ritual behavior. In one of the few experiments performed in any kind of a controlled manner on the experience of meditation, Deikman (1969) notes that one of the phenomena common to all subjects was what appeared to be simultaneity of conflicting perceptions during relatively advanced meditation states. He states:

> . . . the subjects' reports indicated that they experienced conflicting perception. For example, in the third session, subject B stated, about the vase, "it certainly filled my visual field" but a few minutes later stated "it didn't fill the field by any means." In the seventh session referring to the landscape he commented, ". . . a great deal of agitation . . . but it isn't agitating . . . it's . . . pleasurable." In general, subjects found it very difficult to describe their feelings and perceptions during the meditation periods—"it's very hard to put into words," was a frequent comment. This difficulty seems due in part to the difficulty in describing their experience without contractions (1969:209).

It appears that, during certain meditation and ritual states, logical paradoxes or the awareness of polar opposites as presented in myth appear simultaneously, both as antinomies and as unified wholes. This experience is coupled with the intensely affective "oceanic" experience that has been described during various meditation states, as well as during certain stages of ritual. During intense meditative experiences such as yogic ecstasy and the *unio mystica* of the Christian tradition, the experience of the union of opposites, or *conjunctio oppositorum,* is expanded to the experience of the total union of self and other or, as it is expressed in the Christian tradition, the union of the self with God.

We note what appears to be a different neurophysiological approach to essentially the same end state following meditation and ritual behavior. In both cases the end point appears to be the unusual physiological circumstance of simultaneous strong discharge of both the ergotropic and trophotropic systems, involving changes in the autonomic system and the onset of intense and unusual affective states, coupled with the sense of union of logical opposites, usually the self and a personified force or god. It appears that during meditation one begins by intensely stimulating the trophotropic system. There is a marked decrease of sensory input, the attempt to banish all thought and desire from the mind, and the attempt to maintain an almost total baseline homeostatis state with only enough intrusion of the ergotropic system to prevent sleep. The spillover in the case of meditation is from the trophotropic to the ergotropic side with the eventual result in strong discharges from both systems.

Ritual behavior apparently starts from the *opposite* system. Ritual is often performed to solve a problem that is presented via myth to the verbal analytic consciousness. The problem may be dichotomized as good and evil, life and death, or the disparity between god and man. The problem may be as simple as the disparity between man and a capricious rain god or as subtle as the disparity between man's existential contingent state and the state of an all-knowing, all-powerful, unchangeable "ground of being." In any case the problem is presented in the analytic mode, which involves ergotropic excitation. Like all other animals, man attempts to master the environmental situation by means of motor behavior. The motor behavior man chooses goes far back into his phylogenetic past. It usually takes the form of a repetitive motor, visual, or auditory driving stimulus, which strongly activates the erogtropic system. Even the cadence of words and chanting contributes to this repetitive quality. The slow rhythm of a religious procession or the fast beat of drums or rattles all serve to drive the ergotropic system. With prayers and chanting this system is often driven in two ways. The myth may be presented within the ritual prayer and thus excite by its meaning the *cognitive* ergotropic functions of the dominant hemisphere. The rhythm of the prayer or chant, by its very rhythmicity, drives the ergotropic system independent of the meaning of words. If the ritual works, the ergotropic system becomes, as it were, supersaturated and spills over into excitation of the trophotropic system, resulting in the same end state as meditation but from the opposite neural starting point.

The difference between meditation and ritual is that those who are adept at meditation are often able to maintain an ecstatic state for prolonged periods of time. The ecstatic state and sense of union produced by ritual are usually very brief (often lasting only a few seconds) and may often be described as no more than a shiver running down the back at a certain point. This experience may, however, be repeated at numerous focal points during the ritual. Furthermore, the ecstatic states produced by ritual, although they are usually extremely brief, seem to be available to many or most participants. The ecstatic states attained through meditation, although they may last for hours or even days, require long practice and intense discipline.

In any case this unusual physiological state resulting from both approaches produces other cognitive effects besides a sense of union of opposites. Numerous reports from religious traditions point to the fact that such states yield not only a feeling of union with a greater force or power but also an intense awareness that death is not to be feared, accompanied by a sense of harmony of the individual with the universe. This sense of universal harmony may be the human cognitive extrapolation from the more primitive sense of union with other conspecifics that ritual behavior excites in animals. In point of fact the feeling of union with conspecifics carries through to human ritual as well. Even if the feeling is elaborated on a higher cognitive level to become a feeling of harmony with the universe (and a lack of fear of death), most human religious rituals also produce an intense feeling of union with the other participants. This oneness has contributed to the feeling of "a holy people," " a people of God," "a people set apart."

Thus, we see that the phylogenetic origins of ritual carry through in an unbroken line to the most complex human religious ritual. However, on these primitive functions are grafted other adaptive functions—namely, those of higher cognition. In point of fact, man is not simply the sum of neural mechanisms independently evolved under various selective pressures. Rather, man functions physiologically as an integrated whole. Although his higher cognition may have evolved as a very practical adaptive problem-solving process, this cognition carries with it, indeed, requires, the formation of myths that orient the person toward certain problems, problems rendered soluble through ritual. When ritual works (and it by no means works all the time), it powerfully relieves man's existential anxiety and, at its most powerful, relieves him of the fear of death and places him in harmony with the universe. It is no wonder that a behavioral phenomenon so powerful has persisted throughout the ages. Indeed, it is likely to persist for some time to come.

To summarize this rather complex argument, we are simply stating that, given an organism in which the neural mechanisms for abstract thought have evolved, which require causal and antinomous thinking as a highly adaptive trait, that organism must necessarily use these mechanisms in an attempt to explain his existential situation. Such explanation involves the obligatory structuring of myths, complete with the organization of the world into antinomies and with the positing of initial causal termini of strips of observed reality that man calls gods, spirits, demons, and the like. These mechanisms are not a matter of choice but are necessarily generated by the structure of the brain in response to the cognitive imperative. Once the problem is presented in myth form, man, in common with all animals, attempts to solve it (i.e., to master the environment) via motor action. In the presence of a problem presented in myth, and with the inherited ancient ritual mechanisms still intact, ritual becomes the motor vehicle by which the problem is solved. Indeed, ritual behavior is one of the few mechanisms at man's disposal that can possibly solve the ultimate problems and paradoxes of human existence. Thus, although ritual behavior does not always "work," it has such a powerful effect when it does work that it is unlikely ever to pass out of existence within a social context, no matter what the degree of sophistication of society. Religious ritual behavior may take new forms within the context of highly developed Western technological societies. But whether in new form or in old, it is much too important to the psychological well-being of a society to lapse into oblivion.

This essentially ends what has necessarily been a rather sketchy outline of a theory of the evolution of religious ritual that takes into account the evolution of multiple, interrelated neural subsystems. We feel that we have presented a discussion that allows one to understand the evolution of the neural basis of human ceremonial ritual, as well as the *primary* pressures operating on the selection and maintenance of this behavior in human societies. It would be erroneous in the extreme to assume that this is the whole story or that the adaptive advantage of human ceremonial ritual presented in this chapter exhausts its adaptive potential. On the contrary, ceremonial ritual (religious or otherwise) possesses a number of highly adaptive qualities, which, under specific circumstances, may respond to selective pressure from the environment even more strongly than the primary evolutionary components we have been considering in this chapter. Specifically, we have not considered the relationship of ceremonial ritual either to the establishment of cognitive structures or to the institution and maintenance of social structures. Furthermore, we have not considered certain ancillary but very important aspects of human ritual in maintaining social well-being, such as the establishment and maintenance of ordered authority and the distribution of available resources in times of scarcity. The next four chapters devote themselves specifically to these topics. We would urge the reader to bear in mind, however, that, no matter how complex the function of ceremonial ritual in any given society, under a specific set of environmental circumstances it cannot be adequately or fully understood apart from the evolution and function of those neural structures underlying ritual behavior, many of which arose far back in man's phylogenetic past, and some of which are responsible for his becoming *Homo sapiens.*

References

Abraham, R. 1976. "Vibrations and the Realization of Form," in *Education and Consciousness: Human Systems in Transition* (E. Jantsch and C. H. Waddington, eds.). Reading: Addison-Wesley.

Adler, H. M. and V. B. O. Hammett. 1973a. "The Doctor Patient Relationship Revisited, and Analysis of the Placebo Effect," *Annals of Internal Medicine* 78:595.

—— 1973b. "Crisis Conversion and Cult Formation: An Examination of a Common Psychosocial Sequence," *American Journal of Psychiatry* 30:861.

Alema, G. and G. Rosadini. 1964. "Données cliniques et E.E.G. de l'introduction d-amytal sodium dans la circulation encéphalique, l'état de conscience." *Acat Neurochir* (Wien) 12:241–258.

d'Aquili, E. G. 1972. *The Biopsychological Determinants of Culture*. Reading, Pa.: Addison-Wesley Modular Publications.

Basso, A., P. De Renzi, L. Faglioni, G. Scotti, and H. Spinnler. 1973. "Neuropsychological Evidence for the Existence of Cerebral Area Critical to the Performance of Intelligence Tasks." *Brain* 96:715–728.

Becker, E. 1973. *The Denial of Death*. New York: Free Press.

Bogen, J. E. 1969. "The Other Side of the Brain, II: An Appositional Mind." *Bulletin of Los Angeles Neurological Society* 34:135–162.

Bourguignon, E. 1972. "Dreams and Altered States of Consciousness in Anthropological

Research,'' in *Psychological Anthropology*. 2d ed. (F. L. K. Hsu, ed.). Homewood, Ill.: Dorsey Press.

Chance, M. R. A. 1965. In *Primate Behavior* (E. DeVore, ed.). New York and London: Holt, Rinehart and Winston.

Deikman, A. J. 1969. ''Experimental Meditation,'' in *Altered States of Consciousness* (C. T. Tart, ed.). Garden City, N.Y.: Doubleday.

Gazzaniga, M. S. 1970. *The Bisected Brain*. New York: Appleton-Century-Crofts.

Gazzaniga, M. S. and S. A. Hillyard. 1971. ''Language and Speech Capacity of the Right Hemisphere.'' *Neuropsychologia* 9:273–280.

Geertz, C. 1973. *The Interpretation of Cultures*. New York: Basic Books.

Gellhorn, E. 1967. *Principles of Autonomic-Somatic Integration: Psysiological Basis and Psychological and Clinical Implications*. Minneapolis: University of Minnesota Press.

Gellhorn, E. and W. F. Kiely. 1972. ''Mystical States of Consciousness: Neurophysiological and Clinical Aspects.'' *Journal of Nervous and Mental Disease* 154:399–405.

Gellhorn, E. and W. F. Kiely. 1973. ''Autonomic Nervous System in Psychiatric Disorder,'' *Biological Psychiatry* (J. Mendels, ed.). New York: Wiley.

Geschwind, N. 1965. ''Disconnection Syndromes in Animals and Man.'' *Brain* 88:237–294; 585–644.

Harvey, O. J., D. E. Hunt, and H. M. Schroder. 1961. *Conceptual Systems and Personality Organization*. New York: John Wiley and Sons.

Hess, W. R. 1925. *On the Relationship Between Psychic and Vegetative Functions*. Zurich: Schwabe.

Hommes, O. R. and L. H. H. M. Panhuysen. 1971. ''Depression and Cerebral Dominance.'' *Psychiatric Neurological Neurochir*. 74:259–270.

Jay, P. 1965. ''The Common Langur of North India,'' in *Primate Behavior* (E. DeVore, ed.). New York and London: Holt, Rinehart and Winston.

Laughlin, C. and E. d'Aquili. 1974. *Biogenetic Structuralism*. New York: Columbia University Press.

LeGros Clark, C. W. E. 1963. *The Antecedents of Man*. New York: Harper and Row.

Lehrman, D. S. 1965. ''Interaction Between Internal and External Environments in the Regulation of the Reproductive Cycle of the Ring Dove,'' in *Sex and Behavior* (F. A. Beach, ed.). New York: John Wiley and Sons, Inc.

Lévi-Strauss, C. 1963a. *Structural Anthropology*. New York: Anchor Books.

—— 1963b. *The Savage Mind*. Chicago: University of Chicago Press.

—— 1964. *Mythologiques: Le Cru et Le Cuit*. Paris: Plon.

Levy-Agresti, J. and R. W. Sperry. 1968. ''Differential Perceptual Capacities in Major and Minor Hemispheres.'' *Proceedings of the National Academy of Science* 61:1151.

Livanov, M. N., N. A. Gavrilova, and A. S. Aslanov. 1973. ''Correlations of Biopotentials in the Frontal Parts of the Human Brain,'' in *Psychophysiology of the Frontal Lobes* (K. H. Pribram and A. R. Luria, eds.). New York: Academic Press.

Lorenz, K. 1966. *On Aggression*. New York: Bantam Books.

Luria, A. R. 1966. *Higher Cortical Functions in Man*. New York: Basic Books.

—— 1973. ''The Frontal Lobes and the Regulation of Behavior,'' in *Psychophysiology of the Frontal Lobes* (K. H. Pribram and A. R. Luria, eds.). New York: Academic Press.

Manley, G. H. 1960. Unpublished doctor's thesis on displays of the Blackheaded Gull. Oxford.

Maranda, P. 1973. *Mythology*. Baltimore: Penguin Books.

Maranda, P. and K. Maranda. 1971. *Structural Analysis of Oral Tradition*. Philadelphia: University of Pennsylvania Press.

Murdock, G. P. 1967. "Ethnographic Atlas: A Summary." *Ethnology* 6.

Nebes, R. D. and R. W. Sperry. 1971. "Hemispheric Deconnection Syndrome with Cerebral Birth Injury in the Dominant Arm Area." *Neuropsychologia* 9:247–259.

Ornstein, R. E. 1972. *The Psychology of Consciousness*. San Francisco: Freeman.

Pribram, K. H. 1973. "The Primate Frontal Cortex—Executive of the Brain," in *Psychophysiology of the Frontal Lobes* (K. H. Pribram and A. R. Luria, eds). New York: Academic Press.

Rosadini, G. and G. F. Rossi. 1961. "Richerche sugli effetti elettroencefalografici, neurologici e psychici della somministrazione intracarotidea di amytal sodico nell'uomo." *Acta Neurochir*. (Wien) 9:234.

Rosenblatt, J. S. 1965. "Effects of Experience on Sexual Behavior in Male Cats," in *Sex and Behavior*. (F. A. Beach, ed.). New York: Wiley.

Schein, M. W. and E. B. Hale. 1965. "Stimuli Eliciting Sexual Behavior," in *Sex and Behavior* (F. A. Beach, ed.). New York: Wiley.

Smith, W. J. n.d. Chapter II in *The Spectrum of Ritual: A Biogenetic Structural Analysis* (E. G. d'Aquili, C. Laughlin, J. McManus, G. R. Murphy, eds.).

Sperry, R. W., M. S. Gazzaniga, and J. E. Bogen. 1969. "Interhemispheric Relationships: the Neocortical Commissures; Syndromes of Hemisphere Disconnection," in *Handbook of Clinical Neurology* (P. J. Vinken and G. W. Bruyn, eds.). Vol. 4. Amsterdam: North Holland.

Terzian, H. and C. Cecotto. 1959. "Su un nuovo metodo per la determinazione e lo studio della dominanza emisferica." *G. Psichiat. Neuropat*. 87:889.

—— 1960. "Amytal intracarotideo per lo studio della dominanza emisferica." *Riv. Neurol*. 30:460.

Tinbergen, N. 1951. *The Study of Instinct*. London: Oxford University Press.

Tinbergen, N. 1965. "Some Recent Studies of the Evolution of Sexual Behavior," in *Sex and Behavior* (F. A. Beach, ed.). New York: Wiley.

Trevarthen, C. 1969. "Brain Bisymmetry and the Role of the Corpus Callosum in Behavior and Conscious Experience." Presented at the International Colloquium on Interhemispheric Relations. Czechoslovakia, June 10–13.

Walter, V. J. and W. G. Walter. 1949. "The Central Effects of Rhythmic Sensory Stimulation." *Electroencephalography and Clinical Neurophysiology* 1:57–85.

Walter, W. G. 1973. "Human Frontal Lobe Functions in Sensory-Motor Association," in *Psychophysiology of the Frontal Lobes* (K. H. Pribram and A. R. Luria, eds.). New York: Academic Press.

Whitehead, A. N. 1927. *Symbolism: Its Meaning and Effect*. New York: Macmillan.

Six

Ritual and Ontogenetic Development

John McManus

Cognitive processes seem to be at once and the same time the outcome of organic autoregulation, reflecting its essential mechanisms, and the most highly differentiated organs of this regulation at the core of interactions with the environment, so much so that, in the case of man, these processes are being extended into the universe itself.

Cognitive adaptation is an extension of general biological adaptation but that its proper function is to attain such adaptive forms as are unattainable on the organic level owing to their infinite power of assimilation and accommodation and to the stability of equilibrium between these two subfunctions.

Jean Piaget, *Biology and Knowledge*

This chapter relates the phenomenon of ritual to an emerging theoretical perspective in psychology—one embraced by biogenetic structural thought. This perspective, associated with the Swiss epistemologist Jean Piaget, centers on the question of ontogenesis and knowledge. The principal thesis of this chapter is that ritual can be understood in the same terms as the genesis and development of the human intellect. Indeed, as we have made clear in chapter 1, ritual cannot be understood apart from the question of cognition.

A great deal of attention has already been focused on the nature and evolution of ritual and on the function of ritual in establishing and maintaining social coordination. What is now required is a closer scrutiny of the processes of cognitive on-togenesis operating in socialization and providing the mechanisms by which the organism constructs its cognized environment through time. It would not be stretching the point in the least to view ritual as an adjunct to the cognitive system itself, one of a set of functional adjuncts that stand between productive adaptation and psychological disintegration of a social being. Just as the process of self-construction by the cognitive system allows man the capacity to comprehend reality—to make sense out of a "booming, buzzing confusion" (James, 1890)—the belief in and performance of ritual imposes an order for man that is at once both adaptively efficacious and phenomenologically satisfying. In sum, ritual may operate to complete the cycle of the cognitive imperative.

The capacity to act instrumentally upon the operational environment (E_o) is crucial to the affective state of the organism (see Beck, 1967; Pribram, 1971; Seligman, 1975; Weiss, 1972). But to act instrumentally, the organism must be able to construct an adaptively isomorphic cognized environment (E_c) out of a countless number of seemingly unrelated events and stimuli. Interruption of the cycle of self-construction of the E_c leads to stress in the organism (see chapters 7 and 9). It is argued here and in the next chapter that ritual provides a barrier to the disruption of the cognitive imperative cycle and is thus integral to the cognitive process. Let us now turn our attention to a more thorough understanding of this process.

The Ontogenesis of Human Thought

The genetic epistemology of Jean Piaget attempts to reconcile the dual nature of living systems, the seeming paradoxes implied in permanence and change, in conservation and transformation.[1]

---

1. Explication of Piagetian theory and research is an enormous task that can only briefly be schematized here. For more nearly complete treatments, the reader is referred to Furth (1969), Flavell (1963), Piaget (1951, 1954, 1970a, b, c, 1971, 1972, 1973), Piaget and Inhelder (1969), and Wolff (1963).

Genetic epistemology, empirically derived from observations of the ontogenetic development of intelligence in children, reflects Piaget's training as both biologist and philosopher. The principal thesis of Piagetian theory is that human knowledge is a construction rooted in the most basic biological functions, and out of which the structures of intelligence are constructed by man himself. This process of construction is an autoregulation function, isomorphic with the functions of all living organisms whose specific defining characteristic is that they regulate themselves through intrinsic operating principles.

This position differs from preformationism, which states that such structures are wired-in or instinctive, and form empiricism, which states that all that is in the mind is left there by environmental input. For Piaget intelligence and knowledge are constructed at the interface of organism and environment through the actions of the structured organism on the environment. The outcome of this interaction is the progressive self-construction of the operational structures of intelligence. These structures, in combination with instincts and experience, constitute man's three forms of knowledge (Piaget, 1970c, 1971). This knowledge, broader than commonly considered, includes knowing how to, as well as concepts and specific information.

Piaget sees two basic functional invariants as common to all living systems: organization and adaptation.[2] All life is internally organized and regulated and adapts to the environment in which it must exist. The adaptive function itself has two poles: *assimilation* and *accommodation*. Assimilation is the activity that uses the environment on the organism's terms, as when food is transformed[3] by the digestive system. Environmental input is trans-

2. Adaptation can be seen from a variety of perspectives (McManus, 1975), and here the Piagetian (1971) position is emphasized wherein adaptation may consist of biological survival or, at the psychological level, comprehension.

3. Piaget has implied a more sophisticated and complex definition of the concept of *transformation* than other structuralists have. He implies three classes of transformation, one of which is diachronic and two of which are synchronic. All three are intimately related to and influenced by the operation of the others. The three forms of transformation are: (1) *Developmental Transformation*. This refers to reorganizations of structures over time to newer and more complex organization. This is the most important type of transformation from the

formed or changed to fit the needs and structures of the organism. The opposite functional pole, accommodation, is that process through which the organism is modified to fit the specific characteristics of the environment. Organismic adaptation is the result of the assimilation-accommodation balance.

Morphological structures arise out of the activity of the invariant functions of organization and adaptation and come to constitute the organs of those functions. Progression is the transformation over time from a global, undifferentiated state to one of articulation, differentiation, and specialization. Finally, the specialized organs are interrelated into a total interacting, interdependent system. Such a system is called living when its functions and structures are internally regulated. In Piaget's words, "life is essentially autoregulation" (1971:26). It is autoregulation that not only gives a system its unique approbation of life but also allows it to equilibrate both internally and in its contact with the environment. Living systems also grow and develop. Equilibration is the diachronic equivalent of the notion of synchronic equilibrium—the former referring to the process, the latter to the state.

Piaget has, through application of the scientific method, addressed the problem of how man comes to know (Piaget, 1971, chapter 2). The problem revolves around the two-sided issue of man's similarity to and difference from other living things. Piaget maintains that such questions can be addressed productively through the genetic method, by watching how the development of knowledge and knowing takes place within a temporal framework. This, then, has been the study of the ontogenesis of knowledge and the structures or organs of knowing. Within Piaget's broad definition of epistemology it is the very nature of life to "know."[4]

The ontogenesis of the intellect has two principal facets; the

---

point of view of ontogenesis and is discussed at length. (2) *Surface Transformation*. This is the type most common to anthropologists and refers to the rearrangement of elements or content within a given level of structural organization. (3) *Sensory Transformation*. This refers to the effect exerted on sensory input by the internal organization of the structure.

4. Piagetian theory is a non-copy theory of knowledge wherein what are recorded in structures are the actions of the organism upon its environment and particularly the generalizable characteristics of those actions (Piaget, 1971).

functional invariants of organization and adaptation and the structures created out of these functions, which become the organs that perform the functions. Structures, unlike the functions themselves, develop in stages.[5] That is, structures in development proceed from relatively simple principles of organization through a *fixed sequence* of increasingly complex organizations (Piaget, 1970c; Inhelder and Piaget, 1958, 1969; Feldman et al. 1974). In this way the organism constructs a model of reality, one that we have termed the E_c and that is virtually identical for each human being in its formal characteristics, if not in its rate of development or its final stage of development (Piaget, 1971; Inhelder and Piaget, 1958; Langer, 1969). Each successive stage of cognitive organization is more flexible and stable than its preceding stage and allows the construing of reality in progressively more complex terms (Piaget, 1971). Complex structures allow the development of more sophisticated E_cs and increase the probability that the E_c approximates the E_o.

The earliest structures to develop in human children are formally equivalent to those in other mammals and consist of coordination between motor and sensory systems (Piaget, 1952, 1954, 1970, 1971). Subsequent structures beyond these initial ones seem peculiar to *Homo sapiens,* although evidence is accruing that suggests that some of the earlier *conceptual* structures may be applicable to the great apes (particularly chimpanzees), dolphins, and perhaps even canids (see Laughlin and McManus, chapter 3). It is important to stress here that what differentiates the human infant from simpler organisms is not its existing structure or capacity but its *potential* structural development.

What follows is a brief description of the process of ontogenesis as seen from the Piagetian perspective. Of necessity,

5. Stages are defined by two conditions. (1) They must be defined to guarantee a constant order of succession. (2) The definition must allow for progressive construction without entailing total performation (Piaget, 1970c:710). More clearly, these criteria are as follows: (1) each stage of functioning is a necessary result of the previous one and prepares the following one; (2) each stage must be defined by a unity of organization that characterizes conduct at the stage; (3) the organization of the functional structures at each stage integrates the preceding structures; and (4) the succession of the stages must be universal in order if not in rate of development (Langer, 1969:8; Piaget, 1971).

much is left out of this discussion, and the reader is referred to the original works of Piaget, and others, for complete elaboration.[6]

The Sensorimotor Period

Intelligence develops out of the coordination of the two functional poles of adaptation: assimilation and accommodation. Development consists of bringing these poles into equilibrium and thereby stabilizing the internal mechanisms of the organism—the organization function. The internal, organizational nature of the adaptive function is a causally cybernetic, interactive system. Equilibration is initiated from the intrinsic, biological activity of the organism itself and from the results of the action accommodated to the structures existing at the time. All stimuli in the external world are defined and given meaning in terms of their relationship to existing, internal structures. These structures are extremely elementary at birth, constrained biologically to motoric action. Only that stimulation motorically corresponding, at least in part, to the inherited motor structures (reflexes) exists for the infant. A partial match between stimulation and internal structures brings the other functional pole, accommodation, into play. Stimuli that are "recognized" through a partial match, but that are not directly assimilable, induce a self-imposed modification of the infant's structures, altering the internal organization. This in turn sensitizes the infant to a slightly wider range of possible stimulation.

The sensorimotor period lasts for the first eighteen months of life and can be divided into six substages. In the first stage, simple reflexes are exercised and begin to assimilate the first sensory data and to modify themselves to fit that data. The first habits develop in the second stage in terms of some consistency of re-

6. General theoretical material can be found in Furth (1969), Langer (1969), Piaget (1970a, b, c, 1971, 1973), Piaget and Inhelder (1969). Specific material on very early development can be found in Piaget (1929a, b, 1952), and Wolff (1963), on learning in Inhelder et al. (1974), on abstract thought in Inhelder and Piaget (1958), Piaget (1972). The subject of perception can be found in Piaget (1960), Piaget and Inhelder (1971). Memory and its relation to intelligence is discussed in Piaget and Inhelder (1973), and the development of representation and the syymbolic function in Piaget (1951). We now turn to the periods of development.

sponse to a narrow range of stimulation. The coordination between vision and prehension starts at stage three (about four and one-half months). In stage four, the first real signs of intentionality appear. The infant sets out to produce a result, independent of the means of execution. In the previous stage, result and means were fused together. Only existing motor schemes are used to reach ends, the invention of new means to an end appearing at stage five (about one year of age). Finally stage six, which closes the sensorimotor period, is characterized by internalization of schemes resulting in insight of a sort. This substage is the transition from a purely motoric intelligence to one characterized by comprehension.

What are encoded in the child's internal organization are not the characteristics of the objects he encounters, but the effects of his actions on those objects. The internalization of these action-object relationships, not reality, constitutes the mechanisms of adaptive intelligence. Reality, as encoded, is a transformation of the external data in terms of the existing organizational properties of the organism at the time of encounter. The internal system is further developed through a partial match between internal organization and external reality. Through the function of accommodation,[7] the internal organization is modified—stretched to include hitherto nonassimilable properties of objects. This functional interplay constructs the organs of thought and regulation over time. These organs or structures, begun with motor coordinations, increasingly expand throughout the sensorimotor period. It is only at the end of this period, with the appearance of the symbolic function, that truly human thought is initiated, built out of behavioral coordinations and freeing itself from some of the initial, biological constraints (see Piaget, 1951, 1952, 1954, 1970c, 1971, 1973; Piaget and Inhelder, 1969; Furth, 1969, 43ff; Langer, 1969; Wolff, 1963).

7. There are various types of assimilation in the Piagetian system, running from pure functional activity without modification to assimilatory activity, which differentiates the organism. Accommodation is often better seen as a subfunction of the overall assimilative function.

The Preoperational Period

The transition between the sensorimotor period and the next major period depends on the development of the capacity to represent a stimulus within the internal system. Until the end of the sensorimotor period, behavior is limited to reaction to stimuli that are physically present. Such behavior begins to change during the second year of life with the appearance of the semiotic function, which includes imagery and language, the mechanisms allowing the representation of objects not currently in the immediate perceptual field. This function can be observed in the appearance of five new phenomena: deferred imitation, symbolic play, drawing, mental images, and verbal evocation of events not currently happening (Piaget and Inhelder, 1969; Piaget, 1951).

The mode of transition between the sensorimotor period and the new preoperational period is thought to be imitation. This first occurs during the sensorimotor period in a representation of physical acts, which eventually become detached from specific contexts and form the basis for representation. Beginning with this mechanism, the constructions of the sensorimotor period are reconstructed during the years two to seven on the plane of perception and language. The internalization of imitation is thought to underlie the development of language and mental imagery. Imitation itself is a form of accommodation, wherein behaviors or emerging representations conform to characteristics of reality external to the child. Play, on the other hand, is a form of assimilation wherein "reality" is made to conform to the perspective of the child. Neither assimilation nor accommodation ever exists in pure form; they always appear together, albeit with the common emphasis of one much more than the other.

The general coordination of the two invariant functions at each progressive level increases the adaptability of the organism to the external world and also transforms the internal structure of the organism. During this process reality is progressively decentered from the phenomenological perspective of the child and constructed as a system separate and outside him. This happens first at the motor level, second at the level of representation. The reconstruction in the preoperational period (ages two to seven) is the representational equivalent of that done during stages one to three in the sensorimotor period. Early conceptualizations of practical physics (Piaget, 1930), number (Piaget, 1952a), time (Piaget, 1946), and space (Piaget, 1956) are constructed during this period, as are the elementary structures of language (Piaget, 1973). Through this process the initial constraints of biology are progressively broadened and loosened. An operational system linking elements of the new symbolic capacity into a coherent system is still lacking at this stage (see Piaget, 1951, 1954; Piaget and Inhelder, 1973).

Concrete Operational Thought

The term *operation* refers to actions that take place in thought. They are considered to be reversible transformations; that is, they are invertible in operation, as the effect of adding five to a number can be negated by subtracting five. Operations themselves allow flexibility in behavior in that mental actions can be substituted for actual motor action. Reversible operations enable the individual to try out things mentally, to "see" their effects and consider alternatives. Actions that are nonreversible do not permit flexible, "trying-out" strategies. It is in the two major operational periods of life that true thought, in its commonsense meaning, comes to fruition. Operations make possible the development of a true, integrated thought system.

The first such system, *concrete operational* thought, begins to appear after the age of seven years in European cultures but may appear later, depending on factors such as nutrition and environmental stimulation (Dasen, 1972, Piaget, 1972; Greenfield, 1966). It is characterized by two forms of reversible mental actions: inversion and reciprocity. The two faculties allow a flexibility not attainable in the preoperational period, where operations are nonreversible. The concrete operational period reconstructs at the representational level what was initially constructed during the last three substages of the sensorimotor period. During this stage, concepts of mass, weight, and volume develop in sequence, about two years apart, corresponding to developments at the motor level such as perception of object constancy. Concrete operations allow mental manipulation of the elements of reality but are bound to reality as it exists for the individual. Even fantasy and speculation involve the rearrangement of known entities. Language progresses to the use of comparisons such as "longer" or "greater" in contrast to preoperational language, which is restricted to the use of simple positions such as "long" or "big." Many adults appear to progress no further than concrete operations except perhaps in a very restricted range of experience (Piaget, 1972).

Formal Operational Thought

The last stage in the development of the formal properties of thought is called *formal operations* (Inhelder and Piaget, 1958). This is a fully flexible system of thought characterized by operations to the second power, or operations on operations. Propositional logic is now possible in the formally operational thought system, which is freed from the constraints of less developed systems. Where concrete operations are tied to subjectively existing reality, formal operations can deal with possibility. The real can be seen as a subset of the possible, owing to the appearance of two new reversible operations resulting from the coordinations of the previous two, reciprocity and inversion, into an overall system. The two new elements produced are the *inverse of the reciprocal* and the *identity operation.* This new, coordinated thought system makes possible operations upon operations or thinking about thought. When this level is attained, thought has burst many of the biological constraints imposed at earlier levels, although it still functions in terms of elaborated, biologically based laws. A formally operational thought system is considered to be both a deeper organization of the self and a more flexible, stable adaptive system oriented toward the outer world.

A number of points should be stressed in reference to this all too brief description of intellectual development.

First is the role of *repetition* in development, referred to as reproductive assimilation. The innate activity of the organism encompasses the functional repetition of elementary schemes, and through this process the schemes are both strengthened and extended as new objects are encountered (Piaget, 1971, 1973; Wolff, 1963). These schemes are the early manifestations of autoregulation. They are differentiated vis-à-vis external objects and begin to coordinate among themselves the process of reciprocal assimilation, which is similar to the concept of entrainment as used by Chapple (1970) and Lex (chapter 4). Coordinations of this sort continue through the functional exercise of structures up through each of the subsequent periods or stages on a representational and eventually conceptual level, forming systems at each level. The same "objective" reality is differently experienced and interpreted by each subsequent structural organization. Indeed, the definition of a proximal stimulus itself is redefined at each new level.

Secondly, this ontogenetic process is due to four factors: inheritance, physical experience, social experience, and autoregulation. The first three cannot explain development alone (Piaget, 1970b, 1971). Only the inclusion of the autoregulative principle of equilibration will account for this complex phenomenon. The interplay of the functions of assimilation and accommodation, tending toward equilibrium, becomes progressively coordinated during development. Each stage or period represents a nodal point of *relative* equilibrium that is subject to disequilibrium by intrusion of sensory data. As the organism attempts to reestablish equilibrium by assimilating and accommodating to new sensory data, it extends its own range and develops new sensitivities in the process. Formal operations or operations to the second power are the most stable equilibrium state yet identified. As each stage is attained, the subsequent stage becomes more probable, the predecessor being a logical necessity for the successor.

Thirdly, the sequence of stages in this development is fixed, but the age of attainment and the final stage are not (Feldman et al., 1974; Piaget, 1972). That is, the rate of development is variable, depending on the environment in which development occurs. An optimal cultural and physical environment is apparently necessary for the construction of formal operations. Since the rate of development is predictable but variable, a complete explanation cannot be found in inheritance or maturational theories of development (Piaget, 1971). The creation of novelty, and of structures that are enriched compared to data ascertainable from objects themselves, rules out the exclusive influence of the environment. Only construction through interaction of internal structures and the environmental surroundings by autoregulation is capable of explaining development, in concert with the other variables.

Fourthly, each stage of development is built out of and incorporates the structure immediately preceding and is, in its turn, incorporated by succeeding stages. The outcome is one of structures, reorganized and incorporated into developmentally more advanced structures—structures nested within structures. At each stage the biologically based functional invariants of organization and adaptation remain. At each level these functions utilize morphologically more complex structures as their functional organs—structures that increase in their range, flexibility, and stability and are progressively free of constraints extant at birth.

Finally, intelligence develops out of coordination of basic biological acitivity intrinsic to living organisms. Further, thought grows, not out of language, or even perception, but out of a coordination of actions (Furth, 1966; Piaget, 1971, 1973, chapter 6). This coordination is facilitated by perception and language, but these arise out of motor coordinates rather than the reverse. It is with this fact, as well as with the developmental implications of coordinating action schemes and concepts or operations developed out of them, that the link to ritual may be forged.

Ontogenesis and Structural Transformation

Armed now with both a biological definition of ritual and Piaget's biological conception of cognitive development, we may profitably turn to the question of the role of ritual in ontogenesis. It will help us toward that to note Chapple and Coon's (1942) description of ceremonial ritual as manifesting three distinct stages:

1). *Separation*—where individuals are separated from normal activities and interpersonal interactions.

2). *Transition*—where new behaviors and cognitions are learned.

3). *Incorporation*—where individuals are reintegrated with new interactions and roles.

Ritual, in this sense, amounts to an initial desynchronization of ongoing social relations, learning of new behaviors, and the integration of these individuals and behaviors into another interaction system. What Chapple and Coon have described at the level of interorganismic coordination has also been delineated by Piaget (1971:216) in intraorganismic coordination, by Charles Tart (1975) for transition from one state of consciousness to another, and by Weiss and others in embryology. The three stages may be generalized as follows:

1). *Discrimination*—through the action of assimilation in contact with the resistance of diversity.

2). *Differentiation*—through accommodatory activity such as imitation.

3. *Functional reintegration*—establishment of new structures, better equilibrated and more adaptable.

These three stages of structural transformation entail the following five steps:

1. Interruption of the ongoing functioning of a structure or intrusion into the operating system.

2. A comparison process between the intrusion and the structure currently operating.

3. Alternation in judgment and in behavior indicating an attempt to reconcile discrepancy.

4. A resolution of the system—intrusion discrepancy leading to stasis, synchronic transformation, or developmental transformation.

5. A consolidation phase (incorporation) whereby transformations are consolidated into the overall operating structures through repeated functioning in the new mode.

This five-step basic model of transformation is an abstraction modeled on the formal properties of psychological systems and their self-construction. Such systems are synonymous with structures that are semiclosed in respect to the environment; that is, they have permeable boundaries that act in exchange with the environment while maintaining their own identity. They are self-regulated, equilibrated by internal operations of the structures themselves (Piaget, 1971; Laughlin and McManus, 1975b). At this starting point they are in an active state of equilibrium (von Bertallanffy, 1968; Piaget, 1970c, 1971), which simply means that they actively compensate for actual or anticipated intrusions from the environment. Equilibrium is maintained through constant activity, that is, continual functioning of the structures in the state at which they have equilibrated. As such, their operation is generally outside the purview of consciousness (for exceptions see Laughlin and d'Aquili, 1974; Piaget, 1973; Inhelder and Piaget, 1958; Pribram, 1971), and only the results of their operation are generally open to awareness.

Structures operating in an equilibrated state are congruent with the criteria Piaget sets for stages of ontogenesis (Piaget, 1970c, 1973; Wolff, 1963; Furth, 1969; Langer, 1969). They are in a state of relative adaptation with their environment. For transformations to occur,[8] disadaptation in some form must occur in the attempted match between internal structure and its environment. This may be of two sorts: either a conflict between the content within a system and sensory input, leading to the possibility of synchronic transformation, or conflict between the respective structure and input, leading to potential diachronic transformations. It is to the latter transformation that we now turn our attention.

Maintenance of Structure
The two phases of the mechanism of assimilation by which structures are consolidated are *repetition* and *habituation*. It will be seen that assimilation is the principal element of conservation in cognitive development and in ritual. Repetitive (functional) assimilation strengthens the structure through self-generated exercise by controlling the process of sensory transformation that subordi-

8. Disadaptation occurs when encounter with the environment necessitates modification or new behavior on the part of the organism. It implies novelty in the environment.

nates input characteristics to the requirements of the operating structure. Strengthening of a structure involves relative closing of its boundaries to modification from the environment. In other words it amounts to the exertion of constraint upon the empirical modification cycle from within the organism similar to the effect of neurognosis (Laughlin and d'Aquili, 1974; Laughlin and Mc-Manus, 1975b).

In principle there should be an optimal range of such consolidation of a structure through functional repetition. That is, a structure that is insufficiently consolidated or closed to environmental input is too open to capricious modification due to fluctuation in the environment. It will overaccommodate to that variation and remain unstable. Similarly, structures can be excessively closed through overassimilation, insensitive to environmental variation, and hence place themselves at adaptive risk. Such extremes in functioning, particularly overassimilation, have been elsewhere proposed as the initial criteria for a definition of psychopathology (McManus, 1975; Harvey, Hunt, and Schroder, 1961).

From a systems viewpoint, organisms are said to be adapted when the operating structures cease to transform themselves diachronically, restricting transformations to those of a synchronic nature. In effect, ontogenesis has come to a halt. In such a state of relative equilibrium, active compensations for sensory intrusion continue to occur but in such a manner as to inhibit development toward greater structural complexity. This can be done by overassimilation, repetitive or habitual action that distorts input so as not to conflict with the E_c expectancies; by exposure to suboptimal environmental variation, preventing further differentiation of the structure; and by a neurognostically constrained ceiling on development (Laughlin and McManus, 1975a, b; and chapter 3 in this volume). Given relative constancy in the environment, such a state can be seen as adaptive in the more traditional sense if it continues to survive successfully in its ecological niche. Overassimilation per se tends, however, to minimize this possibility and decreases adaptive outcomes as shifts in the E_o become more probable (Laughlin and Brady, 1978; and Laughlin and Mc-Manus, 1975a).

Repetition, implicit in the notion of assimilation, as well as of ritual behavior, strengthens the structure and closes the empirical modification cycle (EMC) of the structure to environmental input that threatens the integrity of the structure as a whole. As mentioned earlier, structures constitute a discrete reality model, the E_c, and repetitive assimilation is the functional mechanism by which the borders are closed to intruders. When carried to extremes, it also keeps out friends who would facilitate development through optimal conflict with the structure's construing of reality.

The consolidation process as expressed in the concept of assimilation is an active one. Functional repetition is an activity on the part of the organism that is action and not re-action. Indeed, the definition of what has traditionally been called the stimulus is a consequence of the functioning of existing internal structure expressed in assimilative activity (Piaget, 1970c; Wolff, 1963). The concept is extendable to the notion of habituation itself, which had previously been perceived as a relatively passive adaptation to repetitive stimulation, principally physiological. This view is no longer supportable (Sokolov, 1963; Pribram, 1971), and current perspectives allow incorporation of the concept of habituation within the more generic phenomenon of assimilation.

Habituation to stimulus input allows the organism to sample selectively from that input stimulation relevant to its own survival or existing needs. If all stimuli were treated equally, determination of those relevant to survival would be exceedingly difficult. The nervous system operates to prevent this situation by placing limits on the amount of stimulation processed. Now these limits create the need to establish priorities among stimuli to be fed into the neural system. This is done by defining a proximal stimulus (Pribram, 1971), to which responses, internal or external, are directed. Other stimulation is placed under a system of control whereby it does not register until it changes (Powers, 1973; Pribram, 1971; Sokolov, 1963). A neural tonic ground appears to be created against which relevant stimulation or figure is attended to and evaluated. The creation of a ground of nonattended stimulation may come through the ability of the nervous system to model that stimulation both cortically and in centers lower in the nervous system (Pribram, 1971; Powers, 1973). These lower level control systems would appear to work on a system of anticipations (feed-forward) that matches expected sensory input to the internal neural model. As long as nothing changes, that is, input matches the model, the stimuli can be ignored while the organism attends to more important matters. Minimal changes in the stimulus configuration are potentially handled by control mechanisms lower in the nervous system that deal with that change before it intrudes into consciousness and thus maintain the adaptive focus of the organism. If change in the controlled or background stimulation overwhelms the lower level control systems, the stimuli intrude into awareness, attracting attention and initiating adaptive action.

It seems that thresholds are not created, but what is created is a neural model or expectancy for incoming stimulation. Sokolov noted that when any change occurs in a stimulus to which the organism has habituated, an array of physiological responses occurs with reference to that stimulus. That is, the nervous system has not habituated itself, but some control system, some model of the stimulus environment, has been confirmed or validated through repeated stimulation. Change in that stimulus refutes the model and the organism responds. This change can be a shift of intensity (less as well as more) or pattern of stimulation. The response to this change has come to be known as the orientation response.

Habituation is the consequence of a mechanism for consolidating input into the existing model or assimilation. This appears to occur through repetition—the repeated *action* of the receiving organism upon a repeatedly presented stimulus and assimilation into the structure. The locus of occurrence seems to be among the interneurons rather than in the input neurons of the system (Pribram, 1971). Repeated activation of the habituation process, repeated matching of the internal reality model, consolidates the incoming data into that model.

The effect of habituation is to create information redundancy, conceptual certainty, and a feeling of necessity. Redundancy and uncertainty are related concepts. Neurologically, redundancy refers to the number of neural fibers carrying the same sensory

199

input. A redundant situation is one in which a large number of fibers carry the same input, that is, redundant information. This is a situation of relative certainty. Reduction in redundancy means these same fibers carry a variety of information, and there is a reduction in certainty about the situation (more conflicting information). What changes here is not the amount of neural firing but the pattern. As Lindsley (1961) suggests, neural elements become *separated* functionally when redundancy is decreased, and this indicates a decrease in synchronization within that neural system and is reflected in EEG recordings. In general, habituation increases redundancy within a particular neural channel, creating greater certainty. In global terms, reality has a homogeneous, necessary quality about it. The consequence of this process is a removal or distancing of the stimulation from conscious awareness, a fading into the background. Its existence is assumed.

Dishabituation based on a mismatch between input and neural model constitutes the orientation reaction. This reaction desynchronizes the channel and increases uncertainty. Habituation itself frees the organism to ignore the repetitive stimulation and attend to deviance or novelty. New sensitivities to stimulation are thus created by habituation, and in biological servomechanisms this constitutes a developing spiral effect: stabilization through increased control and certainty, receptivity to alternative stimulation, and eventual habituation or adaptive action. This spiral effect is at least analogous to the ontogenetic course of cognitive development in human beings (Piaget, 1970c, 1971; Langer, 1969; Pribram, 1971; Seligman, 1975) and in nonhumans (Fox, 1974).

The stabilization aspect of this process is important for the understanding of both ontogenetic development and ritual, elaborated more thoroughly later in this chapter. At this point it is sufficient to say that continued habituation leads to a more stable, equilibrated model of the external world. It is against this stabilized model that the orientation reaction operates.

In sum, assimilation subsumes a number of phenomena having the effect of consolidation and coordination of the E_c with reference to the E_o. It includes the phenomenon of *repetitive action* and its cause within itself and constitutes means by which structures maintain their identity and continue to regulate behavior. The locus of regulation changes with the ontogenetic (and phylogenetic) status of the organism.

Structural Modification-Separation

The adapted, habituated, or consolidated action patterns (including the actions of thought) continue to operate, largely out of the bounds of awareness (Laughlin and d'Aquili, 1974; Laughlin and McManus, 1975b), until events initiate a state of disadaptation (Tart, 1975; Wolff, 1963; McManus, 1975). In this case the ongoing adaptive pattern is interrupted, knocked out of equilibrium, and the internal organization suffers a threat to its own coordination. Assimilatory activity vis-à-vis input is forced to modify itself to some degree by the characteristics of the material being assimilated. The response of the organism is equivalent to what is normally called the orientation response, in which realization of the inadequacy of the currently operating structures penetrates through habituated lower level systems (Powers, 1973) and often enters consciousness. This is the first step in the modification of a structure. The E_c, or a portion thereof, is disconfirmed, bringing the cognitive imperative into play and altering the operation of the empirical modification cycle.

What has happened in such cases is that the structure has become uncoordinated or dissonant in some sense; patterns of organization within the structure have become *separated* from each other. Such dissonance is functionally equivalent to the orientation response as already mentioned. When a deviation occurs in the stimulus situation or when novel stimulation occurs, the organism attends to that event—it orients toward it. This orientation response occurs in two phases: (1) *scanning* behavior or an attempt to identify the stimulus and (2) *registration,* which has visceral correlates. The latter leads back toward habituation, through confirmation of the stabilized model. Lack of confirmation maintains arousal of the neural system and brings attempts to control the new input—that is, to reduce uncertainty. These attempts at control may be expressed behaviorally through acting on the environ-

201

ment, or internally, by adjusting for reequilibration without overt action. Among these internal controls is action exerted by the cortical system on sensory systems. Such attempts to control effectively reduce redundancy or increase it. Controlling sensory processes to reduce redundancy opens the organism to other stimulation in the environment. Increasing redundancy in this fashion closes the organism to alternative input from the environment and focuses it on its own internal processes (Ornstein, 1974; Pribram, 1971).

Changes that elicit the orientation reaction can occur in two localities. The more obvious is a change in the E_o stimulus situation, but a less obvious source also exists. This is a change in E_c stimulus situation, which entails a change in the stimulus-defining mechanism or structure itself. A change in the internal organization of the organism can result in the redefinition of the stimulus by two possible routes. A superficial (content) change such as that acquired in the traditional view of learning can alter stimulus definition. Profound (structural) changes likewise lead to stimulus redefinition or creation through the development of new sensitivities vis-à-vis the operational environment.

Orientation, then, is the mirror image of habituation and the mechanism underlying change counterpointing the mechanism of conservation that makes it possible. The more habituated an act or behavior, the greater the sensitivity to variation (within a range). A preoperational child will see no alternative to his inflexible interpretation of reality. This is particularly true in the early, uncoordinated phase of this period. With increased consolidation of the preoperational structure (five to six years), the probability of attending to conflicting data increases. When this happens, the thought system that took approximately five years to develop and consolidate has begun to develop new sensitivities through those very coordinations and begins to lose organization again in its attempts to resolve the newly found uncertainty. A habituated, redundant, and certain stimulus situation becomes progressively redefined, generating uncertainty and, under optimal conditions, further development.

The modification of a structure is initiated by an orientation response of the internal structure or its subsystems, either through development of a sensitive period in the consolidation of the structure or by variation in the environment. Accommodatory activity on the part of the organism is the result of this event, and this is evidenced by conceptual and behavioral alternation. Elements of the internal organization have begun the process of separation.

Transition

We have just seen that structures are disrupted when there is a perceived conflict between the structural organization of the E_c (and its encoded content) and activity occurring outside that structure. Such disruption can occur for any operating structure up to and including abstract cognition. Conflict is system specified; that is, the incoming stimulation is partially defined in terms of the system itself and occurs within a specific range of mismatch with the internal model. The mismatch can be termed disadaptation (Wolff, 1963) and indicates an imbalance between the adaptive range of the structures and that condition in the E_o to which the organism is attempting to adapt. The orientation response occurs and disrupts the ongoing adaptive cycle. This has internal, physiological consequences often experienced as emotion.

Pribram (1971:212) suggests that affect (either emotion or motivation) "expresses the relationship between perception and action." The organism experiences motivation when action appears feasible in relation to the E_o; it experiences emotion when action does not appear feasible. The organism attempts to assimilate the novel or conflicting situation into its structure. A number of courses can be taken to reduce the attendant uncertainty: (1) the structure can move toward accommodation and resultant assimilation and thus modify the structure toward development; (2) constraint may be exercised over the activity of the EMC tending it toward overassimilation, in which case the process leads back toward habituation or distortion of sensory input (McManus, 1975), and no profound structural modification takes place; or (3) modifications of surface content, a synchronic transformation, may occur, leaving the properties of the basic structure intact (see the following chapter for a synchronic analysis).

203

Initiation of this process should be signaled by *alternation* in the operation of the structures, a vacillation between functioning at the original structural level and the emergence of functioning more characteristic of the next, most complex, developmental level (Harvey, Hunt, and Schroder, 1961; Inhelder, Sinclair, and Bovet, 1974).

Alternation

Alternation, as discussed here, deals with the coexistence of opposites within a temporal framework; that is, the opposites are sequential. It is comparable to the opposition of habituation and orientation just discussed and can exist at any level of phylogenetic or ontogenetic complexity. Each increasing level of development provides greater opportunity for complexity in alternation. The range of possibility provided by a sensorimotor structure is far more constrained than that provided by a structure that is formally operational. The former is limited to behavioral alternation, the latter constrained only by the scope of the conceptual apparatus. Sensorimotor systems do not ask the existential questions discussed by d'Aquili and Laughlin (chapter 5), but formal operation systems often do.

A sensorimotor system, well developed at stage three, has begun to habitutate to the question of how the hand can be coordinated with the eye. The coordination has begun to become automatic. The child now wants to "ask" how it can cause the rattle in its hand to make that noise again, or how it can once more bring a distant object within its grasp. Such a child frames these questions, not with concepts, but with sensorimotor schemes. Why is the question asked? Because the conflict earlier present in the relatively independent operation of hand and eye has been resolved by their coordination. Effective coordination essentially eliminates the question. By the very elimination of such questions, new questions arise. How *can* I make that noise again? How *can* I bring that candy closer?

Alternation may also be understood in terms of the functional invariants: assimilation and accommodation. Over the course of ontogenetic development in *Homo sapiens,* these functional invariants continue to obtain at each level of development. Their interplay constitutes the process of equilibration, the way in which the child organizes the internal structure and adapts to the external world. As development proceeds, these two adaptive poles come into finer, more regulated coordination. Within each major stage of development a course ranging from lability to stability is transversed (Piaget, 1951, 1971); that is, alternation between the two poles becomes less extreme and more coordinated. As this occurs, adequacy of adaptation increases. This can be observed in the alternation between play and imitation, the former constituting a prime example of assimilation, the latter of accommodation.

Early in each structural level, the two poles are extreme as reflected in behavior. In the preoperational period both play and imitation are marked. Symbolic play allows the child to assimilate reality to its own structures, as boxes become houses, ships, or mountains. Sticks become guns, spears, snakes, or whatever else is needed. Similarly, a child can exasperate parents with constant mimicry and imitation. But behavior at each pole occurs separately. Vast swings between the two poles can be seen, but they are not united. As development progresses, they are gradually brought together with the assimilation of reality to self and the accommodation of self to reality.

Resolution

Alternation in behavior marks structures in transition (Harvey et al., 1961; Inhelder, Sinclair, and Bovet, 1974). Transitional structures are characterized by internal conflict between different modes of functioning and perceiving. The locus of the conflict is often between the stage of development out of which the organism has begun to progress and the adjoining level toward which it is progressing (Harvey, et al., 1961). Within a given structure, conflict can appear among elements of content, resulting in fluctuations in behavior. This phenomenon has been extensively examined in the psychological laboratories (see: Festinger, 1964, 1957; Brehm and Cohen, 1962; Abelson et al., 1968; Feldman, 1965, among many others). Here we are primarily concerned with structural conflict, while this phenomenon is primarily an issue of synchronic modifications.

Structure is a major determinant in the definition of conflict.

Whatever the nature of the conflict, it demands some resolution. More abstract structures are known to possess the capacity to tolerate greater conflict than concrete structures (Schroder, Driver, and Streufert, 1967). This is adaptively significant in that it allows the preservation of conflict within the system long enough for resolutions of a complex sort to be worked out mentally. Simple structures demonstrate what is called "quick closure." This means that the cognitive imperative demands a quick and simple (but maladaptive) resolution to conflict and thus reduces threat to the internal organization. Resolution in development can have more than one consequence. It can facilitate, inhibit, or regress development, contingent upon environmental conditions.

To facilitate development, conflict must not be too threatening or too complex in terms of the existing structure. An environment optimally interesting and slightly more complex than the existing structure aids the developmental process (Turiel, 1966, 1968; Harvey, et al., 1961). Environments that threaten too much or are far too complex can drive a structure in transition backward to the originating structure. Cases whose resolution is relatively easy and obvious and that generate a satisfactory resolution in terms of the existing structure may arrest development between stages. This is characterized by double readings of the stimulus situation, in which no real resolution is accomplished, but rather the "resolution" maintains the conflict situation indefinitely. It must be stressed that development is ultimately influenced not by single discrete events, but by the overall pattern that obtains in the organism-environment relationships (Piaget, 1971; Harvey, et al., 1961).

When the environment presents too much redundancy, with insufficient variation to the individual, development begins to grind to a halt. Such variation can fail to occur in any stimulus domain (see Menzel et al., 1963; Fox, 1974, for animal examples of the effect of restricted rearing environments). Such a mechanism is thought to account for differential rates and end points in development (Dasen, 1972; Piaget, 1972; Feldman et al., 1974). Increased development effectively expands the knowable universe, and lack of stimulation, or overstimulation, nutritional energy, or redundancy limits the discoverable properties of reality. Hypothetically, development in the sphere of social reality is more vulnerable to such arrest than physical reality is. A sufficient amount of variation needs to exist so that general principles can be abstracted from the situational variation (Furth, 1969; Langer, 1969; Piaget, 1954, 1971). Too much variability allows too little experience with common features and, at the same time, insufficient opportunity to see that such features fit a general rather than a specific category. It is *acting* on variation, rather than the mere passive perception of it, that leads to development. Symbols are formed in just this developmental fashion.

Concrete operational thought requires a variety of *things* on which to operate, while formal operational thought depends for its development on a corresponding variety of alternative *concepts*. There are two dimensions involved in this concept of variation: spatial and temporal. Both are important. It is a common mistake to consider variation and diversity only in spatial terms. Environments can present sequential variation over time, as well as diversity within the same period. Change over time in a given social structure can act on development of its inhabitants as change does in the short run (see next chapter for complete discussion). Too rapid a rate of change exerts a negative influence, particularly on concrete or simple structures; behaviorally, the consequences can approach very severe extremes, as seen by Turnbull (1972) for the Ik of northeastern Uganda.

Resolution, then, is the process of closure within conflicting tendencies and a return coordination. The organism has, in a sense, decided on one mode of operating rather than another. When a new mode is adopted, it is initially fairly unstable and "inexperienced" in application to the surrounding environment. It must be consolidated or "cooked" into stability.

Incorporation
Whatever the direction of the resolution, the final phase of transformation is incorporation of the resolution into structure. The cycle of transformation, in other words, completes itself. What seems to vary within the cycle is the point at which incorporation occurs. If

assimilation early in the sequence is extreme, no development takes place. If development is delayed because conditions are optimal for facilitating transformation, the cycle is prolonged, and transformation results in a new, more complex and stable structure. In principle, this should apply to synchronic (surface), as well as diachronic transformations. The final stage of incorporation recapitulates the process by which the structure originally maintained its identity, repetitive assimilation. The structure's boundaries thereby become less permeable as the structure consolidates itself through repeated functioning.

The final phase of incorporation and consolidation necessitates a closing of the EMC through a balance of the functional poles of assimilation and accommodation. The structure has adapted at a new level subsequent to the transformation. It will open again only after optimal consolidation has taken place, and the structure has extended its range of application through the exercise of assimilation amid diversity in the environment. If optimal diversity is absent relevant to the structure at hand, further transformations will be synchronic only. Limitation of diversity relative to the content encoded in the structure similarly will reduce the range of synchronic transformations as well.

Ritual and Ontogenesis

The model of transformation in ontogenesis just outlined may be applied to an understanding of ritual behavior. Specifically, one finds that the five steps of transformation are represented in ritual by the following five phases: (1) a breaking up of patterned activity, (2) a comparison of stimulus situation (E_o) with internal model (E_c), (3) alternation in thought or behavior, (4) a resolution of the cause of alternation, and (5) consolidation of the resolution through functional repetition. A number of points should be noted here. First, the temporal span in which this sequence occurs may be relatively extended or so contracted it may be difficult to observe. Second, the two transitional steps of alternation and resolution should be much more marked in new situations, such as learning new rituals or performing infrequent rituals, than in well-learned, often-performed rituals. Third, the sequence principally derived from a diachronic view of transformations may be more easily apparent in a diachronic situation than in a more synchronic or content situation. Finally, the sequence can take place at varying levels of systemic organization (neural, behavioral, psychological, or social).

The five phases of transformation may now be examined in the context of Chapple and Coon's (1942) three stages of ritual: separation, transition and incorporation. To simplify our discussion at this point, we refer specifically to the more complex forms of human ceremonial ritual, while implying at all times that the discussion may be applied as well to formalized ritual in man and other species.

Transformation Through Ritual

1. *Separation* includes phases one and two of transformation: pattern breaking and comparison. The disruption of the ongoing pattern of activity is equivalent to the orientation response, including the phases of orienting and comparison with the internal model (E_c). In ceremonial ritual this involves orienting to the change in the situational demand, whether the ritual is in response to regularly scheduled performance or to some environmental change. There is perception of a change—it's Christmas, there has been no rain for a period of time or A's health has changed for the worse—and comparison of the detected change with an internal model. In the absence of a prescribed ritual response to the ambiguity or zone of uncertainty, lower level systems come into play in an attempt at adaptive conservation. That is, there is a reliance on habitual, adaptive responses by these lower level structures to regulate the internal milieu or adapt to external variation. These conserving responses, in most cases, are relatively automatic, such as motor patterns or adaptors described by various authors (Chapple, 1970; Fox, 1974).

The problem for the transition, subsequent to this orientation and separation, is to realign all levels of systemic organization within the individual or group. The initial orientation can be begun at any one of these levels. The expectation (after Powers, 1973; Pribram, 1971; among others) is that each level of organization has tolerance limits set for deviation from coordination with adjoining systems. When exceeded, the adjoining system detects the deviance and responds in an attempt to control or entrain with the deviating system. The results may or may not lead to the rest of the sequence.

2. *Transition* includes phases three and four of transformation: alternation and resolution. It is here that the actual transformation between equilibrated states occurs. This transformation requires that the sensory transformation of environmental input remain open, that is, not distorted to match expectancy through automatic overassimilation. This allows movement toward either synchronic or diachronic transformations, depending on whether the locus of the mismatch is relevant to content or structure. The latter generally requires many such disconfirmations over relatively extended time, while the former may be almost instantaneous (Inhelder, Sinclair, and Bovet, 1974).

Alternation, however brief, indicates that the operating structure is vacillating between two conflicting interpretations or ways of functioning. Novice meditators usually experience this alternation when attempting to reach a meditative state, alternating between habitual, ergotropic functioning and the desired trophotropic functioning (Lex, chapter 4; Ornstein, 1974). In the transition to ritual this should also occur, most markedly when the ritual is a relatively new experience (this is more thoroughly developed in the following chapter). Even well-practiced ceremonial rituals often have mechanisms to put the participant in the proper frame of mind (see chapter 10). These take the form of departures from everyday activity but are basically antecedent to the ritual proper. Often, they would be expected to take the form of preliminary tuning devices in the sense used by Lex (chapter 4).

Resolution is the climax of the transitional stage and the outcome of alternation. In ritual it marks the completion of transition from habitual functioning to that recognized as ritual. One can be physically in the temple while one's mind is still in the street or alternating back and forth. Resolution marks the point where mind remains in the temple and should be discernible by a number of indices such as posture or autonomic functioning that differ from previous states. A decision has been made at some level of systemic organization to apply the assimilative structures to incorporate the new situation into the activity of the organism and to accommodate those structures to the demands of the situation. The structures are now operating in a new, or at least different ("altered"), E_c.

3. *Incorporation* completes the transformational sequence. New behaviors acquired in (say) rites of intensification, having been practiced, are now used. They are part of the new behavioral repertoire of the individual, and he is part of that new system. Functional assimilation has once again taken over; repetition, habituation, synchronization are back in control, although things have changed. The rhesus monkey stomps and grunts and pops his eyes at a threatening male. The handshake is familiar and passes into the background, unnoticed and forgotten as the stock market becomes the mutual focus of attention. The nervous system begins to settle into a relatively coordinated pattern commensurate with the familiarity of the new activity and appropriate to it. Repetition runs on, the situation is structured, expectations are confirmed, and the situation is regulated, synchronized. The EMC has begun to close down a bit now in this area, functioning more openly in others. The new cognitive structure has begun to establish its boundaries and begins anew to apply its organization to the new world it now perceives. The individual is in a different world now, and it seems right, appropriate, *necessary*.

Finally, a couple of points need to be mentioned in passing. First, nested within a ritual may be more molecular rituals, each demonstrating the sequence discussed previously. It may even be possible to trace the process of transformation down to the level of the simple formalization. Second, thought in the individual goes through a limited series of major transformations of its major organization (i.e., from sensorimotor through perhaps formal operations), and subsystems within the total thought structure go through many more. The study of patterns of transformation in ontogeny takes many years, and this is why there has heretofore been a disproportionate interest in synchronic, or surface, trans-formations, whose study may be completed comparatively quickly.

Conclusions

Ritual serves as a supportive organ in the self-regulation of organic, cognitive, and social systems and the interaction of these systems with the E_o. It operates through its effect on the empirical modification cycle of individual and collective cognitive systems by controlling the transformations undergone by those systems. Overall, this constitutes the process of equilibration by which infor-mation from the E_o is assimilated into the E_c while simultaneously conserving the integrity of the E. The principal function of ritual is equilibration biased toward conservation rather than change, even though this conservative function can be handmaiden to change at adjoining levels of systemic organization.

The manipulation of transformational activity in ritual would seem to follow the five-step model posited as the basis for trans-formations in cognitive functioning. It can be seen as assisting the cognitive transformations as well as functioning along these prin-ciples itself. In addition, ritual would seem to reflect a continuum of systemic complexity that follows the same pattern seen in the ontogenesis of cognitive structures. As with cognition, ritual can be arrayed on a dimension from simplicity to complexity, the latter subsuming and coordinating nested substructures, which them-selves are more molecular rituals. Again, paralleling cognition, the range of phenomena controlled or affected by a given ritual is a function of its structural complexity, ceremonial ritual coordinat-ing more subsystems and adapting to a more extensive E_o than simple rituals or animal ritualizations. Not only is assimilation of the E_o to E_c more conserving, that is, more stable in the more complex forms of both cognition and ritual, but also accommo-dations of the E_c to the E_o are more adaptive in that they are more permanent because of a greater range of conservation at these levels and have a capacity for precorrection that allows modifica-tion of the E_c before the impact of the E_o.

Ritual and Ontogenetic Development

The correspondence between cognition and ritual, then, is both functional and structural. Both are organs of equilibration that vary in scope and effectiveness along a dimension of structural complexity. Each coordinates a more molecular set of structures into a system that facilitates adaptation to its surrounding milieu. The principal difference is that ritual is a creature of organic structures, aiding their conservation and their development. Ritual is the behavior generated by the central organic or cognitive structure, and its effect is to stabilize that structure. This would seem to hold true at any level of organization, from the neurological, through the behavioral and cognitive, to the social. At each more complex level of organization, a more complex form of ritual is necessary to effect equilibration.

References

Abelson, R. et al. 1968. *Theories of Cognitive Consistency: A Sourcebook*. Chicago: Rand McNally.

Beck, A. 1967. *Depression: Causes and Treatment*. Philadelphia: University of Pennsylvania Press.

Bertallanffy, L. von. 1968. *General System Theory*. New York: George Braziller.

Brehm, D. and A. Cohen. 1962. *Explorations in Cognitive Dissonance*. New York: Wiley.

Chapple, E. 1970. *Culture and Biological Man*. New York: Holt, Rinehart and Winston.

Chapple, E. and C. Coon. 1942. *Principles of Anthropology*. New York: Holt, Rinehart and Winston.

Dasen, P. R. 1972. "Cross-Cultural Piagetian Research: a Summary." *Journal of Cross-Cultural Psychology* 3:23–40.

Feldman, C. F. et al. 1974. *The Development of Adaptive Intelligence*. San Francisco: Jossey-Bass.

Feldman, S. 1965. *Cognitive Consistency*. New York: Academic Press.

Festinger, L. 1957. *A Theory of Cognitive Dissonance*. Evanston, Illinois: Row Peterson.

—— (1964). *Conflict, Decision and Dissonance*. Stanford, California: Stanford University Press.

Flavell, J. 1963. *The Developmental Psychology of Jean Piaget*. Princeton, New Jersey: Van Nostrand.

Fox, M. W. 1974. *Concepts in Ethology*. Minneapolis: University of Minnesota Press.

Furth, H. 1966. *Thinking Without Language*. New York: Free Press.

—— 1969. *Piaget and Knowledge*. Englewood Cliffs, N.J.: Prentice-Hall.

Greenfield, P. 1966. "On Culture and Conservation," in *Studies in Cognitive Growth* (J. S. Bruner, R. Olivet, and P. Greenfield, eds.). New York: Wiley.

Harvey, O. J., D. E. Hunt, and H. M. Schroder. 1961. *Conceptual Systems and Personality Organization*. New York: Wiley.

John McManus

Inhelder, B. and J. Piaget. 1958. *The Growth of Logical Thinking from Childhood to Adolescence*. New York: Basic Books.

Inhelder, B., H. Sinclair, and M. Bovet. 1974. *Learning and the Development of Cognition*. Cambridge, Mass.: Harvard University Press.

James, W. 1890. *Principles of Psychology*. New York: Holt.

Langer, J. 1969. *Theories of Development*. New York: Holt, Rinehart and Winston.

Laughlin, C. D. and I. Brady. 1978. *Extinction and Survival in Human Populations*. New York: Columbia University Press.

Laughlin, C. D. and E. d'Aquili. 1974. *Biogenetic Structuralism*. New York: Columbia University Press.

Laughlin, C. D. and J. McManus. 1975a. "Multivariable Cognitive Development: Implications for Anthropological Theory and Research." Paper presented to the New England Anthropological Association meetings. Potsdam, New York.

—— 1975b. "The Nature of Neurognosis." Paper presented at the Anthropological Association meetings, December 4, 1975. San Francisco.

Lindsley, D. B. 1961. "The Reticular Activations System and Perceptual Integration," in *Electrical Stimulation of the Brain* (D. E. Sheer, ed.). Austin: University of Texas Press.

McManus, J. 1974a. "Ontogenetic Development: The Diachronic Dimensions of Structuralism." Paper presented at American Anthropological Association meetings, Mexico City.

—— "Implications of the Schroder U-curve Hypothesis for Social Responses to Resource Deprivation." Paper presented at American Anthropological Association meetings, Mexico City.

—— 1975. "Psychopathology as Errors in Cognitive Adaptation." Paper presented to the American Anthropological Association meetings, December 4, 1975. San Francisco.

Menzel, E. et al. 1963. "Effects of Environmental Restriction upon the Chimpanzee's Responsiveness in Novel Situations," *Journal of Comparative and Physiological Psychology* 56(2):329–334.

Ornstein, R. 1974. *The Psychology of Consciousness*. New York: Viking Press.

Piaget, J. 1929a. *The Child's Conception of the World*. New York: Harcourt, Brace.

—— 1929b. *Judgment and Reasoning in the Child*. New York: Harcourt, Brace.

—— 1930. *The Child's Conception of Physical Causality*. London: Kegan Paul.

—— 1946. *The Child's Concept of Time*. New York: Basic Books.

—— 1950. *The Psychology of Intelligence*. New York: Harcourt, Brace.

—— 1951. *Play, Dreams and Imitation in Childhood*. New York: Norton.

—— 1952a. *The Child's Concept of Number*. New York: Humanities.

—— 1952b. *The Origins of Intelligence in Children*. New York: International Universities Press.

—— 1954. *The Construction of Reality in the Child*. New York: Basic Books.

—— 1956. *The Child's Concept of Space*. London: Routledge and Kegan Paul.

—— 1960. *The Mechanisms of Perception*. New York, Basic Books.

—— 1970a. *Structuralism*. New York: Basic Books.

—— 1970b. *Genetic Epistemology*. New York: Columbia University Press.

—— 1970c. "Piaget's Theory," in *Carmichal's Manual of Child Psychology* (P. Mussen, ed.). New York: Wiley.

—— 1971. *Biology and Knowledge*. Chicago: University of Chicago Press.

—— 1972. "Intellectual Evolution from Adolescence to Adulthood." *Human Development* 15:1–12.

—— 1973. *The Child and Reality*. New York: Grossman.

Piaget, J. and B. Inhelder. 1969. *The Psychology of the Child*. New York: Basic Books.

—— 1971. *Mental Imagery in the Child*. London: Routledge and Kegan Paul.

—— 1973. *Memory and Intelligence*. New York: Basic Books.

Piaget, J., B. Inhelder, and A. Szeminska. 1960. *The Child's Conception of Geometry*. New York: Basic Books.

Powers, W. 1973. *Behavior: The Control of Perception*. Chicago: Aldine.

Pribram, K. H. 1971. *Language of the Brain*. Englewood Cliffs, New Jersey: Prentice-Hall.

Schroder, H. M., M. Driver, and S. Streufert. 1967. *Human Information Processing*. New York: Holt, Rinehart and Winston.

Seligman, M. E. 1975. *Helplessness: On Development, Depression and Death*. San Francisco: W. H. Freeman.

Sokolov, E. N. 1963. *Perception and the Conditioned Reflex*. New York: Macmillan.

Tart, C. 1975. *States of Consciousness*. New York: E. P. Dutton.

Turiel, E. 1966. "An Experimental Test of the Sequentiality of Developmental Stages in the Child's Moral Judgments," *Journal of Personality and Social Psychology* 3(6):611–618.

—— 1968. "The Developmental Process in a Child's Moral Thinking," in *New Directions in Developmental Psychology* (P. Mussen, J. Langer, and M. Covington, eds.). New York: Holt, Rinehart and Winston.

Turnbull, C. M. 1972. *The Mountain People*. New York: Simon and Schuster.

Weiss, J. M. 1972. "Psychological Factors in Stress and Disease," *Scientific American* 226(6):104–113.

Werner, H. 1948. *Comparative Psychology of Mental Developments*. Chicago: Follett.

Wolff, P. 1963. "Developmental and Motivational Concepts in Piaget's Sensorimotor Theory of Intelligence," *Journal of American Academy of Child Psychiatry* 2:225–243.

Seven

Ritual and Human Social Cognition

John McManus

> The difference between man and the higher-order animals
> lies not so much in the ability to learn or to utilize the mean-
> ings of a large number of stimuli, but rather in the ability to
> learn and to utilize alternate meanings of the same stimulus
> and to build up and use different patterns of interrela-
> tionships within the same set of meanings. This change,
> from lower to higher levels of thought, is a matter of de-
> gree, paralleling the evolutionary scale across species and
> developing with age (to an upper neurological limit under
> optimal environmental conditions) within species.
>
> **H. M. Schroder, M. J. Driver, and S. Streufert,**
> *Human Information Processing*

In this chapter we turn to the question of how ritual functions in relation to human social cognition. Our theoretical focus now shifts from the genetic epistemology of Piaget, which is more concerned with physical, rather than social, reality,[1] to several neo-Piagetian approaches more conducive to social analysis. Our present discussion assumes, however, that the principles discussed previously are still operating. These include adaptation and organization, transformation, autoregulation, and invariant stage development, to mention but a few. Specifically, we show that ritual functions biologically and psychologically as an effective tool in the process of equilibration between the cognitive system and its surround. To demonstrate this, we shall view the cognized environment (E_c) as an information-processing system and

1. The major exception is Piaget's *Moral Judgment of the Child* (1932).

ritual as a behavioral and symbolic buffer between that system and the operational environment (E_o).

Cognition as Information Processing

Conceptual systems theory (Harvey et al., 1961; Schroder et al., 1967; Schroder, 1972) is a neo-Piagetian theory that treats the E_c as an information-processing system, one concerned with an individual's social environment. Stages of development are assumed to proceed in an invariant sequence from relative undifferentiation to high articulation and organization.

Each successive stage is distinguished from its predecessor by its greater structural complexity and by its more efficient and more nearly comprehensive information-processing abilities. Thus, each stage is thought to be able to consider greater amounts and diversity of information (Schroder et al., 1967) and therefore to make more realistic adaptive decisions. Complexity of conceptual stages has been shown to be age related in the same fashion as Piagetian stages. Complexity is defined in terms of the number of units or dimensions of information considered and the degree to which these units are integrated into a system (Schroder et al., 1967). Conceptual systems theory distinguishes four nodal stages following a state of relative disorganization:

Stage 1: relatively fixed perceptions or hierarchical organization.

Stage 2: emergence of alternative perceptions of the same dimensions.

Stage 3: complex rules for simultaneously comparing and relating perspectives.

Stage 4: generation of complex relationships among rules of comparison. In schematic form the different stages are depicted in Figure 7.1.

Functionally speaking, one can express the interaction between the organism and its environment in the form of an inverted U-curve (see Figure 7.2). This relationship has been verified re-

Figure 7.1. Stages in the Development of Social Conceptual Systems Levels of Integrative Complexity of Information Processing Structures.
After H. M. Schroder, M. Driver, and S. Streufert, 1967, pp. 515 ff.

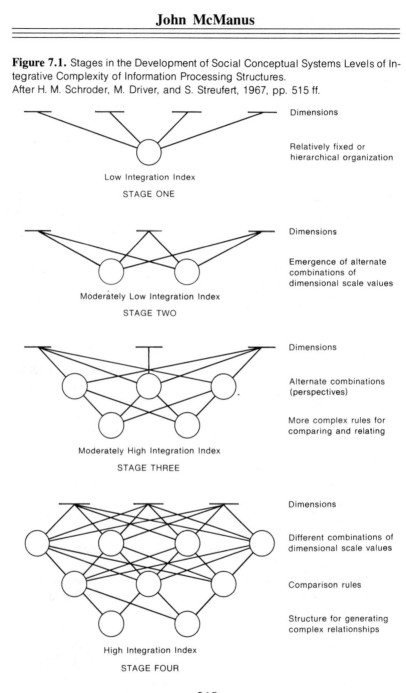

Figure 7.2. General Relationship Between Environment and Behavioral Complexity.

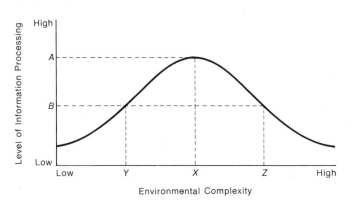

peatedly in experimental situations (Schroder, 1972; Schroder, et al., 1967; Suedfeld and Streufert, 1966; McManus, 1971). The outcome of this disposition-environment interaction is the functional capacity of the organism to process information. As the environment increases its complexity in terms of diversity of information or its intensity in terms of positive or negative consequences, the operational capacity of the organism to read the environment increases to an optimal point. Once that point is reached, continued increments in complexity or intensity diminish the organism's information-processing capacity until baseline is reached. The potential distance from baseline to the asymptote of the U-curve parallels the structural, developmental course of that person. The maximum potential operational capacity of a given individual is set by the developmental level attained. An individual who has developed conceptually to stage four in a given cognitive domain has a much greater capacity than a person who has reached only stage one. The shape of the functional curve remains the same for each person, varying among people only in its amplitude. The inverted U-curve, then, describes the relationship between the person and his or her environment in terms of the person's functional capacity to read that environment. The greater that capacity, the more information is considered and integrated into an overall

219

judgment about the nature of what is perceived. A person who can read the environment in multiple dimensions and integrate these into a complex judgment about reality is in a better general adaptive position than one who responds to a single, immediate stimulus.[2]

Such a method for analyzing the thinking process concerns itself with *how* a person thinks rather than *what* he or she thinks. The distinction is between the information-processing structure and the content that it processes. The information-processing structures range between boundaries of concrete-abstract, rigid-flexible, and stimulus controlled-stimulus controlling. Simple undifferentiated structures tend to be oriented toward external standards, authority, and categorical thinking (right/wrong, good/bad) and tend to avoid ambiguity and conflict (*within* the cognitive system). In Piagetian terms the adaptive balance is toward assimilating reality to the organism's own standards, needs, and structure. Also characteristic of such simple structures are "dependence on fixed standards; greater tendency to standardize judgments in novel situations; inability to interrelate perspectives; a poorer delineation between means and ends; the availability of fewer pathways for achieving ends; a poorer capacity to act 'as if' and to understand other people's perspectives; and less potential to perceive the self as a causal agent in interacting with the environment" (Schroder, 1972:257).

Compared to such simple structures, complex structures possess attributes of flexibility and mobility. They are less stimulus bound in the sense of requirements or rigidity of response to a given stimulus. Complex structures can generate multiple perspectives of a given situation and multiple solutions to problems (Streufert et al., 1967). Tolerance for ambiguity is greater in people characterized by complex structures, as is the ability to generate their own internalized standards, to empathize with others' feelings and perceptions, and to adapt to changing environmental situations.

2. The adaptive value of each stage must be considered in terms of individual functioning within the range of a specific, impinging environment, so that this is not necessarily true in each *specific instance*.

Adaptively, complex information-processing structures would seem to be generally superior, particularly in environments characterized by novelty and change. Since adaptation is always a relationship between the adapting organism and its environment, complexity of thought may not always be adaptive, at least in the short run. The army private who is complex and flexible and generates his own standards may find himself less adapted to rigid, authoritarian army life than his less complex friend. Similarly, cultures or social organizations that do not change and that present few novel situations may not elicit the development of complex structures (Piaget, 1971, 1972; Kohlberg and Gilligan, 1972). The definition of adaptation as the relationship between the complexity of the environment and the organizational sophistication of the organism must always be kept in mind. While greater complexity may generally be most adaptive over the long run ontogenetically or phylogenetically, it may not be so in the short-run situation. There are occasions when simplicity or ignorance is optimally adaptive.

Differences in structural complexity can be seen in the functional capacity of the organism. Functionally, these differences can be expressed as a family of the previously discussed U-curves (See Figure 7.3). Note here that, at any given level of environmental complexity or intensity, the more complex structures

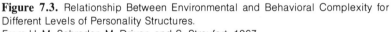

Figure 7.3. Relationship Between Environmental and Behavioral Complexity for Different Levels of Personality Structures.
From H. M. Schroder, M. Driver, and S. Streufert, 1967.

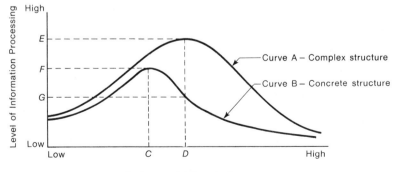

221

demonstrate a greater functional capacity, that is, greater ability to read the environment in multidimensional, integrated terms. These functional differences are greatest at the optimal levels of environmental complexity for each structural level (Schroder et al., 1967). Hypothetically, this optimal level should consist of greater environmental complexity for each more complex structure. Differences begin to disappear at the extreme ends of the curve, where environmental input is suboptimal (unstimulating) or superoptimal (overstimulating). Both suboptimal and superoptimal stimulation reduce the functional operating level of the organism and thus its adaptive flexibility. The simultaneous functioning of two structurally different people can be made to converge at two separate extremes: understimulation and overstimulation.

Conservation of the Cognitive System

The cognitive system, like any biological system, functions to conserve itself, to protect its integrity. While such a system can be threatened by either endogenous or exogenous factors, our principal concern here will be with threat from outside the system. The question is, what constitutes threat for a cognitive system? A threatened system is one that is in danger of losing its internal organizational capacity or its adaptive capacity toward the outside world. Threat to internal organization would be any factor that promotes disintegration of the relationships among the elements of that system. The elements of the cognitive system are the basic units of information, while the relationships among these elements are the system's rules of combination. The combinatory rules constitute the system's structure, while the level of internal equilibrium of the structure is synonymous with the complexity of these combinatory rules. As we have seen in Figure 7.3, two aspects of the environment can reduce the functional level of a given structure: complexity and intensity. Each of these can have a positive or negative effect: a minimum of either is needed for the structure to function; an optimum is needed for optimal functioning, and an overload of either can be injurious to the structure's functioning.

Ritual functions as a buffer preventing disintegration of the cognized environment in relation to stress. Stress is defined as either too much or too little information, as represented by the extreme ends of the inverted U-curve (Figure 7.2), or too great or too little intensification of that information.

The next question to consider is, what does an unorganized cognitive system look like? Within the framework of conceptual systems theory, such a cognitive system would be the preorganized, "sub-one" level. Developmentally, a sub-one system is described as unsocialized and can be considered to have a very limited adaptive capacity. Adaptation is always short run, in response to direct stimulation. People whose development is arrested at this level are highly constrained by their immediate environment. Their inability to tolerate frustration and their extremely egocentric perspective prevent productive cooperation except when it directly satisfies their own needs. The sub-one has no really integrated cognitive system at all; only a set of compartmentalized response tendencies or unconnected substructures. Such people can be disruptive in any social organization.[3] Even sophisticated cognitive structures can be driven down to this functional level under sufficient stress, whose logical outcome may be behavior patterns such as those displayed by the Ik (Turnbull, 1973).

Lack of predictability in the E_o (perhaps as the result of disaster; see chapter 9) breaks down that environment in the perception of individuals who must then create structure from within their own E_cs. People with complex cognitive structures possess greater capacity to do this, and so environmental stress is relatively less threatening to the complex than to the simple system. Someone whose operational capacity is at stage one may be totally destructured, in a functional sense, by a level of stress that reduces a stage four's functional capacity to, say, a stage two. A mechanism that forms a buffer between stage one functioning and a sub-one

---

3. Data collected by the author, including samples of delinquents and drug-addicted persons, show a disproportionate number of sub-one persons. Studies by Montague and Victor presented at the Workshop on Differential Treatment, 1974, Iowa City, Iowa, tend to validate this notion.

state would be extremely useful adaptively, since stage one is an irreducible minimum for corporate response. Ritual provides precisely such a mechanism. The problem of adaptation is twofold: to maintain the internal system and to cope with the outside world. Ritual provides a mechanism that allows for both operations simultaneously—by offering ways to deal with the problem in a group and by facilitating habituation to stimulus in an overload situation. Of particular interest at the moment is ritual's capacity for protecting the match between the E_c and the E_o. This process of system maintenance constitutes something of a continuum in the following way:

1. Complete or almost complete matching between the neurological model and incoming stimulation results in habituation (Miller, Galanter, and Pribram, 1960; Pribram, 1971) or control by lower level systems (Powers, 1973). Such stimulation remains outside the bounds of awareness and generally results in no initiation of behavior directed either toward the environment or toward internal processes. Stimulation so anticipated and controlled allows the organism to ignore it and thereby remain alert to deal with more pressing problems. The repetition of behavior often found in ritual facilitates this process within the ritual situation itself, allowing the individual to attend to and experience the affective consequences of this state or to attend to particularly salient stimuli.

2. When incoming stimulation fails to match the existing model, an orientation response occurs (Sokolov, 1963; Pribram, 1971). Such a mismatch can raise previously ignored stimulation into consciousness (Piaget, 1973) and trigger an evaluation of that stimulation. Subsequent to this evaluation, behavior may be initiated to bring the stimulus in line with the model or the model in line with the sensory data (Miller et al., 1960; Hunt, 1963; Pribram, 1971). The action taken can be external, operating on the stimuli or its source, or it can be internal, directed at reorganizing or controlling internal events (Pribram, 1971; Festinger, 1957; Brehm and Cohen, 1962). The second alternative occurs when the model is modified to fit the stimuli.

3. The mismatch between sensory input and the internal model may be extreme, in which case the internal model may

be completely revised or the stimulation warded off, grossly distorted, or not consciously perceived. Such a gross mismatch can occur in situations such as disaster (chapter 9), where the response of victims may include a complete reformulation of the reality perspective, as in religious conversion, or a destruction of the model itself, resulting in an entropic state. Acute paranoid schizophrenia may be a case of a sharp mismatch where the resolution is the alternative involving extremely gross distortion of sensory data to fit the existing model. Here the internal organization solidifies around a mode of the self concept and the peripheral parts of the model, reformulated to support that concept. Incoming data are overassimilated to match the model, resulting in an extreme, if solipsistic, equilibration between organism and environment that is adaptive in the short run and only in terms of maintaining the internal system.[4] This sort of adaptation generally sacrifices coordination with the world-out-there for equilibrium of the world-in-here. In restricted settings it can accomplish both equilibrations nicely (Rokeach, 1964).

4. Individuals differ in their ability to maintain consistency between internal models and sensory data (Suedfeld, 1964; Harvey, 1962; Schroder and Crano, 1965; Coffman, 1967). The differences tend to be developmental and involve the complexity of the information-processing apparatus in the content area (Schroder et al., 1967; Schroder, 1972).[5]

5. Extreme resolutions of mismatch, by either model modification or sensory distortions, may take the form of short-term adaptations at the cost of longer term maladaptation. Massive accommodation of the internal model can destabilize the internal system, while massive overassimilation may preserve that

4. Overassimilation of incoming data tends to distort it in an inflexible way, promoting a rigid, simple-minded orientation that inhibits consideration of conflicting information. Such a process is maladaptive, as conditions change, and such change is leveled out or not permitted into the operating structure. Adaptive action is based on an E_c's bearing increasingly less correspondence to the E_o and thereby becoming more vulnerable to threat from that environment (E_o).

5. Two transformational processes are involved here. One way of maintaining the internal model is to overassimilate or distort incoming information to match the existing model, reading out any conflicting information. The other process involves manipulation of cognitions already in the system or reality model, distorting or compartmentalizing these so that they are congruent or noncontradicting.

system at the cost of an inaccurate reading of the stressing situation. Internal tension is dissipated at the same time but leaves the organism vulnerable to events occurring outside itself.

6. Under conditions of continued and extreme stress, it may be expected that the internal structure will continue to diminish in its functional level (Werner, 1957). Taken to a logical extreme, the structures themselves could disintegrate, leaving the organism in a relatively permanent state of disorder. At very low levels of functioning comparable to the sub-one stage, complex interpersonal functioning is highly unlikely. At best an "every man for himself" philosophy obtains, making cooperative action impossible. Even in cases where such an approach allows a specific individual to survive, it does so at the cost of the integrity of the internal system. When such disintegration first occurs, the individual should be maximally vulnerable, disorganized, and confused. Steps are likely to be taken that, though they appear meaningless and inappropriate to the external threat, serve to restore the organism's internal equilibrium (see chapter 9).

Any system has its limits of tolerance beyond which the system will fail to maintain itself and will become disorganized. Stress that is itself less than traumatic could efficiently reduce the majority of a population, particularly one composed of proportionately simple structures, to a very low functional level. Cultures able to construct artificial organs of regulation that could protect their members from such a state would be in a relatively better adaptive position both for the cultures and their individual members. Ritual, apparently a cultural universal, would seem to be such an organ.

We hypothesize that a principal adaptive function of ritual is to stand as a barrier between that part of the U-curve (Figure 7.2) descriptive of stage one functioning, or minimal cognitive organization, and sub-one functioning, or the absence of a coherent structural organization. This hypothesis is compatible with descriptions in the previous chapter and by Lex in chapter 4, which deal with establishment of a figure-ground relationship or the process of habituation against which a single, salient perspective is highlighted. Such a state, although not necessarily flexible or maximally adaptive in an individual sense, still maintains the properties of an organized conceptual system.

Ritual has three components that can assist in preventing collapse of the cognitive system: repetitive behavior, a cognitive matrix (myth or dogma), and an affective state. The physiological concomitants of rhythmic or repetitive behavior have been covered in chapter 4. In shielding the cognitive system, the practice of ritual itself can place the broad choice of executable behaviors into a subset under automatic control and out of the realm of cognitive choice and thereby reduce the decision universe. This coordination and the accompanying affective states themselves aid internal equilibration for the individual.

The cognitive component of ritual can have two aspects: definition of the situation and prescription of appropriate action. An individual confronting stress who is initially operating only at stage one is minimally capable of providing his or her own structure. The ritual-myth complex as an institution in a society can provide that structure externally, interpreting reality and creating information redundancy. Stage one persons are oriented to a single interpretation of reality, heavily reliant on external standards, prone to accept authority, and fearful of internal conflict and inconsistency (Schroder et al., 1967:16–17).[6] Ritual maintains their functioning under a remarkable range of adversity, owing to the extensive power of the human intellect to accomplish adaptation to mythically structured cognition.

In addition to defining the situation cognitively, ritual can reduce the stress of overload by prescribing appropriate action consonant with the E_c. Interpreting reality by selecting and integrating sensory data is only one source of uncertainty or stress. Another is deciding what to do about it. If the myth is acceptable as an accurate model of reality and incoming data are assimilated to it, the task remains to reduce the uncertainty due to behavioral choice. Rituals can model action that is appropriate to the internalized cognitive model. As long as this behavior is perceived as reason-

6. A major characteristic of stage one functioning is to look outside oneself for external standards and guidelines for behavior (Harvey et al., 1961; Schroder et al., 1967; Schroder, 1972).

able and effective in dealing with the environment, failures can be explained through assimilation and cognitive maneuvering, making them consistent with beliefs (Festinger, 1957; Festinger, et al., 1956; Brehm and Cohen, 1962; Festinger, 1964). This general coordination of cognition and behavior should generally be capable of maintaining an internal system with which it is compatible.

Consistent with our discussion in the last chapter, we view emotion as a consequence of the coordination between the E_c and E_o. Emotion can act on the cognitive-behavioral level as environmental stress and thereby increase or decrease functional level in the same fashion as E_o stimulation itself can. Coordinations accomplished at the cognitive and behavioral levels can modulate emotion and thereby regulate the stress factor inherent in emotion.

Ritual as Communication

Our discussion thus far has emphasized two points: One, complex cognitive functioning is maximally adaptive and better equilibrated and provides the best situation for accurate reading of the E_o. Two, ritual functions under conditions of stress to protect minimal cognitive structure from total disintegration and entropy. We wish to show now that ritual operates adaptively under other circumstances by *reducing* the functional level of the cognitive system.

Not only do individuals have to adapt to a physical environment, but also they generally must do so in a social context. To do this, they must have an understanding of societal rules and contingencies, strategies of social coordination, and the social import of external events. All of these are part and parcel of the E_c. We have previously examined the construction of the E_c in relation to physical epistemology (chapter 6). We now examine the process by which the individual constructs his social epistemology, a process that, not unlike that of physical epistemology, seems to progress structurally somewhat independently of the cultural surround.[7]

7. Structural development is seen as independent of the cultural surround only in regard to the specific surface transformations or content of that culture. Development is thought to be

Structures and Socialization. Socialization is the imposition of culturally sanctioned beliefs, values, and ways of acting upon the members of the social group. As such, it includes the individual member's world view as well as the many societal rules for interaction and obligations to the group as a whole. It is through socialization, as well as individual ontogenesis, that the world becomes known. Through the socialization process the world becomes known in a culturally acceptable way, as compared with structural ontogenesis, whereby it becomes known in an adaptively acceptable way. Socialization, then, is the socially sanctioned epistemology whose criteria for reality reside in the culture itself or in the chosen representatives of that culture. The task of socialization is to persuade or coerce each member of the society to accept the group-cognized environment and to follow the behavioral dicta implicit in that reality model. Coordination among a society's members is accomplished by means of the socialization process, as well as by means of individual, conceptual ontogenesis. This is a major cultural role of ritual in each individual's adaptation to the E_o and is principally concerned with the content, as opposed to the structure, of experience.

Socialization presents some problems of an operational sort. To transmit the content of a culture, each individual must be reached and convinced. The individual's attention must be elicited and maintained, and information must be transmitted in a fashion that leads to its initial and continued acceptance. Such information must overlap to a considerable degree among individuals and be absorbed by them in the terms in which it was initiated. Meaning must be maintained both generationally and interindividually. Finally, culturally relevant information must be cognitively and affectively controlled in each individual's psychological makeup. Ritual's role in the socialization process is that of mediator or regulator, having characteristics that facilitate solutions to the problems of socialization. This mediation function is accomplished in a manner similar to that which preserves the

---

influenced by various patterns and practices within a society in that these can facilitate or arrest development either by providing too much or too little differentiation in the E_o or by inhibiting sufficient autonomy in explanation of that E_o.

cognitive system—by regulating the functional level of the individual seeking to adapt to or equilibrate with the external world.

The attracting and maintaining of each individual's attention can be accomplished within the ritual context through processes previously discussed. Individuals must first be encouraged or coerced into participating in ritual, the first step in attracting their attention. The next task, gaining and holding their attention within the ritual itself, can be accomplished through a variety of techniques designed to tune the cognitive and biological systems. Such techniques, discussed in chapters 4 and 6, generally include features of rhythm and repetition. The goal is generally the creation of a stage one (fixed-perspective) neurological and cognitive state. Procedures such as this would be expected to be common both to situations geared to initial socialization and to those designed to reinforce socialization (see chapter 10 in relation to the Roman Mass).

The process just outlined embodies two elements of tuning: the cognitive and the physiological systems. These are separate but interrelated processes. Each is capable of functioning separately or in combination. A coordination between the two might be similar to the concept of entrainment used by Lex and also by Chapple (1970). Theoretically the purely physiological level of organization can be reached independently from the cognitive, and vice-versa. In practice, the two are likely to be interdependent. Overstimulation of the neurological apparatus is likely to act as stress on the cognitive system, for example, and thereby tends to reduce its functional level. Similarly, conceptual tuning is likely to have consequences in the neurological system. In either case the experienced affect may be negative—experienced as anxiety. Placed within a positive context, such as is provided by the symbolic aspects of ritual, the physiological events may then be experienced as excitement or euphoria, experienced affect being a joint function of an arousal and cognitive set (Schacter and Singer, 1962). This seems to be the case even at the level of direct cortical stimulation (Valenstein, 1973; Weiner, 1973; Lazarus, 1966, 1974; Lazarus and Opton, 1966; Mahl et al., 1964). Coordination or entrainment of the two levels may lay the basis for various forms of religious experience where the univariate cognitive set provides certainty and "meaning" for the experienced neurological activity.[8] Such a coordination would seem to be ideal for reinforcing the experience, its behaviors, and the cognitive-symbolic messages therein.

The outcome of this process of coordinated neurological activity and a conceptual stage one state may be an overall experience of "unity." In such a state, uncertainty and the attendant anxiety are eliminated and subordinated to the certainty of dogma and tradition. Coupled with an optimal neurological state and given meaning by the cognitive state, a feeling of certain knowledge or unity may be attainable in its extreme form. Even at less intense levels the experience should tend, not only to perpetuate the ritual practice itself through its intrinsic reinforcing properties, but also to cement belief in the accompanying myths, dogma, or teachings. In this fashion, transmission of culturally sanctioned beliefs and norms can be optimally transmitted. In addition, new elements of belief and proscribed behaviors can be introduced within the context of the traditional. As long as these can be made to seem consistent with the established beliefs, the new elements can be taken in by the individual and integrated with the traditional (Sherif and Sherif, 1967; Sherif, Sherif, and Nebergall, 1965; Heider, 1958). Properly handled, new adaptive information can be communicated within the context of the old and in a situation maximally conducive to its acceptance.

To this point we have dealt with ritual's role in attracting and maintaining the individual's attention to communicate a socially sanctioned world view. Also considered to some extent was the mechanism by which this information transmission might be accomplished, its belief ensured, and continued practice made probable. The discussion has been limited thus far to resocialization, that is, communication to those already socialized into the

8. Meaning is provided by assimilation of sensory data into an operating structure. It can be "fallaciously" provided through distortion of that input (overassimilation), making the match of input to internal model a "forced" or distorted one. The experiential effect of such meaning is, however, essentially the same as when less distorted information actually is congruent with the internal model.

symbolic system and beliefs of the culture and into a general model that ignores structural, ontogenetic differences. The model must now be extended to include these two exceptions.

Ontogenetic Variations. The model just discussed ignores differences among people in the structural complexity of their thought processes. Available research indicates that such differences strongly affect reception and interpretation of a communication. Very simply, a communication structured at a given level of complexity or organization is differently received and interpreted by individuals at varying levels in their own structural complexity in that stimulus domain. An edict of ethics or morality is interpreted differently by someone who is at a stage one conceptual level than by a person at stage three. The former interprets such a communication in categorical terms of right-wrong, good-bad. Social rules are seen as having an existence of their own, outside the individuals who practice them. They are likely to be seen as rigid and unmodifiable. The stage three person, on the other hand, may be able to see the issue from multiple perspectives and as differently applicable in different situations. The stage one person applies a moral code identically to all situations without consideration of such things as other people's intentions or mitigating circumstances. There is also a tendency to interpret the communication in terms of one's own beliefs, values, and preferences. Implicit in the stage one person's interpretation is an overassimilation of the input, in Piaget's terms, distorting its meaning to fit the existing cognitive model. One consequence of this process can be reception of a communication in terms very different from the meaning intended by the communicator. A frequent example is seen in a kind of study done every few years by psychologists who present items from the U.S. Constitution or the Declaration of Independence in the form of a poll to which people are asked to agree or disagree. A frequent result is a high rate of disagreement if the source of the quotation is unknown. Working the other way, the Constitution is often used to justify unconstitutional arguments.

Such a cognitive manipulation has been produced by Rosenberg (1960) through hypnosis. Here subjects were measured on their attitudes toward black people. Changes in each individual's feelings about black people were hypnotically induced. Subsequent post-tests in the realm of beliefs rather than feelings indicated that subjects changed their cognitions to bring them into line with their experimentally acquired feelings. Such internal balancing, as well as distortion, of incoming information is common in the psychological literature (Hastorf and Cantril, 1956; Festinger, 1957; Feldman, 1965; Festinger et al., 1956).

More specific to the issue in question is a study done by Turiel (1966), which used Kohlberg's levels of moral development, a structural, developmental system similar to conceptual level and comparable to Piaget's preoperational, concrete operational, and formal operational stages, but in the sphere of moral issues (Kohlberg, 1963, 1969). Moral development has been shown to relate to conceptual level in a Markov fashion, whereby conceptual development in the social sphere is a necessary but not sufficient condition for development in the moral sphere (Sullivan, McCollough, and Stager, 1970). In other words, to possess an abstract conception of morality, one must have developed sufficiently in the social domain. Those extremely abstract or developed on the Kohlberg measure also demonstrate such development on measures of conceptual level. All those who are complex in conceptual level are not necessarily abstract in Kohlberg's terms. Using the Kohlberg procedure, Turiel measured a number of children to determine their level of moral structures. He then presented each child with a moral dilemma and moral arguments pro and con, constructed either one stage below, one stage above, or two stages above the child's own level. He then examined whether the children understood, preferred, or accepted the moral arguments to which they were exposed. The results are intriguing.

Turiel's children, when exposed to an argument *one level below* their own, demonstrated, through retelling, that they (1) understood the argument; (2) saw it as inadequate, silly, or juvenile; or (3) rejected it. Children exposed to arguments *one level higher* than their own (1) demonstrated some understanding of the argument or (2) stated that they saw it as somehow preferable or superior to their own. Those children exposed to reasoning *two levels above* their own showed that they understood it only in terms of the level at which they were currently functioning; that is, they reformulated the reasoning back into concepts equivalent to their own and different from those presented. This example is put forth to demonstrate the different consequences of variation in the thought structures underlying any communication. Its import for socialization and communication in ritual should be obvious. Unless communications are phrased at, or slightly above, the structural capacity of the recipient, they may either be rejected out of hand or revised into a message different from that intended. The word of God as expressed in the Catholic catechism may be perfectly appropriate for the stage one individual but may seem vaguely ludicrous to the stage four person. Similarly, Teilhard de Chardin may excite and convince the stage four person but be lost on the stage one individual.

Ritual can be seen as an organ of regulation that aids in the solution of the problem of how to communicate to individuals differing in conceptual structure. There would seem to be two general solutions: (1) communicate differently to people of different structural complexity and (2) employ techniques that, at least temporarily, induce similar functional levels in all recipients. A great deal of experimentation has been done in education using the former technique (Hunt, 1971; Hunt and Sullivan, 1974). Ritual, we hypothesize, tends to use the second approach.

Through the neural and cognitive tuning built into ritual, participants are moved toward functioning at a stage one level. Rather than produce a variety of communications within itself that are appropriate to more complex, as well as to concrete, participants, the practice of ritual moves the recipients of the communication toward a similar receptive level. In this way, only one level of structure is necessary in communicating social norms and values to a potentially wide variety of cognitive structures. Continued practice of ritual may allow even more complex individuals to remain concrete when considering religious questions. This would be an example of multilinearity of development posited by Werner (1957) or *decalage* posited by Piaget (1971) and Inhelder and Piaget (1958). By this it is meant that individuals develop differently in different content areas, so that a physicist, complex in his or her area of specialization, may be conceptually concrete in reference to religion.

Even in the short run encompassed by the ritual itself, the communication can be appropriate to the temporarily re-trogressed structure of the ordinarily complex communicator. Through processes such as those illustrated by the Rosenberg study, the cognitive content can be manipulated and fleshed out after it returns to the habitual level of functioning. This may take place with relatively little effort, be compartmentalized, or initiate further epistemic exploration. In the last case, conflict between the cognitive content of ritual (and its attendant affective state) and the more complex reality model of the individual may institute a discrepancy thought to initiate intrinsically motivated behavior (Hunt, 1963; Pribram, 1971; Laughlin and d'Aquili, 1974). This might lead to further attempts to understand or elaborate the model. If the attempt leads to a study of Teilhard de Chardin, it will elaborate and reinforce the work of ritual. If it leads to Sartre, however, the work of ritual may be undone, as it so often is in con-temporary Western society. The pressure in most societies will be toward maintenance of the existing reality model, and in most cul-tures few Sartres may exist. Traditional cultures would seem to present the fewest alternatives to established dogma and there-fore are most likely to perpetuate the cognitive models es-tablished and confirmed within the context of ritual. Creation of such models is the core of socialization, and the process has two elements: (1) ontogenesis of the thought structures relatively in-dependent of the specific content of the culture and (2) transmis-sions of the cultural content itself, within the context of the individ-ual thought structures.

Ontogenesis and Socialization. The ontogenesis of human thought was extensively covered in the preceding chapter. The nature of an individual's culture appeared to influence the rate of development and perhaps whether or not the more complex, for-mal operational structures appear at all (Piaget, 1972; Kohlberg and Gilligan, 1972). The latter question is still a subject of debate and may involve the issue of *decalages* or abstract development within very narrow stimulus domains in a specific culture. The universality of such development, at least through concrete operational stages in both knowledge of physical reality and moral abstractness, has been repeatedly validated (Dasen, 1972; Feldman et al., 1974; Kohlberg, 1969). Nothing in the structural developmental approach itself demands that the most abstract structures appear in every individual or even every culture. It only maintains that such development follows a specific *sequence* and that an optimal environment is necessary, in interaction with the endogenous structures themselves, to promote further development. The nature of the environment, its complexity and diversity, influence the rate of conceptual development. Such environmental influences have been similarly implicated in the development of perceptual differences (Witkin et al., 1962).

In order for a given individual to be considered socialized, development must have reached at least a level of stage one in conceptual systems terms. The stimulus-bound, externally controlled, and completely egocentric[9] sub-one person is presocialized. He or she has not yet learned the rules of the game and has no really organized internal system. The sub-one person lives only for the moment and the self. The rule structure of the surrounding world has not yet been learned or assimilated. Rules are seen as impediments to happiness or success unless they facilitate satisfaction of current needs and are considered in terms of specific rather than of general instances. To be considered a socialized individual, one must first develop the capacity for understanding rules and authority. Rules must be seen as having some purpose and as necessary for the common good. In other words, socialization of the cultural content first requires conceptual development to at least a stage one orientation.

Those who have achieved a stage one level of cognitive structure orient themselves positively to rules of some sort and see rules as necessary and desirable. In Western culture they tend to conform to rules, although not necessarily those of the ex-

---

9. Egocentric here is equivalent to the Piagetian use of the term, meaning perceptions based on the individual's structural reference point, rather than the popular use of the term, meaning excessive interest in self per se.

isting society. Rules to such individuals seem to have an existence of their own, apart from the people who made them—they are prescriptive. Socialization in the broad sense includes development of the thought structures up to and including stage one, as well as transmission of cultural values and practices. In the more narrow sense, socialization refers to the second process—the transmission of the culture per se. Development is the term referring exclusively to the former process—ontogenesis and progression beyond stage one is seen as postsocialization, often undoing the work of socialization in the sense of freeing the individual from some social constraints.[10] As development proceeds beyond stage one, the individual begins to make his or her own decisions about what is right, wrong, or preferable. Rules begin to appear as useful but subjective, made by others rather than existing for them. The consequence is often rebellion against those values that the socialization process aimed at inculcating in the members of the culture.

Achievement of a stage one level of development is thought to depend on a modicum of predictability in the environment (Harvey et al., 1961). Consistency of parental behavior and the response of others to the child's behaviors allow the child to establish a pattern of reality. The relationships between acts and their consequences and means-ends relationships can thereby become established. Ritual, through its repetitive patterning of behaviors and symbols, can aid in the development to a stage one level; that is, through imitation and rehearsal, the child can begin to internalize the ritual behaviors and elementary aspects of their meaning.

The problem of socialization is often complex. The child must assimilate, not only content appropriate to his or her contemporaneous role in the society, but also those attributes (or many of

10. Progression past stage one in development is thought to involve a change or transformation that allows multiple perspectives of a situation and transferral of standards from external source to the individual's internal reference system. In this sense there is a change from mere conformity to a consideration of external standards as they relate to the self. In this sense it could be said that the strict notion of socialization (operationalized as conforming beliefs or behaviors) is undone in favor of a more internalized, but potentially more viable, approach to social values and beliefs.

them) appropriate to later roles to be fulfilled in the future. Ritual, and particularly ceremonial ritual, provides, not only an arena for ontogenesis into structural stage one, but also a standardized, repetitive source of age-specific role models.

Recreation of the Cognitive Model. At some point in the life of each individual there comes the time to enter into adulthood. In most cultures this period is marked by rituals signifying the passage from child to adult. Such rituals have been described in Eliade's *Rites and Symbols of Initiation* (1958). It would seem that the role of ritual in this transition is similar to its role in maintaining and reinforcing an existing cognitive model. In the latter case ritual's function is conservative. In rites of initiation or transition its function is one of transformation of the model of reality. Not only is the model of the world-out-there subject to transformation at this point, but so, too, is the model of self—the world-in-here. The initiate must be provided, not only with a new, more complex world view, but also with a new perspective of self and its role in the world-out-there. How might this be accomplished with the aid of ritual?

Probably the clearest example of socialization into adulthood is provided by the bush school, used in many cultures. Bush schools and their attendant rituals are an extreme form of the socialization that, in much modified form, exists in Western cultures in the form of confirmation and Bar Mitzvah. The essential elements of the bush school as a socialization technique are (1) separation of the initiate from his or her former role and environment; (2) hazing or harassment practiced by the initiators; (3) prohibition of previously practiced behavior patterns; (4) introduction of new versions of reality via myths and stories; (5) initiation of new prescribed behavior patterns, particularly those essential to passing of an initiation test; and (6) reentry into the social life of the culture in the role of an adult.[11]

The first three elements in the initiation sequence are culturally induced stressors that operate to destroy the existing reality model of each initiate. The combination of isolation, harassment, and prohibition of standard coping practices acts as stress

---

11. See Chapple and Coon's stages, discussed in the previous chapter.

on the cognitive system. Such an increment in uncertainty reduces the functional capacity of each individual. Threat and uncertainty produce an effect similar to that produced in the Schroder studies (Schroder et al., 1967; and the sensory deprivation work of Suedfeld, 1964). All environmental support for the old reality model is removed through isolation. This further heightens the threat embodied in harassment, making it both more salient and stressful. The implicit goal of such activity is to drive the level of cognitive functioning downward toward an entropic state through creation of unpredictability, lack of external structure, and increase in autonomic arousal. The latter can be both a direct anxiety reaction to the threat and a product of the processes posited by Pribram (1971), in which inability to act on the environment in an instrumental fashion results in ability to exert control on the internal system, which is felt as emotion. Increased affective response acts further to reduce the person's functional capacity, driving it ever downward.

As this process is continued over time, the cognitive reality model begins to disintegrate. Learned versions of reality and previously instrumental responses repeatedly fail the initiate. Confusion and disorganization ensue until the point demarcating minimal (stage one) structure obtains. Pursuing the process further disintegrates the reality model, introducing a relatively entropic state. At this point the individual should be searching for a way to structure or make sense out of reality, and in terms of the initiation, his search constitutes the launching point for the transformation of identity. This parallels the route of ontogenetic development itself, wherein transformation of the cognitive structure seems to be initiated by a retrogression to a lower level prior to conceptual reorganization.[12]

Retrogression in the level of functioning is an integral part of

---

12. (Langer, 1969:179.) Such retrogressions have been identified by Blatt and Kohlberg (1970) and by D. E. Hunt (1973; personal communication). Generally these retrogressions can be expected to occur when the individual is introduced into a highly salient and novel environmental situation. They would be maximally probable at ages when the individual is entering a conceptual transition as a result of normal growth. These would tend to coincide with periods of life change, in our culture ages seven to nine and eleven to fifteen. It is probably not coincidental that First Communion and Confirmation also occur at these junctures.

the initiation procedure. Conditions are established to maintain uncertainty, and the individual is prepared to be reprogrammed. This would be a hyperintensive version of the normal ritual procedures, but the goal may include allowing the individual to pass the fail-safe point, where ritual normally acts as a barrier. Eliade describes this process as a "symbolic retrogression into chaos," symbolic of death of the old modes of behaving and a return to the natural or infant-like state. This is true in a very real, structural sense, as well as a symbolic one. The internal organization of the individual's cognitive apparatus has been retrogressed to an earlier, infantile mode of functioning, tracing backward the course of ontogenesis itself. The individual is now ready for rebirth and a new identity.[13]

At this point, ontogenesis is reconstructed in a new form—the new birth—by infusing the elements of the new model of the world-out-there. This can be accomplished through additional ritual techniques, including repetitive, regulated behavior and new mythic content. The goal here would be recreation of the stage one state in terms of the new myths. As in other contexts, ritual sets up the receptive state, centered on authority through creation of a unidimensional information-processing mode. Reality is re-created outside the person, handed down through the authority of the elders. Uncertainty is reduced and redundancy created. The consequence is recoordination of the neural and cognitive apparati in the new mode. In this context newly prescribed behaviors can be assimilated with maximal efficiency and credence on the part of the initiate. The model of reality is transformed into new terms, the new birth initiated, and the new plane of existence attained. The profane world of the child is thereby left behind, shattered beyond repair along with its attendant cognitive mode; the sacred world of the adult entered on the heels of the new construing of reality.

---

13. This is not a true regression in that the structural organization is not dismantled. Here it is retrogressed under environmental stress, and transformation in content, what the structure organizes, is carried out. The structures themselves should bounce back to their dispositional level with the alleviation of stress, and the new content, over time, may be elaborated at the dispositional level.

The initiate, himself or herself, must also believe in the new identity provided by the elders. It is here that the severe tests of initiation come in. Participating successfully in any of the severe initiation rites can easily confirm the new model of self, which is explainable within any one of a number of psychological balance models (Festinger's dissonance theory is particularly applicable here; Festinger, 1957, 1964). Important in such a process is that the initiate perceive himself or herself as undertaking the onerous task of his or her own volition. Successful participation is a process of model confirmation wherein the logical relationships are set up as follows: "He who passes this test is a man; I passed this test; therefore I am a man." Failure refutes the syllogism, and forced compliance allows alternative explanations to the self and possible lack of confidence. Having passed through the ordeal and absorbed the new knowledge, the initiate indeed is a new person. The world and the self no longer resemble the youth spirited away from the village.

Most cultures using such practices also prolong isolation until the new model solidifies or completes itself. Reintroduction into the social fabric is often accompanied by various forms of social support designed to reconfirm the newly established cognitive model.

The initiation process has been historically viewed as the transformation from child to adult in symbolic terms. Viewed in a diachronic, structural sense, the transformation becomes one of fact. It is a material as well as a symbolic reality. The symbolic retrogression and transformation are paralleled by a structural retrogression and transformation. Within the model of biogenetic structuralism this parallel extends downward into transformations in the neurological system. Such a view is supported by the neurophysiological models of Pribram (1971) and the genetic epistemology of Piaget. What in fact may take place is a complete overhaul of the system at various parallel levels, from the neurological mechanisms themselves, outward through corresponding transformation of the fixed action patterns and cognitive structures. In light of the more recent bioanatomical work following Rosenzweig et al. (1962) and the parallel biochemical work of

Weis (1969), such transformations begin to leave the realm of epiphenomena and enter the domain of the real. The important consideration is that the same functional and structural principles appear to hold true at every level, varying only in their range and complexity as they move from biology to cognition.

The Individual, Ritual, and Society

Both the individual cognitive system and the social system can be discussed in the same structural terms. It is merely the level of analysis that changes. Social systems, then, are considered extensions of biological and cognitive systems characteristic of individuals, organizing these more molecular systems and constrained by them. The relationship of the social system to the cognitive system parallels the relation of the cognitive system to what has traditionally been considered the biological or physiological system. We must stress again here that the differentiations between biological and cognitive systems are only analytical distinctions, holding as we do to the position reflected by Piaget (1971) and Laughlin and d'Aquili (1974) that cognitive structures have physiological reality and are extensions of biological systems.

Social structures exert constraint upon the structural organization of individual cognitive systems, as well as upon the content organized by cognitive structures. This effect is exerted through the society's impact upon ontogenesis of the structures of cognition. As previously discussed, the rate of development and the final structural state of an individual's cognitive system are contingent upon an optimal match between that system at a given point in time and characteristics of the environmental surroundings. Both the structure of the environment and its specific content, such as approved child-rearing practices, influence the developmental processes. Societies that are homogeneous, static, and intolerant of diversity should tend to inhibit development through insufficient stimulation, comparable to suboptimal input in the Schroder U-curves (Figures 7.2 and 7.3). Similarly, a society

242

whose structural characteristics are overly complex, or describable as chaotic, should act on the cognitive system in a fashion analogous to superoptimal stimulation. Societies that exhibit a pluralistic nature, combined with effective institutions for conceptually and behaviorally organizing such diversity, should produce the greatest proportion of conceptually complex members. Departure from this condition should reduce this possibility and suggests that some societies may produce few, if any, really complex conceptual structures.

To stimulate complexity with E_c, complexity and diversity must exist in the E_o. To protect the development of such E_c complexity, institutional structures must exist to modulate and organize environmental complexity to prevent superoptimal stimulation. Ritual, as discussed in this chapter and the last, is one of these institutions. Just as the social organization exerts constraints on individual cognition from without, individual cognition can constrain the actual or functional complexity of the social structure from within (McManus, 1974, a, b.). Constraint can take both developmental or synchronic form. Limitations in conceptual complexity among members of previous generations over time can constrain the development of the social structure as passed on to the current generation. If, for example, all or most previous members of a society failed to develop past, say, the stage one level, we would expect the transmission of a social structure that could be described as no more than stage one in its complexity (reasons for this statement are discussed later). The active involvement of more developed individuals in the formal construction of the society would be seen as essential in producing a complex social order.

In addition, the developmental level of those who hand down the tradition and social organization likewise exerts a ceiling effect on the social structure so transmitted (Laughlin and McManus, 1975). As with the Turiel (1966) results cited earlier in this chapter, the passage of information through an individual cognitive structure exposes that information to potential transformation in its structure. If the Constitution of the United States had to be transmitted orally from one generation to the next, its complex structure would be subject to distortion by the cognitive systems of the storytellers. If such individuals are cognitively simple and if the oral tendency is away from ritual verbatim repetition of the words (as exists in a number of West African societies), toward interpretation, the Constitution would eventually be lost and replaced by a system structured at stage one.

Finally, individual cognitive systems constrain the functional level of a social system. Data summarized in Schroder et al. (1967) clearly demonstrate that, at least for small groups in complex situations, the functional level of the group is constrained by the level of its individual members. In all the data collected by the Schroder group, in no case did a group exceed the developmental level of its most complex member in terms of its behavior in complex situations. The suggestion is, then, that, even if a complex social structure is passed on by previous generations, to function as such, it requires the participation of people equal to it in complexity.

Two factors can reduce the probability that the structural potential of a social structure will be actualized: (1) the dispositional level of those individuals in the society, especially those most intimately involved in its operation, and (2) the stress on these individuals, which determines their contemporaneous level of functioning. Some of this is discussed in the following chapters. Very briefly, stress on individual members of a society inhibits their capacity to actualize the potential adaptability of the social structure as it does with individual cognitive systems. Stress reduces flexibility of decision making, rigidifies the operation of the system, and probably encourages the use of previously adaptive approaches to problem solutions, whether or not they are appropriate to existing conditions. Economic stress or personal crisis impinging on individual cognitive structures in a democracy (for example, the German Weimar Republic) inhibits the full actualization of that social organization, sometimes resulting in its destruction. Again, rituals can act as a buffer or "fail-safe" point here. While they may, in some cases, inhibit the development of really complex and flexible functioning, they do act as an organ of conservation, maintaining at least minimal structural organization and providing the glue to hold the structure together in rough weather.

In sum, human cognitive systems exist between purely bio-logical systems, in the sense described by Piaget (1971), and social systems. Cognitive systems exert constraint upon both ad-joining levels of systemic organization and are constrained by them. They are the bridge between pure biology and traditional anthropology, and all three are part of a continuum of levels of structural organization. Ritual plays essentially a conservative role in the autoregulation of these systems, preserving and maintain-ing their integrity. Rituals establish the basis for part of the on-togenesis of human cognition, the socialization of members within the society, and the protection of the individual cognitive systems in times of stress. Ritual forms part of the matrix that organizes people into the social structure, and provides the glue that holds the social and cognitive structures together. It does so by con-trolling the information capabilities of the individual at the structural level and by influencing the selection of information so handled (i.e., surface transformations or cultural content). While ritual's role is essentially conservative, it can play some role in progression and transformation, as it does, for instance, in sociali-zation. Its principal function, it must be concluded, is to provide what we have called the stage one state: the state that maximizes a single, univariate orientation to reality at any level of analysis—physiological, psychological, or social. We now turn to a more de-tailed examination of this principal function in respect to social action and stress.

References

Abelson, R. et al. 1968. *Theories of Cognitive Consistency: A Sourcebook*. Chicago: Rand McNally.

Blatt, M. and L. Kohlberg. 1970. "The Effects of Classroom Discussion Upon Children's Level and Moral Judgement." Mimeo.

Brehm, D. and A. Cohen. 1962. *Exploration in Cognitive Dissonance*. New York: Wiley.

Chapple, E. 1970. *Culture and Biological Man*. New York: H. H. Rinehart and Winston.

Coffman, T. L. 1967. "Personality Structure, Involvement, and the Consequences of Tak-ing a Stand," in *Personality Theory and Information Processing* (H. M. Schroder and P. Suedfeld, eds.). New York: Ronald.

Dasen, P. R. 1972. "Cross-Cultural Piagetian Research: A Summary." *Journal of Cross-Cultural Psychology* 3:23–40.

Eliade, M. 1958. *Rites and Symbols of Initiation.* New York: Harper and Row.

Feldman, C. et al. 1974. *The Development of Adaptive Intelligence.* San Francisco: Jossey-Bass.

Feldman, S. 1965. *Cognitive Consistency.* New York: Academic Press.

Festinger, L. 1957. *A Theory of Cognitive Dissonance.* Evanston, Ill.: Row Peterson.

—— 1964. *Conflict, Decision, and Dissonance.* Stanford: Stanford University Press.

Festinger, L., H. Rieken, and S. Schacter. 1956. *When Prophecy Fails.* Minneapolis: University of Minnesota Press.

Harvey, O. J. 1962. "Personality Factors in the Resolution of Conceptual Incongruity." *Sociometry* 25:336–352.

—— 1964. "Some Cognitive Determinants of Influencibility." *Sociometry* 27:208–229.

Harvey, O. J., D. E. Hunt, and H. M. Schroder. 1961. *Conceptual Systems and Personality Organization.* New York: Wiley.

Hastorf, S. and C. Cantril. 1956. "They Saw a Game: A Case Study." *Journal of Abnormal and Social Psychology* 49:129–134.

Heider, F. 1958. *The Psychology of Interpersonal Relations.* New York: Wiley.

Hunt, D. E. 1971. *Matching Models in Education.* Toronto: Ontario Institute for Studies in Education.

Hunt, D. E. and E. Sullivan. 1974. *Between Psychology and Education.* Hinsdale, Illinois: Dryden.

Hunt, J. M. 1963. "Motivation Inherent in the Processing of Information and Action," in *Motivation and Social Interaction* (O. J. Harvey, ed.). New York: Ronald.

Inhelder, B. and J. Piaget. 1958. *The Growth of Logical Thinking from Childhood to Adolescence.* New York: Basic Books.

Kohlberg, L. 1963. "Moral Development and Identification," in *Child Psychology 62nd Yearbook of the National Society for the Study of Education.* (H. Stevenson, ed). Chicago: University of Chicago Press.

—— 1969. "Stage and Sequence: the Cognitive Developmental Approach to Socialization," in *Handbook of Socialization Theory and Research* (D. Goslin, ed.). Chicago: Rand McNally.

Kohlberg, L. and C. Gilligan. 1972. "The Adolescent as Philosopher: The Discovery of Self in a Post-conventional World." *Daedalus* 100:1051–1086.

Langer, J. 1969. *Theories of Development.* New York: Holt, Rinehart, and Winston.

Laughlin, C. and E. d'Aquili. 1974. *Biogenetic Structuralism.* New York: Columbia University Press.

Laughlin, C. and J. McManus. 1975. "Multivariable Cognitive Development: Implications for Anthropological Theory and Research." Paper presented to the NCAA Meetings, Potsdam, New York.

Lazarus, R. 1966. *Psychological Stress and the Coping Process.* New York: McGraw-Hill.

—— 1974. "Cognitive and Coping Processes in Emotion," in *Cognitive Views of Motivation* (B. Weiner, ed.). New York: Academic Press.

Lazarus, R. and E. M. Opton. 1966. "The Psychological Study of Stress: A Summary of Theoretical Formulations and Experimental Findings," in *Anxiety and Behavior* (C. D. Spielberger, ed.). New York: Academic Press.

Mahl et al. 1964. Cited in Pribram, K. 1971. *Languages of the Brain.* Englewood Cliffs, N.J.: Prentice-Hall.

McManus, J. 1971. "The Relationship of Cognitive Complexity and Involvement to Social Judgement." Unpublished thesis, Syracuse University.

—— 1974a. "Ontogenesis: The Diachronic Dimension of Structuralism." Paper presented in Studies in Biogenetic Structuralism, American Anthropological Association meetings, Mexico City.

—— 1974b. "Applications of the Schroder U-curve Hypothesis to Anthropology." Paper presented in Socio-cultural Responses to Resource Deprivation, American Anthropological Association meetings, Mexico City.

Miller, G., E. Galanter and K. Pribram. 1960. *Plans and the Structure of Behavior.* New York: Holt, Rinehart and Winston.

Piaget, J. 1932. *The Moral Judgment of the Child.* London: Kegan Paul.

—— 1970. *Structuralism.* New York: Basic Books.

—— 1971. *Biology and Knowledge.* Chicago: University of Chicago Press.

—— 1972. "Intellectual Evolution from Adolescence to Adulthood." *Human Development* 15:1–12.

—— 1973. *The Child and Reality.* New York: Basic Books.

Powers, W. T. 1973. *Behavior: The Control of Perception.* New York: Aldine.

Pribram, K. H. 1971. *Language of the Brain.* Englewood Cliffs, N.J.: Prentice-Hall.

Rokeach, M. 1964. *The Three Christs of Ypsilanti: A Psychological Study.* New York: Knopf.

Rosenberg, M. 1960. "Cognitive Reorganization in Response to the Hypnotic Reversal of Attitudinal Affect." *Journal of Personality* 28:39–63.

Rosenzweig, M. R. et al. 1962. "Effects of Environmental Complexity and Training on Brain Chemistry and Anatomy." *Journal of Comparative and Physiological Psychology* 55:429–437.

Schacter, S. and J. Singer. 1962. "Cognitive, Social and Physiological Determinants of Emotional State." *Psychological Review* 69:379–399.

Schroder, H. M. 1972. "Conceptual Complexity and Personality Organization," in *Personality Theory and Information Processing* (H. M. Schroder and P. Suedfeld, eds.). New York: Ronald.

Schroder, H. M. and W. Crano, 1965. "Complexity of Attitude Structure and the Processes of Conflict Resolution." In *Personality Theory and Information Processing* (H. M. Schroder and P. Suedfeld, eds.) New York: Ronald.

Schroder, H. M., M. Driver, and S. Streufert. 1967. *Human Information Processing.* New York: Holt, Rinehart and Winston.

Sherif, M. and C. Sherif, eds. 1968. *Attitude, Ego-Involvement and Change.* New York: Wiley.

Sherif, M., C. Sherif, and R. E. Nebergall. 1965. *Attitude and Attitude Change.* Philadelphia: Saunders.

Sokolov, E. N. 1963. *Perception and the Conditioned Reflex.* New York: Macmillan.

Streufert, S. 1966. "Conceptual Structure, Communication Importance, and Interpersonal Attitudes Toward Conforming and Deviant Group Members," *Journal of Personality and Social Psychology* 4:100–103.

Streufert, S. et al. 1965. "Conceptual Structure, Environmental Complexity, and Task Performance," *Journal of Experimental Research in Personality* 1:132–137.

Suedfeld, P. 1964. "Attitude Manipulation in Restricted Environments: 1. Conceptual Structure and Response to Propaganda," *Journal of Abnormal and Social Psychology* 68(3):242–246.

John McManus

Suedfeld, P. and H. M. Schroder, eds. 1972. *Personality Theory and Information Processing*. New York: Ronald.

Suedfeld, P. and S. Streufert. 1966. "Information Search as a Function of Conceptual and Environmental Complexity," *Psychonomic Science* 4:233–236.

Sullivan, E. V., G. McCullough, and M. Stager. 1970. "A Developmental Study of the Relation Between Conceptual Ego and Moral Development." *Child Development* 41:399–412.

Turiel, E. 1966. "An Experimental Test of the Sequentiality of Developmental Stages in the Child's Moral Judgments." *Journal of Personality and Social Psychology* 3(6):611–618.

Turnbull, C. 1973. *The Mountain People*. New York: Simon and Schuster.

Valenstein, E. 1973. *Brain Control*. New York: Wiley-Interscience.

Weiner, B. 1973. *Theories of Motivation*. Chicago: Markham.

Weis, P. A. 1969. "The Living System: Determinism Stratified," in *Beyond Reductionism: New Perspectives in the Life Sciences* (A. Koestler and J. Smythies, eds.). New York: Macmillan.

Werner, H. 1957. "The Concept of Development from a Comparative and Organismic Point of View," in *The Concept of Development* (D. Harris, ed.) Minneapolis, University of Minnesota Press.

Witkin, H. A. et al. 1962. *Psychological Differentiation*. New York: Wiley.

Eight

Ritual and Social Power

Tom Burns and

Charles D. Laughlin, Jr.

In one sense it is quite erroneous to speak of the concept of
the external world of the man of action if we mean to imply
thereby that it is ever made the object of his conscious
thought. Strictly speaking he has none. In the main he un-
hesitatingly accepts the form which the thinker has given to
ideas. This holds more particularly for all those questions
connected with the shape, configuration, and origin of the
world around him. The man of action follows the lead of the
thinker or at least repeats somewhat mechanically what the
thinker has to say on these matters because his interests are
centered not upon the analysis of reality but upon the *orientation of reality* and the proofs for its existence.

Paul Radin, *Primitive Man as Philosopher*

In this chapter we present a model and a language for investigating collective action and social control. Using this model, we
discuss the relationship between ritual—particularly religious
ritual—and social control and power. As has been repeatedly
emphasized in earlier chapters, ritual serves as a form of communication uniting members of a group in corporate action. We
expand on this idea, pointing out a variety of social control functions played by ritual in human society. In particular we underscore the role played by ritual in the maintenance of social rela-

We are grateful to Richard Downs and Steve Reyna for their comments and criticisms of an earlier draft of this chapter.

tionships and social structure. Finally, we examine ritual as a power resource in human society and the role it may play in both stability and change.

Past discussion by theorists has revolved more or less around five functions of ritual that are political in the broadest sense of the term: as a mechanism for social control, as a means of resolving conflict, and as a device for maintaining social solidarity, stratification, and political structure.

1. *The Role of Ritual as a Mechanism for Social Control.* Ritual is seen from this perspective as a public or semipublic display of "correct," or "right," behavior for the benefit of individual group members. In some cases ritual may be used to expose "wrong" behavior on the part of one or more members and may even negatively sanction or punish them for moral infractions (see Radcliffe-Brown, 1922:325; Laughlin and Laughlin, 1972; Wilson, 1959:66; Nadel, 1951:138).

2. *Ritual in the Resolution of Social Conflict.* Several "conflict theorists," among others, have viewed ritual as a social process or device for the acting out of social dysfunction, antagonism, factional dispute, and the like. It drains hostile emotions while at the same time providing channels for reunification and reconciliation (see Firth, 1967:80, on "privilege ceremonies;" Gluckman, 1963; Wilson, 1959:217; Nobeck, 1963).

3. *Ritual in the Maintenance of Social Solidarity.* Ritual may function in directing and sanctioning corporate activity, defining group identity, supporting the "moral order," and mitigating against rampant entrepreneurism (see Fortes and Evans-Pritchard, pp. 21–22, and Wagner, p. 217, in Fortes and Evans-Pritchard, 1940; Balandier, 1970:111; Wilson, 1959:216; Firth, 1961:239; Nadel, 1951:362; Radcliffe-Brown, 1922:234; Wallace, 1966:126).

4. *Ritual in the Maintenance of Social Stratification.* In this case ritual activities may "mirror," model, legitimize, define, or otherwise sanction a status difference between segments of society. The status hierarchy may consist of the dichotomy between "royal" and "common" clans, a system of social classes, or a system of relatively fixed castes. Emphasis has also been given to the role of ritual in the marking and legitimization of transition from

one social status category to another (see Chapple and Coon, 1942; Richard in Fortes and Evans-Pritchard, 1940:111; Leach, 1954:10ff; Fortes, 1959; Wilson, 1959:216; Van Gennep, 1908).

5. *Ritual in the Maintenance of the Power Structure.* Those who emphasize this function of ritual point to the restricted access to ritual by persons in authority. Positions of central authority may have originated from the ascendance of ritual specialists (e.g., heads of "rainmaking" lineages may become clan or tribal chiefs). "Divine" kingships may be defined as a special relationship between the leader and one or more supernatural beings—a relationship manifested in public or "secret" ritual. Members of society are described as looking to their leader(s) for critical rituals both on a fixed schedule and during times of stress (see following chapter). The mythic structure may be said to legitimize power relations, and ritual to point up the continuity of political structure—a structure compatible with a corresponding and proper universe (see Fortes, p. 259, Gluckman, pp. 30ff; Schapera, pp. 59, 70, Richards, p. 99, and Wagner, p. 234, in Fortes and Evans-Pritchard, 1940; also see Richards, 1960; Mair, 1970:214ff; Vansina, 1966:32; Leach, 1954; Balandier, 1970:99ff; Middleton, 1960; Laughlin and Laughlin, 1972, 1974; Wilson, 1959:49, 66, 216; Firth, 1961:236; and Nadel, 1951:140).

While the political and integrative functions of ritual are emphasized in the literature and in our chapter, there are other views of ritual, for instance, those seeing its relationship to one or more universal human needs (see chapter 7). For example, Kluckhohn (1942:79) views ritual as a cultural product that provides (along with myths) systematic "protection" against supernatural dangers, the threat of ill health, threats of the physical environment, antisocial tensions, and the pressures of a more powerful society. In general, "ritual is an obsessive repetitive activity—often a symbolic dramatization of the fundamental 'needs' of the society, whether 'economic,' 'biological,' 'social,' or 'sexual.' The all-pervasive configurations . . . of act symbols (rituals) and word symbols (myths) preserve the cohesion of society and sustain the individual, protecting him from intolerable conflict." Turner (see Horton, 1964) views ritual as a way human beings satisfy the universal need for representing and expressing pure existence or the "pure-act-of-being." He argues that ritual cannot be reduced to its functional meaning, "economic rationality," or calculated value.

Horton (1964) considers ritual as a means whereby human beings understand things. In particular, he views ritual as part of theory building, an aspect of the attempt to explain and influence the working of one's everyday world by "discovering the constant principles that underlie the apparent chaos and flux of sensory experience." Horton argues that ritual, in the sense of approach to mystical powers, is a frequent accompaniment of *rites of passage,* because a corporate group is apt to be defined in terms of the personal beings who are "behind" the coordinated activities of its members, and changes of role or status usually involve incorporation into a new group or a new set of relationships. "It is these beings who keep the group flourishing, or weaken it in response to breaches of group norms. Because membership in the group implies having one's life partially controlled by such beings, becoming a member logically involves a process of being put under their control." Similarly, he argues that, because the strength and welfare of corporate groups is seen as intimately bound up with their members' close observance of their moral norms, "the spirits that underpin the various corporate groups of a society nearly always support the moral norms of such groups; and their strengthening action is conditioned upon observance of these norms. When a group assembles to approach its guiding spirit, it is therefore appropriate that its members, in their behavior toward another during the ritual, should demonstrate their readiness to observe group norms."

Leach (1972) also emphasizes the knowledge and communication aspects of ritual but with a focus on collective knowledge. He distinguishes two types of information: (1) information about nature, that is, about the topography, the climate, usable and dangerous plants, animals, inanimate things, and so on; (2) information about society, the relations of men to other men, the nature of social groups, the rules and constraints that make social life possible. The performance of ritual stores and perpetuates such knowledge, which is essential for the survival of the performers.

Still others see ritual as a way human populations regulate their environment; that is, in our terms, ritual serves as a source of power over the environment. Rappaport (1967), in particular, argues that ritual helps to maintain biotic communities existing within their territories, redistributing land among people and people over land, limiting the frequency of fighting, facilitating trade, and so forth.

The function assigned to ritual in any particular social theory obviously depends on the orientation of the social theorist. Some social theorists emphasize social system stability; once institutionalized, the system is predominantly "morphostatic"—that is, it tends to maintain its characteristic structures. Others assume models in which "morphogenic" processes prevail; that is, stability is threatened by ever-present tendencies for structures to reform, change, or evolve (Buckley et al., 1974). If the theorist is concerned with the maintenance of the status quo, then the homeostatic functioning of ritual is likely to be emphasized. On the other hand, if the analyst is concerned with social change—possibly rapid and revolutionary change in political structure—then emphasis is on the role played by ritual in "rebellion" or "revitalization" (see Wallace, 1966:209ff). The outline that follows is a framework that allows social systems to manifest both morphostatic and morphogenic processes—processes that are often working at odds with one another. Ritual may contribute to one or the other or both of these processes.

Action Systems, Social Control, and Corporate Action

Before proceeding to our discussion of ritual and social power, we need to introduce several concepts of social action that will contribute to the analysis and understanding of the political functions of ritual.

Individual Interests Versus Collective Interests

In this book we have been interested in how organisms (including man) alternate between individuated action and corporate action and how ritual behavior affects this alternation in certain adaptively critical situations. The literature pertaining to collective action, at least for man, suggests a variety of situations and conditions conducive to individuation in which, from the group perspective, corporate action would be optimal. Elsewhere (Buckley et al., 1974) attention has been focused on several social situations in which cooperation is problematic because self-interest contradicts group or collective interest: competitive panics, the "commons problem," and the *n*-person prisoners' dilemma.[1] In each case the persons or groups involved typically recognize that they would benefit from cooperation, but each individual perceives that he, personally, is better off if he does not cooperate. In the absence of social control processes, such situations lead to individuation.

1. *Competitive Panics.* Competition is a social process in which each actor tries to gain, or to avoid the loss of, some good, service, or valuable. Competitive panics (extreme competitive action motivated by strong emotion) in social action systems occur under the following conditions (Brown, 1965): The actors involved wish to gain or avoid the loss of some important valuable. The valuable is perceived by the actors as scarce, and what one actor does to retain the valuable has negative implications for other actors. Thus, the use of an escape route in a burning theatre by *A* may reduce *B*'s chances of escape. Simultaneous attempts by many actors to use the escape route further reduce its effectiveness. Competitive panics, then, are likely to occur when those involved have a limited opportunity to gain (or to avoid loss of) a valuable and when those who act first have the best opportunity. There is also an absence of social controls (enforced rules, normative sanctions, presence of authorities) to limit actors' self-interest. Ex-

1. In the examples discussed here each actor perceives that he is personally better off if he individually does not cooperate. His refusal to cooperate is perceived by him as making little or no difference to the ultimate outcome, and, in any case, the benefits of collective action will come to him without the cost or burden of participation. If others refuse to cooperate as well, he would still perceive himself better off in that his own individual effort would not alter the ultimate outcome, and participation would entail substantial and uncompensated cost. And yet, the persons or groups involved typically recognize that they would all fare better by cooperating than not cooperating.

amples of such situations are the following: a burning building with too few fire exits; a sinking ship with too few lifeboats; a collective demand for subsistence that is greater than the food supply (see Laughlin and Brady, 1978); a supply of perishable goods that far exceeds demand but that sellers must dispose of; a bank undergoing a "run" that has insufficient cash on hand to pay off depositors; catastrophes leading to a "breakdown of law and order" and looting; gold and land rushes. The common theme in all these examples is that a perceived scarcity leads to an intensification of competition, followed by increased fear and panic.

2. *The Commons Problem.* In medieval England the commons were lands open to all community members for the pasturing of privately owned livestock. As long as each herdsman limited the size of the herd he brought to the commons, all could benefit from the common pasture. However, each herdsman's expansion of his herd worked to his advantage, since he gained additional grazing without any cost. As long as each herdsman had only a small herd, such an increase had little or no noticeable effect on grazing. However, the expansion of everyone's herd increased grazing but lowered the capacity of the commons to support grazing. Furthermore, any herdsman who restrained expansion of his herd not only failed to gain anything further from the commons but also lost in the short-run exploitation of commons doomed to ultimate ruin by acts of his neighbors. Hardin (1972) considers this problem a prototype of many modern problems. The air, fresh waters, the oceans, and natural resources such as the earth's supplies of minerals and oils are all commons and are vulnerable to the same pattern of overuse.

3. *The N-Person Prisoners' Dilemma.* The well-known problem of the prisoners' dilemma has been described by Luce and Raiffa (1957:95) in the following terms: Two suspects are taken into custody and questioned separately. The district attorney (DA) is confident that they are guilty of a specific crime, but he does not have sufficient evidence to convict them at a trial. Each prisoner understands that there are two options: to confess to the crime or not to confess. If they both keep silent, the DA will book them on some minor charge and they will each get one year in the peniten-

tiary. If both confess, they will be prosecuted but will receive eight years in the penitentiary—that being less than the most severe sentence. If, however, one turns state's evidence and the other does not, then the one who confesses will receive three months in jail, while the other will get the maximum penalty—ten years in the penitentiary. The situation is obviously conducive to individuated, or self-interest, decisions on the part of each prisoner.

An *n*-person example of the prisoners' dilemma is provided by Luce and Raiffa (1957:97). Consider the case of many wheat farmers where each farmer has, as an idealization, two alternatives: "restricted production" and "full production." If all farmers use restricted production, the price is high, and individually they fare rather well; if all use full production, the price is low, and individually they fare rather poorly. The strategy of a given farmer does not, however, significantly affect the price level—this is the assumption of a competitive market—so that, regardless of the strategies of the other farmers, he is better off in all circumstances with full production. Thus full production dominates restricted production; yet, if each acts rationally, they all fare poorly.

Individuation has the potentiality in situations of the type just described of causing social disaster or serious harm to persons and to group continuity. However, for most social groups at most times a number of social control processes are operating consciously or unconsciously on the actors involved to prevent or resolve collective action problems (Goodenough, 1963:95ff; Buckley et al., 1974). Social control processes operate on the various components of action, structuring perceptions, evaluations, action possibilities, decision procedures, and therefore, the likely interaction patterns of those involved. Social controls may take the form of institutional controls (controls imposed from outside the action situation), as well as controls inherent in established or emergent relationships between actors (controls developed within the action situation).

Concepts of Social Action

In order to model and analyze the problem of collective action and the role of ritual in dealing with collective action problems, we introduce several societal-level concepts. Of particular importance are social control processes that shape collective action. These processes operate on the various components of action: value or preference structures,[2] action or "opportunity" sets,[3] and decision procedures[4] (Buckley et al., 1974; Burns and Meeker, 1975).

Social Structuring and Transformation of Individual Preference Structures. There are two ways in which social influence on preference structure occurs: (1) operation on the outcomes of acts through selective sanctions that alter the values of outcomes and thus individual preferences and (2) influences on individuals' perceptions and evaluations of outcomes.

Social sanctions change the outcomes of acts and, thereby,

2. *Preference or Evaluation Structures.* Such structures are order relations on a set of items, for example, a set of action alternatives or action outcomes. Actors are assumed to evaluate actions and outcomes from different frames of reference. Evaluation on the basis of tradition differs markedly from evaluation based on utility or intrinsic value. The result is a variety of preference structures with different origins. Thus, in a given situation an actor may have to evaluate and choose between alternative, often conflicting, evaluation structures. This entails higher order processes, metaprocesses, discussed in footnote 7.

3. *Actions.* Each actor in the system has a finite set of possible action alternatives. This set is composed of finite subsets that are considered for choice in any given situation. Associated with each action alternative is a set of *perceived* (and cognized) outcomes (results, payoffs). *Actors* may be individual persons, groups, factions, parties, governments, social subsystems, and so forth. Organized groups possess goals and objectives in interaction with other groups and have the capacity to carry out corporate acts (realizing, of course, that there also exist endogenous group interactions).

4. *Decision Procedures.* Choice on the part of an actor consists of selecting an alternative from among a set of alternative actions. There are numerous bases for such choice: selection on the basis of the actor's goals or values, selection prescribed by tradition or authority, selection of alternatives other than those prescribed by tradition or authority, random selection, no selection possible, selection necessitated by the demands of personal or group survival, and so on. We list these merely to indicate the multiplicity of motivations in choice behavior.

Decision procedures that entail consideration of actual or predicted outcomes may be contrasted with those in which little or no consideration is given to outcomes, only to "proper" action (e.g., when tradition or authority stipulates that the actor "do this, not that").

The latter is a key consideration in our later discussion of ritual. As Prattis (1973) has pointed out, the range of decision strategies available to actors is wide and the particular strategy selected will depend on a number of variables operating in the situation—and this, of course, entails metaevaluation and metachoice (Burns and Meeker, 1975). Also, as we have already seen (see chapter 7), the range of alternative strategies perceived by the actor will depend on the complexity of cognitive-perceptual structure attending the choice situation.

preference structures. If the outcome of an act is made impossible, or made to look antisocial, illegal, or illegitimate to an actor, it will reduce the weighting of that act in the actor's preference structure (on the assumption, of course, that his name is not Simon Templar). In general, members of a group receive social approval or avoid disapproval by conforming to anticompetitive and cooperative norms. For example, among the So of Uganda, herdsmen who violate the rules governing the use of commons set aside for the use of calves during the height of the dry season are open to public ridicule and judicial action by the governing body of the tribe (Laughlin and Laughlin, 1974). Also, norms and sanctions against rate busting in factories, apple polishers and teachers' pets in schools, and stool pigeons and informers in groups of any kind represent social disapproval of (and control of) conduct that advances individuation at the expense of the group (Blau, 1964:255).

Cooperative behavior and compliance with anticompetitive norms are more likely, the more power the group has over the individual member. Group power over a member is greater (1) the greater the number and extent of power resources controlled by the group in relation to the member, (2) the longer the member's relationship to the group endures, (3) the more he depends on group authority to guide his behavior in situations of relative ignorance and uncertainty on his part, and (4) the more stress is present in the environment of the group.[5]

The group may influence the perceptions and outcome analyses of its members. Individual outcome analysis will be altered by knowledge and concerns about the feelings and goals of others in a group toward which a member has a positive social orientation (self/other orientation).[6] The more positive the orientation and the

---

5. As is shown in chapter 9, there is a direct relationship between increased stress on a group and a tendency toward greater centralization of authority; see also Laughlin and Brady (1978).

6. Social orientations among actors in an action system operate as metaprocesses (see footnote 7) that impose relative, higher order values on the various evaluations or outcome analyses of actors. Actors with pure self-orientations concern themselves only with personal outcomes, while actors with self/other orientations focus on outcomes preferred by both self and other. Other orientations relate to rivalry or competitiveness, equity, distributive justice,

concomitant feelings, the greater the likelihood that individuals would exclude purely self-oriented outcomes.

As we have seen in chapter 7, socialization plays a major role in developing and fostering positive social orientation. In societies a premium is placed on trustworthiness and cooperative behavior. Members are socialized to orient strongly toward the group (be it family, lineage, political organization, secret society, or other group) and to curb personal ambitions, self-orientation, and competitiveness in the interest of the collective. Such cooperative behavior has been a major factor in the failure of many Western development schemes—schemes that have depended in one way or another on individuation, for example, personal accumulation of wealth and capital. In many "target" societies the accumulation of wealth for its own sake and failure to share that wealth with group members are considered wrong or evil actions and may receive strong and negative sanction (see Goodenough, 1963:488ff; Foster, 1962:92). In general, social control over the perception of action alternatives and outcomes can bring about the same result—a structuring of preference relations. It is easy to see that group ideology, including mythology and attendant ritual, may structure and coordinate the perceptions, evaluations, and actions of members and, thus, constitute major social control mechanisms (see chapter 5). The belief or perception that everyone else is cooperating—a view propounded in a public ritual and its covering mythology—typically enhances the likelihood of an actor's co-

---

masochism, and the like. Incumbents of social roles are usually socialized (or in Levi-Strauss's sense, "cooked") into certain social orientations vis-à-vis other actors in the system and are also subject to social controls maintaining or enforcing the orientations. To put this another way, actor A's behavior toward B may reflect a preference structure prescribed by the group of which A is a part. Hence, A's orientation toward B, his display of cooperation, his contribution of gifts and services, and so forth, are grounded in a social and institutional setting and may have very little to do with the behavior of a particular recipient (B).

This conception can be extended to cover cases in which A and B are *both* normatively constrained to interact with one another in particular ways; that is, they have certain orientations and obligations toward one another. Such systems of mutual orientation (including, we should say, most human action systems) are maintained by social control processes. Actors who for one reason or another deviate from the prescribed orientation or behavioral expectations in situations in which they are appropriate experience personal embarrassment or shame and are subject to group disapproval and sanction.

operation. Information to the contrary, of course, erodes the system of compliance. Yet, as is shown in the next chapter, a lack of cooperation in, say, the economic sphere may be offset by perceived or actual cooperation in the ritual sphere.

Groups seeking to foster cooperative behavior try to eliminate as much uncertainty, lack of information, and distrust as possible, since these tend to elicit individualized or uncoordinated behavior in situations requiring collective action. In the case of the "fire in the theatre" problem, one might note the institution of regular fire drills in public buildings and the emphasis on social awareness of the danger of panic responses. Also, shouting "FIRE" in a crowded theatre, as Justice Oliver Wendell Holmes, Jr., pointed out, is an abuse of "freedom of speech."

In general, social solidarity, and norms and sanctions opposing noncooperation, extreme competitiveness, cheating, and the like, among group members alter preference structures so as to reduce the likelihood of competitive or conflictive preference structures' occurring among members. Groups induce members to evaluate outcomes in terms other than self-orientation (and to experience shame and guilt for inequitable outcomes where self takes advantage of others). Groups may also emphasize and enforce "correct action," inducing members to pay more attention to the propriety of their acts than to their consequences. Thus, social controls directed at preference structures *may act to transform a "competitive" preference structure into one more conducive to cooperation.* Social controls are thereby viewed as higher order processes or metaprocesses by means of which one preference structure is transformed into another.[7] The existence of such *metaprocesses* favoring solidarity and self/other orientation over individuation may have an evolutionary basis as has been shown in an earlier discussion (see chapter 3). Robert Trivers in developing an evolutionary model for the origin of "reciprocal altruism," states:

7. *Metaprocesses.* The selection of preference structures or their modification so as to remove inconsistencies or to decrease indecisiveness, the choice of a decision procedure, and the search for new action alternatives or outcomes are examples of processes typically extraneous to decision or game theoretical models of human action (see Burns and Meeker,

If an "altruistic situation" is defined as any in which one individual can dispense a benefit to a second greater than the cost of the act to himself, then the chances of selecting for altruistic behavior . . . are greatest (1) when there are many such altruistic situations in the lifetime of the altruists, (2) when a given altruist repeatedly interacts with the same small set of individuals, and (3) when pairs of altruists are exposed "symmetrically" to altruistic situations, that is in such a way that the two are able to render roughly equivalent benefits to each other at roughly equivalent costs. These three conditions can be elaborated into a set of relevant biological parameters affecting the possibility that reciprocal altruistic behavior will be selected for (1971:37).

In fact, and as has been emphasized numerous times in this volume, the fostering and maintenance of social control metaprocesses that ameliorate individuation are the sine qua non of any adaptive strategy dependent on collective action—regardless of the species (see also Count, 1973; Teleki, 1973, n.d.).

Social Structuring of Action and Interaction Conditions. Social structure and institutional constraints, including constraints on the exercise of power, determine the range of possible conduct—the action alternatives available in a given context. In particular, group constraints may make exploitative interactions such as those depicted in the commons problem, *n*-person prisoners' dilemma, and fire in the theatre situations difficult or unlikely. For

1975). Such processes, in that they determine "how things are to be viewed and evaluated," "what is to be optimized," "which game is to be played," and so forth, entail evaluations, decisions, and operations of a higher order. To emphasize this difference we identify such processes by the generic term "metaprocesses."

We note that this distinction is not absolute. A metaprocess in one context may be an action outcome in another. The total system is essentially hierarchical (Burns and Meeker, 1975). The higher order processes of evaluation, decision, and operation shape the lower order evaluation and decision activities by selecting, synthesizing, and in general controlling the components of the evaluation and decision activities: the preference structures, relevant action possibilities, and decision procedures.

Many components enter into the metalevel analysis and operations: the actor's knowledge and experience, perceptions, personal and social values, and his social relationships. When these are compatible (convergent in their value indications), evaluation and decision making are not difficult or stressful (i.e., decision time, ambivalence, equivocation, confusion, and so forth, are minimal). On the other hand, whenever important conflicts or incompatibilities occur, actors display ambivalence, indecisiveness, and increased decision time, typically generating metalevel activities that may or may not lead to a solution.

one thing, group members may be denied the option of non-cooperation or even nonparticipation whenever others cooperate or participate, for example, by compulsory membership in age sets, universal taxation, or mass migration. Interaction situations themselves may be structured to mitigate competitive panics. For example, in a theatre, the larger the number and size of exits and escape routes to the exits, the less likelihood of panic. In other words, an increase in the supply of a valuable may have the effect of reducing *perceived* scarcity. Another way groups may operate to exclude noncooperation is by expanding the set of cooperative action alternatives. This expansion may have the effect of generating more satisfactory outcomes, both from the individual and the group perspectives. Such an option, again, is at a metaprocess level and *acts to transform a structure of alternative actions having a likelihood of individuation in selection to a structure having little likelihood of individuation.*

A final example of such a metaprocess acting upon the selection of action alternatives is offered by the institutionalization of collective decision procedures. If individual members are allowed to make decisions about action alternatives outside the group context, they may take a self-oriented course of action such as we have depicted in the prisoners' dilemma situation. However, by mandatory collective decision making (that is, the decisions made in group context are binding on the action of the members) the actors as a group gain greater control and, thus, greater power to achieve collectively advantageous outcomes. Self/other-oriented decision making under collective decision procedures becomes more rational in prisoners' dilemma-type settings than self-oriented decision making. Clearly, all of these metaprocesses affecting the selection of action alternatives depend heavily on social conditions such as solidarity, the nature of the relations among actors, cultural understandings, and norms prescribing such procedures and enforcing their results.

Social Power. There are three types of power that an actor *A* may exercise over another actor *B*: [8]

8. Actor *A* is defined as having power over actor *B* (where the actors may be individuals or groups) if *A* can exercise *behavioral control* over *B*—that is, when *A* is able to produce

1. *A* has *constraint power* over *B* whenever he has the capacity to limit *B*'s action opportunities. Examples of constraint power are parents (*A*) placing a child (*B*) in a playpen to constrain his activities, and the removal by a government (*A*) of "enemy aliens" (*B*) to concentration camps in time of war.

2. *A* has *persuasive power* over *B* when he has the ability to influence *B*'s cognitive and affective orientations toward his environment (i.e., *B*'s perceptions, evaluations, associations, and decisions in relation to his environment). *A* may exercise this power in a number of ways. He may be in a position to control the information received by *B* pertaining to action alternatives or outcomes. Research on persuasion (Hovland, 1954; Klapper, 1960; Sears, 1969) has shown that the source of a message greatly influences its effectiveness. If an actor (*A*) possesses competence, status, or prestige in the eyes of *B*, then his messages will usually carry more weight than if he lacks these qualities. Other factors of importance in persuasive influence are the influencer's reputation for objectivity and credibility, as well as the possession of skill in constructing effective messages or controlling their use.

3. *A* has *sanctioning power* over *B* when *A* controls some valuable or set of valuables (*X*) desired by *B* (Burns and Cooper, 1971, 1972). Using his control over the valuable *X, A* may reward

---

an intended effect (change in *B*'s behavior). This entails *A*'s making *B*'s actions conform to *A*'s expectations with a probability greater than that if *A* had not attempted to influence *B*'s action. This conception of social power involves the following conditions and considerations regarding the interaction between *A* and *B:* (1) *Intentionality. A* may influence the behavior of *B* without intending to do so. In such a case we may rightfully say that *A* had a causal effect on the behavior of *B,* but we may not say that *A* exercised control over *B.* Power, then, implies intentionality on the part of *A.* (2) *Disparity of Goals.* In a power relationship, *A* has a preference structure over *B*'s actions and outcomes that, in general, is not congruent with *B*'s. Thus, if *A* did not exercise control over *B,* then *B*'s actions and outcomes would not coincide with the goals and expectations of *A.* (3) *Potentiality.* Power may be potential, as well as actual. This is important because the failure to distinguish power potential (control of behavior through control of power resources) and actual behavioral control (direct constraint of *B*'s behavior by *A*) has led to much confusion and needless polemic in the discussion of social power.

These aspects of power are interrelated and can usually be separated only analytically. The relationships between the types and the processes by which they are organized in an action system are discussed elsewhere (Buckley et al., 1974).

or punish *B* for compliance with or failure to comply with the action alternative directed or desired by *A*. For example, an employer may gain compliance from an employee through his control over promotion, salary increases, bonuses, continued employment, and the like. The valuables *A* controls may be other actors (including supernatural or mythical actors such as ancestors, gods, or spirits), or they may be special knowledge or skill, goods or services, or property.

A's sanctioning power in relation to *B* requires that he have the capacity and the willingness to make decisions and take actions pertaining to *X* in relation to *B*. In most real social situations there are constraints (usually social) on *A*'s control over valuable *X*.

The set of valuables (*X*) that is the basis for *A*'s power over *B* is a *power resource.* Such power resources may be either material (e.g., money, cattle, land, gold, shelter, food) or nonmaterial (e.g., freedom, sanction, approval, well-being, accreditation). In sum, such power resources may be anything that *A* controls and *B* values. In many, if not most, societies with primitive technologies, nonmaterial power resources are of utmost importance. Both types of power resource are, however, found in all societies.

A's power over *B* is typically relative. That is, *B* may control, for example, some valuable (*Y*) desired by *A*. Thus, *B* has a certain power over *A*. *A* has a relative power advantage over *B* when the power *A* may exercise over *B* is greater by some measure than the power *B* may exercise over *A*.

Of the three types of social power, we are most concerned here with sanctioning and persuasive power. The full efficacy of ritual is evidenced in the realm of indirect control of behavior. As we shall see, this is especially the case with persuasive power, where control over ritual as a power resource is a major factor in the institutionalization and augmentation of power positions in any action system.

Ritual and Social Control

While ritual may serve a variety of human needs (see footnote 2), one of its main functions is to structure actors' perceptions and orientations, decision procedures, and action opportunities, that is, the components of action discussed previously. It thereby structures interaction patterns of those involved. In this sense ritual operates intentionally or unintentionally as a social control device, contributing to the creation and maintenance of patterns of collective action and social structure. We discuss specific ways in which ritual does this, providing what appears to be a parsimonious interpretation of ritual in social life, linking phenomena that have typically been viewed as unrelated.

Tuning Effect

Professor Barbara Lex, in her discussion of the tuning effects of ritual trance (chapter 4), has established a basis for understanding ritual as social control over actors' perceptions and orientations. Her thorough discussion requires little amplification here. We only emphasize that neurophysiological tuning in the central nervous system of the individual and synchronization of the tuning effect among all members of the group probably participate heavily in the other functions of ritual examined later. There is probably a significant tuning component to rituals of social orientation (discussed later), wherein the collective action is directed to the accomplishment of some effect (curing, wholesale exorcism of epidemic, and the like). Recent research in the medical sciences has shown the enormous importance of placebo effect on incidence of curing, a point also emphasized by researchers on "folk" or ethnomedicine. In writing about Australian aboriginal medical practice, John Cawte (1974) notes:

The question is often asked by Western observers of primitive society: How is the deceit practiced by the native doctor in creating his mystique and in conjuring his medicine stones compatible with his sincerity? The Spanish missionaries are interested in this paradox, themselves having little doubt that although the removal of a *tjagolo* might depend upon deceit the doctor himself has sincere faith in the act. They put it: he himself is deceived by his deception. A sick doctor will consult another doctor for removal of the *tjagolo,* an act that he knows is one of legerdemain. They suggest that it is like a sacrament, and that is what matters. If faith and hope are healing emotions, the doctor mobilizes them as do priests and therapists in other cultures (pp. 64–65).

Cawte quotes one aborigine who had been watching a curing ceremony as saying, "Of course you don't believe it, but you know what: that man got better. You know why: Make 'im glad, eat 'im tucker straight away. From his heart he feel glad and get better" (p. 33).

The point to be emphasized is that, in the process of tuning, the ritual process may also have the effect of orienting or reorienting the perception and drive toward alternative actions and outcomes. And, as we shall see, the ritual sequence may act to constrain antisocial or noncooperative acts by giving vent to hostility and aggression between members of the group and thus permitting concerted and effective action at a later time (see Kluckhohn, 1942).

Behavioral Modeling of Ideal Sociocosmological Relations

Ritual may function as a model of ideal actions and relations in the social and cosmological world of group members. In this sense, ritual may be viewed as the motor expression of the ideational system. If the ritual is cosmologically expansive, then it tends to be the behavioral embodiment of the group's mythic repertoire. Ritual not only becomes an enactment of the ideational system but also functions hypothetically to reinforce the ideational system through action (see chapter 5).

But more than that, ritual in which ideal roles and relationships between roles are acted out "as they should be" may function as a model of the group's social structure. In other words, such ritual may model, act out, and reinforce the structure of social stratification and often provides cosmological justification for the structuring. As Wallace (1966) puts it:

Thus, belief in high gods mirrors the existence of great differences in rank among living people; belief in malevolent witches mirrors the existence of interpersonal conflicts in an unorganized social group; belief in a morally concerned pantheon mirrors a social structure in which private ownership and personal debts are an important consideration in human relationships. Ritual complements the social structure by providing additional procedures that are necessary to make the whole system work, but which are unavailable in interpersonal relationships. Thus the rituals in honor of the high gods require a public acceptance of differences in rank in human society because the high gods themselves are ranked and because they are believed to endorse human ranking; the practice of witchcraft, and fear of it, tends to curb precisely trespasses that the social structure fails to prevent; and rituals of salvation, directed toward a morally concerned god, entail the settling of debts as a condition of grace.

Perhaps most germane to our present topic, ritual functions to represent and reinforce the prevailing political structure, by requiring acknowledgment of, and respect for, leaders by participants in the ritual.

As a model for proper social relations, perhaps bolstered by cosmological considerations, ritual encourages actions consistent with, or isomorphic with, the action patterns and preferences acted out in the ritual. In sum, ritual functions as a metaprocess through which noncooperative preference structures are transformed into cooperative ones. It is also possible that there is a carryover from the ritual tuning process to motivation, outcome analysis, and action selection outside the ritual context.

Locus of Normative Control and Social Sanction
Ritual may function as a process of social control in a more direct fashion. Ritualized collective action may highlight behavior that is not in line with behavior deemed proper by the group. In extreme cases noncooperative members may be actively sanctioned by exclusion from ritual participation. Exclusion may be couched in such terms as "He (or she) is 'polluted.' " "He (or she) has violated this or that 'taboo.' " "He (or she) is a 'witch.' " There may exist collateral rituals for the "purification" and reinclusion of the member into participation.

Ritual may focus social approval on acceptable alternatives and disapproval on unacceptable ones. Those who choose alternatives unacceptable to the group may be held up to ridicule or may be directly sanctioned by the effects of public ritual. Among the So of northeastern Uganda a thief may be dealt with by the public "casting away of his soul." After a member of the group (children may constitute such a group) renders a curse upon the thief (identity usually unknown), each member simultaneously throws a stone into the air, symbolizing the soul that has thereby been confiscated. Wallace (1966:193 ff) has presented some data indicating a correlation between such sanctions and differences in wealth and related status in societies:

Contrary to some popular impressions . . . even the most primitive peoples often regard violation of the moral code as entailing the threat of supernatural punishment. But there is, nonetheless, a significant association . . . between economic advancement and the supernatural rationalization of morality. Supernatural sanctions for morality are more likely to be invoked in societies where there are, between persons, considerable social differences derived from differences in wealth. The presence of social classes, of widely prevalent debt relationships, of private ownership of important property, of primogeniture, and of the raising of grain crops— each is significantly associated with the belief in supernatural sanctions for morality. The most significant relationship of all is between social classes and supernatural morality.

A ritual sequence may be so structured as to encourage, constrain, and then mediate internal tensions within the group. This factor has been heavily emphasized by conflict theorists like Gluckman (1963) and Nobeck (1963), as well as by other theorists concerned with ritual. They suggest that, within the context of some rituals (variously termed "privilege ceremonies" by Firth, 1967; "rituals of rebellion" by Gluckman, 1954; "rituals of conflict" by Nobeck, 1963), hostilities and other pent-up feelings are released and given structured expression, for example, role reversal (Leach, 1961), sexual license, suspension of common norms, or open commission of, and amnesty for, crimes. An excellent example of this kind of ritual is offered by Robert Dirks (1978) for Christmas festivities among slaves in the British West Indies during the eighteenth century. During these festivities the absolute barrier between slaves and plantation owners was dissolved. Slaves felt free to don their finery and eat at the table, speak with planters on equal terms, commit crimes with impunity, and openly ridicule the planters. Runaway slaves who returned during this period were granted amnesty.

While such rituals provide a "safe" context for the acting out of tensions inherent in the social system, they *simultaneously un-*

derscore by juxtaposition the types of behavior (i.e., the action alternatives) strongly disapproved of by the group at any other time and thus *model improper behavior.*

Focus of Structural Socialization

That ritual is not only important in the stages of development in the child but also, as performed in adult society, a major environmental factor in the development of cognitive processes has been stressed by John McManus (see chapter 7). We point out that, as ritual expresses the ideal model of adult sociocosmological reality, as well as sanctions against improper behavior, so too does it model these elements and relations for the child. We have already mentioned the importance of socialization in generating positive social orientation, collective decision procedures, and proper, cooperative actions and outcomes. For the child participating in or observing ritual, the ritual sequence portrays in microcosm an ideal universe of social roles, social relations, and authority structure, as if he were watching a play on a stage. It is highly likely that such rituals will be reenacted by child peer groups in their play and will be a special focus for mimicry and role play during the child's formative years. It seems to us significant that initiation of young adults into "secret" societies [9] whose rituals have not been observed publicly by children—that is, have not been a factor in their environment—tends to be associated with long and intensive periods of indoctrination (so-called bush schools) before admission of the initiate into full membership. Such formal indoctrination periods are less in evidence in societies in which children are involved in one way or another with rituals from an early age.

Process of Social Orientation Toward Collective Action

Ritual has a powerful effect on group orientation. As was suggested in the introductory chapter of this book (see also chapter 5), ritual acts upon the affective and perceptual faculties of the or-

9. Examples of such societies are Poro in West Africa (Harley, 1950; Little, 1949), the Kovave cult among the Elema of New Guinea (Holmes, 1902), Kwakiutl Dancing Societies (Boas, 1897), and aboriginal secret societies (Elkin, 1964:177).

ganism, directing attention toward one orientation and away from other possible orientations. It also consolidates a common orientation among all or most of the members of the group. This orientation has important ramifications for social control. Many rituals (e.g., fertility rituals, rituals invoking supernatural protection, production rituals, or warfare rituals) have as their explicit purpose the attainment of some phenomenal goal (these include what Wallace has termed "technological rituals," 1966:171 ff). Clearly such rituals place severe constraints upon the behavior of actors. Alternative actions and expected outcomes are often defined quite precisely in terms of the "public good." In cases where all members of a group have a role to perform in the ritual, nonparticipation becomes socially unacceptable.

Rituals have long been interpreted in one way or another as sociocultural markers (e.g., "rites of passage," Van Gennep, 1908; "rites of intensification," Chapple and Coon, 1942; "rites of desacralization," Leach, 1961). That is, a cycle of time (day, year, lifetime) is divided into segments demarcated by ritual (agricultural phases, seasonal phases, birth-adulthood-marriage-death). These rituals may act to orient the attention of the group to the beginning of one phase and the end of the previous phase, affectively and perceptually, and orient group members to a new, appropriate set of tasks or responses to the new phase. Just as a ritual may mark the transformation of a youth into an adult, so too it may mark the ascension of a person to a higher (or for that matter, lower) political status, as in the accession ceremonies accompanying the crowning of a new king, or the succession of a junior age set into the ruling grade.

In sum, ritual may function as metaprocess influencing collective action by defining or institutionalizing collective decision procedures. If selection of action alternatives by actors in particular circumstances is socially constrained to occur during public ritual, then the effect is mandated collective decision making, and this inhibits or prevents individuated outcome analysis.

Ritual and Social Power

Because ritual serves as a social control device structuring action and interaction, individuals or groups gaining control over significant ritual in a society have the potential means of controlling to a greater or lesser extent the evaluations and actions of others in the society. The extent to which an actor or group of actors (A) may exercise social control over other actors (B) in an action system through manipulation of ritual as a power resource depends on several factors: (1) the extent of A's control or monopoly over the ritual, (2) the constraints upon A's freedom to manipulate ritual, (3) the existence of competitive sources other than A for ritual, and (4) the susceptibility to influence through ritual or the amplitude of demand on the part of B for the ritual.

Ritual may be used as a basis of sanctioning power, as well as a resource for persuasive power.

Ritual as Sanctioning Power

All that is required in any society for ritual to become one of a set of power resources is that access to, or control over, ritual be limited to actor(s) A, and that actor(s) B value or have a demand for the ritual. We assume, of course, A's intention to influence the action of B. The existence and use of ritual as a power resource is, in fact, a worldwide phenomenon, one found in societies of every conceivable complexity.[10] Among the Australian aborigines, control of ritual is the exclusive domain of adult males (Elkin, 1964; John Cawte, personal communication). Likewise, control of important ritual in the medieval Catholic Church was (and to some extent still is) in the hands of a select priesthood. Among the So of

10. For ritual to become a power resource in the relationship among actors in a social system, it must be perceived as valuable to certain actors (B) and come under the control of other actors (A). Hence, in a given society, some ritual may function as both social control process and power resource, while other ritual functions solely as social control process. Examples of ritual as solely social control process might be the vision quest among certain plains Indian groups or replenishment ritual after killing an animal among the Bushmen. Examples of ritual as both social control process and power resource might be ritual controlled by an ancestor cult, rainmaking ritual controlled by a "rainmaking clan," or a press conference controlled by a public relations counsel.

Uganda the most important rituals are controlled by a ghost cult composed of the oldest males in the tribe (Laughlin and Laughlin, 1972). In all these cases the rituals controlled by a select group of actors are desired, if not by the entire population, then by a signif-icant number of actors (*B*'s) in the society who have no direct access to the benefits of ritual through those in control. Acquisi-tion of control over ritual has typically proved a potent means of obtaining or consolidating political power. Such is the case in the transition from *gumlao* to *gumsa* political structure in Kachin, where the *gumsa* "chief" accrues both ritual status and functions that, in *gumlao* structure, are more widely spread among group members (Leach, 1954). In traditional Zulu political structure, ac-cumulation of control over ritual has been a conscious strategy in the consolidation of political power, as when "Shaka expelled all rainmakers from his kingdom, saying only he could control the heavens" (Gluckman in Fortes and Evans-Pritchard, 1940:31).

If access to ritual is controlled by *A,* then it may become a scarce resource for *B*. For example, if the "skill" of divination is known to, and practiced by, a select few in a society, and other members wish knowledge pertaining to future events, the diviner may be in a position to demand significant material recompense. Even more, the diviner, although holding no institutional political office, may nonetheless acquire substantial political influence in his community (see Leach, 1954:183, on the diviner in Kachin so-ciety).

But access to, and use of, ritual as a power resource is rarely, if ever, free of constraints. That is, the extent to which *A* may give to or withhold from *B* the benefits of a power resource *X* is usually limited by one or more factors such as competitive sources of *X* available to *B,* institutional constraints upon the role of *A,* possible violent confrontation between *A* and *B,* and, perhaps most impor-tantly in the case of ritual, constraints imposed by the mythic-ideological system, which gives credence, importance, and meaning to ceremonial ritual. This is quite clear when ritual is defined by the ideological system as occurring in a calendrical cycle. In the slave society in the British West Indies, referred to earlier, planters were constrained not to hinder the annual

272

Christmas festivities of the slaves for fear of upheaval and violence in reaction (Dirks, 1978). More generally, the annual cycle of agricultural rituals in many societies, although they may be controlled by leaders who are ritual specialists, must nevertheless be performed or members of the society would likely take some form of reprisal or seek alternative sources for the ritual. The situation is similar when certain ritual duties are defined as part of the obligation of office. For example, leaders in many societies are expected to look after the general welfare of the community. This constrains to a greater or lesser extent their decisions and action possibilities.

Through the control of ritual, a leader may threaten or bring about supernatural sanctions against those who oppose his goals as a punishment (negative sanctions) and in favor of those who support his goals as reward (positive sanctions). For instance, the leader may be in a position to produce rain needed for prosperous agriculture through the initiation of ritual. He may direct the rain to the gardens of his followers and away from the gardens of his antagonists. Or if the leader controls death ritual, he may be in a position to ensure or block the transition of the dead into ancestorhood. A specialist in divination may render judgments about the future and the past that are favorable to his friends and unfavorable to his enemies. By manipulating ritual in such ways, *A* often succeeds in forcing *B* into compliance with action alternatives desired by, or favorable to, *A*. More than that, *A* may have the option to exclude *B* from participation in ritual, or bring *B* to ridicule, to force compliance with *A*'s aims. It is instructive to note that the shaman in many Eskimo societies is asked from time to time to indicate, through trance and communication with spirits, the cause of misfortunes befalling the group. He can easily implicate those who have incurred his disfavor and thus censure the behaviors of which he disapproves.

Ritual as Persuasive Power

More prevalent still is the use of ritual on the part of *A* to influence *B*'s orientation toward his environment—that is, to influence *B*'s perceptions, evaluations, and decisions relative to actions and outcomes. We have seen that the source of information greatly influences its acceptability and effectiveness. If the information relevant to a particular decision situation for B is perceived as derived through the mediation of ritual, then the actor(s) A in control of that ritual has persuasive power over B. Take, for example, the influence a specialist in divination may have over the information imparted to B. The diviner may structure the information he relays in such a way as to increase the probability of choice favorable to the diviner's aims. Consider also the demonstrable placebo effect of curing rituals. Depending on how the medical practitioner structures the ritual and attendant information, the patient may be left in a positive or a negative state regarding his malady.

But the most effective use of ritual in persuasion comes with the initiation of collective action. For the reasons already encountered, ritual may be used by leaders to reinforce ideal, proper social relations and social values; redirect social orientation toward tasks or goals desired by leaders; establish collective action (as in warfare ritual); and provide a politically "safe" arena for the acting out of hostilities and tensions that otherwise might threaten the position or goals of leaders. As we have also seen, the initiation of ritual may provide a public display of proper authority relations between actors, reinforcing the position, rights, and privileges of the leader(s). And through its socialization function, ritual displays transgenerationally an ideal model of authority relations, as well as the cosmological justification for those relations. Finally, leaders may establish, initiate, or hinder collective decision procedures by invoking or failing to invoke ritual, as when members of the ruling age set among certain African tribes are able to hasten or delay succession of power to the next age set by their control of succession ritual. As is shown in the following chapter, leaders may display social and political efficacy while their social system is under the stress of warfare, severe resource deprivation, disaster, or catastrophe by invoking ritual responses over which they have control. Under such conditions the tuning function of ritual reveals its greatest potency.

In short, through the manipulation of ritual, leaders (A) may orient or reorient B's perceptions, affect, and outcome analysis and thereby influence B's preference structures in relation to some set of action alternatives. In fact the enactment of the ritual itself may determine B's actions and outcomes. The influence of leaders over the evaluative processes of B is particularly strong when full participation in ritual is preceded by socialization through intensive ordeals and indoctrination in "bush schools" and initiation into well-structured "secret" societies. In developmental terms leaders may be in the position to create extreme stress or a noxious environment for the initiate, leading to a weakening of cognitive structure while ideal authority relations and ritual participation are being inculcated. This may have the overall effect of conditioning concrete structure in the socialized individual vis-à-vis power relations, ritual, and social role, especially if the indoctrination is associated (as it usually is) with "religion," that is, with belief in the efficacy and sanctions of supernatural beings and their approval of the ideal sociopolitical structure.

All of this gives leaders control of a powerful mechanism for stimulating collective action. Ritual procedures (e.g., fire drills or military drills) may initiate collective action, with its attendant visual cooperation and authority structure, before the actual need for such collective action unrelated to ritual and directed toward an actual event. As we show in the next chapter, ritual may thus be used to maintain social solidarity and the appearance of cooperation when collective action or cooperative behavior is *declining* in other sectors of society.

Ritual and Social Change

Ritual may often play an important role in sociopolitical change. Nowhere is this more evident than in so-called millenarian, nativistic, or revitalization movements, which inevitably contain a large ritual component (see Wallace, 1966:209 ff). Indeed, as is often the case, it is completely or partially through the scrupulous adherence to ritual procedures that the aims of the revitalization movement are to be reached by members.[11] This important role of ritual in change is further explored in the following chapter. Ritual

11. For example, see Wallace (1969); Jarvie (1967) on cargo cults; Mooney (1896) on the Ghost Dance movements.

may also play a role in power competition and changes in power relationships. We mention here three ways in which the transition commonly occurs:

1. *Competitive Sources for the Same Ritual.* There may exist or emerge an actor or set of actors C who control, or claim control over, the same power resource controlled by A in relation to B. This may have the effect of lessening or even negating the influence over B enjoyed by A if B reorients toward C as a source for X (in this case ritual). This situation may be schematized in the following way:

We see that C is in competition with A for allegiance and acceptance as a (the) source of ritual (arrows indicate the direction of relative power). Examples of this are found in cases where a new "religious leader" or movement appears (e.g., Luther and other leaders of the Reformation). Also, secular leaders may establish competitors to a religious elite A to erode their power (again, the Reformation provides many examples of kings' [e.g., those of Sweden and England] establishing a religious power base dependent on themselves rather than on external authority, the Roman Catholic hierarchy centered in Rome).

2. *Competitive Rituals.* There may also emerge an actor or set of actors C who control a competitive ritual or set of rituals (X^*) that are portrayed as being in some sense more efficacious than the traditional set (X). This may likewise lead to a lessening or negation of the influence A has traditionally enjoyed over B if B perceives the new ritual to be superior to the old:

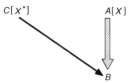

Missionary activities under colonialism have often led to such competition, as has the emergence of revitalization movements in innumerable societies.

3. *Competition Between Ritual and Nonritual Power Resources.* Ritual, as we have explained, is one of a set of types of power resources available for manipulation in the power relationship. There may emerge, therefore, an actor or set of actors *C* who control a nonritual power resource (*Y*) that they claim to be more efficacious than traditional ritual (*X*). In such a situation the nonritual resource may lead to a lessening or negation of the influence *A* has over *B,* if *B* perceives the new resource as preferable to the traditional ritual:

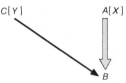

$C[Y]$ $A[X]$

B

This condition may arise in competition between new technology and traditional ritual, for example, pesticides versus fertility ritual, modern medicines versus healing rites, mass media versus ritual communication, or modern weapons versus ritual defense. The situation may also arise in competition between police and law on the one hand and supernatural sanction on the other, for example, police investigation versus divinatory ritual, and ordeal or prison and capital punishment versus ritual sanctions directed by traditional leaders.

The fundamental point here is that, under conditions of sociopolitical change, the very functions of ritual that, under one set of conditions lead to maintenance of the status quo, may also combine to make ritual an important factor for change.

References

Balandier, G. 1970. *Political Anthropology.* New York: Vintage Books.

Blau, P. 1964. *Exchange and Power in Social Life.* New York: Wiley.

Boas, F. 1897. "The Social Organization and the Secret Societies of the Kwakiutl Indians." *Annual Report of the Smithsonian Institution, 1894–95,* pp. 311–738.

Buckley, W., T. Burns, and D. Meeker. 1974. "Structural Resolutions of Collective Action Problems." *Behavioral Science* 19:277–297.

Burns, T. and D. Meeker. 1975. "A Multi-Level, Structural Model of Social Behavior." *Quality and Quantity* 9:51–89.

Burns, T. and M. Cooper. 1971. *Value, Social Power, and Economic Exchange.* Stockholm: Samhallsvetareforelaget.

—— 1972. "The Melanesian Big Man and the Accumulation of Power." *Oceania* 63:104–112.

Cawte, J. 1974. *Medicine Is the Law*. Honolulu: University of Hawaii Press.

Chapple, E. D. and C. S. Coon. 1942. *Principles of Anthropology*. New York: Holt.

Count, E. W. 1973. *Being and Becoming Human: Essays on the Biogram*. New York: Van Nostrand.

Dirks, R. 1978. "Competitive Transformations in British West Indian Slave Societies," in *Extinction and Survival in Human Populations* (C. D. Laughlin and I. Brady, eds.). New York: Columbia University Press.

Elkin, A. P. 1964. *The Australian Aborigines*. Garden City, N.Y.: Doubleday.

Firth, R. 1961. *Elements of Social Organization*. Boston: Beacon Press.

—— 1967. *Tikopia Ritual and Belief*. Boston: Beacon Press.

Fortes, M. 1959. *Oedipus and Job in West African Religion*. Cambridge, England: Cambridge University Press.

Fortes, M. and E. E. Evans-Pritchard. 1940. *African Political Systems*. London: Oxford University Press.

Foster, G. M. 1962. *Traditional Cultures and the Impact of Technological Change*. New York: Harper and Row.

Gluckman, M. 1954. *Rituals of Rebellion in Southeast Africa*. Manchester, England: Manchester University Press.

—— 1963. *Order and Rebellion in Tribal Africa*. London: Cohen.

Goodenough, W. R. 1963. *Cooperation in Change*. New York: Russell Sage Foundation.

Hardin, G. 1972. *Exploring New Ethics for Survival*. New York: Viking.

Harley, G. W. 1950. "Masks as Agents of Social Control." Cambridge, Mass.: Papers of the Peabody Museum of American Archaeology and Ethnology 22(2).

Holmes, J. 1902. "Initiation Ceremonies of Natives of the Papuan Gulf." *Journal of the Royal Anthropological Institute* 32:418–425.

Horton, R. 1964. "Ritual Man in Africa." *Africa* 34:85–104.

Hovland, C. I. 1954. "Effects of the Mass Media on Communication," in *Handbook of Social Psychology* (G. Lindzey, ed.). Cambridge, Mass.: Addison-Wesley.

Jarvie, I. C. 1967. *The Revolution in Anthropology*. Chicago: Henry Regnery.

Klapper, J. T. 1960. *The Effect of Mass Communication*. Glencoe, Ill.: Free Press.

Kluckhohn, C. 1942. "Myths and Rituals: A General Theory." *Harvard Theological Review* 35:45–79.

Laughlin, C. D. and I. Brady. 1978. *Extinction and Survival in Human Populations*. New York: Columbia University Press.

Laughlin, C. D. and E. R. Laughlin. 1972. "*Kenisan*: Economic and Social Ramifications of the Ghost Cult Among the So of Northeastern Uganda." *Africa* 42(1):9–20.

—— 1974. "Age Generations and Political Process in So." *Africa* 44:266–279.

Leach, E. R. 1954. *Political Systems of Highland Burma*. Boston: Beacon Press.

—— 1961. "Time and False Noses," in *Rethinking Anthropology* (E. Leach, ed.). London: Athlone Press.

—— 1972. "Ritualization in Man in Relation to Conceptual and Social Development," in *Reader in Comparative Religion: An Anthropological Approach* (W. A. Lessa and E. Z. Vogt, eds.), 3d ed. New York: Harper and Row.

Little, K. 1949. "The Role of the Secret Society in Cultural Specialization." *American Anthropologist* 51 (2):199–212.

Luce, R. D. and E. Raiffa. 1957. *Games and Decisions*. New York: Wiley.

Ritual and Social Power

Mair, L. 1970. *Primitive Government*. Baltimore: Penguin.

Middleton, J. 1960. *Lugbara Religion*. New York: Holt, Rinehart and Winston.

Mooney, J. 1896. "The Ghost Dance Religion and the Sioux Outbreak of 1890." *14th Annual Report of the Bureau of Ethnology* (2). Washington: U.S. Government Printing Office.

Nadel, S. F. 1951. *The Foundations of Social Anthropology*. London: Cohen and West.

Nobeck, E. 1963. "African Rituals of Conflict." *American Anthropologist* 65:1254–1279.

Prattis, J. I. 1973. "Strategizing Man." *Man* (n.s.) 8:46–58.

Radcliffe-Brown, A. R. 1922. *The Andamen Islanders* (1964 ed.). York: Free Press.

Rappaport, Roy A. 1967. "Ritual Regulation of Environmental Relations Among a New Guinea People." *Ethnology* 6:17–30.

Richards, A. I. 1960. "Social Mechanisms for the Transfer of Political Rights in Some African Tribes." *Journal of the Royal Anthropological Institute* 90(2).

Sears, D. O. 1969. "Political Behavior," in *The Handbook of Social Psychology*, Vol. 5 (G. Lindzey and E. Aronson, eds.). Reading, Pa.: Addison-Wesley.

Teleki, G. 1973. *The Predatory Behavior of Wild Chimpanzees*. Lewisburg, Pa.: Bucknell University Press.

—— n.d. "Primate Subsistence Patterns: Collector-Predators and Gatherer-Hunters." Ms.

Trivers, R. L. 1971. "The Evolution of Reciprocal Altruism." *Quarterly Review of Biology* 46(1):35–57.

Van Gennep, A. 1908. *The Rites of Passage* (1960 ed.). Chicago: University of Chicago Press.

Vansina, J. 1966. *Kingdoms of the Savanna*. Madison: University of Wisconsin Press.

Wallace, A. F. C. 1966. *Religion: An Anthropological View*. New York: Random House.

—— 1969. *The Death and Rebirth of the Seneca*. New York: Random House.

Wilson, M. 1959. *Communal Rituals of the Nyakyasa*. London: Oxford University Press.

Nine

Ritual and Stress

Charles D. Laughlin, Jr.
and Eugene G. d'Aquili

> What does it mean to be a self-conscious animal? The idea is
> ludicrous, if it is not monstrous. It means to know that one
> is food for worms. This is the terror: to have emerged from
> nothing, to have a name, consciousness of self, deep inner
> feelings, an excruciating inner yearning for life and self-
> expression—and with all this yet to die. It seems like a
> hoax, which is why one type of cultural man rebels openly
> against the idea of God. What kind of deity would create
> such complex and fancy worm food? Cynical deities, said
> the Greeks, who use man's torments for their own amuse-
> ment.
>
> Ernest Becker, *The Denial of Death*

The pivotal role of ritual in human adaptation is nowhere more evident than in societies under one form or another of stress. In the
present chapter we concern ourselves with the operation of ritual
under stress, particularly as manifested by societies under severe
ecological stress. *Ecological stress* may be defined as any threat
to the survival of all or most of the members of a society posed by
a decrement in the quantity or quality of basic resources. The
decrement in resources may be caused either by change in the
environment or by change in the interaction between the society
and its environment. In general biological terms a decrement in
basic resources may be caused by change in the incidence or
type of predation, by the inception or exacerbation of competition

280

between groups of conspecifics, or by environmental events affecting the availability of resources.[1]

Ecological stress may be contrasted with *psychological stress,* which may be defined as the reduction of the functional capacity of the individual organism (see chapter 7). The occurrence of ecological stress in a society may or may not entail an incidence of psychological stress. That is, a severe decrement in basic resources may or may not cause a decrement in the functional capacity of actors in their response to the event. As we have already noted in our earlier discussion of cognitive functioning under excessive stress (see chapter 7), one of the major functions of ritual during periods of ecological stress is to serve as one of a set of collective action alternatives that operate as buffers between extreme environmental change and potential psychological stress. Ecological stress, if it does not lead to extinction of the social group, stimulates adaptive equilibration in social structure, economic structure, and other aspects of society (see Laughlin and Brady, 1978). Successful societal equilibration is, however, largely dependent on successful or optimal equilibration of the individual cognitive system in relation to the stress conditions. The psychological-cognitive effects of ecological stress depend on a number of factors operating in the ontogeny of group members. We may say that the ontogenesis of any particular group member exists in a mutual feedback relationship with the process of social equilibration.

To put it another way, we show that the major variable affecting successful social equilibration to ecological stress is the degree to which the stress is predictable (i.e., is perceived as redundant, expected, "in the nature of things"). This perception depends largely on the process of modeling of environmental events that occurs during the ontogeny of actors, and the correspondence between cognitive models and actual environmental events (that is, whether or not environmental events confirm expectations generated from cognitive models; see Laughlin and

1. Throughout this chapter "basic resource" is taken to mean those raw materials present in the environment and technologically available to the society on which the survival of a viable reproductive population depends (see Laughlin and Brady, 1978).

d'Aquili, 1974, pp. 84ff). Where the actual and conceived probability of ecological stress is high, we would expect to find a heavy reliance on collective action alternatives, particularly ceremonial ritual, because of its effectiveness in modeling social and cosmological organization, in anticipating change in either or both realms and in tuning affect to stimulus, as emphasized in previous chapters (see chapter 4).

To further our understanding of ritual, it is necessary to examine these relationships in greater detail. We shall consider the variety of change confronting various societies and then go into the distinction between expected and unexpected change in greater depth. We shall study the functions of ritual in societies under stress and end our discussion with the role of ritual in the revitalization process.

Varieties of Ecological Stress

Ecological stress is a change in the environment resulting in a threat, or a potential threat, to the survival of a society. Obviously, the degree of stress varies from society to society and from time to time in the same society. Probably the most important variable in the severity of stress is the actual discrepancy between maximal (or "normal") and minimal (or "scarce") quantities of basic resources. The degree of vacillation between these points is also a critical factor.

For most societies at most times, ecological stress is minimal or nonexistent. We have innumerable descriptions in the literature of societies that face a seasonal "crisis"—that is, a more or less mild fluctuation in basic resource availability over the course of the annual subsistence cycle. Thus, slash-and-burn agriculturalists may experience a yearly shortage of foodstuffs around the end of the growing season, when reserves have been nearly exhausted, and the new crop is not harvested. In pastoral societies there may be a period during which few animals are lactating and during which people must supplement their diets through hunting, herb gathering, fishing, crop planting, and the like. Indeed, most of the world's societies rely on a variety of subsistence activities and thus optimize their subsistence strategies for all seasons. Under most of these circumstances, economic equilibration to resource fluctuation is so smooth and effective that stress is not apparent. And, of course, there are some societies that experience little or no fluctuation in basic resources. This is the case among the Pygmies of the Ituri rain forest in Central Africa, where there exists an unending abundance of resources (Turnbull, 1961), or among the many groups in Africa, Asia, and elsewhere that practice irrigation and intensive agriculture and thus enjoy a year-long sequence of growing seasons.

Cyclical Versus Noncyclical Change

A critical variable in ecological stress is the extent and duration of the period of resource deprivation. The greater the discrepancy between the normal and deprived levels of resource availability, and the longer the deprivation lasts, the more severe the ecological stress confronting a society. The most severe stress tends to follow in the wake of environmental shifts of cataclysmic proportions. If one looks at a worldwide sample of societies, one can isolate an enormous variety of events with potential for extreme stress. A partial list includes epidemics of human disease, lava flows and volcanic eruptions, earthquakes, hurricanes, tornadoes, crop blights caused by fungi and insects, drought, disastrous loss of food resources or technological implements needed to produce them, blizzards, floods, unpredictable climatic shifts, warfare, bushfire, tidal waves, and livestock epidemics. Any and all of these may take their toll in human life, either directly or by resultant famine. Many of these events may also take a serious toll in the destruction of shelter and property, a factor that may or may not be important in inducing psychological stress, as we shall see.

A major consideration in the analysis of the effects of any change in the environment on a society is the incidence of that change, that is, whether the change is unique or occurs cyclically.[2] This is doubly important where environmental change rep-

---

2. For a general discussion of the different effects of unique and cyclical environmental change on social infrastructures, see Laughlin and Brady (1978).

resents an ecological stress. Any of these disasters may recur often in particular localities, while elsewhere they may occur only once in the history of a people. For instance, the Tikopia face the probability of a hurricane once in every ten to twenty years (Firth, 1959:3), the Kaiadilt of Bentinck Island off the coast of northern Australia face severe and cyclical shortages of fish due to tidal activity (Cawte, 1972:129), and the Bushmen of the Kalahari confront periodic extreme drought (Kaufman, 1910:159). By contrast, the Easter Islanders experienced a sudden raid in the 1860s by Peruvians, who captured hundreds of persons, including major political leaders and important religious figures. These persons were taken to islands off the coast of Peru, where they were forced to dig guano. Some years later, seventeen of the captured Easter Islanders were repatriated, but some were infected with smallpox and brought a widespread and devastating epidemic back to Easter Island (Routledge, 1919:205ff). This series of events was, to say the least, unique to the ecology and the experience of the Easter Islanders.

Expected Versus Unexpected Change
As was stressed in the early chapters of this book, a major function of the brain—the cognitive function of the organism—is to model the environment with sufficient accuracy to ensure survival of the organism. Thus a certain degree of "fit" or isomorphism emerges between events in the E_o, and events within the E_c, of the organism. We have already introduced the notion of the cognitive imperative in chapter 1. We may recall that the first reaction of the brain to a novel stimulus is to identify it—that is, to match sensory input with models of the environment already stored in memory. This recognition operation is usually done before the organism assigns an appropriate affect or response to the stimulus. As we show later, this is precisely what victims of a disaster initially attempt to do.

When one considers the crucial function of the cognitive imperative in the evolution of *Homo sapiens,* it becomes clear that a sizable selective advantage would result from the capacity to anticipate severe shifts in the environment, changes that portend potential extinction of the individual or of the group. Of more advantage still would be the capacity to communicate such expectations transgenerationally to members of the group who have not directly experienced the event, but who, nonetheless, porceeded forewarned.

An organism's cognitive apparatus models its environment by creating redundancy in the sensory information it receives about the environment. In part, it does this through the recognition of patterns recurring in the information. With due emphasis on the limits of any particular cognitive apparatus, any organism will likely recognize and code recurrent fluctuations rather than merely react to them. At the most rudimentary physiological level, this would seem to be a major biological function of so-called biological clocks or circadian rhythms (see Luce, 1971).

We would suggest, therefore, that the cognitive imperative operates not only in the identification of entities and events in the environment, but also in the identification and coding of recurrent patterns of events. Where an adaptively significant change in the environment occurs cyclically, that pattern of recursiveness is perceived and stored and thus creates an expectation of cyclical events that is matched to future events as they occur and that is communicated transgenerationally through socialization (see Laughlin and Brady, 1978).

Lest our account seem too simplistic, a major consideration must be broached at this point and kept in mind throughout the remainder of the chapter. Recursiveness in the environment is not necessarily coded conceptually in the same detail or arrangement in different individuals.[3] Indeed, if the individuals are from widely

3. Although the issue has been discussed at length in a previous chapter (see chapter 6), it needs to be repeated that a model, in part or in whole, may not be apparent to actors in the system. A model may remain unperceived by actors and yet operate through behavior to ensure adaptation to change in the environment. This situation may obtain where actors are aware only of the content or elements of the model while the structure or organization of the model remains unconscious or where the model is embedded in the structure of social relationships, and shifts in those relationships occur over a period of time. In general, the longer the periodicity of a recurring series of environmental events, the less likelihood of that recurrence's being apparent to actors. To offer a more concrete example of what we mean, suppose we have two recursive environmental series that are adaptively significant to

disparate sociocultural backgrounds, we would expect a great deal of discrepancy in surface detail. Considering our distinction between "operational" and "cognized" models of the environment introduced in chapter 1 in a more structural vein, we would consider the operational and cognized models of the environment to be transformations of the same structure.[4] The key is the statement made by Rappaport (1968:237) that: "The two models are overlapping, but not identical"). This consideration saves the distinction from being a simple replication of the emic/etic one, a dichotomy that merely asserts the discrepancy between the reality perceived by the anthropologist and the reality perceived by his subjects.[5] For our purposes the point of greatest structural overlap between operational and cognized models is precisely the nature and quality of adaptively significant recursiveness in the environment. Indeed, it would seem highly unlikely that any such environmental cycle could exist without being modeled, it being assumed that the organism has lived in that environment long enough for recursiveness to manifest itself and that the cycle involved does not

---

a population, one of which has a period of one year (say, the alternation between wet and dry seasons), and the other of which has a period of twenty years (say, the occurrence of serious earthquakes). We would expect the conceptual model of the first series to be largely conscious to the actors, while many of the conceptual and social aspects of the model for the second series would remain unconscious to most actors. The major difference here is that in the first instance (seasons) each individual in the society has the opportunity to experience the environmental cycle directly and assimilate that series of events into his own conceptual system, while in the second instance (earthquakes) only the oldest members of the society will have experienced the periodicity of the event *as a cycle*. Yet the model of the periodicity of earthquakes may be incorporated, in part, in the conceptual systems of younger members of the society through socialization, or the model may be embedded in the structure of social relationships so that proper collective action in the event of earthquake is assured, in spite of the lack of general, direct or indirect awareness of the impending event.

4. For many reasons discussed elsewhere (Laughlin and d'Aquili, 1974) we would argue that the operational model is more likely to be the more empirically accurate of the two.

5. The emic/etic dichotomy is taken by analogy from the distinction between phonemics and phonetics. The "emics" of a situation is as perceived and conceived by the actors themselves, while the "etics" of that situation would be as described by an outside observer (scientist). As often used, the distinction implies little or no overlap between an emic and an etic description (model) of an event.

transcend the neurophysiological capacity of the organism to generate structures.[6]

The most obvious example of this modeling process, both at the cognitive and social levels, is the anticipation and expectation of seasonal changes in the environment—this being for most societies an important factor in adaptation. In traditional Aleut society, adaptation required a delicate balance between demographic stability and economic organization on the one hand and seasonally available resources on the other. Before Russian interference with the Aleuts, the latter were sea hunters "unusually well adapted physically and culturally to the difficult and inhospitable environment which the Aleutian Islands offer" (Bank, 1953:415). They were also keenly aware of the fluctuation of resource availability from periods of relative abundance to periods of extreme deprivation, when, as the Aleuts put it, "they gnaw on straps." In anticipation of the lean months the Aleuts stored fish and other foodstuffs on which they relied during periods of shortage.

This is a strategy that is repeated over and over again in the literature on human subsistence patterns. And in many societies each shift in the cycle of seasonal events is marked by appropriate ritual that functions to model socially in isomorphic display the sequence of seasonal events. Such is the case with traditional Tikopia ritual. Here each step in the economic response to seasonal fluctuations is marked by a ritual—the complete cycle of ritual being termed by Tikopia "Work of the Gods" (Firth, 1940). Each ritual event is determined by one or more environmental cues, such as the phase of the moon or direction of the wind. We find the same type of calendrical sequence of ritual regulating highly organized agricultural production among traditional Maori in New Zealand (Best, 1925: 15), where each stage in the ritual cycle was determined by religious specialists and enforced by chiefs. In these cases, and in many others we could cite (see Tur-

6. We are quite aware that human beings are capable of conceptualizing cycles that have no objective referent in the environment or cycles that once were isomorphic with the environment but are no longer so. But consideration of this type of cognitive modeling is out of place in the present discussion (see Laughlin and d'Aquili, 1974).

ner, 1973), each step in the ritual cycle anticipates a seasonal shift in climate and emphasizes, collectively organizes for, and conceptually prepares for appropriate economic response on the part of actors in the system.

We suggest that adaptively significant and cyclical changes in the environment of a society (or an individual) are modeled by *diaphatic* equilibration of that society's infrastructures and by the interaction of the infrastructures with the environment. Diaphatic equilibration, or simply *diaphasis,* is defined as the capacity of an organism or system of organisms to change adaptive strategy in a repetitive and cyclical or recursive manner. In diaphasis the organism is seen to change, but if observed long enough, there is a return (more or less) to the original state. Diaphasis among organisms is generally and initially a response to recursiveness in the environment. Examples of diaphasis are the coat color change of many animals in response to seasonal changes, alternating activity and hibernation of bears and frogs, alternating localization and mass migration of driver ants, and the seasonal atomization and aggregation of sea gull populations (for a complete discussion of diaphasis, see Laughlin and Brady, 1978).

Diaphasis may be noted in the social infrastructures of human societies, and many of these diaphatic structures may represent an adaptive accommodation to fluctuations in basic resource availability. Among the Bushmen, for whom the availability of water is the paramount variable determining their conscious adaptive strategy (Lee, 1966:152), there exists a marked fluctuation in social cohesion between the three- to four-month rainy season, during which individual bands disperse and travel their separate ways, and the summer period, during which available water is fairly restricted to a few permanent waterholes and bands coalesce around these in larger groupings. Likewise, among traditional Ojibwa there occurred a seasonal atomization and recoalescence of hunting bands, depending on the availability of salmon in the Great Lakes (Bishop, 1970). Also, Holmberg (1950:21) mentions for the Siriono a tendency toward greater social cohesion during the rainy season and loose cohesion or lack of cohesion during the dry season. All of these examples illustrate the behavioral results of cognitive models that are engendered in society members through socialization and that facilitate and even determine an anticipation of change in the environment and thus allow for rapid and appropriate collective response.

As important as diaphasis is in adaptation to season fluctuations in basic resources, it is even more important as an adaptive strategy when a society is confronted by cyclical and ecologically stressful conditions of the sort noted in the previous section. It seems obvious that a society expecting a potentially catastrophic event will fare far better than one that is not expecting the event. Indeed, we feel that expectation of the event is probably the most critical variable in determining the reaction of a society to that event. If the event is wholly unexpected, it may well result in partial or total social upheaval. On the other hand, if the event is perceived to be cyclical in its occurrence and is expected in the cognitive structure or model of the environment of group members, the effects of the event are not likely to amount to social upheaval. Elsewhere, for example (Laughlin and Brady, 1978), a tendency in societies has been demonstrated under severe resource deprivation toward a reduction of reciprocity and reciprocal altruism. Under extreme conditions this tendency may extend to allowing marginally productive members of the society to perish. For example, Bushmen under the pressure of extreme drought leave the old, the sick, and the women and children behind in their quest for water (Lebzelter, 1934:11,31). The same has been recorded for the Ik (Turnbull, 1972) and the Siriono (Holmberg, 1950) during periods of extreme food scarcity when the old and post-weaning children are left to fend for themselves. Margaret Mead (1930:65) mentions for the Manua of Samoa that famine resulting from hurricanes may be so severe that "the weak, the young, and the least wanted of society die from lack of nourishment." Finally, Aranda mothers will not rear children during a time of severe drought. The infant will be killed at birth, and there is some evidence that the infant's corpse may on occasion be eaten (Chewings 1936:12). While from an ethnocentric point of view these cases may appear to be shocking inhumanites, the fact remains that such behavior is eminently adaptive biologically and demonstrates a type of diaphatic equilibration to a periodically marginal resource base.

The distinction between expected and unexpected ecological stress cannot be overemphasized. It is precisely in the opposition of the two types of situations that we see the interaction between ecological and psychological stress. More particularly, we would predict that *the more effective the social diaphasis in maintaining an accurate expectation model of future ecological stress and in providing a course of collective action expected by the actors to be effective, the less likelihood that ecological stress will lead to a significant incidence of psychological stress* (see also chapter 7).

This hypothesis gains some support from laboratory experiments with animals and human beings (see Seligman, 1975). In a series of controlled experiments on rats, the effects of predictability of stress were explored by Jay Weiss and his associates (Weiss, 1972). In brief, rats were randomly selected in sets of three. One rat acted as control subject and received no electric shocks, another rat was given electric shocks at random with no control over whether he had been previously shocked or not, and the third rat was given a variety of cues (depending on the experiment), by means of which he could predict and avoid the shock. After being subjected to shocks, or potential shocks, for an extended period of time, all three animals were killed and examined for extent of gastric ulceration.

As was expected, the control rats that received no shock developed very little gastric ulceration or none. A striking result of the experiment was that rats able to predict when the shocks would occur also showed relatively little ulceration, whereas those that received the same shocks unpredictably showed a considerable amount of ulceration. In short, the results demonstrated clearly that the psychological variable of predictability, rather than the shock itself, was the main determinant of ulcer severity (Weiss, 1972:106).

In more elaborated studies Weiss also demonstrated that the effects of environmental stress in the form of shocks on ulceration decreased as the quantity of information the animal received relative to effective coping increased. In still another set of studies

Weiss et al. (1972) measured the level of norepinephrine in the brains of rats subjected to the same experimental regimen just described. Elevation in the level of norepinephrine in the brains of human beings has been implicated in brain activity associated with purposeful activity, whereas depletion of norepinephrine has been implicated in the onset of depression. Weiss et al. found that "animals able to avoid shock showed an increase in the level of brain norepinephrine, whereas helpless animals, which received the same shocks, showed a decrease in norepinephrine" (Weiss, 1972:113). Probably the most significant study relevant to our present discussion was done by Ronald Champion of the University of Sydney and James Geer et al. at the State University of New York at Stonybrook (reported in Weiss, 1972:112). In their series of experiments human subjects were given inescapable shocks, but half of them were told they could terminate the shock by some action like pushing a button, while the other half were told to do the same action but that it would have no effect on the duration of shock. The subjects who thought they had some control over the duration of shock evidenced less arousal (as measured by galvanic skin response) than those who thought they had no control.

It is our position that ritual often serves as one of a set of alternative, collective procedures for the effective response of a group to ecological stress and that it provides a medium for the active expression of the coping response and also provides assurance that the response is effective. But in order for ritual to provide this function, the ecological stress must be expected (anticipated, predicted). To explain fully the efficacy of ritual in this regard, we shall look in more detail at situations in which ecological stress has been totally unexpected and later contrast this with a detailed examination of conditions in which the stress has been fully anticipated.

Disaster

The literature is replete with sociological and psychological studies of disaster and disaster-related events (see Demerath and Wallace, 1957; Wallace, 1956a, 1966, 1970; Fritz and Williams, 1957; Katz et al., n.d.; Fritz and Marks, 1954; Grinspoon, 1964).[7] It is not our intention to present a complete survey of the disaster data but only to extract from it information relevant to ritual. For present purposes we consider "disaster" to mean unexpected ecological stress and center on some of the more important ramifications of such events.

The data suggest that the more abrupt the disaster, the more disruptive the consequences (Demerath and Wallace, 1957:7). And the consequences of disaster may be grouped roughly into two categories, psychological and social. We look at the psychological effects first because they have immediate effects on the social structure and collective action of victims. Extrapolating from innumerable interviews with, and observations of, disaster victims, Wallace (1970: 202, in Demerath and Wallace, 1957:23) has defined what he terms the "disaster syndrome."

In the first stage, the individual is described as being "dazed," "stunned," "apathetic," "passive," "aimless." He is (literally) apt to be insensitive to pain, to be almost completely unaware, consciously, of his own injuries or of the seriousness of visible damage. First stage victims will do trivial things, such as sweeping off the doorstep of a flattened house, or will leave seriously injured kinfolk in order to chat with neighbors. In the second stage, the individual is no longer dazed, but he becomes pathetically eager for support and reassurance that known persons, structures, and institutions have survived. Personal loss is minimized; concern is for reassurance that the community is intact. Persons in this stage can be easily led and formed into work teams, but they are not effective in leadership. In the third stage, a mild euphoric altruism obtains: the individual enthusiastically participates in group activity designed to restore and rehabilitate the community. Observers remark on the high morale and selfless dedication to be seen on all sides. Finally, as the euphoria wears off, there is full awareness of the long-term effects of personal and community loss. Complaint and criticism against public agencies, bickering with neighbors, and dismay over the personal cost of the disaster attain full consciousness. This syndrome has been repeatedly

7. A complete set of studies of disaster was published as the Disaster Study Series by the Disaster Research Group, National Academy of Sciences, National Research Council. These sources are presently out of print.

identified in the aftermath of both natural and wartime disasters and in the responses of target groups in cultural crises (Wallace, 1970:202).

The conditions leading to the disaster syndrome are instructive in further understanding of the importance of the cognitive imperative in relation to stress. As one disaster researcher has put it, "seeking cognitive orientation in the early period of impact, the individual tends to perceive and interpret disaster cues by reference to those causal agents and other features of his immediate environment with which he is familiar" (Demerath in Demerath and Wallace, 1957:28). The more ambiguous the cues, it would seem, the more likely the individual will be to misinterpret sensory input in terms of his conceptual world (Demerath and Wallace, 1957:16). Lester Grinspoon (1964) has demonstrated that in some cases the victims of a disaster block out input contradictory to their established conception of the world, even in the face of seemingly overwhelming evidence that their conceptions no longer apply (this being characteristic of stage 1 functioning in conceptual systems theory terms; see chapter 7). Grinspoon argued that in such situations merely imparting the "truth" was insufficient to counteract inappropriate conceptualization and behavior on the part of victims, a point also made by Kilpatrick (in Demerath and Wallace, 1957:21). Although their ingenious study of a modern millennial movement is not directly related to disaster, Festinger et al. (1956) demonstrated much the same process of conceptual system boundary maintenance in response to unequivocal disconfirmation.

The picture that emerges from the various disaster and other studies is the likelihood that the initial cognitive response of most individuals facing disaster is to interpret the novel sensory input by assimilating it into previously cognized models of reality (see Katz et al., n.d.). Every attempt is made to maintain these models, even at the expense of ignoring, "shutting off," or rejecting anomalous input. At one point or other during the experience, however, the overwhelming and contradictory input is accepted as real, and this causes disruption of previous models—the models thereafter becoming (at least for a time) inoperative. As a number of scholars have noted (see Wallace, 1970; Laughlin and d'Aquili, 1974; Powers, 1973; Piaget, 1971; Levi-Strauss, 1966), cognitive models are extremely complex systems, and a massive disruption of a part of a model usually affects the entire structure of the model. As Wallace (in Demerath and Wallace, 1957) has noted, the perception of destruction of a portion of a victim's culture is, for a period of time, interpreted by the victim as the destruction of the entire culture. In other words, the perceived failure of a part of the individual's system of expectations is conceived as a failure of the *entire* system. Thus, during the early postdisaster period, most victims are either conceiving a traditional world that is no longer applicable or are stunned by a world of apparently total chaos (stage zero in conceptual systems terms; see chapter 7).

There is certainly ample anthropological evidence from all over the world that this process obtained to some degree or other in the wake of the contact of non-European peoples with European society. One of the most devastating effects of contact for many of the world's traditional societies has been epidemics that were unexpected by all concerned. Thus the smallpox epidemic among the Easter Islanders of the latter half of the nineteenth century appears to have completed the process of social decimation begun by the Peruvian raiders (Routledge, 1919:205ff). The great influenza epidemic of 1918 in Samoa killed roughly 20 percent of the population, including most of the important elders (Keesing, 1934:96). Likewise, influenza caused widespread death among the Maori in the 1890s (Best, 1924:39), while massacre by Russian traders, combined with smallpox and other diseases, wiped out incredible numbers of Aleuts previous to 1900 (Bank, 1953:415ff). Epidemics around European mission stations had much the same effect among the Yahgan of Tierra del Fuego (Gusinde, 1937:1003, 1004) and caused the near extinction of the Vedda on Ceylon by the end of the first decade of this century (Spittel, 1945:67; Seligman and Seligman, 1911:307). Epidemics were again the legacy of European contact both with the Bushmen (Thomas, 1959:123) and with the Tikopia (Firth, 1959:33). The latter were fully aware of the association of communicable disease and an influx of external influences, but they explained these as "mainly supernatural" (Firth, 1930–31:378).

This depressing roll could be extended to literally hundreds of traditional societies around the globe, but the point is that, aside from the other effects of contact with Western society, the seeming inevitability of epidemics of communicable diseases created a situation for these societies approaching disaster proportions, events for which they were immunologically, cognitively, and socially unprepared. All of these groups had, of course, their own methods of curing (normally in the form of ritual procedures). However, although the data are often scanty and based on historical hindsight, they suggest that traditional methods of coping with sickness were, so to speak, overwhelmed by the extent of death and disruption. This would have caused many actors to perceive their models of reality as failing and thus would have led in many cases to widespread anxiety, frustration, and depression—and, as we shall see, to either the complete breakdown of society or to attitudes potentially fertile for the inception of revitalization movements.

Studies of disaster have also proved instructive relative to social processes, especially as they pertain to authority structure. In general, the data show that societies hit by sudden and unexpected ecological stress tend to be unprepared for effective corporate action. Very often the day-to-day social structure breaks down completely or, at best, proves ineffective in meeting the widespread need for rescue and restoration operations (see, for example, Spiegel, in Demerath and Wallace, 1957:3ff). Such cases are often marked by the emergence of spontaneous leadership from the ranks of the populace (Form et al., 1956; Demerath and Wallace, 1957:29). Whether the leadership arises from the predisaster social structure or from postdisaster "spontaneous" leadership, leaders themselves seem to have one trait in common—*they have previously experienced extreme stress.* The previous stress need not have been of the same type, however. Leaders may, for example, emerge during a flood who had previous experience in a combat leadership role (see Fritz and Marks, 1954, and Spiegel, in Demerath and Wallace, 1957). Usually such leaders do not exhibit the disaster syndrome and are effective in rallying rescue and work teams to cope with the emergency.

The data from many sources show that it is virtually axiomatic that groups under stress tend toward greater centralization of authority. Studies in social psychology are relevant here. Fiedler (1962), who performed three laboratory experiments and one study of natural groups, found that highly directive leadership is more effective under stress, while nondirective leadership is more effective under pleasant circumstances. Hamblin (1958:334) offers data from research on twenty-four laboratory groups supporting the idea that "leaders have more influence during periods of crisis than during non-crisis periods. . . ." The data presented by Tuckman (1964) on the relationship between level of cognitive complexity (see chapter 7) of group members and the tendency toward social hierarchy showed that, the less the complexity, the greater the tendency toward hierarchy. As we have shown in chapter 7, the effect of extreme stress is to lower the effective level of cognitive complexity. As Schroder et al. (1967:77) put it, "too much noxity[negative complexity] stress may induce a decrement in *all* aspects of structure, particularly of internally generated dimensions (thus leading to more complete stimulus-boundedness)." Schroder et al. (1967:101) also reported that "our research has shown that, like individual systems, group systems become hierarchical under stress. . . ."

Although it is clear that groups under stress tend to look to authority figures or leaders for guidance, it is also clear that such groups are quick to replace leaders they perceive to be ineffective. At the very least, group members will complain about ineffective leadership. As we indicated in our discussion of the disaster syndrome, this tends to occur as the initial psychological effects of the catastrophe wear off. The challenge to authority happens largely because ecological stress defines within rather narrow limits the problem confronting leaders, and attention of actors is focused on their leaders' capacity to solve problems. Hamblin (1958:334) found, for instance, that "groups tend to replace their old leader with a new leader if the old leader does not have an obvious solution to a crisis problem." Sherif and Sherif (1969:534) also show support for this conclusion in their research and discussion of leadership roles in social movements.

Groups or systems of groups under severe stress and without effective leadership may also atomize—that is, individuals may cease to act for the collective good and begin to compete with one another for individual reward. We described the general collective action problem in the preceding chapter and need only to mention that the tendency toward individualization is increased under the conditions of ineffective leadership. Of relevance here is the work of Muzafer Sherif and his group (Sherif, 1967; Sherif and Sherif, 1953, 1969). In a series of important experiments (called the "Robbers Cave" experiments), they demonstrated that the major variable in causing intergroup cohesion is the presence of what they termed *superordinate goals*. These are defined as "goals which are compelling and highly appealing to members of two or more groups in conflict but which cannot be attained by the resources and energies of the groups separately" (Sherif, 1967:445). Groups (or, for that matter, individuals) will unite around such goals, and continued cooperation thus engendered has the cumulative effect of reducing tension and conflict, reducing competition, and generating intergroup identification (again, this may be related to the findings of the conceptual systems group; see chapter 7). On the other hand, rewards or incentives for individual achievement may be experimentally interjected into group interaction with the effect of disrupting cooperation, reducing the orientation toward superordinate goals and creating an "every-man-for-himself" schism, even at the intragroup level. The experiments conducted by Alexander Mintz (1951) on "nonadaptive" group behavior support the same conclusions by showing that presence or absence of cooperative behavior is proportionate to the reward structure attached to competition versus cooperation.

Disaster and Ritual

To clarify just what may be learned about the functions of ritual in situations of ecological stress, let us summarize the characteristic psychological and social reactions of individuals and groups confronting disaster:

    1. The initial cognitive reaction of individuals to disaster-related cues is to make sense of them in relation to previously formulated models of reality.

    2. Previous models of reality become overwhelmed with contradictory input that finally causes the failure of the entire cognitive system.

    3. Disaster often exposes the relative incapacity of the social structure to cope effectively with the stressful situation. Leadership may emerge spontaneously from the community to fill the vacuum. Whatever its source, effective leadership tends to be derived from individuals who have previous experience with stressful situations.

    4. Groups under stress tend toward greater centralization of authority. But if leaders are perceived to be ineffective in coping with the situation, they will be promptly replaced.

    5. In the absence or failure of superordinate goals (closely related, of course, to the absence or failure of effective leadership), groups tend to fragment, and even (see chapter 8) to follow individual competitive goals.

The key to the social and cognitive reactions to disaster just mentioned is the lack of cognitive and social preparedness in the group facing the disaster. Disaster is a relatively unexpected event, and there is usually nothing in the past experience of most actors that leads them to model a world inclusive of such stress. There exists no cosmological, mythological, or attitudinal justification for the event, and, therefore, there exists no ritual response appropriate to it.

Moreover, the sociopolitical organization of the community is *not* diaphatically structured so as to respond flexibly to the abrupt change in the environment while at the same time maintaining social unity. Speaking metaphorically, the social structure is insufficiently elastic. It is too "brittle" to withstand the pressures of disaster—and it "cracks." Returning now to the issues discussed in the last chapter, we may say that, having no appropriate ritual as one of his set of power resources, the leader is hard pressed to take determined and effective action.[8] He founders under the tension of enhanced demand for action; at worst, he is replaced, at best, he is ignored. In a very real sense the sociopolitical structure of the community proves to be an inaccurate isomorphic model of the environment and thus compounds the disruptive effects of the disaster. In communities lucky enough to include individuals who have past experience in stress conditions, such persons may take over effective leadership for a time and be able to provide some effective action (whether this is ritual or by some other alternative depends on the society involved and the conditions facing it).

Even in societies that cope effectively through ritual response to certain types of stress, unexpected disaster may be so overwhelming that even ritual previously perceived as effective is now perceived as ineffective (see the final section on revitalization). Such was certainly the case in many of the already mentioned societies confronting wholesale epidemics with curing rituals previously directed at individual incidents of disease and injury. In the case of the Easter Islanders, most of their ritual specialists were taken away to work in the Peruvian guano deposits. In short, ritual response to unexpected ecological stress—that is, disaster—is often nonexistent or perceived to be ineffective by society members. This is in stark contrast, as we shall see, to the functioning of ritual under conditions of expected ecological stress.

Recurrent Stress

Probably all human societies experience some degree of fluctuation in basic resource availability. Just how significant fluctuations are in terms of adaptive strategies varies widely, of course, from place to place and from time to time. Many societies in the world need only to make a shift in production strategy to avoid any

---

8. In modern industrial societies, the leader may potentially have other and more effective (scientific, technological), but functionally equivalent, courses of action available to him. But, as the disaster research in many societies points up, leaders may not, in practice, be able to avail themselves of these alternatives.

debilitating resource deprivation whatsoever, while many others experience a brief period of resource deprivation at some point in the yearly cycle. Still other societies confront extreme fluctuations in resource availability or devastating events in their environment at frequent, if not annual, intervals. It is in the latter two cases that socioeconomic diaphasis—that is, recursive change in the structure of society—becomes marked and the role of ritual in diaphasis becomes, for the observer at least, more pronounced.

The critical variable in societal adaptation and psychological adjustment to severe ecological stress is anticipation of the impending event. We hypothesize that *any society confronting expected cyclical, ecological stress will be diaphatically structured in anticipation of that event.* We further hypothesize that *the diaphasis will facilitate the maximization of basic resource availability, social unity, and collective action and the minimization of psychological stress.* Social diaphasis may be more or less obvious, depending on the duration of time encompassed by the structure. Diaphasis may literally encompass entire generations, as is the case among both traditional Aleuts and Bushmen. In these societies we see an alternation of dependence by generation in an adaptively significant way. Among the traditional Aleuts, the adult females and children were totally dependent on the male hunter. But even the hunter realized that the day would come when he was too old to support himself and his family and that he would have to depend on his progeny for support. Thus, no matter how scarce the basic resources became, adults would always make sure that the children had first crack at the food. Like the Aleuts, the Bushmen conceive of the adaptive process as extending over a lifetime—hence, what one does today may well affect one's chances of survival in twenty-five years. They realize that the children they provide for today will provide for them in old age (Thomas, 1959). Neither group, of course, would endanger group survival during extreme stress to help members too old or too sick to migrate.[9] Such incidents were, however, rare, and the process of alternating dependence maintained a transgenerational continuity over periods of extreme stress.

9. This is speculative in the case of traditional Aleuts.

In contrast, transgenerational dependency was not found to be operative in Siriono (Holmberg, 1950), where there existed a perpetual state of basic resource deprivation leading to an "everyman-for-himself" and "take care of the present, the future will take care of itself" strategy. Children were fairly well on their own after weaning and had to collect what food they ate. Old people were allowed to die, for it was felt that they were of no utility to the group (Ibid., p. 85), a situation one also encounters in the literature pertaining to Ik (Turnbull, 1972).[10]

The changing temporal structure (diaphasis) of nonindustrial societies in response to cyclical stress relies heavily on the strategic design and scheduling of ritual. In a very real sense, ecological stress offers a controlled test of the functions of ritual outlined and discussed in previous chapters, that is, socialization, tuning, sociopolitical coping, social control, and the like. These functions examined in relation to stress may be conveniently grouped under the following four roles of ritual: (1) defining the crisis, (2) modeling ideal cosmological and social reality, (3) modeling the dynamic environment, and (4) preparing actors for confrontation with stress.

The Definition of the Crisis

It was David Schneider (in Demerath and Wallace, 1957:10ff) who, in the midst of a collection of reports on disaster research, noted the essential differences between peoples' reactions to hurricanes on Yap and peoples' reactions in the aftermath of most disasters covered in the disaster literature. In contrast to other cases he found no evidence of disaster syndrome and attributed this to the frequency of hurricanes on Yap. The people of Yap were prepared for such events. He also laid the groundwork for a second and critical point: that hurricanes are defined causally in the cognitive structure of Yaps in such a way that their occurrence reinforces social unity, rather than social individuation. "The catastrophes . . . are brought on by a magician when he has been ordered to do so by some chief. A chief, usually only a district chief, is only supposed to order a catastrophe when in his judgment people

10. For a more nearly complete discussion of social diaphasis and stress, see Laughlin and Brady (1978).

have deserved such serious punishment for failing to heed his advice and counsel. A typhoon is, therefore, a punishment meted out to the people by some chief whom they have neglected to heed" (Schneider, in Demerath and Wallace, 1957:12). In present terms the chaos of the hurricane is seen to mirror or isomorphically model social chaos. Thus, instead of socially fragmenting, Yaps become concerned with scrupulous adherence to features in the ideal conception of Yap social order, a reaction characteristic of stage 1 structure (chapter 7). They follow taboo restrictions to the letter, are concerned with rights and obligations, and carry out requisite ritual, whose purpose is to inhibit further catastrophe.

In the conclusion of his study Schneider pointed out that "the unique catastrophe is very different [from the chronic threat]: it is unstructured, and by the time it is structured, it is finished and does not occur again. But the chronic threat, the catastrophe that is long-awaited, takes on distinct meanings and provides a focus for long-standing anxieties, guilts, fears, and hostilities" (p. 15). At least a major portion of the "structuring" that Schneider is stressing is embedded in ritual and attendant mythology and cosmology. Whereas the catastrophe itself focuses negatively on current social ineptitude, ritual focuses positively on proper action within the social order. Ritual participates, therefore, in the definition of the crisis.

Firth gives similar evidence for stress in Tikopia. "For [Tikopia], natural order and prosperity were related to social harmony. Disorder in nature, untoward events [hurricanes, drought, tidal waves, epidemics—all regular occurrences], lack of prosperity, were to be related to social defects such as the religious division of the society or the feebleness of its premier chief" (1959:80). Although Firth observed a general decrement in obligatory exchange and certain types of ritual such as initiation rites, he also noted that even under the worst circumstances the "skeleton" of the society's critical "Work of the Gods" ritual activity was maintained. Again, crisis is defined as resulting from social disorder, and ritual is maintained to reestablish that order.

The examples of this pattern are too numerous to catalogue here. We need only to mention for further documentation that earthquakes, hurricanes, drought, and resulting famine on Samoa are defined as the punishment of angry spirits and gods to which the Samoans respond with appropriate rituals (Mead, 1930:16, 109; Stair, 1897:238). Among the Maori, volcanic eruptions, earthquakes, epidemics, blight, storms, and the like were seen as being caused by gods in reaction to broken taboos, and requisite rituals were performed to placate the gods (Best, 1924:265, 281; 1925:104). Epidemics, storms, and famine were attributed by the Reindeer Koryak to the displeasure of certain spirits, displeasure that was appeased by public ritual (Kennan, 1870:212). Droughts and resultant famine are perceived by the So of Uganda as being caused by the ancestors who are angered by inattention to proper social and religious obligations. Such events (along with all deleterious events) are met by appropriate ritual, the most important ritual being performed by members of an ancestor cult. Important ritual in So also requires collective participation by a significant proportion of the people (Laughlin and Laughlin, 1972). In all these cases the ecological stress is defined perceptually and cognitively in terms of social disharmony, and their incidence has the effect of increasing, rather than decreasing, social cohesion and collective action—in large measure through the medium of ritual.

A Model of Ideal Cosmological and Social Reality

In societies in which cosmological and social harmony are perceived to be isomorphic ritual functions to model ideal, harmonious reality in both. In simple societies that exhibit little social differentiation, ritual may appear so undifferentiated as to be overlooked as ritual. A perfect example may be found in the "dance" and "talk" among the Bushmen. The former include rituals during which healers in trance cure disease (Lebzelter, 1934:47; Marshall, 1962:248), and the latter are occasions in which tensions and hostilities are openly voiced in the group living area (Marshall, 1961:233ff).[11] Bushmen "dances" emphasize the harmony of

11. "Talks" and "shouts" are characterized by the repetitive expression of conflicts and feelings quite distinct from ordinary conversation and may actually lead to semitrance on the part of some participants (Marshall, 1961).

the cosmos and reenact social harmony, but there is virtually no emphasis on social differentiation, other than the distinction between the sexes. By contrast, the rites of protection of chiefs during hard times in Tikopia strongly emphasize the differentiation of Tikopia society into noble and commoner strata (Firth, 1959:264).

In its capacity to model ideal social-cosmological reality, ritual becomes the source of collective action. While the ultimate effects of ecological stress may be felt in a decrement in cooperation and exchange in other sociocultural spheres (e.g., in exchange of foodstuffs between, say, distant kinsmen), within the context of obligatory ritual the community is bound in unity for the completion of corporate action, usually directed toward a single end. The ritual occasion may demand, not only cooperative members, but also cooperative preparation for that ritual—as in the case of requisite honoring of prescribed taboos. Improper or uncooperative action may be emphasized and even underscored during the ritual sequence and thus create strong social pressures for proper action. That is, emphasizing the ideal, ritual broadens the disparity between the ideal and the actual in the perception of participants and may well determine the affective response of participants to those whose actions deviate from the norm.

There are undoubted cases in which mythology and attendant ritual operate to code proper action, which is also adaptively significant action when it is carried out in response to *infrequent* but recurrent stress. Such is clearly the case for Tsimshian and Kaguru survival mythology (John Cove, in Laughlin and Brady, 1978) and for the Buffalo Calf Pipe mythology and ritual among the Dakota (Richard Loder, personal communication). It must be stressed again that *ritual is action and communication*—that ritual is the motor expression of the same cognitive structures that give rise to verbal expression in myth, metaphysics, and cosmology. In participating fully in ritual, individuals are acting in accord with conceived causal relations extant in the universe of their understanding. A fundamental principle in cognitive structuring in any organism is the reduction, wherever possible, of uncertainty. Conceptual uncertainty results in impotence, confusion, and apathy (e.g., the disaster syndrome), whereas certainty tends to result in effective action. The response of organisms to repetitive stimuli in their environment will be a repetitive response. And where regularity is not an objective quality in the event, then some sort of certainty will be imposed upon the event through cognitive patterning.[12] Thus ritualized, collective action in response to ecological stress, accompanied by attendant myth, makes available to participants a model of a perfectly predictable (albeit occasionally destructive) universe and, at the same time, a channel for effective coping with crisis. But more than that, the collective activity in ritual communicates to one and all that the society is well and whole and that one's fellows perceive and concur in the same reality. Thus, one's coping response is bolstered by the action, or at least the approval, of the community.

A Model of Ecological Change

The function of ritual as a marker delimiting initial and final termini of temporal strips of reality has been discussed earlier in relation to cognitive proces__ ; (see chapter 5). An extension of this function becomes apparent in the modeling of ecological change, particularly where such change is recurrent and expected. Recognition of the importance of this function of ritual is indicated by the often-applied distinction between calendrical (scheduled) and noncalendrical (unscheduled) ritual (Wallace, 1966; Titiev, 1960; Turner, 1973). A calendrical cycle of ritual tends to be linked with ecologically and economically essential seasons—the number and duration of *conceived* seasons varying, of course, from society to society. Calendrical rituals operate for participants to focus the attention on: (1) the impending, expected change in environmental conditions, (2) an appropriate change in production strategies in anticipation of these conditions, and (3) potential shifts in basic resource availability, and (4) to maximize through collective action the facilitating qualities of the impending season and minimize debilitating qualities. Thus societies like the So who confront periodic drought resort to ritual to maximize the bounty of the har-

---

12. It was Malinowski (1922, 1931) who first heavily emphasized the relationship between uncertainty in the environment and the incidence of magical ritual. The continued awareness of this connection is reflected in the work of Evans-Pritchard (1937) and Warner (1955).

vest and minimize the likelihood of crop failure. At the first setting of Canopus in the evening sky (occurring at the beginning of winter), Bushmen proffer warming incantations and ritual to shorten the winter and make it milder (Schapera, 1930:174). In some societies living in marginal environments (e.g., traditional Eskimo and Bushmen), collective action and proper preparation in anticipating seasons of scarcity are all that make the difference between living through the "seasonal crisis" and potential extinction. Thus we see that ritual not only models synchronic cosmological and social reality but also may model the diachronic process of ecological change.

Preparation for Confrontation with Stress

By extension from our last remarks, it is obvious that ritual may prepare community members for ecological stress. For ritual to operate, or even be performed, to this end, there has to exist an objective probability of the threatened event's occurring. Where such a probability does exist—at least a probability that some of the participants in the ritual will confront stress—then the ritual may model proper behavior to be performed later under "real" circumstances. We can think of numerous examples of this type of ritual in our own society, where ritual is employed to counteract potential panic in emergency situations, for example, fire drills in schools and aboard ship, first-aid drills, bomb shelter drills, military drills and maneuvers in preparation for actual combat (see chapter 8 on collective action problems).

Examples may also be gleaned from the anthropological literature. In preparation for warfare Samoan priests order special feasts during which sham fights, boxing and wrestling matches, displays of martial skills and (in our terms) neuropsychological tuning for future combat occur (Turner, 1884:20). Similarly, during a prewar ritual, Maori warriors bite the crossbar of the village latrine in affirmation that they will endure any ordeal, no matter how revolting, in pursuit of victory. Warriors also go through a ritual sequence to come under the protection of the war god against supernatural methods applied by their enemies. Buck comments that "after a custom or a ritual has been established, its very performance gives *the feeling that all will be well"* (1952:393, emphasis ours; we have discussed probable neurophysiological mechanisms for such reactions in chapters 4 and 5).

Note, however, that preparedness for stress need not be a conscious factor for the actors involved. Ritual may, for example, play an important role in metabolic regulation and resource use—functions about which actors remain largely unaware (see Rappaport, 1967, 1968; Laughlin and Laughlin, 1972). With Rappaport (1967) we would reject Homans' (1941:172) statement that ritual does not "produce a practical result on the external world." Referring to a number of New Guinea peoples, Rappaport has said: "Ritual regulation helps to maintain the biotic communities existing within their territories, redistributes land among people and people over land, and limits the frequency of fighting. In the absence of authoritative political statuses or offices, the ritual cycle likewise provides a means for mobilizing allies when warfare may be undertaken. It also provides a mechanism for redistributing local pig surpluses in the form of pork throughout a large regional population while helping to assure the local population of a supply of pork when its members are most in need of high quality protein" (1967:182). More than that, in orienting and organizing actors in relation to adaptively critical environmental events, ritual may ensure optimal preparedness within the limits imposed by technological capability. Furthermore, if one conceives of ritual behavior as the result of a dialectic between an organism's conceptual system and its environment, then virtually all ritual has some effect on "the external world," be it direct, as in the case of metabolic regulation, or indirect, as in the case of psychological (and neurophysiological) tuning.

Revitalization

Socioeconomic diaphasis (in general) and ritual (in particular) in response to ecological stress maintain a delicate balance between population adaptation and the vicissitudes of environmental change. The state of isomorphism existing between social and cognitive models and the environment may be disrupted by a variety of disasters such as those discussed already, or by the interference of a superior, belligerent, and exploitative society. We have already seen the chaotic effects on the Easter Islanders of attack by Peruvian slavers. Similarly, we have seen the widespread and devastating effects of contagion that seem to follow inevitably in the wake of Western industrial society. All such situations, along with many others one might cite, pose severely trying conditions for diaphatic structure in traditional societies and may result in political upheaval, loss of morale, loss of confidence in traditional means of coping, and even complete restructuring of society.

As we mentioned earlier, groups under ecological stress tend toward greater centralization of authority. But we have also seen that the data from small group and sociological research, as well as from ethnography, indicate that, if the leadership is perceived to be making an inadequate response to the stressful conditions, the leadership will be replaced. The response of leadership may be interpreted by group members as "having no solution to the crisis" (Hamblin, 1958:334; Sherif and Sherif, 1969:534). The last phase of the disaster syndrome leaves victims in a highly sensitive state with respect to efficacy of leadership during the disaster (Wallace, 1970:202).

If the stress confronting a society is so severe that, not only particular leaders, but also the institution of authority itself is called into question, then the diaphatic structure of the society may fail, and a condition ripe for social morphogenesis or assimilation may develop. Firth (1959) mentions, for example, the emerging attitude among Tikopia that the institution of Chief has deteriorated over the years—this institution had been quite central to Tikopia adaptation to ecological stress in traditional times. Maori attitudes had begun to evidence social disruption under conditions of Western domination when Best (1924:39) recorded the following statement by one of his Maori friends: "I tell you that the Maori is in fault. He has deserted his old goals, institutions, and beliefs; now they have turned against him and are destroying him. How is it possible for us to survive? I say to you that I am resolved to return to the beliefs of my fathers." [13]

Just as the institution of authority itself deteriorates under severe and unremitting stress, so, too, may a traditional ritual response to crisis. In fact, the two would seem to occur simultaneously—in most societies, authority and religious ritual are inextricably linked, an important point emphasized by Goode (1964:138ff). We would repeat here that ritual functions as a buffer between ecological stress and psychological stress only so long as participants perceive ritual action as efficacious. The ritual sequence must maintain an isomorphic "fit" with a dynamic environment. It must, in other words, accurately model the relationship between society and cosmos for community members if their participation in ritual is to have the requisite tuning effect on them. If, however, there develops a perceived disparity between expectations and actuality, either because of external or internal interference with the society's diaphatic structure or because of unexpected intensity and duration of ecological stress, then participants lose their belief in the efficacy of traditional ritual. An alternative way of describing this is that a corpus of anomalous conditions and results begins to build that gradually erodes confidence in ritual response. We have known for a long time that cognitive systems resist erosion from anomalous input (Evans-Pritchard, 1937). But we have also seen from the disaster data that massive anomalous input can overwhelm, at least for a time, cognitive systems built up over the course of a lifetime. We should say, then, that ecological stress, although expected to some degree, for reasons already stated, may approach the effects of disaster.

Loss of confidence in traditional authority structure and ritual response in the face of overwhelming ecological stress creates a condition conducive to assimilation by a dominant society or to radical structural change (these alternatives are actually structurally equivalent as morphogenesis). Indeed, there may emerge a

13. For a causal model of the disruption of social diaphasis in the context of contact with Western industrial society, see Laughlin and Brady, (1978).

transformation of authority and ritual structure by way of a social movement of one kind or another. Anthony F. C. Wallace, who has probably carried the analysis of movements of this type further than any other scholar, has collectively termed them "revitalization movements" (Wallace, 1956b, 1958, 1966, 1969, 1970). Under this rubric he has included (Wallace, 1966:163) a variety of movements, including the so-called cargo cults of Melanesia (Worsley, 1968), *Terre sans mal* movements in South America, Mahdist movements in Islamic societies, millennial movements in Christian societies (Thrupp, 1962), messianic movements in Judaic societies (Wallis, 1943), nativistic movements among North American Indian societies and elsewhere (Linton, 1943), and separatist churches among certain African societies. In so doing, Wallace has recognized the essential structural equivalence[14] of these movements. More importantly, perhaps, he has developed a tentative theory of the origin of all religions based on the process of revitalization. In Wallace's view:

it is attractive to speculate that all religions and religious productions, such as myths and rituals, come into existence as parts of the program or code of religious revitalization movements. . . . Such a line of thought leads to the view that religious belief and practice always originate in situations of social and cultural stress and are, in fact, an effort on the part of the stress-laden to construct systems of dogma, myth, and ritual which are internally coherent as well as true descriptions of a world system and which thus will serve as guides to efficient action (1966:30).

According to Wallace, revitalization movements grow out of conditions of "cultural identity crisis" in which the belief system, religion, ritual, and social structure no longer fulfill the needs of community members. "The sociocultural system is being 'pushed' progressively out of equilibrium by various forces such as climatic

14. By "structural equivalence" we mean that these movements, given different names in different places, have a common cognitive cause. In more structuralist terminology, they form structural transformations that are the behavioral and expressive manifestations of an interaction between common cognitive processes and variant environmental circumstances. For a more nearly complete statement of the causal operations implied by transformation, see Laughlin, 1973.

and biotic change, epidemic disease, war and conquest, social subordination, or acculturation. Under these circumstances, increasingly large numbers of individuals are placed under what is to them intolerable stress by the failure of the system to accommodate their needs. Anomie and disillusionment become widespread as the culture is perceived to be disorganized and inadequate; crime, illness, and individualistic asocial responses increase sharply in frequency" (Wallace, 1966:159). The cultural identity crisis is a crisis of cognitive structure, or "mazeway," as Wallace would term it. The discrepancy between expectations of reality and reality as actually perceived widens to the point where the structures generating the expectations—that is, individual and collective cognitive structures—fail altogether, and the entire conceptual system "bottoms out" or becomes prestructural (see chapter 7). A community of prestructural, individuating, and anomic members is a community quite conducive to the emergence of a socioreligious or revitalistic movement—a movement that is at first a radical departure from traditional society and in competition with traditional socioreligious structure but that later becomes the new way of life for the community. The movement becomes the "culture," and a culture that is perhaps much more in tune with (diaphatically structured in relation to) the conditions that have caused the demise of the old ways.

Ritual is, of course, at the very heart of any religion or religious movement. "Ritual is religion in action; it is the cutting edge of the tool" (Wallace, 1966:102). Ritual inevitably does the work of religion, and for this reason we have stressed the point that ritual does not merely function as a mechanism for maintenance of the status quo (see also chapter 8). As the cognitive systems prevailing in a society change (including myth structure), so, too, will that society's ritual. The revitalization process, if it is sustained in a society, produces more effective ritual (in the perception of adherents) than existed in the old religion.

We find ourselves in partial agreement with Wallace's theory of the origin, development, and fall of religious systems. We would, however, like to combine some of the facets of his theory with those of our own and pyramid them into a conception of dynamic religion and ritual more consonant with our own current thinking.

First, religion and ritual are not static institutions as depicted in some of the older equilibrium theories.[15] They are structures in a process of dynamic interaction (equilibration) with a changing environment. As we have seen (chapter 6), a good deal of the impetus for ongoing change at the level of social systems derives from the process of ontogenesis of individual cognitive systems. The world (E_o), in which the child develops his conceptual system is not precisely the same world in which his parents developed theirs, and so on, generation after generation. The new generation at maturity has equilibrated to an environment somewhat different from that encountered by the previous generations. Obviously, the amount of disparity between generations varies from society to society, and from time to time in the same society, depending in large measure on the rapidity of environmental change. We would expect the *least* discrepancy to exist in the *most* traditional societies.

The point here is that any view of "religion" or "culture" as a rigid and brittle thing that snaps under stress of environmental change is a much distorted view of the process of human adaptation, at least in the light of our understanding of the adaptive development of organisms (see also Waddington, 1957). With reference to ritual, and in Piaget's (1971, 1974) terms, there occurs a gradual transformation over time and over generations of ritual—a transformation that entails both continuity of old elements and arrangements and assimilation of new ones. By this process the "same" ritual may remain efficacious under progressively different environments. Thus, religion, society, and ritual may be said to go through a constant process of revitalization (or "homeorhesis," to use Waddington's term), even while retaining essentially the same structure over time.

Second, what Wallace calls revitalization in his discussion is not merely equilibration in the system but actually morphogenesis of that system. Revitalization in this sense refers to a severe break

15. Wallace (1966) would obviously agree with us here.

in the continuity of the system, as well as the more usual assimilation of new elements into the system.[16] It is significant, we believe, that such movements, when they do occur, almost inevitably follow on the heels of extreme ecological stress—that is, *severe ecological stress appears to be a necessary, but not sufficient, condition for the emergence of revitalization movements.* It is further significant that most recorded revitalization movements develop in the context of intense contact with extremely dominant societies (generally one or more of the Western industrial societies). The nature of the contact has usually been characterized by interference to some degree with the diaphatic structure of the subordinate society, as well as by introduction of communicable disease, extractive exploitation, inaccessible expectation, warfare and massacre, exacerbation of competition for land and basic resources, and active proselytism. It is precisely this type of contact between societies that presents the greatest barriers to effective functioning of traditional ritual. Such contact may (1) variously and actively interfere with the actual process of ritual (e.g., when the British colonial government in Kenya forbade many critical Kikuyu rituals; see Rosberg and Nottingham, 1966; or when Christian missionaires throughout the world forbade the practice of "pagan" ritual they perceived to be in competition with their own), (2) present alternative modes of action that in the perception of members of the subordinate society seem more efficacious than their own traditional ritual (e.g., the introduction of Western medicine), (3) present conditions of stressful proportions with which subordinate society members perceive their own ritual inadequate to cope (e.g., epidemics, superior military capability), (4) generate competitive factionalism and individuation within the subordinate society—competition of sufficient intensity to overwhelm the collective action required for successful ritual.

Third, we suggest that the type of ecological stress requisite for a revitalization movement will either be noncyclical and unex-

16. We are aware that many revitalization movements take the form of a "return" to the "old ways." We would contend, however, that such a return is perceptually and conceptually selective, not objective or actual. The return is to elements perceived as positive attributes, selectively filtered through the contemporary cognized past.

pected (the usual case) or of unexpected intensity, frequency, or duration. Much the same cognitive process is involved in the inception of revitalization movements as is found in the wake of disasters (a point also made by Wallace in Demerath and Wallace, 1957). That is, environmental events become so anomalous in relation to the cognized environment that the cognized models become overwhelmed by input contradictory to common expectations. Traditional ritual response to stress is perceived as increasingly ineffective. This causes the functions of successful ritual (neurophysiological tuning, reaffirmation of ideal social and cosmological reality, channeling of conflict, social control, perception of effective coping behavior) to fail and thus leaves community members in an increasing state of uncertainty, anxiety, apathy, reciprocal conflict and disarray, low morale, helplessness and depression.[17] It is the deterioration of the community's confidence in the coping efficacy of ritual (among other aspects of collective action) and the resultant anomie that creates a condition of extreme susceptibility to alternative modes of coping. These modes may be drawn from a set that includes assimilation into the dominant society, assimilation by the subordinate society of foreign elements from the dominant society, rejection of both the old coping alternatives and those of the dominant society, and the introduction or development of new coping mechanisms through a revitalization movement. If the alternative is the emergence of a revitalization movement, it inevitably encompasses a ritual component that, for a time at least, reestablishes many of the functions that failed with the demise of the old ritual. If the revitalization movement "catches on"—that is, if it maintains its perceived efficacy over a number of years and becomes the new religion and attendant ritual—then the movement, like its predecessor, is involved in the process of equilibration caused by generationally specific ontogenesis. Generation by generation the new religion and new ritual will change, always in such a way as to maintain the conceptual systems and coping behaviors of community members in

17. For a thorough discussion of the importance of expectations and cognitive models in a neurophysiological context, as well as of the relationship between failure of expectations and depression syndrome, see Laughlin and d'Aquili (1974).

314

close alignment with environmental events. And the unexpected, deleterious stress that brought on morphogenesis of the old structure will probably form an expected ("cognized"), if not welcome, ingredient in the conceptual system and ritual action of the new structure.

References

Bank, T. P. 1953. "Botanical and Ethnobotanical Studies in the Aleutian Islands, II. Health and Medical Lore of the Aleuts." *Papers of the Michigan Academy of Science, Arts and Letters* 38:415–432. Ann Arbor.

Best, E. 1924. *The Maori* (vol. I). Wellington, New Zealand: The Polynesian Society.

—— 1925. "Maori Agriculture." *Dominion Museum Bulletin 9*. Wellington, New Zealand.

Bishop, C. A. 1970. "The Emergence of Hunting Territories Among the Northern Ojibwa." *Ethnology* 9(1):1–15.

Buck, P. 1952. *The Coming of the Maori*. Wellington, New Zealand: Whitcome and Tombs.

Cawte, J. 1972. *Cruel, Poor and Brutal Nations*. Honolulu: The University of Hawaii Press.

Chewings, C. 1936. *Back in the Stone Age: The Natives of Central Australia*. Sydney: Angus and Robertson.

Demerath, N. J. and A. F. C. Wallace. 1957. "Human Adaptation to Disaster." *Human Organization* (special issue) 16(2).

Evans-Pritchard, E. E. 1937. *Witchcraft, Oracles and Magic Among the Azande*. Oxford, England: Clarendon Press.

Festinger, L., H. W. Riecken, and S. Schachter. 1956. *When Prophecy Fails: A Social and Psychological Study of a Modern Group That Predicted the Destruction of the World*. New York: Harper and Row.

Fiedler, F. E. 1962. "Leader Attitudes, Group Climate, and Group Creativity." *Journal of Abnormal and Social Psychology* 65(5):308–318.

Firth, R. 1930–31. "Totemism in Polynesia." *Oceania* 1(3):291–321, (4):377–398.

—— 1940. "The Work of the Gods in Tikopia." *Monographs on Social Anthropology* No. 1 and No. 2. London: The London School of Economics and Political Science.

—— 1959. *Social Change in Tikopia*. New York: Macmillan.

Form, W. H. et al. 1956. "The Persistence and Emergence of Social and Cultural Systems in Disasters." *American Sociological Review* 21(2):180–185.

Fritz, C. E. and I. S. Marks. 1954. "The NORC Studies of Human Behavior in Disaster." *Journal of Social Issues* 10(3):26–41.

Fritz, C. E. and H. B. Williams. 1957. "The Human Being in Disaster: A Research Perspective." *The Annals of the American Academy of Political and Social Science* 309:42–5.

Goode, W. J. 1964. *Religion Among the Primitives*. New York: Free Press.

Grinspoon, L. 1964. "The Truth Is Not Enough," in *International Conflict and Behavioral Science: The Graigville Papers* (R. Fisher, ed.). New York: Basic Books.

Gusinde, M. 1937. *Die Vamana: vom Leben und Denken der Wassernomaden am Kap Hoorn.* Die Feurland-Indianer II. Expeditions Series II. Modling bei Wien: Anthropos-Bibliothek.

Hamblin, R. L. 1958. "Leadership and Crisis." *Sociometry* 21:322–335.

Holmberg, A. R. 1950. "Nomads of the Long Bow: The Siriono of Eastern Bolivia." Smithsonian Institution: Institute of Social Anthropology Publication No. 10. Washington, D.C.: U.S. Government Printing Office.

Homans, G. C. 1941. "Anxiety and Ritual: The Theories of Malinowski and Radcliffe-Brown." *American Anthropologist* 43:164–172.

Katz, S. H., E. G. d'Aquili, P. Gottesman, and J. Patys. n.d. "Cognition and Explanation: Responses to the Philadelphia Earthquake." Ms.

Kaufman, H. 1910. "Die Auin. Ein Beitrag zur Buschmannforschung." *Mitteilungen aus den deutschen Schutzgebieten* 23:135–160.

Keesing, F. M. 1934. *Modern Samoa.* London: Allen and Unwin.

Kennan, G. 1870. *Tent Life in Siberia, and Adventures Among the Koraks and Other Tribes in Kantohatka and Northern Asia.* New York: Putnam.

Laughlin, C. D. 1973. "Causality and Transformational Law: A False Dichotomy." Ms.

Laughlin, C. D. and E. G. d'Aquili. 1974. *Biogenetic Structuralism.* New York: Columbia University Press.

Laughlin, C. D. and I. Brady. 1978. *Extinction and Survival in Human Populations.* New York: Columbia University Press.

Laughlin, C. D. and E. R. Laughlin. 1972. *"Kenisan:* Economic and Social Ramifications of the Ghost Cult Among the So of Northeastern Uganda." *Africa* 42(1):9–20.

Lebzelter, V. 1934. *Eigeborenenkulturen in Sudwest—und Sudafrika,* vol. 2. Leipzig: Hiersemann.

Lee, R. B. 1966. *Subsistence Ecology of King Bushmen* (Doctoral dissertation). Berkeley: University of California.

Levi-Strauss, C. 1966. *The Savage Mind.* Chicago: University of Chicago Press.

Linton, R. 1943. "Nativistic Movements." *American Anthropologist* 45:23–40.

Luce, G. G. 1971. *Biological Rhythms and Human and Animal Physiology.* New York: Dover.

Malinowski, B. 1922. *Argonauts of the Western Pacific* (1961 ed.). New York: Dutton.

—— 1931. "Culture," in *Encyclopedia of the Social Sciences IV.* New York: Macmillan.

Marshall, L. 1961. "Sharing, Talking, and Giving: Relief of Social Tensions Among Kung Bushmen." *Africa* 31:231–249.

—— 1962. "Kung Bushmen Religious Beliefs." *Africa* 32:221–252.

Mead, M. 1930. "Social Organization of Manua." Bishop Museum Bulletin 76: Honolulu.

Mintz, A. 1951. "Non-Adaptive Group Behavior." *Journal of Abnormal and Social Psychology* 46:150–159.

Piaget, J. 1971. *Biology and Knowledge.* Chicago: University of Chicago Press.

—— 1974. *Understanding Causality.* New York: Norton.

Powers, W. T. 1973. *Behavior: The Control of Perception.* Chicago: Aldine.

Rappaport, R. 1967. "Ritual Regulation of Environmental Relations Among a New Guinea People." *Ethnology* 6:17–30. Reprinted in *Environment and Cultural Behavior* (1969; P. Vayda, ed.). Garden City, N.Y.: Doubleday.

—— 1968. *Pigs for the Ancestors.* New Haven, Conn.: Yale University Press.

Rosberg, C. G. and J. Nottingham. 1966. *The Myth of "Mau Mau."* Nairobi: East African Publishing House.

Routledge, K. 1919. *The Mystery of Easter Islands*. London: Sifton, Praed.

Schapera, I. 1930. *The Khoisan Peoples of South Africa*. London: Routledge.

Schroder, H. M., M. J. Driver, and S. Streufert. 1967. *Human Information Processing*. New York: Holt, Rinehart and Winston.

Seligman, C. G. and B. Z. Seligman. 1911. *The Veddas*. Cambridge, England: Cambridge University Press.

Seligman, M. E. P. 1975. *Helplessness*. San Francisco: Freeman.

Sherif, M. 1967. *Social Interaction. Process and Products: Selected Essays*. Chicago: Aldine.

Sherif, M. and C. W. Sherif. 1953. *Groups in Harmony and Tension*. New York: Harper and Row.

—— 1969. *Social Psychology*. New York: Harper and Row.

Spittel, R. L. 1945. *Wild Ceylon*. 3d ed. Colombo, Ceylon: General Publishers.

Stair, J. B. 1897. *Old Samoa*. London: The Religious Tract Society.

Thomas, E. M. 1959. *The Harmless People*. New York: Knopf.

Thrupp, S., ed. 1962. *Millennial Dreams in Action*. The Hague, Netherlands: Mouton.

Titiev, M. 1960. "A Fresh Approach to the Problem of Magic and Religion." *Southwestern Journal of Anthropology* 16:292–298.

Tuckman, B. W. 1964. "Personality Structure, Group Composition, and Group Functioning." *Sociometry* 27:469–481.

Turnbull, C. M. 1961. *The Forest People*. Garden City, N.Y.: Doubleday.

—— 1972. *The Mountain People*. New York: Simon and Schuster.

Turner, G. 1884. *Samoa: A Hundred Years Ago and Long Before*. London: Macmillan.

Turner, V. W. 1973. "Symbols in African Ritual." *Science* 179 (4078): 1100–1105.

Waddington, C. H. 1957. *The Strategy of the Genes*. London: George Allen and Unwin.

Wallace, A. F. C. 1956a. "Human Behavior in Extreme Situations, Disaster Study Series 1." Washington, D.C.: National Academy of Science, National Research Council.

—— 1956b. "Revitalization Movements." *American Anthropologist* 59:264–281.

—— 1958. "The Dekanawidah Myth Analyzed as the Record of a Revitalization Movement." *Ethnohistory* 5:118–130.

—— 1966. *Religion: An Anthropological View*. New York: Random House.

—— 1969. *The Death and Rebirth of the Seneca*. New York: Random House.

—— 1970. *Culture and Personality*. 2d ed. New York: Random House.

Wallis, W. D. 1943. *Messiahs: Their Role In Civilization*. Washington, D.C.: American Council on Public Affairs.

Warner, E. 1955. *Trial by Sasswood*. London: Gollancz.

Weiss, J. M. 1972. "Psychological Factors in Stress and Disease." *Scientific American* 226(6):104–113.

Worsley, P. 1968. *The Trumpet Shall Sound: A Study of "Cargo" Cults in Melanesia*. New York: Schocken.

═══════════════ Ten ═══════════════

A Ceremonial Ritual: The Mass

G. Ronald Murphy, S.J.

> **Now as they were eating, Jesus took bread, and blessed,**
> **and broke it, and gave it to the disciples and said, "Take,**
> **eat; this is my body." And he took a cup, and when he had**
> **given thanks he gave it to them, saying, "Drink of it, all of**
> **you; for this is my blood of the covenant, which is poured**
> **out for many for the forgiveness of sins. I tell you I shall not**
> **drink again of this fruit of the vine until that day when I**
> **drink it new with you in my Father's kingdom."**
>
> **Matthew 26:26–29**

This chapter differs from those preceding it in that it attempts to exemplify in a very specific way the major concepts presented in the first six chapters, that is, the pivotal concepts of a biogenetic structuralist analysis of ceremonial ritual. This chapter considers such notions as entrainment, formalization, synchronization, tuning, and cognitive structuring insofar as they apply to a concrete example of human ceremonial ritual, the Roman Catholic Mass. Of course, any ceremonial ritual could have been chosen to apply the analytic concepts presented in this volume. In some ways any number of simpler "more primitive" ceremonial rituals might have lent themselves more easily to analysis within the relatively short space available here. But it was felt that the somewhat abstract concepts developed earlier in this volume might more easily be grasped and tested if a ritual were chosen for analysis that is part of our Western tradition and that carries tremendous emotional importance for millions of people within our own cultural milieu.

The reader is asked to note carefully, not only the several

318

mechanisms used to achieve affective synchronization, but also the numerous occasions when two objects or two points in time are united ritually. The union of opposites and the "warping" of time, which in a sense is a union of opposites (i.e., ambiguity of time present and time past), is exemplified repeatedly in the ritual of the Mass. Ambiguity is an essential part of the union of oppositional dyads. For example, a believer is never sure if the priest or Christ is presiding at any given moment or if the congregation and the "heavenly court" are totally distinct bodies. Similarly, one is never quite sure whether one is present at a church service in the twentieth century, at the last supper, at the crucifixion and resurrection, or for that matter before the Heavenly Throne as presented in the Book of Revelation. The ambiguity is intentional. Furthermore, one is never sure whether the body of the congregants is united with the gifts of bread and wine or whether they are separate. There is also a psychological uncertainty about the status of the bread and wine themselves with respect to the body and blood of Christ. The solution of all these dyadic oppositions, along with the ever-present issue of synchronization of the participants' affect, will undoubtedly be the elements that the reader most clearly notes. It is also our hope that the immediacy of this example may flesh out in a meaningful and concrete way what might otherwise appear to be a sterile intellectual analysis. Accordingly, the tone of this chapter shifts from the primarily analytic stance characteristic of previous chapters to a more synthetic and holistic approach. Although analytic comment is made throughout, in an attempt to relate various parts of the Mass to concepts developed earlier in the text, nevertheless, an attempt is made, insofar as it is possible, to convey a sense of the ritual act of the Roman Catholic Mass to the reader. Obviously, in a strict sense such an undertaking is impossible. For one thing, the written word lacks the repetitive stimulus quality of the ritual itself.

A second consideration is that many readers do not share the belief system on which the ritual of the Mass is predicated and thus do not have access to the ritual "from inside." They may find themselves excluded from the inner effectiveness of the Mass for the believing participant. This should not deter the non-Catholic reader, however, since there seems to be a considerable body of evidence indicating that belief in the cognitive or mythic structure in which a ritual is embedded, though very important if a ritual is going to have full effect, may not be absolutely essential. There are reports of "aesthetic" experiences on the part of individuals observing rituals, whose cognitive content they could not subscribe to. Nevertheless, it appears true that, for the most part, a belief is at least an extremely facilitating circumstance. In an attempt to counteract this difficulty, I present this chapter in a more synthetic mode, hoping that, while I am analyzing this specific ritual, some of its flavor and feeling will be conveyed to all readers. Similarly, to see that our theory is being properly applied to the internal meaning of a ritual, as well as to its external phenomena, the editors wished to have a prime informant apply the concepts to one of his major rituals, one he himself performs. For this reason the scholar who primarily wrote this chapter had to be a Roman Catholic priest.

Obviously the question of the validity of a belief or mythic system is a totally different one from the question of its psychological importance as part of a total ritual act. While atheist, agnostic, and various kinds of believers might differ about the ontological bases of a cognitive or mythic system, nevertheless all can agree, in principle at least, on its *psychological* importance, which has been the main thrust of this volume.

The Entrance Rite of the Roman Mass begins with a ritual enactment of a common model for what the entire Mass is: access to the Inaccessible God. The underlying model for access, "walking toward," is ritually performed by the appointed head of the congregation, the priest, who is the single person able to do it in the name of all. The believers and priest are able to participate in this behavioral metaphor in a nonmetaphoric way since they believe that they already do have access to God, through Christ, at any moment. This belief is embodied in the myth structure, which maintains that "whenever two or three are gathered together in my name there I am in the midst of them." Ritual walking toward the altar requires, not so much a blind throwing of oneself into a metaphor, as an acceptance that what is being acted out is already so, and thus a nonparticipant need not be upset by the apparent casualness with which the ritual can be done. The ritual "walking toward" the altar is not so much an actual traversing of a new path to God as a walking done so as to make the believers' already existing path (Christ) visible and actual. It is an attempt to realize what one already believes to be so, and, since the rite will terminate in speaking to God, it is necessary to approach within "speaking range."

The priest begins the rite of access, ideally, at the rear of the church. He thus starts within the area behind the congregation and outside their sight and conscious awareness. (This is also true, though less effective, if he enters from the sacristy.) Led by the cross and candles, walking through incense and accompanied by the hymn, the priest moves in procession down the aisle, walking slowly through the midst of the congregation. The people rise at the sight of the cross moving through their midst and sing the hymn of entry—thus first beginning to act as a group. The reader will recall the concept of entrainment of cortical rhythms as a response to rhythmic sensory stimuli presented in chapter 4. The importance of this concept to synchronization of the affective states of participants in a ritual act has been emphasized both for animals in chapters 2 and 3 and for man in chapters 4 and 5. The goal of the rhythmic motor movement involved in the entrance procession, as well as of the intrinsic rhythmicity of both the music and the movement of incense in the air, is precisely the sort of alteration of autonomic tuning that results in decreased personal space and a sense of unity of the participants. These concepts were elaborated in detail in chapters 2 through 5.

Beginning *behind* the people's backs acknowledges that the group awareness of the belief that "I am in the midst of them" is at a low level. The ritual accepts this and attempts to raise the level of consciousness through direct enactment of the belief structure in a visible and audible form. That the cross and the priest gradually become visible (to more and more of the congregation) as they progress down the aisle is in itself a quantitative metaphor of a qualitative increase of group realization of the presence of Christ within the group. Thus, according to the notions presented in the first part of this book, not only does the entrance rite provide for synchronization of affect and group cohesion, but also an initial attempt is made at a resolution of an oppositional dyad even at this early stage, that is, the opposition of the congregation as unified entity and Christ himself. The opposition is, of course, one that is present in the mythic system of all the participants and is therefore virtually present from the very beginning of the ritual action, even though not yet explicitly elaborated by the recitation of the myth.

The moving cross, and above all, the moving priest, have gradually become the traversing focus of the rising group's religious consciousness as the priest reaches the front of the congregation. As he approaches the altar rail (a sort of barrier between the sanctuary and the area for the congregation) all eyes are able to see him and group sight has been brought into common focus, an initial affective synchronizing with which it is possible to begin worship. The priest figure focuses attention by using himself to faciliate group identity around a single principal moving person. In this he is a metaphor for Christ, who is the only single person around whom the church believes it can gather, and thus he wears the vestments, not so much to say that he, as a person, is any more Christ than anyone of the congregation, as to indicate ritually that Christ is really here, now, walking in the midst of His people. The ambiguity of the persons of the priest and Christ is here made very explicit, and the resolution of this dyadic opposition (i.e., priest-Christ) is for the first time made possible for those members of the congregation whose "tuning mechanism" is particularly susceptible to the rhythmic presentation of the ritual up to this point. This may be considered the first, or at least one of the first, nodal points of the ritual at which the union of a crucial oppositional dyad becomes possible, at least for some of the more "sensitive" participants. Needless to say, the opposition is not only one of persons, that is, priest and Christ, but also one of time, that is, the present versus the time of Christ (the time of Christ being itself ambiguous—either historical or eschatological, i.e., at the end of time).

The people identify with the motion of the priest figure's approach to the altar, not by moving or by wearing the vestments, but by their singing of the entrance hymn, by which they set the whole tempo of the physical "walking toward" God being performed by the priest and those in the entrance procession, and by their contemplation of the gradual diminishing of the distance between the priest and the sanctuary.

The rite then goes an important step further. The priest gradually transfers the group focus from himself to the altar. When he reaches the head of the group, instead of turning and facing the congregation, he continues forward into the sanctuary, and, with all eyes on him and the music of entry continuing, he bows profoundly or goes down on his knees before the altar. He then ascends the steps that place the altar ritually on a "higher plane" than all other things in the church. He moves forward to it and, bowing his head, kisses it. The simple rite of entry reaches its first climax in a ritually erotic act that terminates a ritual of gradual approach and penetration. The penetration into the realm of the holy is thus shown to be for the sake of living intercourse with the divine, coupled with awe and adoration. The priest then reinforces the atmosphere of divine-human love and communion by filling the sanctuary with incense, a symbol of the presence of the Holy Spirit. He incenses the crucifix, the image of God-man crucified (the prime image of the reconciliation of the divine and human worlds), who performed the first uniting in love of His father with mortal men, and who, in the cognitive belief structure of the community, by His death on the cross effected the penetration from the finite space-time world to the world of the eternal. Then the priest honors the altar, the center of the church, the sacred table by grace of which Christ is able to be present now at the ritual as the divine-human reconciler to which the ritual's models point. The priest incenses the altar, not by standing still, as in the case of the crucifix, but rather by circling around it in an orbiting motion. The stationary incensing of the crucifix speaks of the steady thanksgiving and adoration of the community for the one act of Christ done in the past; the circling is a rhythmic motion acknowledging the dynamic presence of God in time and brings the worship into synchrony with the circling of the planets around the sun, the stars around the galactic center, and even with the heavenly worship conceived of as adoration around the divine throne. The circular motion takes into account the passing of time and sees this also as a manifestation of the divine. Above all, however, rotational motion points to the altar as the central axis of all rotation, the eternal still point. Locating the group's supraordinate center enables a limbic arousal to take place in the midst of the doings of the everyday world and helps the congregation interpret the various motions of its everyday world as a part of the great motion of the entire world around its divine center. Thus the group awareness gradually shifts along its central axis from itself (in the priest) to God.

After this entry, the priest suddenly, as it were, retreats back from the altar area. The incense by now has begun to suffuse the entire church with a visible new atmosphere, and it thus, together with the singing, becomes a tangible expression of the belief in the expansion of the presence of the all-pervading breath (consciousness, spirit) of God thoughout the group and the universe. The priest then goes back out through the gate of the communion rail, almost as though the ritual had forgotten something, and it seems to be begun again. The priest and people together make the sign of the cross on themselves while stating that it is in the name of the Trinity that they are acting, and after a formal greeting, the priest reminds the people that (according to their common belief structure) there is a barrier separating the group from God that is far more effective than that of physical or spatiotemporal distance, that of lack of awareness of the divine presence, namely, sinfulness. The Entrance Rite must now take the moral hesitation of the community about "entering" the sanctuary into consideration, and just as the procession of entry ritual puts the logical left-hemisphere worries about the difficulty of entering "heaven" at rest, now ritual must also quiet the moral scruples that are also primarily a left-hemisphere function.

The Penance Rite does this formally and directly. In accordance with the belief system the barrier of sin is penetrated from the divine side by the offering of forgiveness and from the human side by the accepting of pardon. This sudden intrusion of feelings of unworthiness and of guilt over sin and a need to ask for forgiveness throws a dash of cold water on the solemn joyfulness of the entrance procession. It effectively stops the forward thrust of the entry, but so strong is the fear of entering unworthily, and so strong is the ringing echo of Christ's attack on the pharisee (and his praise of the publican) still in the communal Christian mind, that heads are bowed and three times God's mercy is asked for. Everyone's sinfulness, normally a secret embarrassment, is, through facilitating ritual, openly admitted and confessed, and sinful people feel less embarrassed to be before the sanctuary. One form of the Penance Rite calms by reminding all of known concepts from the Gospel: It is sinners who are the ones to whom Christ calls (and not the upright); it is the sick, and not the well, whom He wishes to heal; and it is He who is the "defense lawyer" pleading for the sinner before the Father.

In an alternate form of the Penance Rite, the priest not only leaves the sanctuary but also reverses his entire path through the center of the congregation, sprinkling everyone with water as he performs a ritual washing, which simultaneously is (1) an evocation of each one's initiation into Christianity (Baptism), (2) a ritually actual sign of the divine grace that activates the "washing" model of forgiveness, and (3) a covering of the sinner as "freely as the rain from heaven." The repetition of the entrance procession in the reverse direction is a retrogression, going back again into the dark recesses of one's background so as to be able to come forward again to enter in with a soul that has morally "returned." The retrogressive steps back to the area of the subconscious and the past are thus accompanied by a gracious rain of forgiveness that was initiated from the front, from the sanctuary, and enables the sinner to return and to enter freely the more sacred parts of the Mass.

The congregation sings an ancient hymn of divine praise: "Glory to God, in the Highest." In singing this hymn, the participants are ritually identifying with the angelic choir of the Christmas story in Luke by singing a hymn that is an extension of the angels' song as given in the Bible. Ritually, the congregation is made to feel, by the very words issuing from their mouths (in view of the cognitive belief structure), that they are a part of the Divine Birth in Bethlehem and that they belong to the choir of spirits who are always in the Divine Presence in heaven praising God to His face. The ritual association of the congregation with angels is made forcefully at this point in the Mass, but this same identification will be repreated at a far more crucial juncture in the liturgy, at the end of the Preface to the Eucharistic Prayer itself.

When the singing has ended, the book of prayers is brought to the priest and the Entrance Rite makes its conclusion in prayer. Theologically, one of the most important facilitating functions of the Entrance Rite is to make prayer possible. It may seem easy for a religious person to say prayers, but it is not really easy to realize the prayers as they are being said. It is not always possible while saying them to coordinate left and right hemispheric activity so as to be able to envision that one has entered into the divine throne room and that God is listening to the words and thoughts being addressed to Him by the person praying. Prayer is the moment when even those of great faith falter, and thus, the Rite of Entry must support the communal faith to the point that the group does not feel that it is patently absurd to address a Divinity that it cannot see, hear, touch, or smell, or walk up to and address. In the ritual, each of these "perceptual requirements," as we might call them, of seeing the holy place, hearing the music of the angels, touching the throne, smelling the celestial atmosphere, and walking up to the Holy One on the throne, has been ritually accomplished. There remains only to speak to God. This the congregation and the priest now do.

The structure of the prayer, with its somewhat rapid alternation of address to the people and to God, coupled with the alternation of silent individual prayer and communal prayer focused in the priest, permits synchronization of affect and communal entrainment. The priest begins the prayer by announcing the Divine Presence to the People, using the following synchronizing structure:

> 1. The priest says ''The Lord be with you'' to the people, verbally reinforcing and repeating the message of the incense, and of the entire rite so far, namely, that the participants are

326

standing where God is and have entered into His presence and must let Him enter their awareness.

2. The priest invites all to pray, to speak individually (silently) to God, as he says "Let us pray." Then follows a period of ritual silence for individual prayer.

3. The priest then stretches out his hands in the gesture that shows he has ceased his individual prayers and now prays as the leader of the group, in and for the congregation. Praying with open hands is common to the Semitic world, but the far-spread hand position as used by all priests of the Roman and Eastern Christian Churches may indicate a universal desire among Christians to suggest ritually that it is "Christ who stretches out His hands on the cross for our salvation," who is peaking to the Father in the prayer of the community.

4. The priest then says explicitly what his hands have been implying visually. The almost doxological prayer ending repeated so constantly in the Roman Rite declares who it is that is giving both priest and congregation vocal access to God. While bringing his hands together slowly in a sweeping, almost circular, gesture of universal unity and completion, he says or chants: *"Through Our Lord Jesus Christ, your Son, Who lives and reigns with You and the Holy Spirit, one God, forever and ever."*

5. The congregation replies with a Hebrew ending that implies that the physical and moral isolation from God have been overcome and that a personal and conversational access to the Throne of God has been accomplished: "Amen."

After the almost excessively active nature of the Entrance Rite, the Service of the Word (listening to the readings from the Scriptures) is a much more passive counterpart. It, too, terminates in prayer, that is, approach to the Divine through speech, but only after a somewhat prolonged period with priest and congregation both in a seated position, listening to Old and New Testament readings interspersed with chants from the Psalms. Sitting down at the end of the Entrance Rite is a way of ritually establishing the fact of arrival and of being "at home" in the church as House of God. It also serves to initiate a period of more relaxed ritual behavior than in the preceding rite. The previous rite is, however, theologically subservient to this one, since through the Scriptures the congregation is being spoken to (instead of speaking to the Divine as in the Entrance Rite), and the basic cognitive belief system is being represented and explained from fundamental sources in the Judaeo-Christian scriptures. The readings are ritually marked by being read from a high place and from a larger, more impressive volume of the Scriptures than the private Christian is likely to have. The first and second readings, one from the Old Testament and one usually from the Letters of Paul, are read with no more ritual marking than that just described. The third reading is, however, clearly marked to stand out from the preceding two.

The third reading is from the Gospel of Christ and is suddenly announced by a singing of Alleluias from the choir. At this the priest or deacon rises from his place and begins to walk toward the Gospel book. The priest pauses before the altar and bows, asking for the ability to proclaim the Gospel well, and proceeds to take the Gospel book and walk with it to the head of the congregation. During all this time, as the reader, book in hand, approaches the people, the Alleluias grow louder and are taken up by the whole congregation. Ritually, the Gospel book and its reader are being "put together" and actualized as one unit. This is not done with the first readings, nor do the readers "walk" toward the congregation. The Gospel book and its reader are identified further as the priest or deacon, before beginning to read, touches his thumb to the beginning of the portion he is going to read. He then touches his thumb to his forehead, lips, and heart and thus prays in gesture that Christ's words may now be his words so thoroughly that they are in his mind (that he understands them—forehead), that they may issue from his mouth as he now speaks Christ's words for Christ (lips), and that there may be a real love between his person and Christ's Gospel (heart). Having done this triple ritual of touching (it is made in the form of small crosses), the priest repeats the formula of Presence used at the Entrance Prayers—"The Lord be with you"—to the participants and then proclaims the Gospel of Jesus written as He delivered it.

Immediately following the Gospel reading, the priest or deacon preaches the sermon. He is ritually responsible for saying Christ's message in the form in which he thinks it is to be said *now.* The ritual is the mystical vehicle for the divine superiority over the time span between *then* and *now.* For the participant in this ritual, the quite obvious time distance between the Christ who spoke to his congregation on the hillside with "Blessed are the poor in spirit" and the congregation at Sunday morning Mass has been bridged through the ritual of the priest's coming to them with the Gospel book, accompanied by the constant chanting of Alleluia. The hearing of Christ's words said again, the bowing request for Christ to speak through the reader, the touching of the book by the reader, and the raising of a voice with Christ's words of long ago—thus is Christ Himself ritually heard speaking again.

This making contemporary the old and the new is so strongly felt that the priest is instructed (despite all taboos against idolatry) actually to incense the Gospel message in the book before reading it, and the congregation is able to reply to the last words at the end of the Gospel. "Praise to *You,* Lord Jesus Christ." At the people's saying this, the reader, repeating the love gesture of the Entrance Rite, kisses the book at the place from which he has read. In the solemn form of the ritual the fuller dimension of the belief is made visible in that the priest or deacon who is to read the Gospel first goes to the throne of the bishop and receives the blessing and is then sent from the throne to preach the Gospel. ("As the Father has sent me so I send you.") This entire ritual "doing" of the Gospel is a vehicle for the mystical belief of the continuing teaching presence of Christ.

The appropriate response to hearing Christ's message (in the cognitive belief structure) should be an acceptance of it in faith and subsequent concern for all mankind as inspired by Jesus. This double effect is ritually expressed through the communal recitation of the Creed and through the Prayer of the Faithful (General Intercessions). This latter prayer before God the Father for the whole world is the ending of the entire introductory section. Both rites are so structured that they enable the faithful to participate in the highest reward of membership in the Church: direct access to the Throne, the ability to speak to God with confidence. The prayer ritual is so structured (ideally) that it is mutually reinforcing and affectively synchronizing for all the participants. The priest calls for prayer in the usual formulaic way: "The Lord be with you." "Let us pray." Then the deacon asks for or reads the concerns and intentions of the people. After each petition given by an individual (or read by the deacon), the deacon calls for communal prayer for the individual with the formula "Let us pray to the Lord," and the people and choir say or sing in harmony "Lord have mercy," or "Lord, hear our prayer."

At the end of the list of concerns the priest himself adds again the ritual prayer ending, which elevates the whole preceding prayer of the faithful to a higher level of consciousness by adding the prayers and concerns in the hearts of the people: "Through our Lord Jesus Christ, Your Son." The priest himself does not usually add intentions in the prayer, but at the end, as the figure robed in the ritual white garment with the long white sleeves of Christ, he stretches out his hands for the community to signify who has been really praying this prayer within the hearts of people. The priest's ritual role in prayer is thus not just to pray but to synchronize the prayers of all participants and to increase the awareness of all to whom it is he is praying in and through the people. The priest is thus an instrument of community realization. The prayer's structure both equilibrates the prayers of the individuals with the concerns of the universal church community and also permits an elevation of awareness through the doxology of the priest at the end. So doing, the expressing of the General Intentions also "gets out" the left hemispheric concerns that, if not voiced, could be a distraction in the sacred rites that follow and might prevent the optimal tuning of right and left hemispheric functions.

The Entrance Rite and the Service of the Word are the two components of the first half of the Mass, both terminating in approach to the Divine Presence and in approach to the Divine in prayer. The second half of the Mass repeats this basic structure but on a much deeper level. The two component parts of the second half of the Mass take place entirely within a culminating prayer and celebrate, not the approach of the participants to the Divine, but the approach of the Divine to the participants. The change is marked by a change in ritual positions. The seated posture of the Service of the Word is replaced by the attitude of prayer and respect and by the frequent kneeling and bowing attitudes of adoration.

In the Entrance Rite the priest (and people, therefore) approached the altar, but at the beginning of the Eucharistic rite proper, it is the bread and wine that are seen approaching the altar. In Roman Catholic, and especially Eastern Orthodox Liturgy, this moment is ritually marked as being of great importance. In the Roman Rite, the priest accepts the bread and wine from deacons or the people, quietly saying a form of the ancient Hebrew blessings over both bread and wine and thus forming a link between the past (Christ's Jewish blessings over the bread and wine at the Last Supper) and the present: *"Blessed are You, Lord, God of all creation. Through your goodness we have this bread to offer, which earth has given."* The bread and wine, as pre-Christian symbols of life, are bowed over and prayers are said that God accept not them but us, and thus they link the community with its Founder and with His fate, which, at this point, the Eucharist recalls with the events of Holy Thursday, Good Friday, Holy Saturday, and Easter Sunday, the Ascension and the heavenly Enthronement.

Once again the omnipresence of the divine awareness (spirit) in all space and in all time is expressed in the ritual by the surrounding of the bread and wine with incense, and then the surrounding of the entire altar with incense, in a circular, orbiting motion (a repetition of the same ritual tone set in the Entrance Rite). But a most important extension of the ritual is made at this time; that is, the priest, the deacons, and all the people are also surrounded by the new Divine Breath—and thus the bread and wine; Christ's life, death, and resurrection (the altar); and the present group of Christian participants are united in an atmosphere that overcomes time-distancing—all this as preparatory coordination for the Eucharistic celebration.

The rite culminates, as before, in prayer, but this time it is the great Prayer of Thanksgiving, which, since it will include the transformation rite of the bread and wine into the Body and Blood of

Christ, must not be entered into without full religious awareness and affective synchronization by the participants.

A staccato series of formalized dialogue statements sets off this prayer effectively as beginning a new, important part of the Mass. In addition, it is often accompanied by its own distinctive chant, and the singing of this dialogue, accompanied by the prayer that follows, marks it as more solemn than the entire preceding ritual. Everyone stands. "The Lord be with you" is repeated again by the priest and met by the customary reply, "And also with you." But this time the dialogue continues with the mystical exhortation: "Lift up your hearts," and its reply "We lift them up to the Lord." The priest then gives the Eucharistic (Thanksgiving) invitation. *"Let us give thanks to the Lord our God." "It is right to give him thanks and praise."*

The Thanksgiving prayer that is then sung once more coordinates the past and the present. It has three basic parts: In the first part thanks are given for the events of the remote past attributed to God the Father—especially the creation of the universe. The past tense is used: "You *made* the universe." The second part is a giving thanks for the deeds and teachings of Jesus Christ. The past tense is used: "He *opened* His arms on the cross; He *put* an end to death." And in the third part, where one expects to find thanks for the deeds of the Holy Spirit, there is a significant *omission* of thanks *to* the Holy Spirit and a sudden switch to the present tense in the verbs. "And so we *join* the angels and saints in proclaiming your glory and *sing:* "Holy, Holy, Holy." Once again past and present are proclaimed as harmonized, the people in the congregation and the people of heaven are proclaimed to be singing with the Holy Spirit (in transtemporal harmony) the same song, the song sung before the throne: the triple-holy song. This, of course, draws upon the vision of Isaiah in the cognitive belief structure for the specific content of the words, but the function of the ritual parallels that of the Entrance Rite—the participants and the population of heaven are identified to express ritually the religious belief that the heaven-earth separation has been overcome and the participants have been brought to heaven. Frequently the choir sings this song in harmony with the congregation and thus makes the harmony between congregation and the heavenly community "audible" to those singing.

After the hymn the people generally assume a full adorational position (usually, though not always, kneeling, in the Western Church) after an appeal again to the omnipresent Spirit of God to consecrate the bread and wine (ritually the bread and wine have been made to include the congregation and its lives) into the whole Body and Blood of Christ. Thus the ritual also identifies participants as part of the Body of Christ and as being of His Blood.

In the ritual of the transformation of the bread and wine, the coordination of the past and the present is expressed, not by tense change in the verbs, but in the synchronization of the ritual actions of the priest's hands with the past-tense account of Christ's life taken from sacred scripture (the source of the cognitive belief system). The priest begins by reciting the narrative of the events of Holy Thursday known to all:

"On the night He *was* betrayed, while they were at supper, He took bread."

At this moment, while the priest's voice is narrating in the past tense, the rubrics (ritual instructions) tell him clearly to *take* the bread into his own hands, and to *raise* it a little over the altar, so that, as the next words are said, regardless of any time coordinates, hands in long white sleeves are again holding the bread before the disciples,

". . . saying: 'Take this, all of you and eat it: this is my Body which will be given up for you.' "

After stepping back into his role as an ordinary believer for a moment to genuflect in adoration, the priest stands and continues the narration:

"In the same way when supper was ended He *took* the cup filled with wine."

The ritual's instruction to the priest at this point carries two thousand years of commitment to Christ's passion behind it: he *takes* the chalice. The priest then raises it and continues speaking:

"He *gave* you thanks, and giving the cup to His disciples, said: 'Take this, all of you, and drink from it.' ''

The priest's gesture at these words, with all eyes on the chalice, makes the invitation to drink proffered two thousand years ago once again a present reality. Together, *past* words and *present* gestures make a ritual *unum per se* that ritually can be reconstituted in any time regardless of the time in which the words were said. The priest bows and continues:

"This is the cup of my Blood, the Blood of the new and everlasting covenant. It *will be* shed for you and for all men."

After repeating the Eucharistic command, "Do this in memory of me," both the people and the priest begin the chronologically structured *remembering* (anamnesis) of the subsequent events of Christ's life of which they are, by extension, now ritually a part.

Within the cognitive belief system the request, "Do this in memory of Me," is the last request Jesus made of His disciples before His death. The last request of Christ, that this meal be used to demonstrate and recall the manner of His death (broken body, spilled blood), a moving request that He not be forgotten, is fulfilled, both by the people (who remember Him by chanting the refrain "Christ has died, Christ is risen, Christ will come again"), but most of all by the offering of the Body and Blood as the sacrifice during this remembering. In the Byzantine Rite the gestures of the priest's hands express the actual *contemporaneous* occurrence of what the narration says occurred in the past. As the priest says (on Good Friday) "We remember His death" his hands slowly pick up the bread and the wine, and, by crossing his hands, he holds the plate and the cup above the altar in the form of a cross. As he continues he extends the remembrance to the subsequent events: "We remember His resurrection from the dead and His ascension into heaven." While speaking, he slowly lifts the bread and the wine above his head. Everyone is on his knees. The ritual link-up between heaven and earth is/was being made. The priest prays that this sacrifice (a life given up for others' lives) may have been/be the union between God and Man that brings the life of the

Sacrificed to all the participants in the ritual, especially those who participate in the eating of the Body and the drinking of the Blood of self-sacrifice.

Since in the belief system Christ is seen as a vine of which His followers are the branches, the ritual elevation of the Body and Blood of Christ (recalling and reenacting the *ascension into heaven*) enables the priest to say to God the Father in the name of all: *"We* offer You (the we is the "I" of the entire "vine" of Jesus Christ in any time era) *His* Body and Blood."

As the priest then lowers the Body and Blood to the altar, he is able again to offer a prayer uniting all believers, regardless of time or space. The Spirit of God (seen now as ultimately present, not just in all the universe, but specifically in the entire Body and Blood) is asked to hold the believers in total harmony—with God Himself (The Father) and with all of the heavenly family. As the Body and Blood remain on the altar, the priest's hands are fully extended to pray for popes, bishops, priests, people, all here present and those absent, the living and the dead, believers and seekers. Most amazingly of all, the angels and the saints of past eras are regarded as here present and as all worshipping the Eternal One within the same harmony of the Divine Spirit, who, in the Gospel, first came upon the Christian community after the ascension of Jesus and is asked now to be here again. Recollection of the past, and consciousness of the present as separate, is assumed to be a kind of mode of perception that is appropriate enough to those confined within the sequence of time events but entirely inappropriate for the consciousness of the One who has ascended over time and with whose eternal mind the Mass is being celebrated. Thus the Eucharistic Prayer embodies, as did its Preface, a transition of tense, this time not from past to present but from present to an implied future that encompasses past, present, and future as one harmonized tense:

"Have mercy on us all;
make us worthy to share eternal life
with Mary the Virgin Mother of God,
with the apostles, and with all the saints
who have done Your will throughout the ages.

May we praise You in union with them
and give You glory
through Your Son, Jesus Christ.''

In an alternate Eucharistic Prayer the time switch is made in even more harmonized terms:

''Father in Your mercy grant also to us, Your children, to *enter into* [cf. Entrance Rite] our heavenly inheritance *in the* company of the Virgin Mary, the Mother of God, and Your apostles and saints. *Then,* in Your kingdom, freed from the corruption of sin and death, We *shall sing* Your glory *with* every creature Through Christ our Lord.''

The whole Eucharistic prayer is brought to a synthesizing conclusion as the Doxology (final glorification) is sung. It is quite revealing, since it does not glorify the glorified God, but rather turns in on itself and glorifies the principles and foundation through which, in this ritual, the worship of the invisible God is made possible.

The priest does not lift up his hands toward God the Father as he has been doing, nor does he bow and bring his hands together in a great circle as is usual for most prayer endings. Instead, he again lifts the plate with the Body on it and the chalice with the Blood and holds them, as though enthroned, above the altar. In the traditional form of the gesture the white circle of the Bread, the Host, is held directly over the chalice and lifted, not in a crossed form, but upright, so as to resemble a rising sun or a human being with body (Chalice) and head (Host). With the whole ritual and the attention of all participants centered on the Body and Blood as they are held up by the priest, he chants the Doxology, never daring once to mention the name:

''Through *Him,*
With *Him*
In *Him*
In the *Unity* of the Holy Spirit,
All glory and honor *is* Yours
Almighty Father,
Forever and ever.''

The people respond with *Amen,* and the Eucharistic Prayer of Christ has been brought to perfection.

The Communion Rite now begins. The Communion Rite assumes that the heaven-earth polarity has been resolved and that either "we are in heaven" or "heaven is here on earth"—an appropriate description of the situation at this point. If we are, therefore, "in heaven," and heaven is before us "on earth," then the description of heaven and heavenly activity found in the Bible (especially Rev. 5, etc.) provides the model for "what to do" in this part of the rite (just as the events of Christ's life, death, and resurrection provided the model for what to do and say during the Eucharistic prayer).

In heaven (according to Revelations), God the Father is enthroned before all—Part I of the Communion Rite will be to address Him. In heaven all men (and angels) are in harmony and at peace within the heavenly kingdom—Part II of the Communion Rite will be the exchanging of the Kiss of Peace among all participants. In heaven the Lamb of God is enthroned on an altar before the throne (Rev. 7:9; this is paradoxically derived from a description of early Christian liturgy). Part III will be the necessary breaking of the Bread above the altar, which will be referred to as the Lamb of God, and is accompanied by the thrice-repeated chant "Lamb of God, you take away the sins of the world, have mercy on us." Part IV will be receiving the Body and Blood described as the Lamb of God.

Having gained access to liturgical place and liturgical time, a ritual facilitation of the realization of the presence of God, and having gained access to the invisible God through Christ and with Christ and in Christ, the congregation now rises to speak directly to God the Father. In some of the Oriental churches, such as the Armenian, not only the priest but also all the people now spread their hands to the full prayer position normally used only by the priest.

In an ultimate act of synchronization of the participants as brothers they stand and say (or chant) the ancient and simple prayer that they were told by "Him" to use in direct access to the divine:

"Our Father,
Who art *in heaven,*
Hallowed be Thy name,
Thy kingdom come
Thy will be done on *earth* as it is *in heaven.* . . . ''

The Our Father as said by all participants not only locates them before the Throne but also locates them completely within the ancient tradition of all those who have said this prayer. Its structural position, after the end of the Eucharistic prayer and at the beginning of the Communion, lets it perform the double service of being a harmonized form of address to God in the mouths of all and of using its petition, "Give us this day our daily bread," to initiate Holy Communion.

The manifestation of heavenly peace on earth is begun by a prayer, not to the Father, but to Christ, which does not allude to the expected "Peace on earth, good will to men" but instead, and more appropriately, to one of the later, postresurrectional appearances of Christ, with which He surprised His disciples when they were gathered together in the upper room. This transfer of an appropriate situation from part of the cognitive belief system to the situation of the congregation in its present-day "upper room" is aimed here, not solely at decreasing the distance between "then" and "now," but also at bringing about a realization of identity on the part of the participants. It is assumed in this part of the Mass that the distance has been decisively abolished; the problem that the ritual is faced with now is this—how to get the participants to realize whom they have become.

Lord Jesus Christ, You *said* [scriptural situation] to Your *apostles* [old identity]:
"I leave you peace, My peace I give to you."
Look not on our sins, but on the faith of Your church [present situation]
and grant us [new identity]
the peace and the unity of Your kingdom [heaven on earth]
where You live forever and ever.
Amen.

The priest then extends his hands toward the people and says simultaneously: "The peace of the Lord be with you always" and thus makes Christ's ancient wish of peace to His original apostles in the upper room after the resurrection a wish extended in the present time to this new group of apostles. In the traditional usage the priest then kisses the altar very close to the Body and Blood (and in some Oriental rites he kisses the Body and the cup), in order to "receive" the Kiss of Peace from Christ, and then extends this greeting from Christ to the participants by ritually kissing (or by touching or shaking hands) the participants closest to him, who in turn pass the Peace from Christ, spreading it throughout the "kingdom" where He "lives forever and ever."

After this ritual of heavenly friendship and greeting, attention is again drawn back to the altar by the priest's beginning to break the bread for the participants' communion. This gesture lends itself to many possible accompanying words on unity and brokenness, one-many, and so forth, which are actually used in Eastern rites. The Roman rite simply begins the heavenly worship of the Lamb of God (broken for the sheep) on His heavenly-earthly "throne" (the altar) within His "kingdom" (the congregation, in heaven and on earth). The priest breaks the bread, mingles the Body and Blood, and all bow profoundly toward the altar while repeatedly chanting "Lamb of God, You take away the sins of the world, have mercy on us," (cf. the heavenly worship in Rev. 7:9–13).

After praying privately, the priest genuflects in adoration to the "Lamb" and invites all now to Communion in Christ. He holds up the bread over the plate as an invitation to the supper and says the words:

> "This is the Lamb of God
> Who takes away the sins of the World
> Happy are those who are called to His supper."

The ritual answer by the participants to this invitation is again an allusion for the sake of realizing the nature of the present situation. The people paraphrase the shocked reply of the Roman centurion when Christ offered to enter into his house:

> [Scripture]: Lord, I am not worthy that You should come into my house, but only say the word and my son shall be healed.
>
> [The Mass]: Lord, I am not worthy to receive *You*, but only say the word and I shall be healed.

As the people then silently throng forward to receive "Him," the priest comes down from the heavenly/earthly altar to them with the Body and Blood of the Lamb for them to eat and to drink. In the meeting that follows, all that the Catholic faith is about is accomplished.

As though nothing ritually adequate could follow upon this, the Roman rite is very brief after the Communion. The people are now conceived of as in full Communion with God the Father, fully made into His Sons (they are body in His Body, His Blood flows now in their veins), and so there follows only a short prayer of thanksgiving after Communion. Significantly, the ritual opening phrase of the Roman prayer structure is omitted ("The Lord be with you") so as to underline that no such wish need be made now. Practical announcements are made, especially about needy causes and people, so that those in communion will know to whom to go with help.

In a reversion to its ancient Jewish origins, the ritual ends with the priest raising his hands in a gesture of blessing over the people in a situational allusion to Christ's last blessing before his final departure in scripture.

> Then lifting up His hands he blessed them. While He blessed them, He parted from them. . . . (Luke 24:51)

The words for the blessing may be found in a parallel place in Scripture:

> Go therefore and make disciples of all nations, baptizing them in the name of the Father and of the Son and of the Holy Spirit.

Thus, even the dismissal situation is made into a transtemporal Christ situation, as the gesture of blessing is made and the words are spoken:

Priest: May almighty God bless you, The Father, Son, and the Holy Spirit.

People: Amen.

Priest: Go in peace to love and serve the Lord.

People: Thanks be to God.

Eleven
Concepts, Methods, and Conclusions

John McManus,
Charles D. Laughlin, Jr.,
and Eugene G. d'Aquili

This way of viewing collaboration among specialists in different branches of knowledge would be the only possible one if we admitted a thesis to which far too many research workers still unwittingly cling—that the frontiers of each branch of knowledge are fixed once and for all, and that they will inevitably remain so in the future. But the main object of a work such as this—is rather to push back the frontiers horizontally and challenge them transversally. The true object of interdisciplinary research, therefore, is to reshape or reorganize the fields of knowledge by means of exchanges which are in fact, constructive recombinations.

Jean Piaget, *Main Trends in Interdisciplinary Research*

The spectrum of ritual is complete. The reader has had theory and prism in hand and, depending on his or her expertise, has perceived varying amounts of light. No single approach could ever do justice to the infinite range of hues in human ritual behavior. Many libraries could be filled with colorful descriptions of the subtle nuances in ritual behavior, and as many libraries could again be filled with endless and fascinating analyses of those nuances. What we have done here is to build an interdisciplinary bridge across which the insights of a number of disciplines might move. It remains only to tie together in some brief and coherent way the main threads in thought presented in the book.

It must be remembered that we have been concerned, not only with the vast expanse of the spectrum of ritual, but also with the manner in which we, as scientists, proceed to our subject of scrutiny, regardless of the nature of that subject. Our summary, then, entails an examination of the logic and necessity for cross-disciplinary research, a statement of progress made in biogenetic structural theory since the publication of the original book by Laughlin and d'Aquili (1974), a reevaluation of science as ritual, a statement of the "penetration hypothesis," and, finally, a return to the question of ritual.

Biogenetic structuralism differs from a number of other approaches in its insistence that behavioral interpretations be consistent with evidence from the neurosciences (see also Pribram, 1971), in its plea for interdisciplinary exchange and effort (see also Piaget, 1971), and in its insistence that human and animal behavior be considered in light of each other as they exist in natural, as opposed to exclusively laboratory, situations (see Lorenz, 1971; Piaget, 1971; Wilson, 1975; Count, 1973; and Schneirla, 1957, 1965).

To begin, we point to three fallacies that we feel have done great damage to the progress of the social sciences and that, if they continue to be entertained, will remain obstacles to the development of knowledge in social and psychological areas of study. These methodological fallacies are:

1. Explanatory monism.
2. Reductionism and emergence.
3. Arbitrary exclusion.

The first of these, *explanatory monism,* is common practice. It has been discussed often, but here we concentrate on the objections to it as articulated by Konrad Lorenz, from whom we borrow its name (Lorenz, 1971:249). Explanatory monism is the consequence of failing to understand that any living organism is a *system* composed of many interacting parts. The concentration for artificial isolation of one of these parts or subsets of parts often leads to an attempt to reconstruct the behaving organism based on *knowledge of these parts alone*. This failure to consider all parts and their interaction or, at the very minimum, their existence, constitutes explanatory monism. One example would be the ortho-dox behaviorist approach to psychological explanation, which or-ganizes itself around the conditioned reflex as the basic explana-tory unit, and which excludes from consideration more complex operations. In Lorenz's words, "explanatory monism blinkers the outlook because it channels investigation into a narrowed range of experimentation which precludes the discovery of other explana-tory principles" (1971:249). Such experimental blinders often lead to a cult of methodology in which quantification becomes more important than comprehension.

Without further belaboring the point, we feel that the tendency to build systems of thought around a single explanatory element artificially constricts the domain of discourse and hinders the de-velopment of a more balanced view. This holds for our own ap-proach as well. All behavior is not explainable from knowledge of structure alone. We simply maintain, along with Piaget, Lorenz, and many others, that, without knowledge of the organizing princi-ples underlying behavior (i.e., structure), no thorough under-standing of behavior is likely to occur.

A second fallacy that we feel is detrimental to the develop-ment of social science is the tendency toward either *reductionism* on the one hand or *emergence* on the other (see Piaget, 1971:38ff). The fallacy of emergence is committed when an analyst attributes the characteristics of a system at one level of systemic organi-zation (say, a first-order differential) to a system at a lower level of systemic organization (say, a second-order differential). This is obviously and intimately related to the first fallacy just dis-cussed. For example, if one deludes oneself into believing that the elements and organization of thought can be reduced to the reflexive, neuronal, or similar elementary unit, one is more likely to fall into the trap of trying to reconstruct thought from only that ele-ment and to ignore competing approaches. Complex systems em-body properties not existing in less complex systems, and ar-tificial attribution of the former to the latter not only prohibits *full understanding* of the complex but also tends to lead to basic *mis-understanding,* not only of the complex, but also of the relation of the simple to the complex.

In similar logical vein, the fallacy of reduction is committed when the analyst suppresses the characteristics of the higher level of systemic organization and attributes to them the characteristics of the lower. Obvious examples here are teleological, rather than telenomic, explanations. Within the delimited range of human cognitive development, sensorimotor systems characteristic of the first year of life simply do not possess many of the properties of subsequent conceptual stages of development such as representational capacity or reversibility of operations. These develop out of the functioning of the sensorimotor system in an environmental context but are not literally present in it.

These two common tendencies, to attribute the lower to the higher and to ascribe to the lower properties of the higher, systematically skew the course of scientific investigation. If we assume the neurons or the genes possess all the properties of higher cognition, we stand little chance of understanding the operative principles actually occurring with these systems. Similarly, if we see no more in cognition than what is observable in the functioning of a neuron or a molecular behavioral unit, we stand little chance of understanding a phenomenon so complex as thought.

Finally, a third fallacy closely related to the previous two is the *fallacy of arbitrary exclusion.* This fallacy is committed whenever we, through ignorance or through adherence to a normative rule, exclude from consideration material efficiently present in the phenomenon being studied. This may be the result of strict adherence to rules of reduction or emergence or, for that matter, explanatory monism. Also, as noted in chapter 1, the fallacy may be committed by defining a phenomenon in such a way that we artificially exclude similarities and connections with related phenomena.

The Rule of Minimal Inclusion is offered as a means of removing the blinders that come naturally to the scientist who is trained in a highly delineated specialty. The rule states that any explanation of a phenomenon must take into account any and all levels of systemic organization efficiently present in the interaction between the phenomenon in question and that phenomenon's environment (Rubinstein and Laughlin, 1977).

Adherence to the Rule of Minimal Inclusion helps in avoiding not only the fallacy of arbitrary exclusion, but also the previous two fallacies. It requires that the analyst consider information pertaining to the phenomenon in question and residing at least one level below and one level above that of the phenomenon. For example, consideration and explanation of ritual has required us to refer to numerous levels of systemic organization, from the neurophysiological to the ecological, especially touching upon the intervening levels of cognition and society.

Interdisciplinary Problems

The principal impediment to refuting the fallacies just discussed is the existence of scientific disciplines. Each distinct science has its own specific problems, defined by the content, and maintained by the culture and social organization, of that science (Kuhn, 1970). Concentration on the issues of one discipline to the exclusion of those studied in other disciplines can have a profound inhibitory effect on the progress of each discipline. To transcend disciplinary boundaries is to recognize the existence of transcendental issues that operate in each discipline and that lay the common groundwork for a potential unification of the disciplines.

We believe that the concept of structure is the most promising means for bridging the arbitrary boundaries of disciplines. In examining the nature of structure, a common language may emerge, by means of which researchers of different persuasions may exchange information for common use.

The Major Problems of Social Sciences
As expressed by Jean Piaget (1970), the principal problems common to the many social and life sciences would seem to be these:

    1. The filiation, evolution, and construction of structures.

    2. The problem of how structures maintain balance and control.

3. The nature of exchanges between structures and the surrounding milieu.

These three generic problems pertain to any field of inquiry in the social sciences and are concerned with two aspects of structures: (1) their functioning as incomplete entities in the process of formation or transformation and (2) their functioning as completed, but active, organizations.

The problem of filiation, evolution, and construction of structures is a *diachronic* one encompassing both phylogenesis and ontogenesis. It involves consideration of structures over time and focuses on change in the organization of behavior. Included within this problem is the source of structures themselves and the construction of structures through interaction between their intrinsic activity and the surrounding milieu. In this volume we have discussed the question of genesis through the concept of neurognosis (also, Laughlin and d'Aquili, 1974; and Laughlin and McManus, 1975), and through the Piagetian approach to construction outlined in chapter 6. Structures create themselves, both ontogenetically and phylogenetically, through interaction. Construction and neurognosis involve systematic change within the system under the impact of the environment. The contemporaneous state of this construction, the level of development, acts as a determinant of the nature of stimulation relevant to the system in question and its adaptive capacity within its environment.

The problem of balance and control (or homeostasis) is *synchronic*. Here the problem is: Given a specific level of structural development, how does the system maintain its internal integrity and how does it maintain the capacity to function? This is a problem more familiar to most social sciences than that of filiation, unless they are actively involved with issues of development. The question is how organization is maintained, rather than how it is achieved.

Questions of exchange are, again, *synchronic* questions that deal with the interaction of a system and its environment. Where balance and control tend to focus on the system itself, exchange shifts the focus to what is extracted from the environment and taken into the system and what that system puts back into the environment. The notion of exchange has a long history in most life sciences.

The Major Concepts in Social Science

In a similar vein, Piaget (1970) has posited three principle categories of concepts that parallel the major problems, as follows:

1. Structure of organization.
2. Function.
3. Information.

Structure is the major defining characteristic of a living system. It is the organization of the functions of that system. The concepts and problems cited by Piaget are intimately intertwined in reality, separable only conceptually. Each structure, with its genesis and construction, with its functioning through balance and control and exchange through information flow, influences and constrains others in the invariant biological functions of self-organization and adaptation.

Problems, Concepts, and Transformations

These basic problems and concepts can be subsumed under the three forms of transformation discussed in chapters 1 and 6:

Developmental transformations encompass the genesis and construction of structures, which, in turn, are the organs that carry out surface transformations in interaction with the operational environment (E_o), through sensory transformations of the information exchange between the internal structure and the E_o. In a sense, then, the nexus of a structural approach to the social and life sciences is the study of transformations and structure itself, and the total coordination of these transformations.

Transformation	Problem	Concept
Developmental	Genesis and Construction	Structure
Surface	Balance and Control	Function
Sensory	Exchange	Information

Biogenetic Structuralism Elaborated

The Spectrum of Ritual, in addition to being an initial attempt to *apply* the ideas developed in *Biogenetic Structuralism,* is also an extension and elaboration of that approach. We briefly outline some of the major elaborations we feel are reflected in the preceding ten chapters.

1. As reflected in Barbara Lex's chapter specifically, the notion of "brain" has been extended to include the *peripheral nervous system.* This is a particularly important elaboration, especially in light of advances in research dealing with control over autonomic activity. A related elaboration is further development of the place of bilateral asymmetry of the cerebral cortex, a subject briefly treated in *Biogenetic Structuralism* and further discussed in chapters 4 and 5.

2. John Smith's chapter 2, as well as Laughlin and McManus's chapter 3, extend the biogenetic structural approach to include *animal behavior.* In light of the relatively recent emergence of ethology and its potential for advancing our knowledge of behavior, this is an essential development.

3. Elaboration of the discussion of *cognition* as originally presented in 1974 is another essential advance. Readers of the first book often did not see the full connection between brain, on the one hand, and society on the other. The link between brain and society lies in the cognitive processes of the individual human being. In chapters 6 and 7, by McManus, and chapter 5, by d'Aquili and Laughlin, this important linkage has been further developed. Of import here is the creation of a continuum in the same conceptual terms between brain and society and the interlinkages between all three levels of organization (also McManus, 1974b; 1975).

4. A greater emphasis on the *diachronic dimension* is an important elaboration. While *Biogenetic Structuralism* placed considerable emphasis on evolutionary development, it neglected ontogenetic development. In chapters 6 and 7 McManus addresses the issue and attempts to abstract some principles that may be applicable to development per se, whatever the range of the temporal dimension (also McManus, 1974a,b).

5. The original explication of structure seemed to leave some readers with the impression that structures were rigid and static (Waddington, 1975). *The Spectrum of Ritual* places greater emphasis on the fact that structures are *active*. Structures, as defined in this volume, are *organic*. They function and are alive.

6. *Neurognosis* is another concept that some readers have found troublesome. In *Biogenetic Structuralism* the concept was used to label the initial state of neural models, which were then modified and elaborated in structure and function as a result of interaction with environment. While in another work (Laughlin and McManus, 1975b) we have examined the concept of neurognosis in greater detail, we have emphasized in the present volume the crucial process of model elaboration through the empirical modification cycle and operations to facilitate the cognitive imperative.

7. The notion of *levels of organization* describable in terms of the same concepts and related to actual structures of the neural and cognitive systems is a major elaboration. Echoing Whitehead, the structural nature of reality and man's knowledge of it can be described as an onion-like set of layers of organization, and the laws of interconnection are inferred from a structural approach (also Rubinstein and Laughlin, 1977).

8. Another advance made by this volume is the initial attempt to *develop and apply* a generic, biogenetic structural methodology. A valid response to *Biogenetic Structuralism* would have been: "That's fine, but how do you do it?" Although the approach outlined in this volume is anything but complete, we can at least say, "This is how you can *begin* to do it, and here are eleven chapters of instructions."

9. Still another important concept is that of *diaphasis,* described by Laughlin and d'Aquili in chapter 9. The means by which social structures adapt to environmental change, particularly in the absence of advanced technological knowledge, are a very important matter, and the concept of diaphatic equilibration not only addresses this topic but also integrates it with parallel phenomena, such as cognitive adaptation, especially as this is considered by McManus in chapter 7 (also Laughlin and Brady, 1978; McManus, 1974b).

10. The borrowing, elaboration, and integration of Rappaport's concepts of *cognized and operational environments* into biogenetic structuralism as widely inclusive, generic constructs is a major development of the approach.

11. Finally, perhaps the most significant addition to the biogenetic structuralist approach is inclusion of an expanded theory of *transformation.* Much of what constitutes the other concepts elaborated in this volume really boils down to transformation of the basic structures themselves in development, to the arrangement of the content organized by those structures, and to the abstraction of information about the environment through structure. Transformation is the mechanism of the empirical modification cycle that, along with neurognosis, constructs each person's cognized environment (E_c). In chapter 6 a generic model of the nature and functioning of transformations is presented, and chapters 7 and 9 (also McManus, 1975) outline the operation of these transformations in an environmental context.

Science as Ritual

In *Biogenetic Structuralism* (chapter 6), Laughlin and d'Aquili advanced the hypothesis that the process of doing science (or "sciencing") was a special application of the empirical modification cycle, a process common to all men everywhere. Sciencing was described as operating via an alternation between induction and deduction to establish, maintain, and modify models of reality. Using the various insights developed in our previous chapters, we expand briefly the discussion of this issue.

The scientific enterprise is the ritualization of the empirical modification cycle. By ritualizing the process of model reformulation already operating to transform the E_c into optimal adaptive isomorphism with the E_o, science is able to make the most, not only of feedback into the models, but also of feed forward or anticipation allowing for precorrection of the models before such modification is necessitated by input from the environment.

Treating science as a ritualization phenomenon allows us to apply many of the tools of analysis used previously to understand other types of endeavor. Thus we may examine the process of sciencing in relation to the five-step transformation model presented in chapter 6, a model, you will remember, involving pattern *interruption, comparison, alternation, resolution,* and *consolidation.* Now picture, if you will, the scientist going about sciencing. In contrast to his everyday E_c, the model of reality of concern to the scientist qua scientist is relatively conscious and explicit and perhaps is stated in a theory and derivative hypotheses he wishes to test. As long as the scientist's observations and descriptions match the assumptions and expectations he has developed on the basis of the model, sciencing proceeds much like Piaget's functional assimilation. It is merely a repetitive application of the model, through behavior, to a variety of phenomena. Just as the cognitive system itself can reject, ignore, or distort data not fitting the model, so the scientist possesses no particular immunity to such faulty assimilation. The scientist remains in a cycle of repetitive action and confirmation of the model until expectancy is violated in one of two ways. The first is discovering that the data do not quite fit the model. Perhaps a hypothesis is disconfirmed. Or perhaps the hypothesis is not quite disconfirmed, but the data look odd. Maybe new variables are suggested by the observations. In general, a mismatch occurs that suggests that the issue should be further pursued. The second is a more basic and profound violation of expectancy because it affects the assumptions underlying the expectation. We refer here to a violation of the *structural* expectations, which are often unconscious. The latter disconfirmation is far less frequent than the former but is subject to the same laws.

With disconfirmation of his expectation, the scientist enters step one of a transformational state. The habitual, repetitive functioning of the empirical modification cycle has been interrupted and desynchronized. Some modification is in order. Minor modifications in content may be made without altering the basic hypothesis. Mismatch may have been due to chance, the influence of a minor variable, or an error in procedure. In other cases the scientist may have to reject the hypothesis, reformulate, and test again. Alternation between various interpretations of the disconfirmation may be evident, and a resolution in the form of a new hypothesis may have to be made. If the new hypothesis is not disconfirmed, consolidation (the fifth stage) is immediately entered and the reality model is appropriately modified. The repetition phase is reentered, and the new variation becomes an assumption (after a respectable number of replications), which, in turn, generates its own contingent behaviors. Most of science proceeds in this manner, small accommodations following one upon the other, slowly modifying, appending, and consolidating the general expectations.

The process of model reformulation under massive disconfirmation is, however, more profound. As with cognition itself, sciencing proceeds through the five-step transformation sequence. At first there is orientation toward and comparison of the discrepant material. In general, the more inductive the approach, the more models of reality are open to modification. This is, however, only a matter of degree. The essential point at this stage is that there is movement from overassimilation of discrepant material to orientation toward and recognition of the fact of discrepancy.

As with thought itself, modifications of the model will be heralded by a phase of more or less severe *alternation* in interpretation and behavior. There is confusion over the relevance and ramifications of the discrepant material, with bipolar attempts to preserve the reality model intact while one is making sense of the new input. There occurs a marked conflict among elements and subsystems within the structure of the model. When the model in question forms the cornerstone of a paradigmatic discipline in Kuhn's (1970) sense, conflict may well arise among practitioners of the discipline about what actually constitutes their science, what are pertinent questions to be asked, and what are appropriate methods to answer those questions.

This conflict can be *resolved* in two ways: One, the new material and ideas may be rejected by a large segment of the discipline holding faithfully to the traditional view. This is tantamount to saying that their conceptual structures remain impervious to modification. Under severe stress of defending the traditional view, one would expect more intense and active resistance, comparable to the functioning described in chapters 7 and 9. Two, there emerges a reorganization of the structure of expectations that leads to a new structure of knowledge, that is, a modified reality model. The new reality model is, like any new conceptual structure, characterized by entirely new sensitivities to events in the operational environment previously not perceived. Through establishment of repetitive observations based on these new sensitivities, an era of *consolidation* begins that completes the cycle of transformation and leads ultimately, if it occurs at the level of discipline-wide acceptance, to the establishment of a new paradigm.

Full recognition that sciencing is the ritualization of the empirical modification cycle is important because the ritual itself may be consciously modified to optimize the recognition of discrepant input and minimize the overdefense of models. In other words the tendency toward premature closure of models and resultant faulty assimilation may be avoided. An obvious example of the ritual of sciencing in operation is the so-called learned society meeting (read, ceremonial ritual). There was a time when the principal function of the meeting was as a controlled forum for exploration of new and old data and ideas. Quite literally speaking, if one could not gain access to a hearing through a learned society meeting, one's observations and ideas had little effect on the prevailing model. Yet, once having gained a hearing, one's (possibly discrepant) observations became a matter of record, and rules of etiquette and exchange required at least a modicum of confrontation between old and new. In modern times this function of the learned society meeting has taken a back seat to other political and economic considerations. Yet the function remains latent in the ritual and, with recognition of its potent effect in facilitating model transformation, could be consciously reemphasized.

The Penetration Hypothesis

The implicit ontology used in biogenetic structuralism and underlying the present application is one of an infinity of levels of systemic organization, each of which must adapt to and be structured by the level immediately molar to it (see Rubinstein and Laughlin, 1977). The Rule of Minimal Inclusion requires that in the present case a number of levels of systemic organization be controlled in our explanation, as illustrated in Figure 11.1. The levels thus far touched upon are the neurophysiological, the cognitive, the social, and the ecological.

Each structural level of organization is seen as having effects on the adjoining levels, organizing the structures lying within it (molecular structures) and adapting to and affecting those structures external to it (equivalent structures and molar structures). A cognitive structure, then, is partially organized by the surrounding social structures and, in turn, exerts an organizing influence on its constitutive structures, for example, behavioral schemes and neurological components. None of these levels may be treated as epiphenomena. They have their existence in the form of systemic coordinations of constituent elements, each a structure, each a

Figure 11.1. The Cognized Environment (E) as the Individual Cognitive System and Its Interactive Relationship to Adjoining Levels of Systematic Organization.

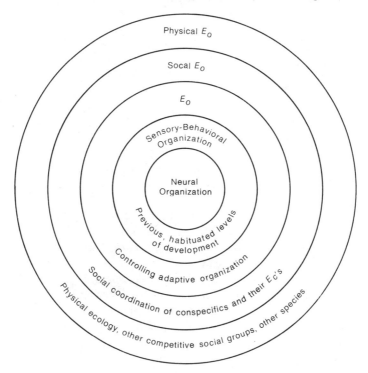

system of transformation, each with its own empirical modification cycle.

This ontology allows us to formulate an important concept by whose use we may come to understand better the interaction between levels of systemic organization. *Penetration* refers to the effect that one level of systemic organization has on another. This is a quantitative concept and may be examined at any level on a continuum from nil to total effect. The *penetration hypothesis* states that each level of structural organization operates as a buffer between structures molecular to itself and structures external (both equivalent and molar) to itself. Thus, social structure stands as a buffer between the physical E_o and the individual E_c. Likewise, the E_c stands as a buffer between the biological (including neurophysiological) system of the organism and the organism's E_o (including both social and physical components). A number of points may be briefly made in relation to the notion of penetration and the penetration hypothesis:

1. The integrity of any structure is directly related to its degree of susceptibility to penetration. Total penetration by the environment precisely defines nonstructure at any level.

2. Structures may be penetrated at any level of organization. Certain aspects of the E_o may affect the neurological system directly without mediation by the E_c.

3. When we speak of a system as having a "boundary," we are really referring to that system's resistance to penetration vis-à-vis its environment. When examining "boundaries," we are typically examining the mechanisms of resistance of the system of reference.

4. Penetration may be in terms of content or structure. With specific reference to the E_c, we may speak of structure (*how* reality is organized) and content (*what* is known about reality). Penetration, then, may be structural in its effects, as with a decrement in structural complexity under stress, or may be of content, as in assimilation of novel material from the E_o.

5. Adaptive structures are, by definition, semisusceptible to penetration. That is, a structure totally closed to penetration will not survive in a changing environment. On the other hand, a structure too open to penetration is vulnerable to internal

disruption and final discorporation. An adaptive structure exhibits a range of permeability appropriately flexible in relation to the vicissitudes of its environment.

6. In general, the more complex the organization and integrity of a structure, the less permeable that structure is to *structural* penetration. More complex E_cs, for example, will admit, assimilate, and organize more information from the E_o than simpler E_cs will. Also, complex E_cs are more stable and flexible (that is, have a greater range of control over penetration) and are less vulnerable to morphogenesis under the impact of the E_o. Under threat from the E_o, more complex E_cs are able to ward off or absorb aspects of the E_o that would destroy simpler structures.

7. Any level of structure is sensitive to a limited range of stimulation in the environment. Human E_cs, then, have sensitivities that are peculiar to that system. Note that neurognostic constraints, as well as the E_o, exert principal influences on the content to which any E_c will attend. A sensorimotor child is not sensitive to most symbolism, most language, and most "culture" content. In contrast, an operational level E_c can think about itself, plan into the future, attend to language and symbolism, and assimilate much "culture" content.

8. A minimum of stress is necessary to stimulate optimal functioning in any structure. An overload of stress decreases functioning in any structure. The interpenetration among adjoining levels of structure will take the form of mutually interacting U-curve functions, the vulnerability of each level of structure being contingent upon the strength and structural complexity at that level. High penetration is signaled by a closing of the adjoining structure to complex or contradictory input, a concretization or rigidification of functioning, and, perhaps, an exceptionally high rate of internal activity.

The penetration hypothesis, then, states that levels or organization of structure are cybernetically, causally linked in a predictable fashion. Activity at one level is diffused into adjoining levels and affects the functioning of those levels in a curvilinear fashion. Some effect is necessary to stimulate activity in the adjoining systems. Too much effect of one structure decreases its functioning in the way developed in chapter 7. Effective stable structures regulate this interaction more efficiently and facilitate the optimal functioning of adjoining structures. In this volume, ritual has been seen as a regulative tool, existing at several levels of organization, which assists in the protection of more molecular structures, allowing these structures to adapt productively to the E_o to the extent that these structures or E_cs reflect comparability to the E_o in some adaptation-relevant terms. Ritual's primary role vis-à-vis systemic penetration is to aid in the conservation of the E_c and subsequently reduce its vulnerability to threat from the E_o.

Ritual: A Summary

The Spectrum of Ritual is the result of applying an emerging analytic approach to what has been a rather stubborn problem in behavioral science. Although the three principal authors bear sole responsibility for imposing the idea of structure on the whole endeavor, the interaction among all authors has, we believe, resulted in a fairly unified and nearly comprehensive analysis of ritual behavior spanning the areas of ethology, neuroscience, psychology, and anthropology.

The preceding ten chapters are dense and complex, and a complete summary of all that they have said about ritual would require far more space than we are allowed. Instead, we would like to influence unity by outlining briefly some major conclusions about ritual that have emerged from the volume. This outline can be roughly expressed in terms of the three major categories: structure, function, and information.

Structure
Ritual behavior can be viewed as a continuum of repetitive, stereotyped, and coordinated behaviors emerging in complexity both in phylogenesis and in ontogenesis. Neurobiologically wired-in, so to speak, ritual retains the same basic defining characteristics at each discrete level of evolutionary and developmental organi-

zation. At the same time, the rigidity of form loosens, the range of application expands, and stability weakens. More complex and extensive rituals are seen as diachronic transformations of simpler and restricted ones. Each stage in the emergence of ritual incorporates the elements of the previous stage, while raising the ceiling for complex expression and expanding to incorporate new elements and relations between elements. With each step up the phylogenetic and ontogenetic scale, the organism expands its repertory of formalizations, rituals, and, finally, ceremonial rituals, and in the adult form may exhibit the entire range of structural complexity that has gone before. The adult human being, capable of abstract, conceptualized ritual, can nevertheless also be seen expressing simple formalizations, sometimes in the context of more complex rituals themselves.

As we proceed outward from the more molecular organization of neural systems through cognition and society, we find increasingly loosened and modified constraints on ritual behavior. Each succeeding level of organization subsumes and coordinates the more molecular levels. Each successively molar level operates as a control system for more molecular levels. Human ceremonial ritual coordinates a multitude of minirituals and formalizations into a larger pattern that extends their spatiotemporal and conceptual domain of relevance. Extreme examples of the organizational capacity of ritual are found in the annual cycles of the Roman Catholic church year (see chapter 10 for an analysis of the Mass itself), and the Tikopia Work of the Gods (Firth, 1967). The degree of spatiotemporal and behavioral elaboration of ritual is contingent upon the structural complexity of the organism that performs it.

Function

From the structuralist perspective, ritual may be seen to perform a number of functions in the service of generating structures at the neural, cognitive, and social levels of organization. The principal function would seem to be the equilibration and regulation of (1) the *activity* of generating structures, (2) the *transformation* of those structures, and (3) the *interpenetration* between levels of structural organization. This does *not* mean that ritual always functions conservatively, for that would be a serious misunderstanding of the concept of equilibration. Ritual quite often coordinates transformation and morphogenesis in structure.

Information

Ritual affects the processing of information by regulating the quantity and diversity of information processed and the selection of specific information processed. In both cases, ritual would seem gradually to increase the redundancy of input into the internal structure or E_c. The coordination of informational exchange with the E_o affects the character of the E_c through the systematic reduction of diversity in input, through confirmation of the already existing model, through repetition, and through provision for a restricted range of content in experience. Information, then, is constrained structurally so as to keep diversity within the bounds assimilable by the structures in question and so as to enable the information from the E_o to match expectations generated by the structure.

Epilogue

Advocating a nontraditional approach to science can be an unsettling experience. It is not easy to depart from the tenets inculcated in our professional training and accepted by so many of our competent and resourceful colleagues. But each of us has felt the demand to do so through individual experience with the limitations of currently accepted theories and methods in each of our separate disciplines. It is much easier for us, however, than it has been for scientists such as Piaget, Lorenz, Pribram, Chapple, and Count, among others, who for years have seen the myopia of accepted approaches and have struck out alone in the exploration of new perspectives and means of study. In this sense we are latecomers.

The increasing proliferation of books and articles in many fields advocating concepts and methods similar to those discussed here signals, we think, a major change in the direction of social science. It is still very much a minority view in each discipline, but one that is very rapidly gaining acceptance. The need to consider the organization of behavior, to see it in an interactive context, and to see it as a patterned whole is currently the most likely thrust in contemporary theory. As researchers and theoreticians in each discipline begin to recognize the overlap between their area of specialization and those of others working in different fields, the probability of significant advances in each field increases. Such progress proceeds not so much by gradual accretion but through conceptual recombination, the construction of a new perspective. In this vein we agree with Sommerhoff (1974:vi) in saying:

The degree of diversification and specialization in brain research and in allied disciplines is such that no one mind can keep abreast of all that is relevant. In consequence, anyone who steps out of the frame of established research to take a fresh look at fundamental concepts or to speculate about the special capabilities of the human brain, is likely to draw the fire of specialists in the many territories he is likely to cross. . . . it is clear that this is a risk one must learn to take in one's stride. Hence I make no apologies for what some may regard as blatant omissions; nor, on the other hand, do I claim finality for my conclusions.

Sommerhoff's thought holds true, not only for brain research, but for the social sciences in general. *The Spectrum of Ritual* is an attempt to stand back and look again at a familiar phenomenon. It is an effort at recombination through interdisciplinary cooperation, providing a view that is different and, it is hoped, more productive than current approaches. Through *its* development, *we* have developed, and as we proceed to other, similar tasks, we hope you, the reader, will be stimulated by this view to rethink your professional interests and to take from this volume something of value that can be applied to your own questions.

References

d'Aquili, E. G. 1975. "The Nature of Structural Transformations." Paper presented to the American Anthropological Association, San Francisco, December 1975.
Count, E. W. 1973. *Being and Becoming Human.* New York: Van Nostrand.

—— 1975. "Languages of the Organism." Paper presented at the Conference on Origins and Evolution of Language. New York, N.Y. September 1975.

Firth, R. 1967. *Tikopia Ritual and Belief*. Boston: Beacon Press.

Kuhn, T. 1970. *The Structure of Scientific Revolutions*. 2d ed. Chicago: University of Chicago Press.

Laughlin, C. D. and E. G. d'Aquili. 1974. *Biogenetic Structuralism*. New York: Columbia University Press.

Laughlin, C. D. and I. Brady. 1978 *Extinction and Survival in Human Populations*. New York: Columbia University Press.

Laughlin, C. D. and J. McManus. 1975a. "Multivariable Cognitive Research: Implications for Anthropological Theory and Research." Paper presented to the N. E. Anthropological Association, Potsdam, N.Y. March.

—— 1975b. "The Nature of Neurognosis." Paper presented to the American Anthropological Association Meetings, San Francisco. December.

Lorenz, K. 1971. *Studies in Animal and Human Behavior*. Vol. 2. Cambridge, Mass.: Harvard University Press.

McManus, J. 1974a. "Ontogenetic Development: the Diachronic Dimension of Structuralism." Paper presented to the American Anthropological Association Meetings, Mexico City, December.

—— 1974b. "Implications of the Schroderian U-Curve Hypothesis for Social Responses to Resource Deprivation." Paper presented to the American Anthropological Association Meetings, Mexico City, December.

—— 1975. "Psychopathology as Errors in Cognitive Adaptation." Paper presented to the American Anthropological Association, San Francisco, December 1975.

Piaget, J. 1970. *Main Trends in Interdisciplinary Research*. New York: Harper.

—— 1971. *Biology and Knowledge*. New York: Basic Books.

Pribram, K. H. *Language of the Brain*. Englewood Cliffs, N.J.: Prentice-Hall.

Rubinstein R. and C. D. Laughlin. 1977. "Bridging Levels of Systematic Organization," *Current Anthropology* 8(3):459–481.

Rubinstein, R., C. D. Laughlin, and J. McManus. n.d. "One Relation of Kuhn's Paradigmatic Science to Cognitive Psychological Theory." Ms.

Schneirla, T. C. 1957. "The Concept of Development in Comparative Psychology," in D. Harris, *The Concept of Development*. Minneapolis: University of Minnesota Press.

—— 1965. "Aspects of Stimulation and Organization in Approach/Withdrawal Processes Underlying Vertebrate Behavioral Development," in *Advances in the Study of Animal Behavior* (D. S. Lehrman, R. A. Hinde, and E. Shaw, eds.). New York: Academic Press.

Sommerhoff, G. 1974. *Logic of the Living Brain*. New York: Wiley.

Waddington, C. H. 1975. "Mindless Societies," in *New York Review of Books*. November 1975.

Wilson, E. O. 1975. *Sociobiology: The New Synthesis*. Cambridge, Mass.: Harvard University Press.

Name Index

Name Index

Name Index

Radcliffe-Brown, A. R., 48, 279; cited, 7, 250
Radin, P., quoted, 249
Rakic, P., 48; cited, 8
Rappaport, R. A., 48, 115, 279, 316; cited, 93, 253, 286, 307; quoted, 13, 39, 307
Rawlings, Richard, cited, 83, 94
Reynolds, V. and F. Reynolds, 115; cited, 99
Richards, A. I., 279; cited, 251
Roberts, J. M., 150; cited, 139
Robey, D., 48; cited, 3
Rokeach, M., 247; cited, 225
Roosevelt, T. and E. Heller, 115; cited, 87
Rosadini, G. and G. F. Rossi, 182; cited, 168-69
Rosberg, C. G., and J. Nottingham, 316; cited, 313
Rose, R. M. et al., 115; cited, 90
Rosenberg, M., 48, 247; cited, 11, 232, 235
Rosenblatt, J. S., 182; cited, 156
Rosenzweig, M. R. et al, 247; cited, 241
Rossi, I., 48; cited, 3
Routledge, K., 317; cited, 284, 294
Rubinstein, R. A. and C. D. Laughlin, 48, 362; cited, 6, 9n4, 14, 25, 346, 350, 354
Rubinstein, R. A., C. D. Laughlin, and J. McManus, 362
Rumbaugh, D. and E. von Glasersfeld, 115; cited, 100
Russell, B., 48; cited, 6

Sade, D. S., 48, 115; cited, 21, 39, 83, 91, 92, 94; quoted, 98
Salmon, W., 48; cited, 7, 25
Samarin, W. J., 150; cited, 128
Sapir, J. D., 78; cited, 74
Sargant, W., 150; cited, 142
Sartre, Jean-Paul, 235
deSaussure, F., 48; cited, 3
Schacter, S., 48; cited, 11
Schacter, S. and T. E. Singer, 48, 150, 247; cited, 11, 133, 134, 230
Schaffer, H. R., 116; cited, 81, 88, 89
Schaller, G. B., 116; cited, 86-87, 94, 97, 107

Schapera, I., 317; cited, 306
Scheflen, A. E., 78; cited, 72
Schein, M. W. and E. B. Hale, 182; cited, 156
Schenkel, R., 116; cited, 85, 97
Schneirla, T. C., 48, 116, 362; cited, 30, 93, 343
Schrier, A. M. and F. Stollnitz, 116; cited, 88n3, 89, 98
Schroder, H. M., 247; cited, 217, 219, 220, 225, 227n6
Schroder, H. M. and W. Crano, 247; cited, 225
Schroder, H. M., M. J. Driver, and S. Streufert, *Human Information Processing,* 48, 215, 317; cited, 4, 206, 217, 218-19 (*fig.*), 221-22 (*fig.*), 225, 227, 239, 244, 296; quoted, 116
Sears, D. O., 279; cited, 263
Sebeok, T. A. and A. Ramsey, 116; cited, 95, 110
Seligman, C. G. and B. Z. Seligman, 317; cited, 294
Seligman, M. E., 116, 215; cited, 88n3, 184, 200, 290
Seligman, M. E. and J. Hager, 49; cited, 21
Semmes, J. et al., 116; cited, 108
Servide, E. R., 49; cited, 7
Shack, W. A., 150; cited, 118
Shaughnessy, J. D., 49; cited, 25n11, 27
Sherif, M., 317; cited, 297
Sherif, M. and C. Sherif, 317; cited, 296-97, 308
Sherif, M. and C. Sherif eds., 247; cited, 231
Sherif, M., C. Sherif, and R. E. Nebergall, 247; cited, 231
Smith, C. U. M., 150; cited, 135
Smith, W. John, 42, 51-76, 80; articles, 49, 78; cited, 28, 29, 37, 58, 61, 64, 67, 74, 75
Smith, W. John, J. Chase, and A. K. Lieblich, 78, 116; cited, 64, 83
Smith, W. John, S. L. Smith, and E. C. Oppenheimer, 49, 78; cited, 68, 83
Sokolov, E. N., 150, 215, 247; cited, 135, 198, 199, 224

Name Index

Sommerhoff, G., 362; cited, 361
Southwick, C. H., 116; cited, 90
Sperber, D., 49
Sperry, R., 150; cited, 124
Sperry, R. W. et al., 182; cited, 172
Spittel, R. L., 317; cited, 294
Stair, J. B., 317; cited, 303
Stevenson-Hamilton, J., 116; cited, 87
Streufert, S., 247
Streufert, S. et al., 247; cited, 220
Sturtevant, W. C., 150; cited, 122
Suedfeld, P., 49, 247; cited, 10, 225, 239
Suedfeld, P. and H. M. Schroeder, eds.,
248
Suedfeld, P. and S. Streufert, 248; cited,
219
Sugiyama, Y., 116; cited, 99
Sullivan, E. V., G. McCullough, and M.
Stager, 248; cited, 233
Sutherland, J. W., 49; cited, 6
Suttles, W., 116; cited, 106

Tart, C., 215; cited, 195, 201
Teilhard de Chardin, P., 234, 235;
Phenomenon of Man, 49, cited, 4, 11
Teleki, G., 116, 279; cited, 99, 105, 106,
107, 109, 261; quoted, 106
Terzian, H. and C. Cecotto, 182; cited,
168
Thomas, E. M., 317; cited, 294, 300
Thrupp, S., ed., 317; cited, 310
Tillich, P., 49; cited, 40
Tinbergen, N., 78, 116, 182, cited, 54, 58,
67, 155; The Study of Instinct, 182,
cited, 155, 156
Titiev, M., 317; cited, 305
Trevarthen, C., 182; cited, 174
Trivers, R. L., 279; cited, 260-61
Truex, R. C. and M. B. Carpenter, 49;
cited, 30
Tuckman, B. W., 317; cited, 296
Tunnell, G. G., 150; cited, 124
Turiel, E., 233-34; articles, 49, 215, 248,
cited, 14, 206, 233, 243
Turnbull, C. M., The Forest People, 317,
cited, 283; The Mountain People, 215,
248, 317, cited, 207, 223, 301
Turner, G., 317; cited, 306

Turner, V. W.: articles, 78, 150, 317,
cited, 74, 140, 253, 287-88, 305; Forest
of Symbols, 78, cited, 54, 74, quoted,
53
Tyler, E. B., 49; cited, 4

Valenstein, E., 49, 248; cited, 11, 230
Van Gennep, A., 49, 279; cited, 40, 251,
270
Van Hooff, J. A. R. A. M., 49; cited, 37
van Lawick-Goodall, J., 116; cited, 93,
94, 97, 98-99, 100-1; quoted, 101-2,
104-5
Vansina, J., 279; cited, 251
van Valen, L., 116; cited, 108

Waddington, C. H., 49, 317, 362; cited, 5,
312, 350
Walker, S. S., 150; cited, 118-19, 122,
134, 137, 138
Wallace, A. F. C.: articles, 49, 279, 317,
cited, 10, 14, 275, 292, 294, 308, 310;
Culture and Personality, 49, 317, cited,
4, 292, 308, 310, quoted, 292-93; The
Death and Rebirth of the Seneca, 279,
317, cited, 292, 310-11; Religion: An
Anthropological View, 49, 279, 317,
cited, 25n11, 26, 38, 88, 121, 130,
250, 253, 270, 305, 310, 311, 312n15,
quoted, 266-67, 268, 310-11
Wallace, R. K. and H. Benson, 150; cited,
138, 138n11
Wallis, W. D., 317; cited, 310
Walter, V. J. and W. G. Walter, 150, 182;
cited, 125, 157
Walter, W. G., 182; cited, 164
Warner, E., 317; cited, 304n12
Waterhouse, M. J. and H. B. Waterhouse,
116; cited, 90
Weidmann, U. and J. Darley, 79; cited,
67
Weigl, E., 116; cited, 108
Weiner, B., 248; cited, 230
Weis, P. A., 248; cited, 242
Weiss, J. M., 215, 317; cited, 184, 195,
290, 291
Weitz, S., 79; cited, 65

Subject Index